FEAR IN ANIMALS AND MAN

FEAR IN ANIMALS AND MAN

Edited by

W. Sluckin

Department of Psychology
University of Leicester

 VAN NOSTRAND REINHOLD COMPANY

New York – Cincinnati – Toronto – London – Melbourne

**Published by Van Nostrand Reinhold Company Ltd.,
Molly Millars Lane, Wokingham, Berkshire, England**

*Published in 1979 by Van Nostrand Reinhold Company,
A Division of Litton Educational Publishing Inc.,
135 West 50th Street, New York, N.Y. 10020, U.S.A.*

*Van Nostrand Reinhold Limited,
1410 Birchmount Road, Scarborough, Ontario, M1P 2E7,
Canada*

*Van Nostrand Reinhold Australia Pty. Limited,
17 Queen Street, Mitcham, Victoria 3132, Australia*

Library of Congress Cataloging in Publication Data

Main entry under title:

Fear in animals and man.
    Bibliography: p.
    Includes index.
    1. Fear. 2. Psychology, Comparative.
I. Sluckin, W.
BF575.F2F4   156'.2'4   79–64
ISBN 0–442–30164–2

Contents

v

Chapter 4 Fear-Evoking Stimuli   **86**
P. A. Russell, *Department of Psychology, Aberdeen University*

Foreword

Psychology at present is very much a cognitively oriented discipline, preoccupied with the study of such processes as perception, memory, learning and thinking, and in consequence conceiving of the individual as primarily an information-processing organism – a kind of bloodless computer that calmly appraises the input from its environment and then acts accordingly in an utterly dispassionate manner. Yet how very different the facts of living are! Every experience has an emotional quality to it, be it pleasure or disgust, satisfaction or anger, confidence or fear. The latter is of particular interest, for not only is it a universal feeling with which we are all personally acquainted but it is also an extraordinarily rich phenomenon, one that can be both a useful warning signal and a crippling form of pathology: a phenomenon that amply deserves study yet one that has proved to be far from easy to analyse objectively.

It is very much to the credit of this volume that it attempts to put right the imbalance produced by our preoccupation with cognitive processes with its powerful plea to attend to the emotional side of human and animal nature. The individual contributions present a most learned and, collectively, a most balanced account of the present-day status of research on fear. Above all, they very quickly make apparent the extraordinarily complex nature of this phenomenon. And no wonder, when fear can be expressed in such utterly diverse ways as panic-stricken flight and frozen immobility, when it manifests itself at both physiological and behavioural levels, when it has both ontogenetic and phylogenetic and both individual and social implications. There are even questions to be raised about the unitary nature of this phenomenon, for the fact that we happen to have a specific word in our language to express it does not necessarily mean that there is 'a thing' in nature that corresponds to the word (a conclusion only too familiar to those acquainted with recent thinking in psychology about such other 'things' as intelligence, aggression, honesty, and so forth). And by the same token, to integrate all the many aspects studied under this heading into one coherent theory is still well beyond us: let the reader be warned that he will need considerable tolerance of ambiguity if he wishes to inform himself of current thinking on this topic.

The study of fear, especially in human beings, presents problems that other psychological functions do not present. For ethical reasons one cannot experimentally induce it to the degree that it manifests itself in real life: to study it in the real-life situation, however, is often not only impractical but also intensely harrowing for the investigator himself. I learned this to my cost when, as a clinical psychologist working in a children's hospital, I studied behaviour on admission: in all the years that I worked in such a setting, at a time when parents were allowed only limited access, I could never quite harden myself to tolerate the intense panic that a young child almost invariably shows on becoming separated from its parents, being looked after by unfamiliar people in unfamiliar surroundings, and having to undergo unpleasant medical procedures – all at a time when, being unwell, such a child would normally cling all the more to its parents. We all have our personal associations with the notion of fear: for me it is those hospitalised children that so vividly attest to the reality of this emotion and that illustrate the difficulty of studying it objectively in its full-blown, real-life form.

Yet whatever personal or conceptual difficulties there may be, the range of experiences and behaviour patterns coming under the umbrella term 'fear' is clearly in need of scientific investigation. There is no other volume presently available that brings together in so complete and competent a manner the work that has been accomplished so far in this vital area; as the various contributors make clear, however, our ignorance of the nature, function and development of fear is still considerable. One of the main aims of this volume ought therefore to be propaganda making: to draw attention to this field in general and to its specific gaps in particular, in the expectation that others will respond to the challenge and take the study of fear further forward. If this is done, Professor Sluckin can indeed be proud of having got this volume together.

H. R. Schaffer
University of Strathclyde
Glasgow, Scotland

Preface

We all know what fear is. We know it from first-hand experience. We know it as an emotion of a characteristic (and unpleasant) quality. We cannot directly observe it in others, but can often judge by their behaviour that a person or an animal is fearful. We can also observe, if we set out to do so, certain physiological signs of fear. Thus fear must be regarded as having three sets of components: experiential, behavioural and physiological.

The experiential component is the most directly known but probably the least readily investigable. It may be submitted to a scrutiny which consists largely of a semantic-philosophical analysis. We could ask, for instance, whether concepts such as fear and anxiety have much in common. We may ask whether the objects of fear are the same as the causes of fear. Have such considerations any bearing on empirical investigations of fear? Questions of this type, aiming at a conceptual clarification of our field of enquiry, are considered at some length in Chapter 1 by Robert Thomson.

Fear in its physiological manifestations is, of course, more tractable than is fear as a feeling. However, difficulties remain. Initially, there is doubt about the correspondence between the experience of fear and the physiology of fear; this doubt has its roots in the uncertainty surrounding the possible meanings of 'feeling afraid'. A problem, too, is whether fear is a physiological entity; some studies suggest that the physiological features of fear in one context may be rather unlike those in another context; for example, that acute fear and chronic anxiety have different physiological concomitants. Perhaps the most important research problem in this area is that of advancing our understanding of the role of the brain in mediating fear. Andrew Mayes gives due consideration to this issue in Chapter 2. More generally, his systematic and critical review covers all the investigations and theorising since the early days of the James–Lange theory which are germane to the physiology of fear.

From the viewpoint of psychology the behavioural aspects of fear are the central ones. Not only is there doubt as to whether fear can be regarded as a physiological entity, but there is also little justification to think of a unitary fear state at the behavioural level. This is a point strongly emphasised by John Archer in Chapter 3. Using the phrase 'behavioural aspects' in the plural seems appropriate because this helps to avoid the implication that something called fear is behind, and activates, the variety of forms of fear behaviour. As Archer maintains, such an assumption is unfounded 'in view of both the low correlations between different measures of fear and the complex nature of behavioural fear responses'. It follows from this that it is

xi

misleading to attempt to measure the degree of fear, as such; and attempts to do this in the past have not taken into account the great diversity of fear behaviours. The basic types of fear response are escape and immobility; but there are very many associated expressive modes of behaviour and social signals, and there are also certain indirect influences of fear reflected in various ways in the rates of eating, drinking, ambulation, defecation, and so on. This point of view, coupled with the ethological perspective characterising Chapter 3, gives special importance to Archer's survey of the behavioural aspects of fear.

Chapter 4 by P. A. Russell on fear-evoking stimuli complements the preceding chapter very well. Russell is in agreement with Archer in regarding fear as 'a heterogeneous collection of interrelated responses each of which may be elicited by a slightly different set of conditions'. A comprehensive taxonomy of the environmental conditions which elicit fear responses provides the structure for Chapter 4. The body of the chapter consists of an up-to-date and detailed survey of knowledge of fear stimuli in animals and man. Thus, our attention tends mostly, but not exclusively, to be directed towards the particular rather than the general. One important way of classifying stimuli is to put them into the categories of 'species predictable' and 'not species predictable'. A discussion of the latter takes us into the realms of learning and psychopathology; and these receive a fuller treatment in later chapters.

My original intention was to produce a contributed volume not so much on fear in general as on the development of fear. Later, it seemed well worth while to broaden considerably the scope of the book. The development of fear in the individual from infancy to maturity is, however, still at the centre of interest of the present volume; and Chapters 5 and 6 may perhaps be thought of as the core chapters. They do complement each other nicely. Chapter 5 by Eric Salzen considers the ontogeny of fear in young animals in broad terms as the ontogeny of self-protective behaviour patterns. Interestingly, Salzen classifies these patterns into protective contact responses, avoidant distance responses and signalling thwarting responses – a very useful scheme for the review of existing knowledge in the area in question. The roles of maturation and experience are especially brought out in the last two sections of Chapter 5. Both this chapter and the next never stray very far from the basic problem of all developmental studies, that of the interaction of maturation and experience. Chapter 6 by Peter Smith surveys and assesses the state of present-day knowledge of the ontogeny of fear in children. Smith does this in considerable detail, beginning with the first six months of life. He pays special attention to such phenomena as the fear of strangers and separation anxiety, which he examines in relation to human cognitive development. He is constructively critical of the different possible theoretical approaches. He looks at such matters as sex differences in fear, temporal stability of fear, etc. The reader will undoubtedly find this chapter to be comprehensive and instructive.

It is perhaps a matter of some surprise that in the first six chapters of the book the role of classical conditioning in generating fear, though given some attention, has not received a systematic and searching treatment. The fact is, however, that it is the clinical psychologists much more than others (such as ethologists or developmental psychologists) who appear to be most concerned with this matter. It is, therefore, fitting that A. T. Carr should deal with fear conditioning in Chapter 7 under the general heading of psychopathology of fear. The view that fear must be rooted in painful experience – the classical conditioning model of fear acquisition – is thoroughly examined in the light of the now available empirical evidence; and it is found wanting. The effectiveness of observational learning and of information transmission in bringing about fear in human beings is stressed. Cognitive processes are considered in all manner of fear acquisition, including classical conditioning. It is perhaps too obvious to need stressing that anticipation of harm is a feature common to all fear states, no matter how they may have been acquired; although this seems to have been lost sight of too often in the past. The cognitive-learning approach appears to provide a wider perspective, and it seems to be more flexible and amenable to continual modification than the more traditional conditioning-theory approach to the explanation of fear acquisition.

Chapter 8 attempts a brief overview of the development of fear, in different senses of the word development. Writing that chapter, as well as this introduction, and generally compiling the present volume, has been a pleasant task. I should like to thank all the contributors not only for the chapters they have written but also for the help they gave me in many ways while I was piecing the book together. I wish to express my special gratitude to David Winsor of Van Nostrand Reinhold for his encouragement and forbearance. Greatful thanks are also due to Margaret Frape for many kinds of secretarial assistance cheerfully given throughout the preparation of this book.

Wladyslaw Sluckin
University of Leicester
July 1978

CHAPTER 1

The Concept of Fear

Robert Thomson

'Fear', 'anxiety', 'apprehension', 'alarm', 'dread', 'terror' are words that occur both in everyday language and in the writings of social scientists. They are defined, somewhat ambiguously, in dictionaries. Obvious definitions, e.g. that fear refers to a present situation, while anxiety refers to a future or past state, do not take us very far. It is a curious fact that when we use these concepts we can easily relate them to our personal experiences; we know what it is like to be afraid or anxious. It is also not difficult for an actor or actress, without speaking any lines, to convey to an audience that a character is afraid or anxious, and moreover to show something quite specific about the quality of this emotion. Yet philosophers and psychologists who attempt to describe and explain fear and anxiety, and to provide a theory, do not find their job at all easy. There are problems when it comes to showing abstractly what fear is.

'Fear' concepts are a species of the genus of words denoting 'emotions' (fear, anger, disgust, pride, etc.). These concepts have certain common features of use, as well as their own more specific job of work to do. What work does a concept such as 'fear' do? What is the analysis of its meanings? This is the basic theoretical issue at the root of any discussion of the concept of fear, rather than any consideration of 'theories of emotion'.

1 A Conventional Viewpoint: Fear as an Inner State

Certain interpretations of a semantic type often lie at the basis of a theoretical approach. A long-established view is that an emotion such as fear is the name of an inner feeling, or similar set of feelings, a type of sensation, an identifiable state of consciousness. The word 'fear' denotes a particular type of sensation or feeling. 'Emotion is bound up with feeling. Were you to produce an off-the-cuff definition of the term, it would probably have some reference to subjective feelings' (Strongman, 1973).

It is also widely held that, correlated with such identifiable subjective states, are specific bodily changes. Fear involves changes in galvanic skin reaction, increase in heart rate, rise in blood pressure, decrease in salivation and secretion of digestive juices, and many complex changes throughout the

1

sympathetic nervous system. These inner changes produce typical 'outward' symptoms – pallor of the facial skin, sweating of palms, trembling of limb muscles, tension in certain muscles of the head, etc. Such 'arousal' is often followed by such behaviour as 'flight' or 'withdrawal'. However, the behaviour is explained as the effect of the inner changes – physiological changes of a determinable kind which are correlated with sensations in consciousness. Inner forces produce observable overt reactions. The emotion concept of 'fear' refers to these inner causes.

This account of fear was favoured by philosophical psychologists in the early years of this century and has been adapted by many psychologists since. It may be questioned as failing to give an adequate analysis of what our commonsense already registers about fear. Is it the case that 'fear' is identifiable in terms of highly specific physical changes of the agent's body? Having clammy hands, pallor of the skin, dryness of the mouth, increased heart beat, may be symptomatic of fear, but equally may be symptomatic of the onset of an infectious disease such as influenza. A student who suffers from diarrhoea prior to an examination may be highly anxious or may, again, be the victim of a bacterial infection. Several of the physiological changes which occur in fear are not tied exclusively to this type of reaction: galvanic skin reaction occurs in startle to a studden noise and also as an accompaniment of sexual arousal. By itself this physical measure does not exclusively indicate fear. Nor do a combination of physical symptoms necessarily differentiate fear from some other reaction. Although Schachter in 1957 used a variety of physiological measures to test reactions to danger (fear) and to provocation (anger) and did find differences in pattern, these differences were small and there was considerable overlap. Later research has tended to confirm the negative side of this approach; patterning reveals *intensity* of emotion but fails to distinguish between different types or qualities of emotion (fear/rage: pleasant/unpleasant). Autonomically one cannot demonstrate precisely a physiological basis for differences between fear and anger.

A second point is that some fears do not appear to be accompanied by any clear-cut physiological changes or physical symptoms, e.g. fear of growing old, fear of not ever getting married, of the next war, of being the illegitimate child of somebody you dislike. These are real fears but do not usually have discriminable and distinctive physical accompaniments tied regularly to these specific fears.

Can sensation or feeling as experienced provide a clear index of a specific emotion? Are feelings of fear or anxiety as distinctive as gnawing toothaches or bruised shins? To teach a child the meaning of the word 'fear' by making it afraid and saying 'Fear is how you felt just then' might not be an effective lesson. Laboratory-induced fear, stimulated by sudden loud explosions, or

2

the sudden presentation of a snake, may produce sensations of a different quality from those experienced in a car crash or when being molested by a maniac. Do the feelings we have in anger, indignation and shame differ from each other in a markedly distinct way? Are the feelings experienced in stage fright, before an interview, or going into the dentist's chair for painful treatment exactly similar? There are surely variations in feeling quality from one fearing situation to another — a fact which gives scope to the descriptive skills of creative writers such as novelists. Sensations are not sufficiently precise, discrete, invariable, to provide the main index of an emotion.

Against this, it might be pointed out that fear is experienced in differing degrees of intensity. There must be some kind of state which varies in quantity? However, differing degrees of intensity of emotion are assessed by utilising two different criteria. We watch for bodily symptoms — gestures, facial expression, bodily posture — and note physiological changes of the kind measured by Schachter.

Equally important are variations in a person's voluntary behaviour and these are subject to a range of individual differences. This point is made clear by Anthony Kenny (1963) in Chapter 3 of his *Action, Emotion and Will*. Fear of heights, Kenny points out, is shown in bodily reactions when a person is exposed on high places; sensations in the stomach, trembling of the limbs, pallor of skin. But this fear is also shown in the energy, persistence and ingenuity with which a person avoids all high places. X may never climb mountains, ascend towers, approach the edge of cliffs. Thus X rarely experiences feelings of fear, or displays its physical symptoms, in relation to heights. His avoidance behaviours, nevertheless, demonstrate the intensity of his fear. Y, on the other hand, may climb mountains enthusiastically, and may occasionally, during a difficult operation, experience spasms in the pit of the stomach, or be in a cold sweat for a moment or two. On any strict count, Y experiences more sensations of fear and exhibits more of its symptoms, in high places, than does X. Yet X's fear of heights is more intense and extensive. The frequency, and especially the significance, of actions is a better estimate of emotional *strength* than an examination of inner feelings and physical symptoms.

Another consideration, in this rejection of fear as synonymous with inner causes, is a general feature of the paradigm case of fearing: that usually fear has an object. We ask 'What is X afraid of?' Fear, or anxiety, is usually directed towards an object. The term 'object' covers a wide variety of things. We fear other people, animals, things that happen to us, such as undergoing surgery or being questioned by police officers as criminal suspects: we also fear complex organism – environmental situations such as the absence of something providing safety and security or the non occurrence of an expected event.

3

In order to specify fear or anxiety it is often necessary to refer to its object. The nature of the object and its possible relationships to the agent make all the difference to the quality of fear.

Fear of falling to death is different from being afraid of a dental extraction, or of not being able to speak one's lines when performing in a play. It is the variety of possible objects, and the different types of relationship between agent and object, which governs the form and content of a fear or anxiety situation. What one is afraid of, and what the significance of the object of fear is, for the agent, is central to the business of being afraid. Being afraid of losing a tennis match, on which one's reputation as the best player in the club depends, can be a genuine fear – keeping the victim on edge or sleepless for days. Yet it is different in many respects from the fear that one is likely to die in the near future as a consequence of a disease one has contracted.

In virtue of the variety and differences amongst possible objects of fear, in humans, and the complexity of possible relationships, there is nothing common to, intrinsic to, basic to *all* possible fears and anxieties. A carefully controlled experiment in which subjects react to controlled 'danger' stimuli will only reveal how people react to *this* specific object, or type of object, in this kind of context. Subjects might have different feelings and exhibit different symptoms and responses to different kinds of fear-evoking object in other contexts.

Equally subject to variation is the behaviour of the person in relation to the object of fear. Even at the commonsense level we know that a man who is afraid may run away, hide himself, stand 'frozen' to the spot, move cautiously and carefully around a given area, or aggressively attack the object of fear with a view to removing or destroying it. Even within these broad categories of action there are wide individual differences. Specific skills may be exhibited in coping with danger, as well as distinctive traits of personality. Reaction to danger has often been regarded as a test of 'courage' and 'character' – implying that behaviour in response to danger, and involving fear, can be assessed on some scale of marking, from 'heroic' to 'cowardly'.

In anxiety, where fear-like reactions are directed to what is not immediately present, the variability of behaviour would seem to be even greater from case to case. Psychiatric case histories of dysthymic or 'anxiety' neuroses often seem to show idiosyncratic as well as some common features.

One reason for the variability of human behaviour under the impact of fear or anxiety is that we have some kind of 'apprehension' or 'misapprehension' concerning the object. How precisely a person perceives, or construes, the object makes a difference to the context. We are only afraid if we believe the object to be dangerous or threatening. At one extreme it is possible to be afraid when the object presents no great danger. Typists in an office building

4

may panic as smoke drifts through the rooms whereas a fireman can see at a glance that the source of the fire is trivial and easily extinguished. Raw recruits may be afraid when they are approaching the battle-front while seasoned soldiers perceive that it is a 'quiet' sector with no immediate danger of coming under fire. Conversely it is possible to remain fearless in the presence of a genuine danger as when a child approaches a colourful but deadly snake with a view to picking it up. Mostly we can distinguish between what is an appropriate object of fear and what is not. Nevertheless, how we interpret an object of fear, and especially its relationship to us, is relevant to how we react. Not only predispositions of temperament, previous experience in similar situations, the expectedness or otherwise of the situation, but any special circumstances of *this* context – and how they are perceived – determine our behaviour.

An important factor in any fearful situation is a person's appraisal of his capacity to cope with the object. An experienced big-game hunter, armed with a good gun and ammunition, is in a stronger situation when faced with a dangerous wild animal than an inexperienced and unarmed traveller. The confidence of the hunter in his experience, skills and capability of killing the animal with his first shots diminish the intensity and affect of his fear. Knowing what to do in order to protect oneself from the danger, and having the skills and the means to apply this knowledge, make for a less limiting fear. The absence of such 'knowing how to cope' is liable to increase the intensity of the 'emotional arousal' dimension and adversely affect avoidance behaviour. What we know about the object of fear, and our practical knowledge regarding how to deal with the object of fear, are important dimensions of the context. They are not, of course, simple dimensions or easy to investigate empirically.

2 Objectless Fear

So far we have been dealing with the standard, or paradigm, case of fear, in which the object of fear is known. There are, however, cases of objectless fear and anxiety. There are 'free-floating' anxiety states and instances of undirected fears for which no object can be found. The first point to make is that, since these are deviations from the standard case, they do not necessarily invalidate what is said of the paradigm. However, there may be ways of trying to relate these 'objectless' fears to the standard case. It may be that in some cases some species of cognitive confusion is involved. There is an object of the fear or anxiety but the agent fails to discriminate it or identify it. Some type of amnesia, inhibition or blockage occurs that prevents the individual from perceiving the situation he is in. Thus a person on waking in

5

the morning experiences fear or anxiety but cannot say what is the object of this. It may be that an event likely to occur in the near future is being blocked from conscious experience, an event with unpleasant associations. On the other hand the state of fear or anxiety may be related to the inability to recall a stupid action committed earlier, the consequence of which may soon have to be faced. Without accepting the questionable metatheories of psycho-dynamic psychologies there may be some truth in descriptions of defensive reactions which cut out of awareness objects of an anxiety-related type.

On the other hand 'free-floating' anxiety may be explicable in terms of behavioural models. Anxiety originally associated with a specific stimulus-object may have generalised widely so that a variety of conditioned stimuli evoke anxiety reactions. There no longer appears to be a specific object since it has become lost in the stimulus-generalisation process. Anxiety does not seem related to the usual definable type of object but to seize on a wide variety of apparently meaningless stimuli.

Finally there may be cases of objectless fear which have causes, of a kind which cannot easily be traced, but no object. Later the distinction between the 'cause ' of fear and the 'object' of fear will be made and thus the possibility of special cases of genuinely objectless fears may be accepted but without weakening the paradigm case of fear in which an object can be determined.

3 Rationality and Fear

The irrationality, or apparent irrationality, of objectless fear introduces another feature of the concept. Fear can be assessed as 'rational' or 'irrational', 'sensible' or 'pointless'. Criteria of rationality apply to fears and anxieties. The significance of this consideration is this. If fear and anxiety, as forms of behaviour, can be appraised according to criteria or rationality, it is unlikely that fear is simply reducible to internal sensations or feelings. Sensations, whether of toothache, rheumatism or fear, simply happen. They are neither rational nor irrational responses. Nor are the physical symptoms of fear − cold sweats, trembling limbs, etc. − rational or irrational as such. They occur in response to certain types of nervous stimulation. If fearing and being anxious can be rational or irrational, then they must involve the dimension of human intelligence at work. In what ways can fear or anxiety be rational or otherwise? It is unreasonable to be afraid if there is evidence that the object of fear does not exist or is different from what one believed it to be. It is unreasonable for the solitary spinster to fear that there is a burglar in the cupboard if the cupboard is empty or if the noise can be shown to be produced by the cat.

Again, a groundless fear can be stated in a proposition, which would be a reason for being afraid if it were true, but which can be shown to be false. It is unreasonable to fear that the building in which one is writing an article is about to collapse and crush one to death if all the evidence suggests it is structurally sound, there is no real possibility of an earthquake, it is adequately searched for the bombs of terrorists, etc.

We also have irrational fears of the kind in which the person agrees that there is no danger – and believes this – but remains afraid. One might be afraid of harmless grass-snakes or toads, having perhaps acquired a sort of conditioned fear to such harmless objects in childhood.

In superstitious fears we give as our reason a true statement which is a weak reason for assuming the existence of threat. A man may feel apprehensive if a black cat crosses his path or he 'reads' disaster in a pack of cards.

Neurotic fears are such, from the logical viewpoint, as when the object of fear is an inappropriate one. To be afraid of being in an open space, or of being at the top of a tower with high railings, or of birds or beetles is to be afraid of what does not threaten one or include any real danger.

It is unreasonable to be afraid when the object is an appropriate object of fear but when one's reaction is exaggerated or excessive. It is reasonable to be afraid of a cobra but unreasonable to scream and faint when one sees one on a film or when it is safely behind glass in a zoo.

These are some of the different ways in which it makes sense to apply concepts of rationality to 'fear' situations. These are logical and not psychological observations but they have significance. 'Fear' includes cognitive elements in some of its basic uses. (See G. Pitcher, 1965.)

Fear unquestionably involves the arousal, on the perception of a situation, of complex reactions in the sympathetic nervous system. This is part of our evolutionary inheritance. It is probable that certain basic fears towards specific types of object – 'primitive' fears – emerge in earliest infancy and form the starting point of developmental processes of considerable complexity.

However, the *concept* of fear in relation to its objects is something which humans learn – what it *means* to be afraid or anxious is identified, both in ourselves and others, in observing what people do in association with 'dangerous-threatening' objects. It is important to know the way our bodies work and how the evolutionary process has provided us with basic adaptive mechanisms. It is important to know how these mechanisms operate in the origin and development of fear and rage in the case of the typical human being. Biological research is relevant and basic to our understanding of fear.

However, there is scope for a wide range of variations in the way these adaptive mechanisms work. Once development gets under way, human intelligence and imagination are involved in the process.

4   Anthony Kenny's Analysis of the Fear Concept

How should the concept of 'fear' be analysed? Anthony Kenny (1963) in his book *Action, Emotion and Will* (Chapter 3, p. 67) suggests that fear is a concept identified by the use of three types of criterion. His analysis seems a useful one:

(1) Firstly, these are fearful circumstances in the human environment – dangerous and threatening objects.
(2) Secondly there are symptoms of fear: physiological changes of the kind discussed in textbooks of physiological psychology in the sections on 'emotion'.
(3) Finally there is action towards the object: intelligent, intentional action (flight, hiding, evasion, combat, etc.). In an ideal case all three criteria can be identified and 'fear' can be applied as an appropriate classification.

(a) If a wild animal approaches, X turns pale, breaks into a sweat, screams, runs for shelter, hides, and later says 'I was scared stiff'. We readily accept 'X was afraid of the lion' as a correct classification.
(b) X displays symptoms of fear and takes action to avoid an object, but there is no genuinely dangerous situation, as in the case of phobias. Here, criterion 1 is absent, but 2 and 3 apply.
(c) X shows symptoms of fear but takes no appropriate action, e.g. when 'rooted to the spot'. Here, criterion 3 is absent, but 1 and 2 apply.
(d) A dangerous situation exists and avoidance action is taken, but there are no symptoms of fear, e.g. X sees a storm approaching and quickly steers his boat into harbour. Here, criterion 2 is absent, but 1 and 3 apply.
(e) Dangerous circumstances exist but there are no symptoms of fear, and avoidance behaviour is absent, e.g. a soldier advances into an area of heavy fire. Later he says 'I was terrified but I did my duty'. Here, criteria 2 and 3 are absent, but 1 applies, supported by subsequent testimony.

However, if none of these three criteria applies, we find it difficult to apply the concept of fear meaningfully. If X says he is afraid but we cannot detect any dangerous circumstances, X shows no symptoms and takes no action, then we ask 'Of what are you afraid?'. Now if X replies 'I am not afraid of anything. I just feel like this every day at this time. Just afraid', then we are puzzled. Has he a reason for being afraid? Does he expect a catastrophe to happen at this time of day – the start of a nuclear war, or the end of the world by divine intervention? If X denies any such 'objects', we conclude either that X is exhibiting a pathological fear or else that he does not know the meaning of the concept. Perhaps he uses 'fear' when other people use the term 'hunger'. Whatever the explanation of this odd case for the psychologist, it serves to show the point of Kenny's three criteria for the application of the concept of 'fear'. One simple implication is that provided we have evidence of some capacity for receiving and decoding information from the environment concerning dangers or threats, and some capacity for learning what are dangerous circumstances (or being provided with innate capacities for registering these), the concept of fear may be applied to animals other than human beings. All three criteria would be applicable: circumstances of threat in the environment; physical symptoms; avoidance behaviour resulting from some perception of 'objects' of fear.

5 Objects and Causes of Fear

It is now time to make a distinction between the 'object' of fear and the 'cause' of fear. It is possible to give a causal account of fear without any reference to its object. 'I became anxious because of overwork.' 'I was irritable because I had to miss lunch.' This does not say towards what objects the anxiety or the irritation were directed – it merely states how these feelings originated. We are frequently anxious about possible future events – about failing our examinations next summer or having to undergo a surgical operation next year. The objects of our anxiety are not causal antecedent conditions. They are events in the future which possibly might *not* happen. I may fear the effects of an atomic explosion in the town where I live – but this is only a possibility in the future. The causes it may be said are 'imagery' or 'words' or other 'thoughts' which represent the feared events. But does imagery cause fear? It is surely what the imagery refers to, or represents, that constitutes the object of fear. The words or visual images used are in themselves no different from any other words or visual images – neither fearful not unfearful objects. It is the unrealised, nonexistent 'events' that are fearful, albeit through the capacity of the human brain to represent possibilities symbolically.

If the building in which I am working goes on fire, I may be afraid. I may never have been in, or even near, a building on fire before now. The causes of

9

my fear are experiences of being mildly burnt – with matches, gas jets, hot plates. I extrapolate from these experiences to the possibility of getting burned in a new and more terrible manner. The kinds of object which are the causes of my fear are different from the present one and are remote in time. These examples may be less convincing than a consideration of two simple questions. Having asked X 'What are you afraid of?' (the dark, disease, bats) one can go on to ask 'Why are you afraid?' (of the dark, of disease, of bats). X knows the objects of his fear but may not be able to say why he is afraid of these things. The causes of his fears are unknown to him. Psychologists may not agree in providing explanations, so we have reasonably secure knowledge, in many instances, of the objects of fear but are less able to determine the causes of the fear under review. We readily accept that the boss may have been irritated during the working day by several distinct incidents (objects of anger) while appreciating that the cause of his irritability may have nothing to do with the office staff and their efficiency (e.g. he had a row with his wife over breakfast).

There are, of course, instances in which a specific situation can serve as both object and cause of anxiety. If a person is anxious about a disease he has contracted, the disease is both the cause and the object of his anxiety.

In many cases, however, object and cause of fear/anxiety are distinct and separate factors. It is one thing to give a casual explanation as to how X came to fear something; it is another thing to give an account of X's relationship to the object of his fear – how he perceives and interprets his situation, how he feels, and how he intends to act. His reaction to the object of fear may not be detached and inferential. It may be quick and behavioural, but intelligent and insightful as is that of an athlete engaged in a fast, competitive sport. The relationship between the agent and the object of his fear is central to any account of this emotion.

We conclude this argument by suggesting that sensations or feelings and the physiologically based symptoms occurring during certain forms of 'arousal' are connected with fear, as a concept, only if they occur in a context of 'action related to circumstances'. Behaviour, in fear, is related to the background of events in which it occurs. Fear is a reaction in which we are alert and intelligently aware. It is true that feelings of certain kinds are closely related to definable symptoms, and, more flexibly, to actions. Behaviour in fear is influenced by many factors. A civilian caught up in a battle area may, under the influence of fear, take flight or hide. A soldier involved in the battle is constrained by his role, and the law, from doing either. He may inhibit tendencies to run away or take cover and thus face danger, obeying orders, even when afraid. 'So feelings are tied to symptoms, and symptoms to circumstances and circumstances to types of behaviour.' But the context brings many factors to bear on the individual who feels,

10

displays symptoms and reacts. It is the whole configuration that determines whether or not a human response is classifiable as 'fear' or not. We must focus on 'behaviour related to objects' as the core factor while not rejecting the feelings experienced or the symptoms manifest in the arousal of the nervous system.

Emotions such as 'fear' are crudely conceptualised in 'commonsense' thought as the eruption of an effervescent-like process which begins somewhere inside the organism and works its way outwards into symptoms and actions. However, fear (and rage) are more complicated than this. Some influences rooted in intelligence and imagination (especially in the case of anxiety) are involved. So also, on occasions, are human values. There are some occasions when the expression of an emotion serves a dual function. It both expresses the emotion and makes an appraisal or evaluation. 'I fear for his safety.' 'I am delighted at your success.' 'I am deeply angered at your conduct.' These all express our emotion, indicate our relationship to an object, but they also express a judgment. To be deeply angry at somebody's behaviour is to express emotion but also to appraise the behaviour as 'cruel', 'insensitive', 'wicked'. To fear for a person's safety is to express one's feelings and to appraise the situation as 'harmful', 'threatening', for the welfare of the person. These are special uses of emotion-concepts. However, the business of using them in relation to implicit value judgments goes wider than this.

Some objects of fear are dangerous or threatening in a basic, almost biological sense. Life may be endangered or severe physical injury is possible or health may suffer from the threatening object. But the concepts of what sort of situations are 'dangerous' or 'threatening' are greatly extended in meaning through the use of criteria of value. A man may pay a large sum of money to a blackmailer out of fear. What he fears is hurt to his reputation, or to his prestige as a model and upright character, or to further advancement in his career, if certain information about him is published. His life is safe, his body and health are in no dangwr, but complex things like status and relationships with other people may change, if he is exposed, and these changes he values negatively. A student may cease to be anxious about his future examinations and the diploma if he comes to believe that the degree and the careers to which it leads are worthless, or even immoral, as defined by newly accepted 'values'.

A whole range of fears and anxieties are dependent on wants and needs that are artificial or contingent upon what we have learned to value: on how we construe certain human activities and employments and relationships. Thus a politician may genuinely fear another fellow member of his political party as a threat to his ambitions of becoming a leader or minister. To the individual politician whose career is set upon attaining high office an energetic rival may be an object of anxiety, if not of fear. The situation is

11

structured in terms of certain 'values' defining 'success', 'fulfilment', 'implementation of specific policies', etc. Without these the individual would have different aims and desires, and therefore would regard his present rival differently. It is not only what is likely to threaten life, injure our bodies, cause physical pain, which is seen as 'dangerous' or 'threatening'. Whatever is construed as contrary to our gratifications, ambitions, fulfilments, can be seen as harmful, distressing, ruinous, according to some criterion of value. This greatly extends the intrusion of value judgements, thus making certain situations into 'threats' and therefore objects of anxiety.

6   Disruptive Fear

So far we have taken only the standard case of the concept of fear. This presents fear as an adaptive response. Circumstances appear which are perceived as dangerous or harmful and appropriate action protects the agent against the harm which is threatened – or at least has this aim.

However, some fear and anxiety seems disruptive of adaptive behaviour. We speak of a person 'paralysed with terror', 'rooted to the spot in fear', 'stricken with panic' or 'overwhelmed with anxiety'. There are some emotional behaviours which Gilbert Ryle, in his *Concept of Mind*, (Chapter 4, pp. 83–115), classified as 'agitations'. Such common expressions as 'shocked', horrified', 'amazed', 'stricken', 'flabbergasted', indicate the commonality of such violent and disruptive responses to circumstances. A highly specific event, often sudden and unexpected, serves as the cause, as well as the object, of emotion. Normal activity is halted – clear thinking, focussed attention, coordinated movement all cease. The agent is disturbed out of his ongoing adjustments, and feels the situation as a shock to the system, cutting across normality. Many agitations are unpleasant – the sight of a sudden accident in which people are injured; the receipt of such news; the explosion of a terrorist bomb. But equally we can be disrupted in a pleasing way – the unexpected return home of a long-absent member of the family; news that somebody is safe and well, having survived in an air crash; the announcement that one has won 'on the Pools'...

'Fear' can be so intense and violent as to prevent effective avoidance of a sudden and terrible threat. Anxiety, as is common knowledge, can be the most crippling symptom in many neuroses, reducing the sufferer to the status of an invalid.

How disruptive, disorganising, maladaptive fear and anxiety occurs, and how this differs from adaptive fear and anxiety, are matters for empirical research. Is the size and the specific organisation of the physiological changes a factor? How far are predisposing personality characteristics responsible for

12

disruptive fears? Is there a kind of confusion involved – the agent not knowing how to cope? What we can note is that 'fear' refers also to a continuum of behaviours. At one end are adaptive actions in fear and anxiety enabling the agent to survive dangers: at the other extreme are behaviours of the contrary maladaptive type. Theorists have sometimes emphasised one or other of these extremes on the emotion continuum. It has been held by M. Arnold, R. Lazarus and P. T. Young that all emotion is disruptive, disorganising of adaptive behaviour. On the other hand, R. Leeper, O. H. Mowrer and D. Rapaport have held that all emotion has a part in organising and sustaining adaptive behaviours. It would seem wisest to hold that it presents a continuum and that it can be either – or, in the middle ranges, neither.

7   Fear as Mood and Sentiment

The concept of fear, in common with other emotions, covers both adaptive and maladaptive forms of behaviour. Other concepts of emotion apply besides these two, for example the concept of 'mood'. Whereas the paradigm cases of emotion refer to an occurrence, a specific set of reactions to specific stimulating circumstances, 'mood' refers to dispositional tendencies over time. Moods last for varying periods. A person can be in an anxious or irritable or frivolous mood for an afternoon, a day, or even longer. To be in an anxious or fearful mood is to be liable to have certain kinds of feelings, to be a prey to certain kinds of thought and cognitive preoccupation, to display certain types of behaviour – the anxious person looks 'tense', is physically restless or fidgety, cannot settle easily to work tasks. Moods do not seem to be directed towards a specific object as are standard emotions, and their causes may be obscure. We are simply anxious or irritable at things in general – all kinds of situations or stimulus objects are liable to elicit anxiety reactions 'while the mood lasts'. Fear as a mood is widely generalised. It is similar to free-floating anxiety, although the latter is usually reserved for neurotic forms of anxiety, while 'mood' is retained for less acute, milder, normal emotion which tends to persist and 'spread'. Ryle described moods as general 'frames of mind' – to be liable to feel and react in a variety of affiliated ways to a variety of stimulation.

In addition to moods we have concepts referring to a variety of emotional habits. Here emotive reaction occurs as a factor or element within a 'complex' of behaviour. Shand invented the term 'sentiment' to mean an 'emotional disposition centered on an object or person'. The terms 'love' and 'hate' are sentiments rather than prototype emotions. If we love another person we have a related set of concepts – beliefs, thoughts, aspirations,

13

memories – associated with that person. We are likely to experience joy and pride when the loved one prospers in achievement, or fear if he is in danger, or grief if he is lost. How we feel about loved ones is closely linked with how we think about them. Love of children, loyalty to our nation, pride in our job, respect for honesty, distrust of radicalism, are all sentiments involving complex fusion of thought and feeling. 'Fear' and 'anxiety' are emotions which readily form part of our basic 'sentiments'. Thus emotions such as fear do not always occur in relatively 'pure' or prototypic form: they probably occur most frequently as part of the complex emotional habits – sentiments, attitudes, prejudices. Again, human rationality is involved, and changes in beliefs and expectations lead to changes in emotional content of the sentiment. The love of a husband for his wife may change to hate and contempt if he comes to believe that she has married him only for his money, has constantly been unfaithful to him, and has said spiteful and mocking things about him to her lovers. As his representational beliefs change so do the emotive contents and one sentiment is replaced by another – in this case a contrary one.

One misleading line of thinking about 'fear' and other emotions has arisen from asking the question 'What do words like 'fear' stand for or name?' or 'What are the essential attributes of fear?'. The answer is narrowed to sensations of a particular kind, or physiological changes located in specific operations of the nervous system. However, our analysis of 'fear' suggests that the term refers to a complex situation of 'action related to context': environmental circumstances, the agent's appraisal of them, states and predispositions of the agent, his actions in relation to the object all being involved. What the concept of emotion does fix upon are the *functional* properties of the action rather than on the causes of the action, or the physical processes of the body which structure and arouse activity. The causes are an important topic of enquiry and so are the physiological processes arousing the agent. But what the concept of 'fear' means is a complex interaction between organism and environment achieving, or failing to achieve, certain results (or 'functions').

8 Fear and Motive

One further general point must be made before turning to more empirical matters. Concepts of emotion such as 'fear' are used to describe reactions to stimulating circumstances. Such concepts can also function as logical terms: they are key factors in giving explanations of actions. We not only experience fear or undergo fear; we act 'out of fear' or 'because we are afraid'. Why did X suddenly strike Y? Y has been provocatively insulting and thereby made X

14

angry. Disruptive emotion leads to impulsive action which is not easily inhibited. Why does X move cautiously and carefully in the shadows and take cover in doorways? He is afraid of being intercepted by enemy agents. Here fear leads to intelligent and adaptive actions.

In this latter case behaviour may be directed towards a goal, viz. getting unobserved to a car, entering it, and driving away rapidly to a secure place. This goal, and the means adopted to achieve it, involves intelligent, purposeful behaviour. It may also have a motive – e.g. to get an important document to a particular official, so that he can take appropriate decisions, and to prevent an enemy from getting this document first. Doing this may be motivated by patriotism, a sense of duty, out of gratitude to one's leader, etc. This we would regard as 'motivated' conduct. There is a reason for acting in this way; it is one which does not imply the most obvious conventional associations, or consequences, of the 'defensive behaviours'. However, it is doubtful if fear is, in itself, a 'motive', or reason of the motive type, for acting. Fear and those 'avoidance of danger' responses, which are part of the criteria for recognising fear, are linked closely with the motivated conduct of 'getting the documents safely to a particular person without the enemy seizing them'. To that extent, to the extent that the same behaviours are both part of the fear reaction and part of the motivated sequence, fear enters into this context of explanation. Fear, anxiety, excitement, relief may involve intelligent, goal-directed behaviour which is linked with motivated behaviour (viz. behaviour requiring explanation in terms of the reasons an agent has for selecting a specific goal and choosing certain means towards its attainment). However, even when this is not the case – as with disruptive emotion, or 'agitated' behaviour – what a person is doing may be explained by saying, for example, 'he is terrified of ...', 'he is acting out of fear of ...', or some similar phrase.

9   Fear and Arousal

The topic of 'motive-type' explanation in comparison with explanation in terms of feelings, desires, intentions, needs, traits, rule-following, etc., is a complex and difficult one. However, all that we need to note is that concepts of fear have both a descriptive-classificatory function (referring to experiences and actions) and a logical-explanatory function relating propositions. If psychologists wish to use the concept of fear they must take such a difference of use into account. To what extent do they wish to use the forms of explanation in which 'fear' operates as a factor? If not, do they wish to retain this concept in their literature? Elizabeth Duffy regarded established concepts of emotion as misleading and useless, and argued for

15

their exclusion from psychology. Behaviour may be regarded as varying in only two ways, direction and intensity. Direction may be defined in terms of selectivity of response, which is based on expectancies and the relationships among perceived stimuli. An individual approaches or avoids a situation in terms of its incentive value or threat value. Intensity is defined in terms of general organismic 'arousal' or energy mobilisation and this can be measured in terms of certain response variables. Emotion is simply a point, or range of points, on the higher end of the arousal dimension. There is no need for different types of emotion – the concept can be expressed in the technical terms of the behavioural sciences. This was the gist of Duffy's case. There could be some point in using technical terms in relation to empirical researches of physiological or behavioural-experimental kinds which are concerned with aspects of what, at the level of ordinary language, we would call 'emotional behaviour'. Psychologists could be dealing with specialised questions about highly abstract aspects of the general phenomenom, and terms adapted from everyday language might only introduce unwanted implications into the reports of results or into hypothesis derived from controlled investigation. If, however, psychologists do wish to investigate the complexities of behaviour, 'action related circumstances', which emotion concepts classify, they are obliged to use such concepts with all the implications they carry. In this case some careful analysis of their conventional uses would seem essential, if only to make clear what specific questions are being asked about the complex behavioural situation denoted. It is a pragmatic question whether or not psychologists need to retain concepts such as 'fear' and 'anxiety' depending on the aims and scope of their specific enquiries. What is important is that we recognise that the concept of 'fear' (and its related terms) is more complex in meaning than appears at first attempts at definition.

10   Empirical Considerations

How does this account of the concept of fear relate to the literature of experimental psychology? Is there anything there compatible with these main conclusions? There are not many experimental researches of much consequence which can be related to our analysis. The work of Schachter is of some relevance, however, and gives some degree of support to the analysis of the concept of fear given above.

Schachter's original work used a variety of measures to test reactions to danger (fear) and to provocative situations (anger). The physiological patterns in the two emotions did differ, but the differences were small and there was considerable overlap. Thus, the autonomic differences between fear and rage were not clear. Schachter put forward the hypothesis that any emotion is named and identified through the situation in which it occurs and in terms of the individual's perception and interpretation of that situation. The nervous system, in emotion, is in a general state of arousal, but it is the cognitive 'labelling' or conceptual activity that organises the individual's response. Schachter and Singer, in their experimental study of 1962, attempted to test this theory. Experimental subjects were told that the experimenters were investigating the effect of a new vitamin compound ('suproxin') on vision. They were to be given an injection of this compound. In fact subjects were injected either with epinephrine or a saline placebo. Epinephrine has known effects: rise in systolic blood pressure, increase in heart beat, respiration and levels of blood sugar. The subject has sensations of palpitation, tremors, flushing, rapid breathing. These reactions closely simulate the physical symptoms of 'fear'. Subjects were divided into four groups:

(1) The correctly informed group was told that the 'new compound' had side effects – these being the actual effects of epinephrine.
(2) The second group was given epinephrine but told that the 'new compound' would produce no side effects.
(3) The misinformed group was given epinephrine and told that the 'new compound' would have side effects, but these were impossible effects of epinephrine: headache, itching, numbness of feet.
(4) A fourth group was injected with the placebo and told it was the 'new compound' and would have no side effects.

The crux of the experiment involved subjects in groups 1 and 3 – those correctly and incorrectly informed about the side effects of the injection they had received. These subjects waited in a room, before the vision test was given, for 20 minutes. Each subject was placed alone with another who was an accomplice or 'stooge' working for the experimenters. The accomplice acted out a series of antics, presumably the effects of the drug. These simulated a high state of euphoria – singing, chatting cheerfully, making jokes, doodling, making a paper aeroplane and throwing it around. Subjects subjected to this 'suggestion treatment' were given a questionnaire with many questions but combining ratings of 'happy feelings at this moment'. It was found that subjects in the misinformed group 3 produced reports of euphoric reactions but informed subjects (group 1) did not. Other subjects from these two groups waited with an accomplice who simulated a high degree of anger, ending with him tearing up the questionnaire form. Again, subjects in group 3, the misinformed group, reported a large number of feelings of anger or irritation but the informed group 1 subjects did not report such feelings.

17

This study, together with a number of others, led the experimenters to conclude:

'It has been suggested first that, given a state of physiological arousal for which an individual has no explanation, he will label this state in terms of the cognitions available to him. This implies, of course, that by manipulating the cognitions of an individual in such a state we can manipulate his feelings in diverse directions. Experimental results support this proposition since, following the injection of epinephrine, those subjects who had no explanation of their bodily states give behaviour and self-report indications that they had been readily manipulable into disparate feeling states of euphoria and anger.'

From this it follows that, given a state of physiological arousal for which the individual has a satisfactory explanation, he will not label it in terms of any alternative cognitions available to him. Experimental evidence supports this expectation. In conditions in which subjects were injected with epinephrine and told correctly what they would feel, such subjects proved immune to the effect of 'manipulated cognitions' or suggestions.

Schachter's findings seem to be supported by other studies. G. W. Hohmann (1962, 1966) studied 25 patients suffering from lesions of the spinal cord. These were divided into five groups on the basis of measures of visceral innervations – the higher up the spinal cord the lesion, the less sensation is experienced. Schachter's theory would predict a decrease in emotion for patients with high-placed lesions. The studies confirmed a decrease in fear and anger responses the higher the lesion. Subjects with high-placed lesions reacted behaviourally to threat or provocation but reported they had no feelings. This result is complementary to an earlier experiment by Maranon (1924). He injected 210 subjects with epinephrine. Their reactions were recorded: 71% reported only physical sensations; 29% reported an emotional feeling but said this was 'false' or 'phoney'. It was as if they were afraid, but somehow unlike genuine fear. However, when a stimulus was presented representing an object of fear (e.g. reference to the death of a relative) their feelings became more lifelike. Maranon's subjects did not have feelings germane to fear, since they lacked any perceptions or information relevant to a threatening or dangerous situation. No objects of fear were present and so they did not interpret their fear-like physiological reactions as fear. Hohmann's subjects exhibited appropriate responses to threat but did not have feelings of fear in virtue of their lack of visceral arousal.

Schachter's thesis has some empirical support, viz. that cognitive reactions are more basic to emotion either than the feelings experienced or the underlying physiological changes. There must be diffuse arousal of the sympathetic nervous system for fear to exist, but this does not markedly structure the emotional response. Any feelings that occur are subordinate and highly manipulable in terms of our perceptions and interpretations of the situation. However, Schachter's account concentrates on inner states – physiological arousal plus cognitive orientation. He does not include actions in his theoretical model, although 'behaviour in relation to the object' is implied. Since 'action related to object' is important in our analysis, Schachter's theory only partially matches it.

Another group of psychologists has held that appraisals, specific cognitive states, intervene between the environmental situation and physiological-behavioural response in emotion. We appraise the situation as to whether it is harmful, or beneficial, or neutral to us. M. B. Arnold and R. S. Lazarus are the most generally quoted psychologists who hold this view. A considerable amount of experimental literature exists to test hypotheses derived from this theory and it seems generally agreed that these results are not sufficiently clear or decisive to be of great help. However, it is interesting that appraisal in terms of criteria of 'value' (that which is beneficial-harmful) is stressed in these studies. Our analysis has taken this as a special case, or derived use, of the concepts of emotion since not all threats and dangers liable to provoke fear are to biologically basic factors.

Beyond this group of experiments there are not many relevant experimental studies relating to our interpretation of the concept of 'fear'*. This is largely because most theories of emotion concentrate either on the physiological changes involved or in the sensations experienced, or on a mixture of both.

11 Fear and the Theory of Emotion

We have already presented considerations against identifying emotion with sensations or feelings. But one might expect the study of the physiological changes involved to be a sound basis for a theory of any emotion such as fear or rage. The search for the physiological bases of emotion has been disappointing so far. It is known that many specific parts of the brain and their characteristic mechanisms are involved, e.g. the limbic system and the endocrine reactions are obviously much involved, but exactly how the mechanisms interact is not known. It is not even quite certain what

---

*See also the review and discussion of this work from the physiological angle by Andrew Mayes in Chapter 2.

19

is the relative function of peripheral as compared with central brain mechanisms, so any purely physiologically based theory of emotion cannot take us far in psychology at present. Yet it might be argued that this is not simply due to the state of play in current research.

Emotion cannot be reduced to, or identified with, physiological changes as such. It is true that emotions can be changed by manipulating physicochemical functioning of the brain. Drugs can reduce or eliminate anxiety or depression. Also the physical symptoms of anxiety may abate after somebody has talked to and 'counselled' an anxious person, offering practical suggestions for coping, and encouraging the person to make decisions to take initiatives in relation to the objects of anxiety, or the cause of anxiety. This presumably produces 'feedback' from interaction with social environment which produces changes in brain functioning.

However, the bodily changes which are fundamentally part of the emotional state are not themselves the emotional state. Such physical changes as are known to occur in fear and anxiety occur in other contexts, and are integrated with a range of different behaviours, and different cognitive orientations. We classify physical states as part of, symptoms of, emotion only in *some* circumstances, not in others. They are basic to emotion, essential to emotion, but do not seem to constitute the whole of an emotion – at least in the sense that they alone supply the criteria of emotion.

If neither theories emphasising 'sensations' nor theories in psychology emphasising physiological changes in arousal are acceptable, what about those which concentrate on behaviour? It might be expected that behaviourist theories of emotion might illuminate the relationships between behaviour and its objects in emotion. On examination such theories turn out to be disappointing. Most behaviourists add little to the theory of emotion explicitly stated by J. B. Watson. This is somewhat a priori account. Watson defined emotion as 'an hereditarily pattern reaction' involving specific types of physiological change. Emotion is similar to instinct: it is an unconditioned response. However, emotion is distinct in so far as the stimuli evoking it come as a shock or trauma, putting the organism into a state of disorganisation or disruption of normal activity. Emotions are limited to 'agitations'. The study of infants led Watson to postulate three basic types of primitive emotional reactions which he called X, Y and Z.

The X-type results from the sudden removal of physical support, from loud noises, and from mild but sudden stimuli occurring when the infant is about to fall asleep or come awake. This is analogous to the adult response of 'fear'. The Y-type reaction results from restraining or impeding bodily movements, and corresponds to 'anger' in adults. The Z-type results from stroking the skin, and corresponds to 'love'. Typical infant responses in emotion are checking the breath, crying, smiling and making distinctive gurgling sounds. These primitive reactions are starting points for a complex conditioning process which results in adult fear, rage and love as the basic emotions. How the adult behaves in the presence of specific conditioned stimuli by producing fear, rage or love depends on his learning history.

One can readily question this theory. Is adult fear, as in the case of submitting to threats in blackmail, identical with the X-type situation of the infant? Are the responses in this fear-situation exactly of the same kind as in infant fear? If not, what developmental processes link them to the X-type reactions? Is fear in blackmail simply a refinement, through conditioning, of X-type behaviour? It would not be easy to demonstrate this implausible hypothesis.

Again, Watson gives the impression of being neutral in labelling certain infant reactions X-type, Y-type, Z-type. Yet he does imply that these are prototypic fear, rage and affection and he does so by referring to the usual criteria for identifying fear or rage: the circumstances in the environment, their effects on well being, the relationships of organism to 'object' of response. We only conceptualise these infant reactions when we regard them as 'behaviour related to circumstances' and so classify them as analogous to 'fear' or 'rage' in adults or older children. Reacting to a sudden noise by startling, holding breath, crying, gives warrant to conceptualise it as 'fear', even if this is called 'X-type' or 'primitive'. Watson illicitly introduces conventional notions of 'emotion' into the premises of his theory.

B. F. Skinner takes a somewhat different view of emotion from that of other behaviourists. 'Emotion is not primarily a kind of response at all but rather a state of strength comparable in many respects with a drive'. Emotion is identified and recognised in others by observing changes in certain learned responses, e.g. approach-avoidance patterns. Again he emphasises that certain types of stimulus characteristically evoke what is labelled 'emotions', viz. shock, restraint of movement, withholding reinforcement. Thus emotion is alternatively defined as 'a particular state of strength or weakness in one or more responses induced by any one of a class of operations'. But what type of response and what class of operation lead us to identify fear, rage, joy? Skinner's criteria, when examined, do not enable us to distinguish between any conditioned response and an emotional response. On his theory any response can be changed in strength by controlling conditions of reinforcement. Either all behaviour is emotional or else it is not possible to discriminate fear from the strengthening or weakening of a pecking response induced by a reinforcement schedule.

12   Some Tentative Conclusions

An examination of existing theories of emotion does not give us much hope of improving on our analysis of the concept of fear. But too much must not be placed on theory construction. It is unlikely that we shall reduce all fearing to a small number of neatly defined and precisely measured indices stateable within a tidy model. There is a great variety of possible onjects of fear and anxiety available in the human environment and these are subject to change (e.g. nuclear war, energy crises, pollution, did not impinge 70 years ago). There is wide scope in individual differences in learning to fear specific objects. There is a considerable range of individual differences in the way people perceive, construe, conceptualise situations, so that what provokes fear or anxiety for some does not do so for others. Predispositions to respond anxiously or fearfully owing to constitutional or personality differences must operate as a factor.

What this amounts to is that emotion concepts, in their descriptive function, refer to *general* conditions, each of which can have a variety of manifestations, and involve a considerable diversity of behaviour. 'Fear' or 'anxiety' are very broad classifications. William McDougall, who had clinical experience as a psychiatrist, did not regard 'anxiety' as a distinctive state. It was, for him, a term reflecting 'ill-defined ranges of experience and feeling'. When one reads case histories of dysthymic neurotics one is inclined to agree with McDougall; whatever common symptoms they might share, they also appear to exhibit considerable diversity of feature – among eliciting circumstances, types of behaviour, types of coping problem, developmental history, relation to other, e.g. psychosomatic symptoms. Not only does a term like 'fear' refer to a highly general condition, but any given state of fear may be changeable, exhibiting within its period of existence differing experiences and different types of reaction: it may not be a discrete reflex-like form of behaviour but unstable and volatile. Moreover, within the classification of 'emotion' there are several distinct subcategories: adaptive emotion, agitated states, moods, sentiments and what A. R. White calls 'feelings of completion', such as feeling well, tranquil, bored, mentally exhausted. All these are slightly different classifications requiring differentiating criteria. Any theory of emotion, or even of fear, would be too abstract and formal to be of any great use. It is more helpful to give an analysis of the ways in which such concepts work, even at an elementary level. Psychologists can survey the alternatives and decide which they wish to retain in their technical discourse, or else decide to avoid using such terms and fall back on specially constructed terms for use in specialised contexts. Which they decide is a pragmatic matter, although linguistic usage and logical rules for description and explanation still apply, especially in the still uncertain areas of the social sciences.

We have tried to synthesise some current thinking as to what constitutes an analysis of the concept of 'fear'. Our analysis is open-ended: it may not be sufficiently exact and rigorous in exposing differences in use, it may have neglected some interesting aspect of the functioning of the concept; it may be mistaken in certain respects and open to revision.

Anthony Kenny's triple criteria for identifying an appropriate use of the concept have been central and some use has been made of cognitive theories of emotion. What has been said may seem simplistic and straightforward. Yet it is in fact corrective of earlier thinking derivative from Descartes, Locke, Hume and the Mills who bequeathed to the earliest empirical psychologists of the 19th century some misleading ideas about basic psychological concepts. Some of this questionable thinking has become part of several contemporary theories of emotion which are discussed in most textbooks. To the extent that some of this long-settled dust has been cleared this somewhat Aristotelian approach is justified.

CHAPTER 2

The Physiology of Fear and Anxiety

Andrew Mayes

1 Introduction

Fear is a complex set of behaviours, patterns of physiological arousal and of cognitions, which has evolved in many species so as to optimise the chances of survival in the face of a wide range of threats and dangers. A paradigmatic example is provided by the prey-predator interaction. Thus, Ratner (1975) has proposed that many prey species, on seeing a predator in the distance, will freeze. If the predator continues to approach, the prey will flee. If this attempt to avoid danger proves unsuccessful and the victim is cornered, he will turn and fight. Finally, in a number of species, if the fight goes badly and the prey is in the clutches of the predator, it may display the death feigning response – now more usually referred to as tonic immobility. Evidence suggests that predators are less likely to kill a death-feigning victim (see Gallup, 1974). These behaviours are accompanied by activation of various components of the peripheral autonomic nervous system and of the neuro-endocrine system. Within an evolutionary context, it is heuristically useful to postulate that such physiological arousal increases an animal's capacity to respond adaptively in danger situations. Physiological research on fear and anxiety must then try to answer two questions: (a) what are the autonomic and endocrine components of fear, and what, if any, are their functions? and (b) how does the brain mediate the cognitive/perceptual, behavioural, autonomic/endocrinal aspects of fear, and their interaction? Although the second question, in a sense, subsumes the first, the distinction is a convenient one because, until recently, research was directed either at peripheral physiological correlates or fear or at central structures mediating it, but not at both in an integrated fashion.

Unfortunately, current answers to the above questions are difficult to review for three main reasons. First, much relevant research has been aimed not explicitly at fear, but rather at phenomena such as stress, avoidance learning, psychosomatic aetiology and emotion in general. Although fear is important in all these phenomena it is difficult to determine whether effects on variables are caused by it, other emotions, or by nonemotional factors. This difficulty may explain why so little research has been couched in terms of fear, and relates to the second reason. There is no consensus about what distinguishes emotions from nonemotional states and what distinguishes one emotion from another. Although Gray (1971b) is probably right to suggest that all emotions are reactions to reinforcing events or signals of such events, this formulation is insufficiently precise to help us determine whether interest, enjoyment or love are emotions, or whether fear and anxiety are the same emotion. Many researchers regard fear and anxiety as identical, e.g. Levitt (1971), whereas, in contrast, Izard (1972) views fear as a fundamental emotion and anxiety as a variable and complex state comprising fear and at least two other basic emotions such as anger, shame, guilt or interest. Even if we accept that these views represent unacceptable extremes and adopt an eclectic position in which anxiety differs from fear in being milder*, longer lasting, often arising from internal rather than external causes, frequently irrational and maladaptive and concerned with future possible threats rather than actual ones, it still has to be decided whether physiologically this is merely a difference of degree. If so, provided the eclectic interpretation is used, anxiety should be associated with less intense but more prolonged physiological and experiential components, and can be traced to the similar way to fear by physiological and biochemical manipulations.

The third reason why it is not possible to give a straightforward summary of current physiological views about fear is the lack of universal agreement about the relationship of its experimental, behavioural and physiological aspects. Major disagreement has focussed on the relationship between fear's physiological and experiential components, and can be traced to the influence of the James–Lange theory of emotion. To consider clearly the nature and relevance of the autonomic and endocrine activation in fear it will be necessary to consider the theorising of James and his epigones.

2 Views on the Interrelationship of Fear's Main Components

James' theory (1884), applied to fear, may be expressed paradoxically as asserting that we are afraid because we run, and not vice versa. For him, the feeling of fear is the perception of feedback from physiological changes initiated by the emotional stimulus. These changes comprise not only autonomic-endocrinal activities but also skeletal ones. In contrast, Lange

---

*This is essentially the position adopted by A. T. Carr in Chapter 7.

(1885), a physiologist, regarded the experiential and motor aspects of emotion as unimportant, and seems to have argues that the vasomotor components of autonomic arousal actually are the emotion. A syncretic version of their views has been very influential in subsequent thinking about emotion and motivation. This version states that the emotional feelings are the perception of feedback from the autonomic-endocrinal activations elicited by emotional stimuli. Different emotions can be distinguished by the experiencer (and presumably experimenter) because they are associated with different patterns of activation. The theory requires such differences in activation pattern not only to be present but also to be perceptually distinguishable. Cannon's (1927) famous critique of the James–Lange theory is based on five objections relating to the alleged undifferentiated responsiveness and insensitivity of the autonomic nervous system. Briefly, he claimed: (a) the latency of visceral changes is too great to be a direct source of emotional feeling; (b) artificial induction of visceral changes does not produce emotion; (c) the viscera are relatively insensitive structures; (d) the same visceral changes occur in all emotions and, also, in some nonemotional states; and (e) blocking afferent feedback from the viscera by deafferentation does not impair emotional behaviour. These criticisms have, in recent years, between subject to a number of qualifications (see Fehr & Stern, 1970; Lader & Tyrer, 1975), some of which will be considered later in this chapter. Nevertheless, most theorists do not accept the unalloyed form of the James–Lange theory. In its place, Cannon advanced a centralist theory in which the thalamus, when released by appropriate stimuli, activated hypothalamic structures which coordinate visceral and endocrine activation, and independently, the cortex, which was held responsible for emotional experience. Subsequent criticisms of Cannon's emphasis on the role of the thalamus (Papez, 1937; Maclean, 1949), stressing instead the importance for emotion of limbic structures, will be discussed later. More germane to the present context are two other features of the theory: first, its separation of the experiential and physiological components of emotion, and, second, his reinterpretation of the physiological arousal as an emergency reaction rather than an epiphenomenon of no significance or a discriminative cue for a given emotional state.

Current researchers have accepted Cannon's suggestion that the emotions such as fear have adaptive significance although his detailed claims have been questioned. Along with Hans Selye's (1952) concept of the 'general adaptation syndrome', which focuses more on longer term physiological adjustments to extreme conditions, it has spawned a plethora of research on stress. His total separation of the experiential and physiological aspects of emotions has, however, been more seriously challenged. In some now classic experiments performed in the 1960's, Schachter (see Sachachter, 1975, for a review) claimed to have shown that the effects of manipulations, such as adrenaline injections or chlorpromazine administrations, depended on the cognitive context in which they occurred*. Thus volunteer subjects, injected with adrenaline and kept ignorant of its visceral effects, became either more angry or more euphoric than several types of control subjects, as a function of whether they were exposed to stooges who either foamed at the mouth about the supposed heinous activities of the experimenter or engaged in a series of apparently impromptu comedy turns. When, with their respective stooges, experimental subjects acted more angrily or more euphorically than controls, and subsequently reported feeling more angry or more euphoric. Although significant, the effects observed were not large and there has been some difficulty in replicating them (Marshall, 1976; Maslach, 1977; and see pp. 265–290 in Zimbardo, Ebbeson & Maslach (1977) for a critique of Schachter's experiments). Related and complementary evidence exists, however, which supports some of Schachter's claims. Thus, although clinical injections of hydrocortisone do not increase the immediate experience of anxiety, they do enhance anxiety proneness (Weiner, Dorman, Persky, Stach, Norton & Levitt, 1963). Furthermore, Valins (see Valins, 1970, for a review) has produced similar effects to Schachter by providing subjects with false feedback about their visceral responses. One study showed that nude pictures were rated as more attractive when subjects were falsely led to believe that their heart rates had increased whilst viewing. Similarly, subjects were deceived into thinking that although their heart rates increased on exposure to shock, they showed no increase when viewing slides of various snakes. Control subjects saw the same slides but knew the tape-recorded beats they heard were not their heart beats. Subsequently, although equally 'phobic', experimental subjects were more willing to approach real snakes (65% actually picked up and held live snakes) and presumably felt less afraid than controls. It would seem that the perception of chimerical visceral changes influenced the intensity of both emotional feeling and behaviour. Critics have, however, pointed out that the false feedback used by Valins may have induced real visceral changes, which influenced his results.

According to Schachter and Valins, perceived physiological arousal, whether illusory of veridical, determines the intensity with which an emotional (or nonemotional) state is felt and how intensely it is acted out. The particular emotion experienced, however, depends on the cognitive context in which the arousal occurs. So whether an adrenaline injection increases anger, fear, euphoria or amusement is contingent on the cognitive

---

*Note how such empirical findings influence the conceptual analysis of fear in Chapter 1 by Robert Thomson.

interpretation of why its physiological effects are present. This view implies that emotions as well as some nonemotional states are all associated with a more-or-less undifferentiated state of physiological activiation, which varies only in intensity. To this extent it is similar to Lindsley's activation theory of emotion (Lindsley, 1951) which gives a central role to cortical arousal by reticular formation influences. The two approaches differ in that Lindsley believes that emotions can be differentiated solely in terms of the arousal's intensity whereas Schachter argues that the emotion experienced is a function of the cognitive appraisal of the situation. In Schachter's view, without perceived physiological arousal an emotion like fear should not be felt even if a situation is perceived as threatening. Conversely, fear should not be experienced if physiological arousal occurs without a concomitant threat appraisal.

The first of these two desiderata of Schachter's theory does not seem to be compatible with two of Cannon's criticisms of the James–Lange theory. Cannon objected both that 'visceral changes are too slow to be a source of emotional feeling', and that 'total separation of the viscera from the central nervous system does not alter emotional behaviour'. Both criticisms point to situations in which emotions seem to occur without visceral activity. Since the work of Sherrington (1900) on sympathectomised dogs and of Cannon, Lewis and Britton (see Cannon, 1939) on sympathectomised cats, many studies have been completed, generally indicating that well learned emotional behaviours, before sympathectomy, remain intact in animals and man. There is, however, some evidence that sympathetic activity facilitates the acquisition of learned emotional behaviour and that sympathectomised animals act but may not feel emotional. Thus Wynne & Solomon (1955) have shown that sympathectomised dogs are slower in acquiring an avoidance response than control animals. Their lesioned dogs also extinguished the response much faster than controls. This rapid extinction did not apply to two animals that had been sympathectomised *after* acquiring the avoidance response. They were just as resistant to extinction as the controls. Although the classic study of Dana (1921) was interpreted by Cannon as proving that humans deafferented by spinal injury are emotionally normal, a more recent and extensive study by Hohmann (1962, 1966) points to a different conclusion. Hohmann divided a sample of 25 paraplegic and quadriplegic patients into five groups according to the height of their spinal damage. The groups represent a continuum of visceral sensitivity, such that the higher the lesion the less the visceral sensation. If Schachter's cognitive theory of emotion is correct the higher the lesion the less will be the experience of emotion. Each of the subjects was given a long, structured interview which concentrated on emotional feeling rather than associated thinking. Subjects were required to recall comparable emotion-arousing incidents from before

28

and after their injuries, and then to assess the relative intensity of the felt emotions. Hohmann's data show that Schachter's expectations are borne out. The higher the lesion, the less was the reported emotional feeling. This relationship held very strongly for fear and, possibly, slightly less strongly for anger. It also held with grief and sexual excitement – interestingly, the sole exception was sentimentality, which was unaffected by the lesion level. Typically, the subjects reported acting emotionally in various situations although they didn't feel it, in order not to be taken advantage of by others. Schachter suggests that the 'as if' nature of the emotions reported by Hohmann's spinal cases bears a contrapuntal relationship to that reported by Maranon's (1924) subjects. Some of these volunteers, who must have been pioneer recipients of adrenaline injections made statements like 'I feel as if I were frightened; however I am calm'.

Even the above cognitive-physiological proposal is correct and the feeling of fear is the result of an interaction between the cognitive appraisal of threat and physiological arousal, certain aspects of how these two components relate to each other and fearful behaviour remain unresolved. A possible route out of this uncertainty is offered by the thorough-going cognitivist approach of Lazarus (1966, 1975a and b). Lazarus contends that the physiological arousal of fear and anxiety arise as a consequence of a situation being appraised as dangerous or threatening and therefore to be avoided. Such fear-eliciting perception in animals may be very concrete, simple and built into the nervous system. Whereas in man, and perhaps other primates, symbolic processes and learning become dominant, vastly increasing the gamut of situations which can be seen as dangerous or threatening. This vastly increased sensitivity to threat helps explain why anxiety frequently seems maladaptive, if it is accepted that the 'fear system' was evolved to cope with immediate dangers rather than distant, vague and possibly imaginary threats. Lazarus goes so far as to challenge Selye's view that the 'general adaptation syndrome' is a response to any noxious stimulus. In contrast, he argues that in many cases, although probably not all, an appraisal of threat has to be made if the adaptation response is to be elicited. For example Symington, Currie, Curran & Davidson's (1955) study implies that unconsciousness and anaesthesia eliminate the adrenal effects of psychological stress. Patients, who had died of injury or disease whilst continuously unconscious showed evidence, at autopsy, of having had normal adrenocortical activity during the period of dying. Patients who had been conscious during this period did, however, show adrenocortical changes. It has, also, been shown that bodily harm does not elicit an endocrine response in unconscious animals, and Gray Ramsey, Villareal & Krakauer (1956) have demonstrated that general anaesthesia (itself, a physiological stressor) elicits no significant adrenal reaction.

Although unconsciousness is an instance where the lack of cognitive appraisal prevents the triggering of the physiological and behavioural components of fear, Lazarus is more interested in those situations where man's cognitive coping strategies enable him to interpret events, which, at face value, are very threatening, in a relatively benign light. This distinction between the nominal and functional significance of stimuli, and the emphasis on the protean and flexible nature of man's cognitive capacities is central to the interpretation of the human physiological literature on emotion. It is nicely illustrated by two studies of Bourne (1970, 1971) and the effects of two combat situations in Vietnam on soldiers' level of 17-hydroxycorticosteroid secretion. In one study, the level of these steroids (known to be elevated in fearful subjects) was assessed by taking 24-hour urine samples from a number of helicopter ambulance crew members who were flying dangerous missions. Bourne found that these hormones were consistently excreted at a rate approximately 20% less than the normal calculated for men of the subjects' body weight. There was no correlation between the rate of excretion and whether the subjects were exposed to the danger of a combat mission or were hanging around the base during a cease-fire period. Bourne, who had gained the men's confidence by flying on missions with them, was able to find out how they coped with their predicament. Two of the men thought they were invulnerable for religious reasons, another had estimated that the probability of being hit on any particular mission was so low that he could disregard it, and yet another controlled his thoughts by repeatedly running through what he was going to do when the battle zone was reached. Clearly, a variety of cognitive coping techniques can all effectively prevent a situation being appraised as threatening and this blocks the physiological response. Military training is in part aimed to control a soldier's thinking in battle so as to minimise the apprehension of threat. Bourne obtained similar results with a 12-man team of the Special Warfare Forces which was exposed to especially risky conditions. Their coping seemed to depend very much on their self-perception as competent, self-reliant and aggressive individuals. The control of fear and anxiety by psychological means has its limitations in the military sphere. It was the officers in Bourne's studies who showed relatively elevated corticosteroid activity. They were, ineluctably, more personally involved than their men because of their role as intermediaries, often having to pass on unpleasant orders from higher command.

Lazarus and Schachter emphasise slightly different aspects of the experiential component of emotion. Lazarus argues that emotion is basically a response-complex to a particular kind of appraisal whereas Schachter sees emotional feeling as something that derives from the interaction between appraisal and physiological activity. If the interpretations are combined and applied to fear the following picture emerges. An individual perceives his surroundings, comparing what he perceives with similar situations stored in memory. If these previous situations have been associated with damage or danger an appraisal of threat will be made. Sometimes these appraisals will not be based on memory but will be 'built-in' to emerge at some stage of maturation. With humans, the possibility of unconscious appraisal of threat must also be considered. However it is reached, a threat appraisal will result in a complex set of activations of autonomic, endocrine and cortical systems. Some of these activations will have sensory effects, which when perceived in the context of threat appraisal result in the feeling of being frightened. Threat appraisal without physiological feedback, or physiological activity without threat appraisal, will give rise to an anomalous feeling of fear which has a 'cold' or 'as if' quality. In certain circumstances, appraisal of threat may be experienced perceptibly before the occurrence of physiological arousal. The latter may only become apparent after the danger is over as when a driver swerves his car to avoid an accident. Normally, however, when fear is felt, the Schachter-Lazarus approach suggests, threat appraisal and the effects of physiological arousal are experienced together.

There are, unfortunately, two basic and related difficulties that require some qualifications to the above approach to fear. The first arises because a large body of recent data suggests that fear may be felt without physiological disturbance and, conversely, that in 'fear situations' little subjective fear may be reported despite the presence of quite marked physiological reactions (Rachman, 1974). The second difficulty concerns the link between threat appraisal and felt fear, and fear expression and behaviour. Most workers regard fear as involving a 'felt action tendency' but do little to explain how feeling afraid leads to fear behaviours.

Much of the evidence for dissociations between fear feelings and physiological arousal has emerged in the clinical treatment of phobic patients. Thus, although presentations of a real or symbolic version of a fearful object may elicit diminished physiological arousal after treatment, patients may continue to complain of unacceptable feelings of fear. A similar dissociation was observed by Fenz & Epstein (1967) in the study of fear among veteran parachute jumpers. Whereas the physiological measures of heart rate, skin conductance and respiration continued to build up steadily until the time of the jump, subjective ratings showed a sharp increase before boarding, but then decreased until around the time of their jump. Interestingly, novices who showed much greater physiological disturbances did not show this dissociation. Their physiological reactions and subjective feelings varied correspondingly. If fear feelings and physiological reactions are imperfectly coupled systems then their coupling seems to improve at extreme levels of fear.

31

Not only are fear feelings and physiological arousal imperfectly coupled, but also neither is coupled perfectly with fearful behaviour. Rachman (1974) points to the fact that even when phobic patients show behavioural improvements, such as claustrophobics being willing to travel on underground trains, they may still report being just as fearful as before treatment. Lang's (1970) investigations have led him to conclude that the subjective and behavioural aspects of fear may be imperfectly correlated. Further corroboration comes from studies which have failed to find a consistent relationship between avoidance behaviour intensity and 17-hydroxycorticosterone plasma levels in monkeys (Natelson, Smith, Stokes & Root, 1973).

What tentative conclusions can be drawn from this salmagundi of findings and theories? Certainly, the components of fear are coupled, although imperfectly so. They are not independent. Indeed, caution is necessary in interpreting studies which suggest that physiological arousal can be decoupled from fear's other components. These studies typically use few physiological measures and it is well known that physiological responses to stress correlate poorly (see Lang, 1970). The degree of uncoupling that does occur can perhaps be explained in two main ways. First, the physiological and behavioural components of fear can probably be independently influenced by conditioning and other kinds of learning. For example, De Toledo & Black (1968) have shown that cardiac deceleration is acquired more slowly than behavioural components on a condition suppression task with rats. One would predict greater degrees of uncoupling in species in which more learning occurs. Second, there is a lack of clarity about the meaning of 'feeling afraid', so that much theoretical disputation resolves into semantic pettifogging. To judge by informal sampling of laymen this unclarity applies not only to theorists. 'Feeling afraid' may be taken to mean (a) some kind of cognitive appraisal of threat, (b) feelings arising from physiological reactions in a threatening situation, and (c) the feeling of a drive to take avoiding action from a threat. It is a mistake to think people always talk about the same thing when they refer to 'fear feelings'. This point applies a fortiori to assessments of the intensity of fear feelings. Such assessments are, anyway, unlikely to be influenced by fine-grained changes of physiological arousal because, as suggested by the studies of Valins (1970), we are relatively insensitive to such arousal changes. In the light of this and the vagueness of usage, poor correlations between fear's components are to be expected.

How the components are coupled is still poorly understood. Threat appraisal influences physiological responding and is, in turn, influenced by the latter. Further cognitions (what Lazarus calls 'secondary appraisals') influence what behavioural actions are taken, and the intensity, direction

32

and efficiency of these are likely to be affected by the physiological reactions engendered by the primary appraisal. It may well be that the role of physiological arousal in fear feelings, and, to a lesser extent, fear behaviour is an acquired one, arising from the frequent association of such perceived arousal with threat appraisal. Such a mechanism could explain individual differences in the interpretation of 'feeling afraid'. Some of us may be more Schachterian than others. In my view, the main deficiency of this picture is that it pays insufficient court to the 'primitiveness' of much fearful behaviour. This is best illustrated by situations where fear is maladaptive, irrational and possesses a 'driven' quality. Lazarus (1966) cites documented instances where, on the battlefield, terrified soldiers were unable to pull the triggers of their rifles or run around out of control in the line of fire. Phobics are capable of rationally judging the object of their fear as foolish and yet obviously are terrified of that object. This suggests that a distinction can be drawn between a rational and primitive type of appraisal, mediated by different parts of the brain, but still interacting. The former could weakly influence the latter and other fear components in the ways argued by Lazarus, but it is the latter which has been evolved as a mode of perceptual appraisal closely tied to subsequent physiological responding, fearful expression and avoidance behaviour. Primitive appraisal could give fear its 'felt' quality and, as will be discussed later, is probably mediated by limbic structures. In contrast, rational appraisal is probably cortically mediated and influences other fear processes more indirectly.

3 The Nature and Functions of the Physiological Arousal in Fear

It was Cannon and his Harvard associates who first demonstrated the sensitivity of the sympathetic-adrenomedullary system to psychological stimuli. These finding led him to formulate the view that the activation of this system served an emergency function, preparing the organism for more efficient struggle in states of fear, pain and rage (Cannon, 1915). Selye's (1952) later emphasis on pituitary-adrenal activity as a result of stress extended the range of reactions studied in fear and stress. It is, however, generally agreed that the pituitary-adrenal system is slower to react, and required higher levels of psychosocial stimulation before doing so, than does the sympathetic-adrenomedullary system (Levi, 1972). In Cannon's view, exposure to various stresses results in the rapid physiological preparation of the body for swift action. Changes include: increases in the rate and strength of heart beat with associated increases in the rate at which oxygen can be pumped round the system; redistribution of the blood supply from the skin and viscera to the muscles and brain; release of oxygen-carrying red blood cells through contraction of the spleen; release of stored sugar from the liver;

33

deeper respiration and bronchial dilation; pupillary dilation; increased coagulating ability of the blood and an increase in the number of lymphocytes to aid tissue repair.

If the stress is prolonged the influence of the adrenocortical system becomes prominent. Under the control of the anterior pituitary adrenocorticotrophic hormone (ACTH) glucocorticoids are released from the adrenal cortex. These hormones, which include hydrocortisone, corticosterone and cortisone, have an anti-inflammatory action as well as modulating glucose metabolism. They facilitate the transformation of nonsugars and increase the deposition of sugar in the liver, thus containing the process initiated in the earlier alarm response to stress, adjusting the body for rapid energy expenditure. The glucocorticoids also act synergistically with the adrenal medullary hormones, adrenaline and noradrenaline, to amplify the reactions of the blood vessels. The anti-inflammatory effects of these hormones are, however, paradoxical within the adaptational framework. The actions include the inhibition of antibody formation, reduced rate of tissue regeneration around a wound, decreases in the number of lymphocytes and eosinophils, and a general reduction in the weight of lymphoid tissues. A natural consequence is an increased susceptibility to infection and a decreased capacity to recover from wounds.

More recent endocrinological research, epitomised by the work of Mason and his associates (see Mason, J. W., 1975 for a review), has enlarged the range of hormonal systems known to be affected by fear-provoking stimuli. It appears that the pituitary-thyroidal, pituitary gonadal, growth hormone and insulin systems, also, sensitively reflect fear reactions. Mason has used a variety of hormonal assays to measure changes in situations where monkeys are required to develop conditioned avoidance responses or be exposed to unconditioned aversive stimuli, or where humans are manipulated so as to be anxious. The detailed nature of the results is complex but the overall impression is that release of hormones prompting catabolic mobilisation of energy resources rises during states of fear and anxiety, whereas anabolic hormones reciprocally decline, only to recover in the aftermath of the emotion when anabolic processes would be paramount. So thyroid and growth hormone activity increase along with increased activity in the adrenomedullary and pituitary-adrenal systems, whereas levels of androgens, oestrogens and insulin decrease. There is, however, some suggestion that when stress is prolonged there may be decreases in thyroid and growth hormone activity. Reliability of assay techniques is still controversial so caution over all these conclusions is warranted. Nevertheless, the results are not contradictory, but rather suggest that acute fear and chronic fear are associated with rather different physiological

34

consequences. The effects of prolonged emotional stress on sexual and reproductive activity are, indeed, well corroborated. Males show a fall in the production of spermatozoa and may have delayed or even suppressed puberty onset. In female primates the menstrual cycle may be disrupted or blocked, and in sub-primate females there may be an equivalent disturbance of oestrus. Associated disruptions include decreases in uterine weight, ovulatory block, an increase in spontaneous abortions and failure during lactation.

Although extending Cannon's original views, the more recently discovered endocrinal responses to fear stimuli do not seem to require a modification of his basic position. The physiological reactions to fear and stress optimise the efficiency of rapid, high-energy expenditure to the detriment of long-term growth, reproduction and disease resistance. A more careful look at the literature does, however, suggest the need for some changes. First, Cannon overemphasises the idea that fear is associated with a rather undifferentiated dominance of the peripheral sympathetic nervous system – the parasympathetic being reciprocally inhibited. Second, he insufficiently appreciates how radically physiological reactions may vary in different fear-eliciting contexts, with different degrees of fear, different individuals and when exposure to fear is over a short or long period. Third, he focuses on the way the emergency reaction prepares the body for rapid action at the expense of considering facilitatory effects on the brain. These points will be considered in turn.

Classic observations by Sherrington (1917) indicate that emotional excitement is associated with both sympathetic and parasympathetic discharges with the dominance of the former producing a sympathetic effect in the intact organism. Thus, dogs exposed to a loud noise show heart rate increases. When the upper spinal cord is cut, abolishing sympathetic but not parasympathetic influences, the heart rate actually decreases. Similarly, it has been shown by Gelhorn, Cortell & Feldman (1941) that cats frightened by exposure to barking dogs show a rise in blood sugar, but a fall when the effect of sympathetic discharges on the adrenal medulla is eliminated. The influence of adrenaline is responsible for the rise in blood sugar, whereas the decrease observed postoperatively appears to be mediated by insulin, under the control of the vagus because the effect is abolished when the parasympathetic vagi are severed. It is also clear, as will be discussed later, that even in normal organisms some parasympathetic responses may achieve dominance in fear. Micturition, defecation and nausea are notorious reactions to fear which occur in many species. Additionally, penile erection, which is at least partially a parasympathetic response, has been associated with acute fear in monkeys and human infants. The response has also achieved lay recognition and has been even noted in the turtle (Hellman,

35

1970)! Relative sympathetic and parasympathetic activity is very much a function of the conditions of fear generation and individual factors. Just how much physiological reactivity varies in fear-eliciting conditions will now be discussed.

It is a central feature of Cannon's emergency reaction and Selye's general adaptation syndrome that the physiological reaction to a range of emotions and stress stimuli is undifferentiated. In contrast, a desideratum of the James-Lange theory is that different emotions must be associated with different patterns of physiological responding. Support for differentiation comes from the everyday observation that anger is associated with a red face whereas fear is accompanied by a white face. Early evidence that this difference is part of a more complex pattern was indicated in a fascinating case study of Wolf & Wolff (1943). They had the chance to investigate an Irish New Yorker called Tom, whose oesophagus had been severely damaged at the age of nine when he drank some very hot clam chowder. It was necessary to make an opening in the abdominal wall so that Tom could feed himself by putting food directly in his stomach. It was noted that his stomach showed two basic reaction patterns under different emotional conditions. It showed either an increased blood supply, mucosal engorgement, increased secretion of hydrochloric acid and increased activity of the stomach muscles or the opposite set of changes. The former pattern of increased activity was found when Tom was angry and the latter pattern of decreased activity when he was afraid or depressed. These observations have since been confirmed by Reichsman, Engle & Segal (1955) in a 6-year-old girl with gastric fistula.

Ax (1953) extended these findings further in a study where 43 subjects were exposed to fear- and anger-provoking circumstances whilst seven physiological measures were being recorded. In the fear condition, subjects, who had been wired up to the recording apparatus, were told that it had a 'high-voltage short-circuit'. In the anger condition, a stooge passing as a technician wandered around the laboratory insulting everyone including the experimental subject. Ax found that seven of the 14 measures taken showed significant discrimination between anger and fear. Diastolic blood pressure rises, heart rate falls, number of rises in skin conductance and muscle potential increases were greater in anger than in fear, whereas skin conductance increases, number of muscle potential increases and respiration rate increases were greater for fear than for anger. It was argued that the physiological response pattern seen for anger is similar to that produced by injections of adrenaline and noradrenaline, and that seen with fear is similar to the reactions produced by adrenaline. This interpretation received corroboration from Funkenstein (1956), who studied the blood pressure response to mecholyl injections of normal and psychiatric individuals whose normal reaction to stress was either one of anger, or one of anxiety or

36

depression. Mecholyl produces a different blood pressure response depending on whether pressure has previously been increased by noradrenaline or adrenaline. Those whose predominant emotional response was anger showed the noradrenaline type of mecholyl response, whereas fearful/depressive responders showed a basically adrenaline response pattern.

Some of the early studies of catecholamine excretion (Elmadjian, Hope & Lamson, 1957; Silverman & Cohen, 1960) produced results compatible with those of Funkenstein – adrenaline seemed to be associated with anxious reactions and noradrenaline with aggressive ones. There even seems to be evidence (Goodall, 1951) that the adrenal medullas of aggressive species produce mainly noradrenaline, whereas those of fearful, submissive species produce mainly adrenaline. It seems unlikely that these physiological reactions are normally perceptually distinguishable or related, in any simple way. to the experiential aspects of emotion. It is more likely that they occur because of the particular response requirement of an emotional situation. High levels of both adrenaline and noradrenaline occur when energy is being expended in large amounts such as in active sports. In contrast, the adrenergic reaction is found where little that is active can be appropriately done, e.g. when undergoing a stressful interview or playing in goal. This view receives support from the results of plasma-catecholamine studies of monkeys by Mason, Mangan, Brady, Conrad & Rioch (1961). They noted that adrenaline output is increased in situations characterised by novelty and uncertainty, but a rise in noradrenaline is found in conditions which are familiar and stereotyped, and also unpleasant. It has also been demonstrated that adrenaline and, to a lesser extent, noradrenaline excretion increases when subjects are watching an amusing film (Levi, 1965). This last finding reinforces the idea that it is the response requirements of a situation, rather than emotional feeling, which are most important in determining the physiological response. It remains to be seen whether this response-demand hypothesis can incorporate two further observations. The first is that the threshold for release of noradrenaline to psychosocial stimuli is generally higher than that of adrenaline. The second is that under pleasant, relaxed conditions associated with reward, decreases in catecholamine and glucocorticoid production occur (Frankenhaeuser, 1975; Coover, Sutton & Heybach, 1977).

Ax (1953), in discussing his results, reported that between-subject variance was significantly greater than within-subject variance, which he pointed out agreed with the findings of Lacey (1950) that there is considerable specificity in individual patterns of physiological responding. Not only may individuals show markedly different patterns of responding to nominally similar stresses, but Lacey (1959) has also claimed that the same individuals respond similarly to a stressor over a 4-year period. He refers to this phenomenon as intrastressor stereotypy of response. Physiological response specificity is characteristic of people in general and what applies to the normal person may be seen more strikingly when psychosomatic pathology is involved. Thus sufferers from Raynaud's disease (in which excessive vasoconstriction of the hands causes pain and other complications) show a very large drop in hand skin temperature when exposed to emotional stress, especially when this is aggravated with cold. Individuals with gastric ulcers show only a very slight drop in hand temperature under the same conditions, but show big increases in stomach acid secretion unlike the Raynaud's disease patients (see Graham, 1972, for a review). A study by Moos & Engel (1962) further indicates how specific response patterns can be. These workers compared a group of arthritics with a group of hypertensives in an emotion-provoking situation. EMG electrodes were placed over the muscle group which had recently been associated with most arthritic pain as well as over a relatively pain free group. Two EMG placements were made in similar sites on the hypertensives, and the blood pressure of both groups was measured. The expected dissociation between EMG and blood pressure changes of the two groups was observed, but the arthritic patients only showed increased EMG reactivity compared to the hypertensive group in the muscle group associated with recent pain.

There is some reason to suppose that a sex difference in physiological reactivity to emotion exists, as well as individual stereotypy. When allowances are made for body weight, no difference remains in catecholamine excretion between the sexes (Karki, 1956). Under stressful conditions, such as performing an intelligence test under time pressure or engaging in an arithmetic task, differences do, however, emerge. Males show significant increases in adrenaline output over that seen in resting conditions, whereas the output of females increases little if at all. Another type of difference has been shown by the Libersons (1975) in a study where men and women were exposed for 1 minute to the maximum electric shock they could tolerate. Although tolerance levels were similar, the men showed a significant increase in systolic blood pressure immediately following the shock period whereas women did not. By contrast, the women showed significant increases in their respiratory rates while the men, if anything, revealed slight reductions. Although individual and sex differences are probably salient independent variables determining the pattern of physiological reactivity in fear-eliciting contexts, caution is warranted. Some of the effects may be caused by individuals conferring different emotional interpretations upon nominally identical situations.

Although physiological reactions are a function of individual and sex differences as well as of different emotional states, it also seems likely that

38

they will vary as a function of the particular fear-provoking contingencies. This might be predicted, if it is accepted that different response requirements elicit different physiological responses, because fear behaviours range from fighting and fleeing to freezing and tonic immobility. Although the former are associated with predominantly sympathetic responding there is some evidence that tonic immobility elicits a more parasympathetic kind of kind of reaction. Nash, Gallup & Czech (1976) have recorded heart rate, respiration and body temperature during tonic immobility in chickens. Heart rate decreased throughout the period, respiration, after an initial increase, showed a similar slowing, and body temperature was lowered throughout the period. Malcuit, Ducharme & Belanger (1968) have reported a steep heart rate deceleration in rats that display freezing prior to shock in an avoidance task. Rats, actively avoiding, show a cardiac acceleration. The deceleration was accompanied by a decrease in overt reactivity to shock. Such changes in somatic and cardiac activity have been interpreted as part of a global response to attenuate the effects of noxious stimulation (Malcuit, 1973). In this and similar situations, the evidence shows that it is unlikely that the cardiac changes are secondary to somatic activity.

Further support for these ideas is provided by work using models of psychosomatic disorders. It is popularly believed that both heart disease and ulceration can result from chronic anxiety or fear. Evidence suggests that noradrenaline, released through sympathetic activity, is a factor in cardiac degeneration, whereas ulceration is primarily a symptom of excessive parasympathetic activity. In a series of studies, Corley and his associates (e.g. Corley, Shiel, Mauck, Clark & Barber, 1977) have testing monkeys in an anxiety-provoking situation where they had to respond repeatedly to avoid shock. Yoked monkeys received shocks whenever the 'executives' failed to respond appropriately, but were given no control over the shock. Two patterns of cardiovascular response were observed. If the subject had some control over the shocks he showed excessive sympathetic activity which if prolonged resulted in cardiac disease. Those subjects who could do nothing about the shock developed a passive kind of anxiety and showed dominance of the parasympathetic system. In one study, the yoked monkeys showed marked physical deterioration and a dangerous degree of heart rate slowing, sufficiently serious in two cases to cause ventricular arrest and death. Voodoo death in man, and its equivalent in animals, seems to be well authenticated (Goodfriend & Wolpert, 1976) and excessive parasympathetic activity is probably its mechanism. Interestingly, cases of dying have also been reported in some animals who have had tonic immobility induced (Gallup, 1974). Weiss (1968), using rats, but similar procedures to Corley, has been able to show that ulceration occurs far more frequently in yoked animals that have no control over their environment. The availability of an effective coping procedure in an anxiety-provoking situation seems radically to alter autonomic activity.

Gellhorn is a worker whose ideas are important to consider in the context of physiological variability in fear situations (e.g. see Gellhorn, 1970). Following the views of W. R. Hess, he argues that autonomic changes are correlated with somatic and cortical ones, forming two major systems. Ergotropic activity comprises increased sympathetic discharges, increased cortical excitation indicated by EEG desynchronisation, and increased activity and tone of the striated muscles. Conversely, trophotropic activity comprises lessening of somatic responsiveness, increased parasympathetic discharges, reduced muscle tone and the presence of sleep-like EEG potentials. Ergotropic activity is believed to be integrated in the posterior hypothalamus whereas the more anterior regions of the hypothalamus control trophotropic functions. Under normal conditions reciprocal innervation operates, such that a stimulus which excites one system decreases the activity of the other. Rebound effects also occur, such that, following high activity in one system, the antagonistic system becomes more sensitive to stimuli. Gellhorn cites evidence that manipulating muscle tension can influence the rest of the ergotropic-trophotropic balance. This implies that different motor requirements in the natural situation will alter the balance. When emotional excitement is great, Gellhorn argues that reciprocity between the two systems breaks down. In fact, he distinguishes three states of sensitivity. In the first, which perhaps corresponds to mild fear or anxiety, reciprocity still holds and there is ergotropic dominance. In the second, corresponding to higher fear levels, reversal phenomena occur such that stimuli which ordinarily excite one system now excite the other. This suggests that more parasympathetic responses will occur at higher fear levels. In the third state, corresponding to very high fear levels, there is increased simultaneous activity of both systems. Gellhorn mentions instances where terror, induced by inescapable shocks or being forced to swim without a chance to escape, led to massive trophotropic discharges (and in the latter case, often a rapid death, not by drowning or exhaustion). Consistent with this view, Gellhorn claims that fright from a sudden shock (e.g. seeing a ghost) is a parasympathetic response. Such sudden frights are often associated with fainting or a retching-vomiting reaction. It is, therefore, reasonable to conclude that the intensity of fear importantly influences autonomic response pattern.

Whether prolonged fear has differential effects seems likely, but requires further investigation. It has been suggested by Malmo (1975) that unlike acute fear, chronic anxiety may produce a long-lasting increase in autonomic sensitivity, such that previously mild fear-eliciting stimuli produce large autonomic effects. This phenomenon probably requires intense and

40

prolonged anxiety. Broverman, Klaiber, Vogel & Kobayashi (1974) have investigated another and apparently opposite effect of prolonged stress. They report experiments where exposure to short-term anxiety-provoking stress facilitates performance of serially repetitive, overlearned tasks such as colour naming, simple addition and card sorting and impairs performances of perceptual restructuring tasks such as the Block Design, Object Assembly and Similarities subtests of the Wechsler Adult Intelligence Scale (maze learning would be an equivalent task for animals). In contrast, long-term exposures were found to have the opposite effects. It is suggested that these effects are related, in part, to the length of exposure of the central nervous system to adrenomedullary and adrenocortical hormones. So short-term exposures are thought to arouse an ergotrophically dominant state, supposedly mediated by a catecholaminergic transmitter, favouring the serially repetitive overlearned tasks. Longer exposures cause a central shift to trophotropic dominance, thought to be a cholinergically mediated state, favouring the perceptual restructuring tasks. The authors cite data that indicate that drugs that stimulate central adrenergic activity facilitate the performance of repetitive, overlearned tasks. Performance is depressed by adrenergic blocking agents. Focus of attention is narrowed by adrenergic stimulants and by moderate stress (Teitelbaum & Derks, 1958; Callaway & Thompson, 1953). Such attentional narrowing would be expected to enhance performance on 'simple' tasks, but impair it on tasks requiring frequent attentional redeployment. Converse performance effects have been shown with cholinergic agents (see Broverman, Klaiber, Kobayashi & Vogel, 1968). A speculative account is proposed to account for the differential effect of exposure duration on the central systems. Stress increases cortisol and decreases gonadal hormone production. Some evidence suggests the former is a more potent monamine oxidase inhibitor. Stress will, therefore, decrease monoamine oxidase activity which will initially increase central adrenergic functioning. In time, however, false transmitters such as octopamine accumulate, impairing function and shifting dominance to the cholinergic system.

Even if the mechanism postulated by Broverman and his associates is wrong it seems likely that long-term exposure to stress can produce at least two kinds of effect. If anxiety is intense, it may lead, in certain predisposed individuals, to a state of heightened ergotropic sensitivity. When prolonged and less intense, it more usually leads to a central state of trophotropic dominance. It can, then, be concluded that although fear states are associated with patterned physiological activation, these are not associated with one condition of sympathetic, let alone ergotropic activity. The pattern varies as a function of fear intensity, duration and the response requirements of the emotion. Particular physiological reactions may be differentially enhanced or

41

inhibited across individuals and between the sexes. It is not known why, but genetic and learning factors are probably important.

An aspect of Broverman's theory that merits emphasis is the dissociation between peripheral and central 'activation' measures in long-term stress. Thus adrenal activity remains high despite central signs of 'restful' trophotropic dominance. Lacey (1967) has made similar observations. He and others have noted that stressful situations produce cortical arousal accompanied by a decrease in heart rate when attention has to be directed towards external events. When attention needs to be focused and perhaps in more intense fear-eliciting contexts, the cortical arousal is accompanied by heart rate acceleration. Lacey & Lacey (1970) have argued that the cardiovascular system forms a feedback pathway to the brain so that in 'over-arousal' increased heart rate reduces cortical arousal and decreases awareness of external stimuli – a protective function. Cardiac deceleration influences the cortex so as to increase the efficiency with which outside events are processed. In contrast to Lacey, Malcuit (1973) has suggested that cardiac deceleration forms part of a global response that reduces reactivity to unpleasant events. He finds decelerations where subjects are 'passively' exposed to electric shocks or when rats freeze in anticipation of shock. It could be that the response serves differing functions depending on the other reactions with which it occurs.

The idea that the autonomic and endocrine reactions of fear influence brain processes so as to improve adaptability has been investigated intensively during the past decade. Lacey's work represents one strand. Many of the cerebral changes are directly mediated through other brain regions responsible for threat appraisal, but autonomic and endocrine factors have an important modulating influence.

It is thought that circulating adrenaline crosses the blood-brain barrier in functionally significant amounts in certain subcortical regions such as the hypothalamus and reticular formation (Rothballer, 1959). Stimulation of these regions indirectly affects the rest of the brain. Thus adrenaline excitation of the reticular activating system induces high-frequency, low-voltage activity in the frontal cortex – an effect abolished by reticular formation lesions (Rothballer, 1959). This 'arousal' effect may be mediated by an ascending noradrenergic system, the dysfunction of which causes sedation and depression (Schildkraut & Kety, 1967). In this context, it is interesting to note that although small doses of adrenaline administered intravenously or intracerebrally produce brief arousal, larger doses induce long-term sedation. There is also direct evidence that adrenaline manipulations affect avoidance learning. Conner & Levine (1969) have suggested that an inverted U-relationship exists between adrenaline levels and active avoidance. Removal of adrenaline by demedullation slows acquisition; small adrenaline doses increase the rate of acquisition in demedullated rats; and large doses impair performance. It is uncertain how these effects are mediated. Finally, pace Cannon, recent data suggest that adrenaline ensures a steady supply of glucose to the brain rather than prepare the muscles for intense activity (see Natelson, Smith, Stokes & Root, 1973).

ACTH and the glucocorticoids have been shown to have somewhat contrasting effects on active and passive avoidance and extinction behaviours. Hypophysectomised rats are impaired in active avoidance acquisition. This impairment is reversed not only by ACTH injections but also by injections of the heptapeptide comprising amino acids 4–10 of ACTH. This ACTH fragment has no adrenal action suggesting that ACTH's effect is a direct one on the brain (De Wied, 1969). ACTH treatment appears to normalise defective avoidance acquisition but does not improve normal avoidance learning (Moyer, 1966). In contrast, ACTH does facilitate passive avoidance acquisition above normal levels. There is also good reason to suppose the effect is an extradrenal one, unrelated to changes in responsivity to electric shock (Guth, Seward & Levine, 1971; Pare, 1969). ACTH or its heptapeptide fragment ($ACTH_{4-10}$) also prolong extinction, whether in an aversive or an appetitive task. This action is also extradrenal, a view which is corroborated with the prolonged extinction produced by adrenalectomy, which raises ACTH levels (De Wied, 1967). Corticosterone injections, however, facilitate extinction. They do not do this by inhibiting ACTH, because the effect occurs in hypophysectomised rats (De Wied, 1967). Further evidence that the sites of action of ACTH and corticosterone are central, when they influence extinction, was produced by Van Wimersma Greidanus & De Wied (1969, 1971). Corticosterone implants speeded extinction most when placed in medial midline thalamic structures (especially the nucleus parafascicularis) and in the lateral ventricles. ACTH (1–10) was also effective in these sites but was also active in the region of the rostral mesencephalon and caudal diencephalon. It remains to be shown whether the hormonal effects on active and passive avoidance are owing to central action. It does, however, seem likely.

Pituitary-adrenocortical hormones may also modulate perceptual processes. Surgical removal of the adrenal cortex produces an increased ability to detect sensory signals, particularly for 'internal' signals arising from taste, smell, hearing and proprioception. In contrast, patients with Cushing's syndrome, who have excessive adrenocortical activity, suffer a marked dulling of the senses. Henkin (1970) has argued that sensory detection and integration is regulated by a feedback system involving the brain and endocrine system. Although adrenocortical deficiency lowers sensory thresholds it impairs integration, making difficult the assessment of

43

loudness and tonal qualities, and disturbing speech perception. Glucocorticoid treatment can restore these functions. Henkin has demonstrated that even the small changes found in the circadian rhythm for corticosteroids is sufficient to influence taste detection in normal subjects.

Patients with Addison's disease, who have a failure of adrenocortical function, display psychological disturbances, which often include a dysmnesia. Such observations are coherent with a growing body of data in which post-training injections of ACTH, ACTH fragments, corticosteroids, adrenaline or vasopressin have been shown either to facilitate memory or to alleviate the effects of a range of amnesic agents such as protein-inhibiting antibiotics and electroconvulsive shock (for example, see Fink, 1975; Crow, Longden, Smith & Wendlandk, 1977; Rigter & Van Riezen, 1975). It has been contended (for example by Flood, Jarvik, Bennett, Orme & Rosenzweig, 1977) that such post-training hormonal activations prolong the consolidation period and hence lead to stronger memories.

The hormones, released in fear and anxiety, have then a range of effects on learning and extinction of avoidance tasks, on arousal, on perceptual function, and on memory. It seems plausible to argue that in many natural fear-eliciting situations these effects will not only increase the efficiency of threat-evading actions but lead to the more reliable retention of useful contextual and behavioural information. Researchers are trying to determine at which sites these hormonal influences are mediated and, to date, the evidence points to the involvement of limbic-midbrain and related structures.

4 How the Brain Mediates Fear and Anxiety

Textbooks usually trace the evolution of ideas about the brain's role in emotion by discussing Bard and Cannon's work, which emphasises the salience of diencephalic structures, and then passing to the Papez–Maclean stress on the limbic system with its repercussions in contemporary research. This hallowed scheme will be briefly followed.

Early studies (e.g. Woodworth & Sherrington, 1904) showed that animals decerebrated below the hypothalamic level growl, spit, scratch and bite when handled roughly. These responses and sympathetic reactions require clear nociceptive stimulation for their elicitation. They were referred to as pseudoaffective behaviours on the assumption that no emotional experience can occur without forebrain involvement. Bard (1928) found that cats, decerebrated above the hypothalamus, displayed very low thresholds for emotional excitation and very much better integrated attack behaviour. In Cannon's (1927) 'thalamic' theory of emotion, it is argued that the hypothalamus integrates the somatic and autonomic components of emotional behaviour under the control of the thalamus. Cannon contended that the thalamic mechanisms are normally inhibited by higher forebrain structures, but that this inhibition is overcome when the thalamocortical system receives innate or learnt emotional stimuli. Subsequent thalamic activation of the cortex led to emotional experience whereas the hypothalamic activation was held responsible for the physiological arousal and behaviour associated with the various emotions.

Although Cannon's views about the hypothalamus have been supported and elaborated by much subsequent research, the thalamus has fallen out of favour as an emotional system. The pioneering work on electrical stimulation of the brain in intact, awake animals by Hess (1957) revealed that relatively few thalamic points gave emotional responses when stimulated. Further, Bard (1928) had found that cats without either cortex or thalamus still showed 'pseudoaffective' behaviours. Just before World War Two the focus of interest switched to the limbic system. A major contributory factor in this shift was the publication of Kluver and Bucy's work on the effects of bilateral temporal lobectomies in monkeys (1937, 1938, 1939). One feature of their eponymous syndrome was a marked reduction of fear and aggression. The other major influence was a theoretical one. In 1937, Papez wrote a speculative paper in which he described, in detail, a limbic-hypothalamic circuit which might mediate emotion. He argued that some sensory information is transmitted from the thalamic relay stations to the hypothalamus. This information is finally relayed to the mammillary bodies where it is integrated with further information from the neocortex. This processed information is then relayed to the anterior nuclear group of the thalamus and from there to the cingulate gyrus where the emotional experience is generated. Transmission is then to the hippocampus via the cingulum where the emotionally coded information is organised and, finally, the fornix relays the information back to the mammillary bodies, thus completing the loop. His circuit represents what Papez called 'the stream of feeling'. One observation that influenced Papez' thinking was that animals that have died from the enraged form of rabies frequently show damage to limbic structures such as the hippocampus. Papez seems to have agreed with Cannon in regarding the hypothalamus as an integrator of emotional behaviours.

Maclean (1949, 1975) has extended and modified the ideas of Papez. He claims that the hippocampus and amygdala are important in the mediation of emotional feeling, and that Papez exaggerated the role of the cingulate gyrus. In his more recent work he has developed the concept of the triune brain. It is argued that, in evolution, the primate forebrain expands along three basic patterns which are characterised as reptilean, paleomammalian

45

and neomammalian. These systems are radically different in biochemistry and structure and, although interdependent, operate to some degree independently. Maclean provisionally identifies the reptilean forebrain with certain basal ganglia structures, the paleomammalian brain with the limbic system and the neomammalian brain with the neocortex and brainstem structures with which it primarily connects. One instance of decoupling between the systems is provided by epileptic seizures originating in the limbic system. These have a tendency to spread in and be largely confined to the limbic system, particularly the hippocampus. Neocortex may show little change during such seizures. Maclean (1975) suggests such limbic-neocortical dissociations may account for conflicts between what I have referred to as primitive and rational appraisal. He sees the neocortical system as performing fine-grain analysis on sensory information from the external world, the limbic system as organising more primitive emotional and motivational feelings, and speculates that the basal ganglia structures may be basic for species-typical behaviours such as those involved in fear-eliciting contexts. Concerning this last idea, although little is known, striatal lesions in squirrel monkeys have been shown to disturb species-typical displays (Maclean, 1972, 1973). It is also significant that the limbic lobe conforms to the striatum like a mold. Could interconnections have provided the route by which emotional feelings trigger species-typical fear responses?

Since the War a massive literature on the limbic system's role in emotion has been created. Little agreement exists about how the data should be interpreted. It appears that all limbic and many related structures have *some* role in emotion. Before trying to review this literature, some further comments will be made about the integrative role of the hypothalamus. These will concern Gellhorn's elaboration of Hess's notions of ergotropic and trophotrophic behaviours. Lesion and stimulation work has established clearly that the former are integrated by structures in the posterior hypothalamus whereas the latter organised in more anterior parts of the hypothalamus. Stimulation of posterior structures elicits not only sympathetic reactions, but also increased somatic tone, cortical desynchronisation, behaviour arousal, and, if continued, flight or fight. Opposite effects are produced by anterior hypothalamic stimulation. The state of sensitisation of these structures determines the intensity of the physiological and perhaps somatic reactions. Their sensitivity can be altered by feedback. For example, the increased muscle activity, often linked to fear, increases posterior and decreases anterior hypothalamic sensitivity. To the extent that this view is correct, the occurrence of one fear component would tend to elicit the others.

The sensitivity of these reciprocally innervated structures also seems to be under the influence of the limbic system. It has been proposed by Isaacson (1974) that the hippocampus normally modulates the hypothalamus in favour of a trophotropic balance. He suggests that hippocampal lesions shift the balance towards ergotropic dominance. It is well known that animals with hippocampal lesions show perseverative responding in various tasks such as passive avoidance. Isaacson argues that the difficulty lies in the initiation of behaviour rather than its maintenance, which is the responsibility of the ergotropic regions of the hypothalamus. Compatible with this view, there is evidence that the hippocampus normally exerts a tonic inhibitory influence over corticosteroid release, although recent evidence suggests that the modulation may be more complex (see Iuvone & van Hartesveldt, 1976, for a discussion). By contrast, animals with amygdala lesions have their greatest problems with response initiation, according to Isaacson. He, therefore, infers that the amygdala normally exerts a tonic influence on the hypothalamic systems in favour of ergotropic balance. If Maclean is right in postulating that the amygdala and hippocampus are both involved in mediating emotional feeling, why do they exert opposing influences on the hypothalamic systems, which integrate so much emotional behaviour? To attempt to answer this question it is necessary to examine the limbic system literature in more detail.

Investigating the source of decerebrate rage, Bard & Mountcastle (1948) found that cats which had ablations confined to the neocortex were actually more placid than normals. This finding suggested that forebrain structures exert both inhibitory and facilitatory influences on the behaviour-integrating system of the hypothalamus. Subsequent work has shown the limbic system to be central for such modulations. Thus, for example, the current consensus is that large lesions of the amygdala, in many species, produce a dramatic taming or quieting effect, and that, at least in rodents, large septal lesions can cause a transient rage syndrome. The effects of amygdala damage apply to man as well as other mammals. Human examples of the Kluver–Bucy syndrome have been documented (e.g. Marlowe, 1975), displaying the symptoms of visual agnosia, amnesia, hypersexuality, undiscriminating orality and marked decreases in emotionality. More specifically, amygdalectomies have been claimed to have 'pacifying' effects in man (Mark & Ervin, 1970). These human observations not only relate the amygdala to fear behaviour but demonstrate that amygdala destruction markedly reduces feelings of fear. This view is corroborated by studies of the effects of human temporal lobe epilepsy and electrical stimulation of human amygdala (see Gloor, 1972). Fear is the most commonly elicited emotion in temporal lobe ictal states and stimulation work strongly indicates that the amygdala is the

47

critical structure involved. Feelings of fear seem to be evoked only by stimulation of the amygdala or overlying temporal neocortex, and not of other neocortical regions.

In animals such as cats, amygdala stimulation may cause emotional behaviour and, if prolonged, leads to complete fight or flight reactions (Fernandez De Malina & Hunsperger, 1959, 1962). Similar effects can be produced more rapidly by stimulation of the ventromedial hypothalamus and the central grey of the midbrain. Further lesion and stimulation work implies that these three structures form a single system with neural influences largely proceeding in a downstream direction from amygdala to central grey. Zbrozyna (1960) and Hilton & Zbrozyna (1963) have claimed that amygdala stimulation no longer elicits these effects following total severance of the ventral amygdalofugal pathway, whereas cutting the stria terminalis, the other main amygdala-hypothalamic tract, has no effect. The role of the former pathway is, however, disputed by Hunsperger & Bucher (1967). Within the system, separate if overlapping sites seem to be involved with fighting and fleeing (see Kaada, 1972).

Some early amygdalectomy studies found, in contrast to later work, that the lesion produced increased aggressiveness (e.g. Wood, 1958). Such results have been explained as effects of irritative stimulation on the periphery of the lesion proper (Green, Clemente & De Groot, 1957). Subsequent work has, however, made it clear that although some parts of the amygdala exert excitatory effects on flight and fight behaviours, others have inhibitory actions (see Kaada, 1972). For example, although Fonberg (1965) found increased tameness in dogs following medial amygdala lesions, increased fighting followed lesions of the dorsomedial part. This latter lesion probably damaged the basolateral division of the amygdala because Fonberg (1968) has shown that stimulation of this structure inhibits fear reactions to pain and direct hypothalamic stimulation. For unknown reasons, with large amygdala lesions the effects of damage to facilitatory systems for fear seem to be dominant.

Stimulation of separable and overlapping amygdala sites not only produces fight and flight reactions, it can also elicit attentional-alerting responses, a wide range of autonomic and endocrine responses, including rapid corticosteroid secretion, and effects on eating and possibly sexual behaviour (see Kaada, 1972). All of these responses are related to emotional or motivational activation and it has been suggested repeatedly that the amygdala is important because it is involved in selecting responses appropriately related to goals (e.g. Rolls, 1975). It has been argued, more specifically, that the amygdala is concerned with the formation and subsequent recognition of stimulus-reinforcement associations. To perform such a function it is necessary that the amygdala should be able to compare analysed sensory information with punishment or reward contingencies present at the time, or associated with previous presentations of similar information. Anatomically, the amygdala is well placed to do just that. Rolls (1975) cites evidence that it receives olfactory input from the pyriform cortex in the rat, visual input from the inferotemporal cortex in the monkey and an auditory input in the cat. Jones & Powell (1970) have shown that each cortical sensory system shows an orderly sequence of projections from primary through secondary to tertiary fields with the final auditory, visual and somatic projections converging on the depths of the superior temporal sulcus, frontal pole and orbital region. Uniquely, there is a very large visual input into the amygdala. It is, therefore, interesting that Downer (1961) has been able to produce many of the symptoms of the Kluver–Bucy syndrome by disconnecting the temporal cortex from the amygdala in the monkey. The evidence suggests that visual input from the temporal cortex is particularly important for arousing fear in primates.

Not only does the amygdala receive much processed information from the neocortex, it also receives information about reinforcement from the hypothalamus with which it has two-way connections. Some amygdala neurones are activated by self-stimulation of hypothalamic and other sites in rats and monkeys. Neurones also respond to eating and drinking elicited by hypothalamic stimulation. Furthermore, it has been shown in many species that amygdala stimulation can be rewarding or punishing (Rolls, 1975).

If the amygdala does act as a comparator to make possible the recognition and learning of stimulus-reinforcement associations, its neurones must reflect this function which should be impaired by lesions. There is some support for these expectations. Thus, Ben Ari & Le Gal La Salle (1972) have shown that single units in the cat amygdala that had habituated to a click began to fire consistently again when the click had been paired with an electric shock to the paw. In monkeys, Fuster & Uyeda (1971) showed amygdala units responded differently to two signals, one associated with reward the other with punishment. In extinction, the number of responding units decreased. Removal of the structure, containing these cells which seem to change their response concomitantly with the formation of stimulus-reinforcement associations, causes difficulties in learning about aversive stimuli. For example, Rolls & Rolls (1973) have shown that amygdala-lesioned rats do not learn normally to avoid a solution of lithium chloride which produces sickness after ingestion. Many studies have found amygdala lesions to produce impairments of active avoidance. The literature is complex but it looks as if selective lesions to the basolateral amygdala may impair passive avoidance and conditioned suppression (see Kaada, 1972).

These avoidance impairments are probably not the result of a general learning difficulty. Rather, they seem to be associated with the development of insufficient fear because it has been shown that rats with small basolateral amygdala lesions, which are slower than normals in acquiring an active avoidance task, also show a lower level of plasma corticosterone during their first avoidance sessions. The lesions caused no change in basal corticosterone levels, so the difference probably reflected a deficiency in fear (see Ursin, Coover, Kohler, Deryck, Sagvolden & Levine, 1975).

What then is the amygdala's role in mediating fear? It seems to be a critical structure in a system which learns to associate stimuli with threat and to recognise such stimuli subsequently as fear-eliciting. It is ideally placed for this function because it is an interface, which receives processed sensory information from the neocortex and information about reinforcement from more 'primitive' regions of the brain, particularly the hypothalamus. When the amygdala is activated by a learned threat-eliciting stimulus, fear is felt. This activation in turn sets in train a series of autonomic and behavioural processes, integrated in the hypothalamus, which lead to active coping with threat. One would therefore predict that the pattern of fear associated with amygdala arousal would be basically ergotropic.There are three points which should be made about this picture. First, it implies that innate fear-eliciting stimuli are, or can be, processed without the amygdala, probably at the level of the hypothalamus. Decerebration results support this view. It does, however, need to be more precisely tested by seeing if amygdalectomy selectively spares unlearned fear behaviours. Second, the amygdala is clearly a functionally differentiated structure and although some of these functions are integrated within some overall behaviour, others seem not to be. It is, therefore, important to state that the active-fear processes are mediated by a subsystem of the amygdala. A separate system, involving the amygdala, which controls passive fear-coping responses, is suggested by the detrimental effects of some amygdala lesions on the acquisition of passive avoidance and conditioned suppression. Both systems would be controlled by those structures whose activity mediates fear feelings. Third, the amygdala is merely the hub of a system which eventually produces fear feelings and active coping. The aim is to understand the flow of information through this system. Given the degree of interconnectivity of the amygdala and the rest of the limbic system, let alone the brain, this is a daunting task.

Two limbic structures that have strong mutual connections with the amygdala and also are themselves interconnected are the septum and the hippocampus. Many workers now believe that these regions form the heart of a system which is responsible for actively blocking behaviour in response to aversive stimuli or stimuli associated with aversive events through conditioning (see, for example, Dickinson, 1974). Dickinson reviewed the literature concerned with the effects of large septal lesions. He argued that lesioned animals show increased persistence of responding in the face of

50

aversive events and frustrative nonreward. Thus, lesioned animals show impairments in a variety of passive avoidance situations as well as a facilitation of performance in a two-way active avoidance task. This latter is hard for normal animals because it also involves a passive avoidance component. Lesioned animals have been shown to be more persistent in many tasks involving the extinction of previously acquired responses. It is contended that these deficits are not caused by a general problem with learning because septally lesioned rats can learn complex mazes as quickly as intact animals. Dickinson also cites evidence that lesions do not disrupt a general response suppression mechanism and that they leave intact the ability to form new associations between stimuli and their response-contingent reinforcement consequences. It is shown that the data on the effects of lesions on escape and unconditional reactions suggest there is an increase in resulting behaviour. The effects on response persistence cannot then be explained in terms of a decreased sensitivity to aversive events. Instead, it is claimed that large septal lesions both decrease the suppressive effects of aversive events and increase their activating effects. A plausible interpretation of these results is that the septum is part of a response-suppression system which exerts an inhibitory influence on a facilitatory system in the amygdala. Supporting this view, Schwartzbaum & Gay (1966) have shown that combined septal-amygdala lesions decrease septal reactivity, but do not affect septal persistence as assessed by elevated responding in the initial segments of a fixed-interval schedule. Septal lesions not only impair response-suppression to aversive events, they cause the disinhibition of an amygdala system which activates responding to aversive events. Actually, because some studies (e.g. Zucker, 1965) find that septal lesions increase reactivity to positively reinforcing events as well, Dickinson advances a slightly more complex model. He postulates that stimuli are first processed for their affective significance: it has, of course, been argued here that this function will involve the amygdala. Processed information of positive and negative valence is then fed into the amygdala's facilitatory system and the inhibitory septal system which modulates it. Only stimuli with negative valence are fed into the septal response suppression system.

The hippocampus has also been linked to the active arrest of responding associated with threat and aversiveness. Thus, following hippocampal lesions it has been shown, in rats, that the ability to suppress responding in the face of conditioned threat stimuli is reduced, as is the ability to hold a stationary 'boxing posture' in intraspecific fighting (see Blanchard, Blanchard, Lee & Fukunaga, 1977). These workers have examined the behaviour of hippocampally lesioned rats in a brightly lit open field situation, using a grid and the amount of line crossing as a means of assessing freezing. On initial exposure the lesioned and intact animals did not differ. It has been

51

shown (Blanchard, Kelley & Blanchard, 1974) that during the initial period, following placement in the open field, frightened animals respond by making abortive attempts to flee. After this they tend to respond to the threat in their surroundings by freezing. Accordingly, Blanchard and his associates found that lesioned animals spent less time freezing after their initial exposure. Interestingly, although they ambulated more than intact rats, they did so in a slower and more leisured fashion. Lesioned rats were also impaired in another threat situation which involved placing them on a small high ledge. They fell from this more rapidly than intact rats because they were unable to maintain a freezing posture. Hippocampally lesioned rats have been shown to react normally when threatened by a cat or given 'shock prods'. The responses in these situations, like the initial fleeing in the open field, are active, and so it is likely that the hippocampus is selectively involved with a wide variety of response-suppressions to threat.

It is widely believed that the septohippocampal system plays a critical role in mediating the orienting reaction (for example, see Isaacson & Pribram, 1975, passim). This reaction involves both behavioural arrest and a series of changes which enhance the ability of the system to process information. Many workers also accept that the system is critically involved in the habituation of the orienting reaction. This reaction is triggered by novel stimuli, which are known to be capable of eliciting fear. It is, therefore, plausible to postulate that this system receives information which is analysed as novel and/or threatening in response to which it blocks ongoing behaviour and alerts sensory systems so as to optimise the processing of the available sensory input. Such monitoring prepares the animal so that it can subsequently cope actively with the threat. The system may also monitor input and determines when it ceases to have a negative valence. In other words, it may unlearn stimulus-punishment associations. So learned fear stimuli can cease to elicit fear. It has been argued by Gray (1970) that, in primates and probably man, the orbital frontal cortex provides the cortical representation of the septohippocampal system. This structure sends an important projection to the medial septal system (Johnson, Rosvold & Mishkin, 1968) and, like septal and hippocampal lesions, damage to it has been shown to impair passive avoidance and extinction of previously rewarded behaviour, but enhance active avoidance (see Grossman, 1967, for a review).

The postulation of this briefly adumbrated system is speculative, leaves salient issues untouched and must be qualified. First, the relationship of the orienting reaction to fear needs clarification. Uncertainty is neither a necessary nor a sufficient condition of fear elicitation. The orienting reaction probably occurs only when fear is mild and the situation uncertain. The defensive reaction (Lynn, 1966) is triggered by more intense novel stimuli and other threat stimuli may elicit other alerting reactions. The orientation reaction specific response suppression is only one of several kinds of suppression that the septohippocampal system mediates. Second, other structures such as the amygdala are involved in mediating the orienting reaction (see Kaada, 1972). Third, it is clear that the system, like the amygdala, serves a complex of functions which are located in different subregions (for example, see Ross & Grossman, 1977). Nevertheless, if the proposal is accepted in outline it remains uncertain whether activity in the system merely activates various response components of fear or whether it is also concerned with fear feelings. There is some evidence that frontal leucotomies do reduce anxiety and the affective consequences of pain (Robin & Macdonald, 1975). Interpretation of such observations is hard because the frontal cortex is interconnected with the amygdala as well as the septohippocampal system, i.e. there may be an indirect disruption of the amygdala's fear perception system. Tanaka's (1973) finding that orbital lesions in monkeys impair escape behaviour supports such a possibility. Ursin, Coover, Kohler, Deryck, Sagvolden & Levine (1975) report that plasma corticosterone levels in septally lesioned rats are a function of their active avoidance performance, and seem normal. Iuvone & Van Hartesveldt (1976) found that in hippocampal rats corticosterone and freezing levels were lower than those of intact rats in an open field. The issue is, strictly, unresolved although the consensus view seems to be that the septohippocampal system is not a mediator of fear feelings. If the system is involved in the unlearning of fear then it presumably must feed back into the amygdala as well as receive input from that structure. Such interconnections exist. It does, however, remain to be shown directly that these structures do mediate the extinction of conditioned fear.

Although other limbic structures have been investigated, the data are very conflicting and interpretation of their role in fear is premature. The literature on cingulate gyrus lesions illustrates this point (see Grossman, 1967), although Ursin and his associates have recently argued that one of this structure's functions may be to inhibit the physiological reactions to fear, once adequate avoidance behaviour has occurred. Their cingulate lesioned rats, even when they had achieved a 90% avoidance criterion, continued to produce undiminished corticosterone levels and 'freeze' in the intertrial interval. Similarly, although suggestive results have been obtained, the role of the habenula (which receives septal projections via the stria medullaris) remains uncertain. Lesions to this nucleus impair one-way avoidance learning but it is uncertain whether it reduces fear or disturbs passive avoidance because the data are conflicting (for example, see Rausch & Long, 1974).

Heimer (1972) has described a pathway from the amygdala to the mediodorsal nucleus of the thalamus. This structure is richly interconnected with the prefrontal cortex (see Robin & MacDonald, 1975). It is, therefore, interesting that stereotactically placed mediodorsal lesions have been reported to reduce anxiety in man (pp. 172–207 in Orchinik, Koch, Wycis, Freed & Spiegel, 1950). Rats with such lesions have been found deficient in active but not passive avoidance learning, freeze less to novel but more to aversive stimuli, and appear tamer than intact rats (see Waring & Means, 1976, for a review). Roberts (1962) has shown in cats that electrical stimulation of certain sites in the dorsomedial nucleus produces fear-like behaviour such as cowering, and that animals learn to avoid such stimulation (which was probably not pain-eliciting). In apparent contrast, Nathan & Smith (1971) have found, in monkeys, that lesions impaired the conditioned suppression of lever pressing without affecting conditioned cardiac changes. These results are confusing but probably reflect the fact that the mediodorsal nucleus receives input from both the amygdala and septohippocampal systems. This could explain its apparent relationship to fear feelings as well as active and passive fear responses – the shade of Cannon may be vindicated yet.

Before concluding this review brief mention will be made of a growing body of data which are consistent with a greater right hemisphere role in the mediation of emotions, particularly aversive emotions such as fear. Several workers have found that left and right hemisphere lesions are associated with different emotional reactions (for example, see Gainotti, 1972). The catastrophic reaction, associated with anxiety, crying, hostility and compensatory boasting is characteristic of left hemisphere damage, whereas the indifference reaction, associated with apathy, jocularity, underplaying and anosognosia, is characteristic of right-hemisphere lesions. These findings are reinforced by the results of studies using dichotic and lateralised tachistoscopic presentation with normal subjects. The data suggest that the advantage to the right hemisphere is increased when affective stimuli are used, particularly when affective memory is involved (see Suberi & McKeever, 1977, for a review). Davidson & Schwartz (1976) recorded parietal EEG activity whilst subjects formed visual or verbal images some of which were of intense past emotional experiences. There was significantly less right hemisphere activity during emotional imagery periods. Dimond & Farrington (1977) used a contact lens designed so that visual information projected only to one hemisphere. Subjects viewed neutral, amusing or unpleasant films wearing these lenses so that the input was directed to either their right or left hemispheres. Heart rate was recorded. The largest increase in heart rate whilst watching the unpleasant film was found when input was directed to the right hemisphere, whereas heart rate increased more when information about the amusing film was directed to the left hemisphere.

Although significant the effects were, however, small. The pattern of the present literature suggests that a right hemisphere system mediates unpleasant affects and a left hemisphere system mediates pleasant affects. These systems mutually inhibit each other so that damage to one leads to overactivity of the other. Why emotional perception should be so distributed remains a mystery.

To understand how the brain mediates fear is to be able to describe the route fear-related information takes through the brain, as it converges or diverges on various nuclei; and to describe how that information is processed at each stage. An essential prolegomenon to this task is a detailed knowledge of neuroanatomy, particularly of the links between limbic structures and neocortex, and between the former and the brain stem and hypothalamus. Such knowledge has increased considerably in the past 20 years, so that we can begin to see that the limbic system functions as a dynamic and integrated whole.

CHAPTER 3

Behavioural Aspects of Fear

John Archer

1 Conceptual Approaches to the Study of Fear Behaviour

1.1 'Fear' in Everyday Speech and in Scientific Terminology

The term 'fear' is used in everyday speech to refer to an emotional state which we all know and have experienced. When I say 'I am afraid', what sort of information does this statement convey? It would, of course, inform you that my feelings and behaviour were different from those involved had I said that I was feeling angry, or hungry, or disappointed. But without supplementary information it would not tell you much about the sorts of behavioural activities I was likely to carry out, or anything about the details of my physiological state. I could have said that I was either 'very frightened' or 'just a little scared', and these statements concerning my degree of fear would have enabled you to make a rough assessment of degree by comparison with your own recollections of similar feelings. Nevertheless, what I may have regarded as meriting the description of 'intense fear' could be different from your perception of what this label means. Thus any statements of degree would only be a rough approximation. For everyday speech, we would only need such an approximation: precise measures of how my fear state corresponds with your past recollections of fear states are simply not necessary considering what our neural and endocrine fear mechanisms have evolved to cope with.

Ultimately, we can trace the mechanisms underlying our feelings of fear to what was necessary to produce the appropriate avoidance behaviour quickly enough in situations where physical harm was the likely result of any failure to do so. Accurate introspection as to the nature or degree of the feelings involved would certainly not have been appropriate. Instead, quick effective action would be the adaptive surviving characteristic. You run or hide first

I thank Dr. D. Broom (Department of Zoology, University of Reading) and Professor R. J. Andrew (School of Biological Sciences, University of Sussex) for their helpful comments.

and ask questions later, if at all. What is likely to have been more important than assessing the degree of fear experienced is any supplementary information about the source of the fear-evoking object: was it, for example, a snake in the grass, or a sudden noise, or a large predator? It is this type of information which would be more relevant for taking effective action.

When a scientist studies the state we label 'fear' in everyday speech, he may be very interested in the question of the degree or intensity of fear, or in the details of its physiological and behavioural accompaniments. It is then that the limitations in accuracy of our everyday descriptions become important, and have to be recognised and overcome.

Broadly speaking, behavioural scientists have adopted one of two types of approach to the study of fear. One concerns the level of fear a person or animal is showing, and the other concerns the precise physiological and behavioural characteristics of the state. These two very different approaches represent experimental psychological and biological traditions respectively. As I have indicated above, neither question is answered very well by looking to subjective reports of our everyday experience of fear.

1.2 Fear as an Intervening Variable

The first of the two questions posed above has been asked by experimental psychologists. 'Fear' in this context has been used as an 'intervening variable' and is often represented as a central change of a single type which can vary over a unitary scale. This would correspond to asking in everyday speech 'How frightened are you? Just a little, or scared out of your wits?' In formulating a unitary scale on which to measure the degree of fear, psychologists have made a number of assumptions, perhaps based originally on the subjective way we experience fear: these require examination before proceeding any further.

The most important assumption is that a unitary scale makes an adequate representation of the various changes occurring when a person or animal experiences fear. This is related to the general question of whether we can usefully represent a motivational system, be it concerned with eating or drinking or fighting or copulation, by values placed along a single dimension. Criticisms of this approach (e.g. Hinde, 1959) regard such a unitary representation as too great an oversimplification to be useful for precise analysis. In fact, the 'unitary drives' approach as it is called, has been criticised on a number of grounds, e.g. that different measures of the same motivational state or drive may not co-vary with one another (Hinde, 1959, 1974), and that the diversity of causal factors known to be involved is not adequately represented by changes in one variable. McFarland & Sibley (1972) have argued that if the behavioural output is simple (i.e. involves a

57

single response measure), as is the case with drinking, it is still possible to choose one (output) variable in the control system which could be represented on a unitary scale: for drinking this would be the final command activating the motor system involved in the action of drinking. Although the rest of the system may be complicated, this one value would produce a simple index of the strength of motivation. This approach may be feasible where there is only one possible type of output and intensity can be measured simply. However, in the case of 'fear', there are several possible types of physiological and behavioural responses, and these may be grouped in a number of alternative ways.

The work of Lang (1970) can be used to illustrate the implications of this point for studies of human subjects. Lang showed that measures of 'fear' were at least partially independent of one another, finding a correlation of 0.41 between the subjects' subjective ratings of their fear state and observations of their avoidance behaviour. The correlation between questionnaire measures and overtly expressed avoidance behaviour was particularly low, since there is here the added problem of whether people exaggerate their fears to minimise them (see also Rachman, 1974, p. 11; Maccoby & Jacklin, 1974, Chapter 5).

Lacey (1967) reviewed more wide-ranging evidence from clinical studies, normal human subjects, and from animal experiments, which showed far greater contradictions between autonomic, electrocortical and behavioural measures of 'arousal' (a unitary concept related to that of fear, but much less specific). Somatic and behavioural indications of 'arousal' were shown to be dissociable components mediated by separate neural mechanisms, but they commonly appeared simultaneously. Differences in physiological response measures also indicated that although the autonomic nervous system does respond to external stimuli as a whole in the sense that all the output measures are changed in the same direction, not all autonomically innervated structures exhibit equal increments or decrements of function. Rank correlations for different somatic measures, e.g. heart rate, muscle potentials, palmar conductance, all gave low values (0.35–0.46), and Lacey concluded that one cannot predict with any accuracy the overall level of other responses from knowledge of any one response.

In investigating the problem of measuring fear in animals, an experimental tradition of devising tests of fearfulness or 'emotionality' became established from the 1930's onwards. The initial problem was seen as devising tests and measures of emotionality (Hall, 1938; Broadhurst, 1957), also called fearfulness (Gray, 1971a) or fear (Lester, 1968). Originally, Hall (1934b) devised the 'open field test' (a misnomer since the apparatus consisted of a closed arena): the animal subject (laboratory rat) was placed into the arena for a short period of time (2 min originally), and testing was repeated over a number of days (14 in the original 1934 study). The presence or absence of defecation and urination was noted on each day and a total score calculated for each measure. More recent studies have used fewer test-periods and simply counted the total number of fecal boli deposited. Hall (1934b) originally also measured whether food-deprived rats ate wet mash placed in the centre of the arena, the rationale for this measure being that fear would inhibit eating (see Section 2.3 for a discussion of this point). In the present discussion, we are more concerned with how closely the measures are related to one another than with the original reasons for chosing particular measures. Hall (1934b) found quite high correlations between the three measures used in the first open field study, and later found a significant negative correlation between the number of days a rat defecated in the open field and its locomotor activity. These two measures, ambulation and defecation, became established as measures of 'emotionality', and have been used extensively in later studies (Archer, 1973a).

Although Hall originally intended the concept of 'emotionality' to be merely a convenient way of describing 'a complex of factors', the notion soon became replaced by a unitary fear state. I have reviewed some of the more recent literature on the open field and other tests (Archer, 1973a), in particular to determine the evidence for the measures being related in a way that would be predicted from a unitary emotionality concept. In the open field, defecation and ambulation showed fairly low negative correlations, generally statistically significant (typical values 0.2–0.6). There were, however, a number of limitations to this general conclusion, depending on the sample size and the early experience and strain of the animal. Other behavioural and physiological measures (e.g. heart rate) taken in the open field showed little evidence of a consistent relationship with defecation scores. The relationship between open field defecation and measures of emotionality taken in other tests (e.g. emergence from a sheltered or familiar environment, active avoidance learning) was particularly poor.

The three lines of evidence outlined above (taken from the work of Lang, Lacey & Archer) all suggest that the response measures associated with the fear state do not change in the same way as one another. This conclusion poses special problems for those experimental psychologists who have defined fear or emotionality in unitary drive terms. Denenberg (1964), Broadhurst (1960), Gray (1971b) and others have argued that emotionality can be regarded in this way. Furthermore they extended their intervening variable concept to one covering longer-term dispositions, and regarded emotionality as a constitutional trait. (I have criticised this conclusion in some detail elsewhere: Archer, 1973a.)

Typical of these positions, but more lucidly presented than most, is that of Gray (1971b), who insisted that estimating the degree of fear is central to the study of this process. I have already pointed out some of the theoretical and practical difficulties of this viewpoint. It is also illuminating that Gray appeals to 'commonsense', i.e. introspection, in justifying his position (Gray, 1971b, p. 34). In contrast, I have argued at the beginning of this chapter that this sort of commonsense is not a good guide for the scientific investigation of fear. In my opinion, Gray's original questions 'Can we estimate the degree of fear?' and 'Can we measure fear?' are inappropriate starting points because they contain implicit assumptions about the nature of fear (derived from 'commonsense'), which are misleading for a scientific analysis. The most important of these assumptions is the idea of a unitary fear state which, as I have tried to show, is not supported by the evidence. In a more general context, Hinde (1974, p. 28) has also pointed out that the use of intervening variables which appear to correspond to subjective experiences, as entities with apparent physical reality, is dangerous and misleading. The latter point has also been made by the philosopher Whitehead, and termed 'the fallacy of misplaced concreteness' (Waddington, 1977, Chapter 1): thus fear is not an entity but a term derived from human experience. The reader is referred to Hinde's work for a more general discussion of the use of intervening variables. With regard to fear, Gray (1971a) provides an example of the sort of erroneous conclusions this approach can produce: here Gray analysed rodent sex differences in terms of 'emotionality': an analysis of these same measures, but in terms of other concepts, produces entirely different conclusions (Archer, 1971, 1974, 1975, 1977).

One question raised by the above discussion is why fear response measures should vary so much in relation to one another. The answer is twofold: firstly the complexity of the mechanisms underlying the fear response, and secondly that many fear response measures are affected by other motivational systems. Considering the first of these two points, Lacey (1967) described two ways in which fear responses can vary: situational stereotypy and individual response patterning. Situational stereotypy refers to the observation that different fear evoking situations produce different types of fear responses. For example, in an experiment on the effects of testosterone on the behaviour of chicks in an open field (Archer, 1973c) I found that when a bell sounded outside the test situation, it induced prolonged 'freezing' with no peeping (distress calls). In contrast, the response of the chicks to the same type of open field containing a bell in the centre, and sounded for the first 5 seconds, produced a much more variable range of responses including prolonged freezing, or peeping accompanied by 'scanning' head movements and locomotion, or jumping, or 'burrowing' at the side walls (Archer, 1976b). The variation found in this second situation also illustrates Lacey's second concept, of individual response patterns, since different chicks showed different types of response to the same situation. Thus, one chick would jump frequently whereas another would remain immobile for the whole three minutes of testing. Similarly, some rats may freeze in an open field whereas others may run around the outside of the arena.

There is little evidence concerning the variables which might produce either the different responses to different external situations or the different responses by different individuals. What evidence is available will be discussed in a later section of this chapter.

A second source of variation in the relation of fear responses to one another arises because many fear responses are affected by other motivational systems. Thus, defecation in an open field is influenced by causal factors other than those affecting the fear state, e.g. food intake (Archer, 1975). Providing that the animals being tested are matched for food intake, this would not generally influence the results of open field testing. But it does influence the results for sex differences (Archer, 1975) and for oestrous cycle changes (Drewett, 1973; Birke & Archer, 1975), since the different conditions are not matched for food intake in these comparisons. Similarly, if treatment or group differences influence general activity or exploration, to use ambulation as a measure of fear would also be misleading; again, the measure would reflect influences other than fear. The rodent sex difference and oestrous cycle literature also illustrates this point: females ambulate more in an open field at oestrus than dioestrus, and females ambulate more than males. Gray (1971a) and Gray & Levine (1964) have used these results to argue that females are less emotional than males and that females are less emotional at oestrus than dioestrus; however, the evidence has been reinterpreted by myself (Archer, 1971, 1975) and others (Russell, 1973; Drewett, 1973) as showing a more general sex difference and oestrous cycle difference in exploration or activity rather than a difference in fear.

1.3 Ethologically-Based Approaches

In view of all the difficulties in attempting to measure the degree of fear by one or more response measures, I suggested that an alternative approach to tests of emotionality should be adopted (Archer, 1973a). Specifically, two sorts of method were outlined, one of which involved measuring the change in frequency of particular types of behaviour over successive exposures to a novel situation, and the other one involved more short-term measures of fear responses taken immediately after the animal had been placed in the fear-evoking situation. Neither measure was based on the notion of a unitary fear state; and both involved more detailed behavioural measures than is customary in the psychological literature. In this respect, they were based on a more ethological or observational approach to the subject of fear.

61

An ethologically-based approach would begin by looking at the details of behavioural characteristic of fear-evoking situations, and would use the term fear not as an intervening variable but as a description (see Hinde, 1970, 1974 for further elaboration of this point). A descriptive label would not imply anything about how one type of 'fear response' measure is related to a second type of fear response measure. It would not, for example, make any assumptions about similarity in their internal control mechanisms. Thus, the same descriptive label could even be applied to two measures which appear to be largely unrelated causally. Having said this, we may then ask why it is considered useful to describe the two responses with the same label 'fear behaviour' if they may not necessarily be causally related.

Three possible answers can be offered to this question. The first is related to the use of fear in everyday speech. We label certain acts as fear because we recognise them as likely to be associated with what we know subjectively as a fear state. Since animals show many similar types of fear behaviour, we may not think we are in too much danger of wrongly classifying fear responses. But it can be difficult to separate, solely on the basis of appearance, responses such as immobility associated with fear, from immobility associated with looking intently at an object, or fast running away from a stimulus from fast running towards a food source. In general, relating an animal's behaviour to what we think are its intentions, judged by our own feelings, is not a sound basis on which to classify behaviour.

Hinde (1970) stated that the case for classifying withdrawal and immobility responses together rests largely on the similarities in the stimulus situations which elicit them. Thus, we might instead classify behaviour as fear because it all occurred in response to the same types of stimulus. In practice, it may be difficult to describe precisely what the stimulus situations producing fear behaviour are, and there is the problem that other types of behaviour may also occur in the same types of situation: e.g. an electric shock strong enough to produce jumping and squealing (fear behaviour) in rats, also facilitates copulation in males when a female is present (Barfield & Sachs, 1968). We cannot really call this copulation 'fear behaviour' simply because it occurs in the same situation as jumping and squealing. Despite such reservations, however, the context or stimulus situation does provide a common way of classifying fear behaviour.

A third way of classifying behaviour as fear behaviour is a functional one. A functional classification relies on both form and situation: but instead of considering them in isolation, form is assessed in terms of how appropriate it is for a given situation. Thus immobility would be regarded as a fear response if it effectively camouflaged the animal in a situation where running was a less effective form of escape. How appropriate a particular form of behaviour is for a given situation cannot be assessed from isolated examples, but only from the typical behavioural repertoire of the species in realtion to its natural habitats. Thus, a functional approach will involve not only the immediate consequences of the act, which may vary from situation to situation, but the ultimate or evolutionary function of the behaviour. Using this approach, fear behaviour is behaviour concerned with removing or protecting the animal from a source of noxious stimulation or from an anticipated source of noxious stimulation. Viewed in an evolutionary context, one can envisage a progression from the most primitive form, escape responses to noxious stimuli, to responses which anticipate noxious stimuli, basing this anticipation on the perception of sudden changes in the environment (Archer, 1976a). Further refinements to this type of anticipation would include responding to other features of the environment indicative of noxious stimuli.

2   Behaviour Associated with Fear Motivation

2.1   Flight and Immobility

Hinde (1970) stated that fear responses comprise a diverse group of behaviour patterns including both those leading to withdrawal from or avoidance of a stimulus, and immobility responses. Thus, there are in behavioural terms two broad categories of fear behaviour, represented by flight and immobility. Both these categories include several different types of response.

Responses concerned with active avoidance (flight) can be said to vary approximately over an intensity dimension. Thus, low intensity active avoidance may be measured by avoidance of proximity: if the animal is placed near to the fear-evoking situation, it will move away. One example of this is what Barnett (1958) referred to as 'neophobia' in rats, the avoidance of an unfamiliar feeding container placed in their home cage. A more intense form of active avoidance would be flight or rapid avoidance behaviour, when the animal runs, jumps, swims or flies rapidly away from the fear-evoking source. A third, high-intensity form of flight is panic behaviour, which is undirected flight or flight that is prevented by a physical object. This may produce inappropriate escape behaviour, i.e. escape behaviour which is not guided by the stimulus configuration of the immediate environment.

Thus some animals show clear-cut escape behaviour, e.g. jumping or flying away. In such cases, it may be possible to measure jumping as a form of escape behaviour, in an open field or novel environment test (e.g. in chicks: Archer, 1973b and d). There are some studies which have recorded the number of escape jumps in a novel environment for mice (e.g.

63

Lieberman, 1963; van Oortmerssen, 1971) and rats (Brannigan, 1972). But in general jumping does not occur sufficiently frequently to have been widely used in this way.

In the absence of specific escape behaviour such as jumping, active fear behaviour has to be inferred from the animal's behaviour in relation to the context: e.g. is the animal moving rapidly away from a noxious stimulus?

Fast undirected movement in a situation where direct escape would be impossible is also usually interpreted as escape bahaviour: e.g. in rats it occurs both in response to electric shock and in an open field (e.g. Livesey & Egger, 1970; Blizard, 1968). It is also known that rats will cross an electric grid to escape from a novel environment to their home cage (Blanchard, Kelley & Blanchard, 1974). It is, however, doubtful whether evidence of this type conclusively demonstrates that the fast running which often occurs when a rat is placed into an open field is escape behaviour. The difficulty is that, when tested, the rat is not only avoiding the open field but is also approaching its home cage – its behaviour may therefore be motivated by either the negative incentive of remaining in the open field or by the positive incentive of returning to its home cage. A single study such as that of Blanchard et al. does not differentiate between these possibilities. There is in any case a great difficulty in inferring that a response is active escape behaviour where the animal shows no specifically recognisable escape behaviour (such as jumping) or where it is not moving away from a clearly localised aversive stimulus.

A different approach to defining active escape behaviour is to consider the associated social and expressive responses: e.g. many animals also emit distress calls or show piloerection and pupil dilation (see Section 2.2). Their occurrence, together with fast locomotion, may be used to define active escape behaviour.

The problem of precisely defining active escape behaviour arises because the usual behavioural act (locomotion) is one which is common to most other motivational systems. Thus, active escape behaviour cannot readily be defined on the basis of form alone, as is the case for other types of behaviour, such as feeding, drinking, copulation and attack. It also appears that there is no clear dividing line between mild preference for one stimulus over another, and avoidance or escaping from a stimulus. These two alternatives may be clear when escape is shown in its most extreme form, i.e. high intensity locomotion accompanied by expressive acts. However, in between the cases of mild preference for another stimulus and rapid escape are many instances where the labels 'escape' or 'preference' are arbitrary ones.

It seems therefore, that a clear case of active escape behaviour would involve the following: firstly, the animal's normal method or methods of locomotion would occur but they would be activated at a high intensity;

secondly,. the direction of the locomotion would be away from a source of potential danger (or it may be undirected if no escape route seems possible); thirdly, locomotion would be directed towards a place less characterised by danger; fourthly, the motor component would be accompanied by physiological changes, which would mostly be sympathetically innervated reflexes, generally associated with preparation for exertion (e.g. increased heart rate and respiration); fifthly, there may be expressive gestures, vocalisations or odour secretion (and many of these may have originated from sympathetically innervated reflexes).

When all these responses occur together, it is clear that the animal can be described as showing active fear and escape behaviour. But when only one or two of these conditions are fulfilled or when activation is at a lower intensity, the descriptive label would not be so clear-cut. We are, therefore, not dealing with one specific behavioural response characteristic of fear or escape motivation but with a complex of reflexes and coordinated actions, which are capable of being organised in many different ways, for the many different fear-evoking circumstances which animals face. Some of the actions and reflexes associated with active escape may also be associated with motivational systems other than fear responding: the most obvious example is locomotion, but others include the distress call of the young chick, which may signal not only fear but also states such as cold or hunger. It seems, therefore, that fear responding involves a flexible repertoire of available responses, many of which are shared with other motivational control systems.

The second major class of fear responses are immobility reactions. There appear to be several overlapping types of immobility which occur in fear-inducing conditions. Perhaps the best known is 'freezing' – relatively short-lived periods of immobility shown by many species of animal to fear-evoking situations: these are usually accompanied by signs of autonomic arousal, e.g. high heart rate and respiration rate, and the animal is likely to be very responsive to external stimuli such as touch. Freezing may be accompanied by a crouching posture. Animals usually show a gradual resumption of activities after freezing, e.g. first moving the eyes, and then the head and finally the whole body (e.g. in buntings, Andrew, 1956b; in chicks, Archer, 1973c, 1976b).

Another similar form of immobility can be termed 'protective immobility', occurring in animals with protective spines or armoured plates or a shell. In these cases immobility is preceded by reflexes which involve the withdrawal of unprotected parts of the body so that they are protected. Examples of animals which behave in this way include the hedgehog, tortoises, bivalve molluscs and the woodlouse, *Armadillidium*.

Periods of immobility are also shown in conflict or frustration situations, and these have a similar appearance to freezing, e.g. in mice (Slater, 1972), in chicks (Archer, 1974c) and in guinea pigs (Pearson, 1970). Whether or not these should be classified as fear behaviour is uncertain. Gray (1972a) has suggested that frustration situations evoke mild fear, because similar responses occur to fear-evoking and frustration-evoking stimuli, and because of the aversive nature of frustration. I have also suggested that fear and escape responses characterise frustration situations, and that these can be casually related to other fear-evoking stimuli (Archer, 1976a).

In practice, it may be difficult to differentiate on the basis of descriptive criteria fear-induced immobility from other forms of immobility. Similar problems to those involved in defining active escape behaviour occur in the case of immobility: fear-induced immobility may be even more difficult to define since the animal does not move in relation to the aversive stimulus.

There is a further type of immobility, tonic immobility, which occurs in a wide variety of vertebrate and invertebrate species in response to physical restraint*. It has perhaps been most widely studied in the domestic chicken (e.g. Gallup, 1974). Tonic immobility has a number of characteristics which differentiate it from freezing: for example, tonic immobility is generally longer-lived and the animal is more responsive to external stimulation. At first, the animal struggles and attempts to escape, but subsequently it assumes a rigid immobile posture which persists even in the absence of further restraint (Gallup, 1974). Termination of tonic immobility is usually abrupt – there is an almost immediate transition from the immobile to the mobile state, usually associated with an attempt to escape from the captor (Gallup, 1974). Tonic immobility corresponds in most cases to death feigning or thanatosis (Edmunds, 1974, Chapter 8), described as an anti-predator defence reaction.

The functional significance of tonic immobility also appears to differ from that of freezing and crouching: the latter lessen the chance of an animal being detected by a predator whereas in the case of tonic immobility the prey has already been caught by the predator. Presumably, tonic immobility lessens the possibility of injury (Vestal, 1975) as well as the chance of being eaten, either by causing the predator to lessen its hold on the prey or even to temporarily release it altogether. Particularly in the case of birds, the sudden transition from apparent death to escape would be sufficient to maximise the captive's chances of escaping. In many solitary mammalian predators, such as the domestic cat, predation is specifically directed towards small moving objects and the prey is not necessarily killed and eaten once it has been

---

* See also Section 4.1 on signalling thwarting-responses: tonic immobility in Chapter 5 by Salzen.

caught. Such a pattern of predatory behaviour would seem ideal for enabling tonic immobility to function as a last-minute rescue device, literally snatching the prey from the jaws of death. Indeed, I have observed such a spectacular escape of a song thrush from my domestic cat: escape was sudden and decisive and the would-be predator startled by the bird's sudden resurrection. More generally, cats have been observed to lose interest in lizards, mice and small birds which become immobile after capture (Gallup, 1974 and personal observations). Gallup (1974) also cited a study of wild ducks attacked by red foxes under natural conditions. The ducks frequently went into a state of tonic immobility, and as a consequence escaped unharmed. In experimental tests, 29 out of 50 ducks survived initial capture and handling by foxes simply through assuming an immobile posture.

Although there are older ideas linking tonic immobility with hypnosis or sleep, most current researchers would view it as a form of fear response, and would probably agree with the anti-predator function I have outlined above. Gallup (1974) pointed out that the fear hypothesis is often used to interpret indirect evidence, e.g. that the response shows habituation (see also Nash and Gallup, 1976; Crawford, 1977), that it is impaired by tranquillisers, and is increased by social isolation, rough handling, novel testing conditions, as well as prior periods of brief electric shock, loud noise, suspension over a visual cliff, or a conditioned aversive stimulus. This again raises the more general issue of whether to consider all fear responses as arising from a single motivational system. It seems that tonic immobility shares a number of features with other so-called fear responses – particularly that it is accentuated by the various noxious conditions listed above – but it also differs in many ways, particularly in its detailed physiological characteristics: for example, it is characterised by decreased heart rate, respiration and body temperature (Nash, Gallup & Czech, 1976). It is perhaps best to regard tonic immobility as one of many different types of fear response, but one which has a number of specific characteristics that fit it functionally for escape from predation: these include the rapid transition from immobility to escape, the lack of impairment of sensory and information-monitoring processes (e.g. the pupillary reflex, EEG activity to stimuli, and the ability to clasically condition all remain intact: Gallup, 1974).

Tonic immobility and similar forms of restraint-induced immobility occur in a wide range of animals, vertebrates and invertebrates alike, e.g. arachnids such as spiders (Crawford, 1977), crabs (e.g. O'Brien & Dunlap, 1975), insects such as water beetles (Ratner, 1977) and crickets (Crawford, 1977), teleost fish (Crawford, 1977), various species of snake (Crawford, 1977), chickens (e.g. Ratner & Thompson, 1960) and predatory birds such as hawks (Crawford, 1977), and mammals (e.g. deermice: Vestal, 1975). Some of the responses described as tonic immobility in the literature seem to represent cases of protective immobility, e.g. in the case of the woodlouse, *Armadillidium*, which forms a protective ball, described by Ratner (1977), and Crawford (1977) as tonic immobility. In other cases, the degree to which the animal shows immobility appears to bear no relation to the death-feigning reaction observed in the wild (Crawford, 1977). It seems, therefore, that what is now referred to as 'tonic immobility' (e.g. Gallup, 1974) may cover several related phenomena (a similar point is also made by Lefebvre and Sabourin, 1977).

2.2   Expressive and Social Behaviour as Fear Responses

Fear behaviour such as escape or immobility is associated with a number of expressive movements, sounds and odours, usually derived either from intention movements or outward manifestations of the animal's physiological state. Many of these have become changed over the course of evolutionary history and have been adapted for a communication function, since fear responses commonly occur in social contexts.

Expressive movements of vertebrates include the erection of dermal appendages, such as hair in mammals, or feathers in birds, or dorsal and ventral fins in fish. Darwin (1872) described these as occuring in conditions of emotion such as fear or anger. The ears are also highly expressive in many mammals, being drawn back as a protective reflex or being erected in the alerting reaction. Facial expressions are likewise important, particularly in primates. Typically, the eyes and mouth are widely opened and the eyebrows may be raised during fear responding.

Sounds are emitted by many otherwise silent animals when in great fear or pain. Darwin (1872) suggested that these may be derived from 'involuntary and purposeless contractions of the chest and glottis' which occur during exertion, or that they may provide some relief from pain or fear. In many animals such sounds are used to communicate a state of distress which covers a variety of circumstances, including those normally thought of as fear-inducing. Andrew (1963a), in contrast, have argued that many mammalian vocalisations have arisen in evolutionary history from *protective* closure of the glottis. He also pointed out (Andrew, 1962) that many mammals 'possess a variety of calls which fall into a series of increasing intensity': low-intensity calls are given, e.g. on recognising a sought-after stimulus such as food (equivalent to 'ah!' in man), and other more intense calls occur in response to frustration or strange objects. In this way vocalisation can reflect a variety of internal states.

In group-living animals, such vocalisations function in communication. For example, in flocks of small birds, when one animal detects a predator it will give an alarm call and all the other members of the flock will dart for cover or freeze. Such alarm calls are similar from species to species because there is selection for a call which is difficult to locate: all employ high frequency sounds with no sharp onset (see Alcock, 1975, Chapter 13). One result of this convergent evolution is that interspecific communication occurs, so that mixed species flocks of small birds may forage together. Similarly, baboons are sensitive to prey species with keener senses, such as antelopes.

Alarm signals may also communicate with the predator itself, thus informing that it has been detected by the prey: e.g. it has been suggested that the 'stotting' (stiff-legged bounding run) of the Thompson's gazelle occurs primarily for this purpose (Alcock, 1975, Chapter 13).

Animals may show a degree of specificity in their vocalisations, for example by emitting different vocalisations in response to different predators. Thus California ground squirrels respond to low flying hawks with a single loud whistle but to mammalian predators with chatters, a more variable vocalisation (Owings, Borchert & Virginia, 1977). Tinbergen (1957) also stated that some species of birds have more than one alarm call, dependent on the type of predator or its behaviour.

Defecation and urination often accompany strong emotions in animals. Darwin (1872) remarked that when in a state of terror, 'a dog will throw himself down, howl and void his excretions'. Increased defecation and urination in times of fear are well known in many other species, and have formed a commonly used measure of fear in rats and mice (in the open field test: see Section 1). Similarly, involuntary defecation may occur in times of great fear in man.

In many species, urine and faeces are commonly used for scent marking. It is possible that this has arisen from the involuntary urination and defecation shown to novel and other fear-inducing stimuli. In other mammalian species, there are specialised skin glands which produce nauseous scents in response to frightening stimuli, and hence function as a defense against potential predators. The skunk is the most famous example, but a similar type of response occurs in other mustelids, such as the polecat.

The wide range of expressive and social responses associated with fear responding again raises some of the general issues discussed earlier, e.g. whether they represent a unidimensional response, and how specific they are to fear evoking situations.

The assumption that there is a set of postures or calls or odours which are specific to fear motivation has been a common one, not only in the psychological literature (see Section 1) but also in the ethological analysis of social displays which may contain a mixture of fear responses and other types of behaviour. A common assumption among ethologists has been as follows: if

69

two or more motivational systems (e.g. sex and fear, or aggression and fear) are constantly activated at the same time in a particular social situation, during the course of evolution this will have resulted in display behaviour, which is a mixture of both types of motivation (see, for example, Tinbergen, 1951; Hinde, 1970, Chapter 16; Blurton-Jones, 1968). Such an analysis assumes that it is useful to focus attention on the overall control of particular responses by separate motivational systems and that behaviour is hierarchially organised with each response subgroup being clearly controlled by such a system. Neurological evidence from research on cats (e.g. Brown and Hunsperger, 1963) is inconsistent with this view since threat displays could be elicited by electrical stimulation of areas separate from those eliciting escape or attack.

A rather different approach (Andrew, 1972a) would be to consider each of the specific responses contributing to such displays in terms of their immediate causation: thus a loud noise or a novel stimulus *simultanelusly* evokes a series of responses such as sympathetic reflexes, protective responses, and withdrawal or immobility. These would vary with the particular situation ('situational stereotypy': see Section 1), and each one would be coordinated with the other in the same way that all an animal's activities are coordinated together. However, in this analysis there would be no clear separation of the control of responses by mechanisms specific to fear or to another type of motivation. Thus the label 'fear behaviour' would refer to a series of specific responses which can be varied and integrated with one another in a whole variety of ways to produce a large variety of finely adjusted responses to a variety of potential dangers. Many of these responses would occur as alternatives to one another and many would occur in other situations which it would be inappropriate to label as fear-inducing.

In general, an approach emphasising specificity of fear responses has not been a popular one in the behavioural literature on fear. It is, however, the approach of Lacey, discussed earlier (Section 2.2), and has also been applied to mammalian displays by Andrew (1972a). Instead of viewing mammalian displays as a result of conflict between major motivational variables, Andrew considered the functional origin of each subcomponent of the overall display. Thus a specific response such as ear-flattening was viewed as a protective reflex against possible danger; therefore, its occurrence would not be specific to fear-evoking situations but it would also occur where there was, e.g. aggressive motivation. In general, Andrew described mammalian display components in terms of responses such as protective reflexes, autonomic reactions, alert responses, responses to novelty, vocalisations, cutaneous secretions and behaviour associated with locomotion and exertion or immobility. Such responses are, in Andrew's analysis, not associated with a particular motivational state such as fear or a type of behaviour such as

70

fleeing, but many will tend to be simultaneously evoked by the same ('fear-evoking') stimuli. This approach to the analysis of behaviour associated with the expression of emotion implies a flexible repertoire of responses by which the animal can communicate an overlapping series of emotional expressions.

2.3 Effects of Fear Responding on Other Motivational Systems

The question of how fear-evoking stimuli affect other types of behaviour is one which has been considered in the ethological literature. Thus Hinde (1970) identified this problem as concerning two questions relating to the interaction between different motivational systems. The first was what decides the particular behavioural outcome when casual factors for more than one type of behaviour are present (Hinde, 1970, Chapter 17). The second (discussed in Chapter 9 of Hinde, 1970) was how the casual factors for two motivational systems might overlap: e.g. how does a mild fear-evoking stimulus affect eating or sexual behaviour? The first question assumes that there is competition for behavioural dominance between the causal factors associated with different motivational systems. Thus the result may be total suppression of one type of behaviour by the other, or interruption of one by the other, or a mixture of the two types of activity, or a blocking of both and the appearance of a third type of behaviour. The second question assumes that rather than competition for behavioural dominance occurring, stimuli normally evoking one type of behaviour have nonspecific effects and may influence (e.g. facilitate) a second type of behaviour from a different motivational system.

In practice it seems that both these assumptions may be correct, but under different circumstances. Under conditions where only weak fear-evoking stimuli are present, it seems that there are relatively nonspecific, usually facilitatory, effects of fear-evoking stimuli on other types of behaviour (e.g. eating or drinking). Under conditions where strong fear-evoking stimuli are present, competition between motivational systems appears to be a more adequate description (cf. Fentress, 1973, 1976, who suggested that lower-intensity stimulation produces a large amount of overlap between causal factors for one system and another, whereas higher-intensity stimulation produces greater specificity).

In this section, I shall discuss firstly facilitation of other activities by fear-evoking stimuli (i.e. cases which fit the nonspecificity model). I shall then discuss the various cases which fit more into a competition model. Several of these are perhaps intermediate between the two: for example, the suppression of both activities and their replacement by a third type of

71

behaviour (a 'displacement activity': Zeigler, 1964) has been explained in a variety of ways, involving nonspecific effects (Tinbergen, 1952; Fentress, 1968), or competition leading to disinhibition of a third type of activity (e.g. Andrew, 1956a; van Iersel & Bol, 1958). Occurrence of activities intermediate between fear behaviour and another type of activity, e.g. in some vertebrate social displays (see Section 2.2) has also been explained in terms of competition between motivational systems, but the alternative explanation offered by Andrew (1972a) involved both specific and nonspecific factors. Total supression of another type of behaviour and its replacement by fear behaviour is the clearest case where the competition model is most appropriate. A related case is that of partial interruption of the other type of behaviour.

These five possibilities, facilitation, displacement activities, intermediate activities, total suppression and partial interruption, are now considered in turn.

2.3.1 Facilitation

It has been found that under certain conditions fear-evoking stimuli may facilitate another type of activity. Hinde (1970, Chapter 9) reviewed a number of studies on rats which showed that an electric shock administered before testing led to increased eating and drinking. Another study, in which shock was administered in the test situation, showed a decrease in food intake as a result of shock. Thus the facilitatory effect of shock on eating and drinking may result from an after-effect of the shock. The exact nature of this after-effect, whether nonspecific or specific (e.g. peripheral) effect, is not clear (see also Hinde, 1970, Chapter 9).

In carnivores, gulls and monkeys (Hinde, 1970, Chapter 9), it has been observed that stimuli which induce a mild disturbance are likely to enhance sexual behaviour. It has also been shown experimentally that painful electric shocks can stimulate sexual behaviour in male rats (Barfield & Sachs, 1968). Again, these are the after effects rather than the direct effects of such stimulation. However, Gantt (1950) observed that the penile erections could be prolonged in many dogs by fear-evoking stimuli, such as removal to a strange room, or a blow or a threatening gesture. In this case, erection appears to occur as an immediate response rather than as an after-reaction, and is accompanied by fear behaviour such as crouching, falling on the floor or trying to run away. Possibly such penile erections represent isolated reflexes given to a wide range of stimuli eliciting emotional excitement, rather than being associated with more general sexual motivation. Even so, they could represent an overlap of casual factors for behaviour from two motivational systems (cf. Fentress, 1973, Fig. 1).

On a more anecdotal level, a shared fearful experience may accentuate human sexual feelings (Wilson and Nias, 1976, Chapter 4).

2.3.2 Suppression of Both Types of Behaviour

Another possible outcome when causal factors are present for fear and another type of behaviour is that both are replaced by another, functionally unrelated, activity, referred to as a displacement or irrelevant activity (Zeigler, 1964). Such activities are usually preening (or grooming), or feeding or drinking. It was mentioned above that their occurrence has been explained either in terms of competition or nonspecific effects: the former included the disinhibition hypothesis, according to which the mutual inhibition of two activities disinhibits a third type of behaviour for which weak causal factors are presumed to be present all the time (Andrew, 1956a; van Iersel & Bol, 1958); alternatively, McFarland (1966) has suggested that as a result of conflict between two incompatible types of motivation or frustration through nonreward, attention is switched to stimuli other than those controlling ongoing activity. Fentress (1968) offered a different type of explanation, in terms of nonspecific effects, one which is reminiscent of the older 'excess drive' explanation of Tinbergen (1952).

Thus when there is a conflict between approaching and avoiding a particular stimulus, displacement activites, such as grooming in mammals or preening in birds occur. There are many examples in the ethological literature: e.g. fighting starlings may stop and preen their wings, and swans may show nest-building during fighting (Tinbergen, 1952).

2.3.3 Intermediate Activities

Another possibility is that behaviour containing features common to both fear and another type of activity may occur. Andrew (1956a) observed that when a hungry bunting flies towards a food source which it also tends to avoid, it flicks its tail vigorously. Tail flicking is an intention movement for taking off and it is appropriate for both approach and avoidance. In this case, the bird showed a behavioural element which was common to both types of behaviour. Such common elements are, however, rare. It is more likely that features from two or more types of behaviour will be combined or alternated with one another, and typical examples of this occur in the displays of fish, birds and mammals. As I remarked earlier (Section 2.2), these displays have often been analysed in terms of conflicting motivation, and whether it is appropriate to do so has been the subject of a long-standing debate in the ethological literature (see Hinde, 1970, Chapter 16; Andrew, 1972a).

Another example of behaviour which reflects two different types of motivation is when two different types of behaviour are alternated with each other.

73

Thus Hinde (1970, p. 401) cited the example of a half-tame moorhen which, when offered food, made incipient pecks and swallowing movements towards the food while almost simultaneously edging away from it. Here components of both fleeing and feeding behaviour occurred in close temporal proximity, presumably indicating incomplete behavioural dominance of one over the other.

2.3.4 Total Suppression

Fear responses typically function to cope with danger in the short term. In order to do so, the animal may have to sacrifice other activities which would normally be involved in maximising its fitness, such as drinking, feeding or sexual behaviour. Thus, fear responses are typically of high priority if the fear-evoking stimulus is strong enough: most other types of behaviour, there-fore, tend to be replaced by fear behaviour in such circumstances.

Hall (1934b), in the original work on the open field test (see Section 1.2), measured the degree of inhibition of feeding in the open field as an index of emotionality. Barnett (1958) also observed inhibition of feeding by wild rats when their food was introduced in an unfamiliar feeding container and in a different place in their cage. He referred to this inhibition as 'neophobia' since it presumably resulted from an inhibition of eating by the novelty-induced fear. Andrew (1956b) investigated the ease with which fear responses were aroused in several species of *Emberiza* (buntings) by recording the latency of water-deprived birds to approach a water dish with a lump of plasticine placed on its rim. All species were inhibited from drinking at first, but later began drinking.

Sexual behaviour is similarly inhibited by high-intensity fear-inducing stimuli. Thus Beach et. al. (1956) found that male rats selected for high sexual responsiveness showed progressive inhibition of mounting a receptive female when subjected to 380 V shocks in a test situation; similar rats given 100 V shocks continued to copulate throughout the 11 tests on which shock was given: they did, however, show a progressive increase in the frequency of incomplete copulatory attempts during successive tests.

Active exploration is also decreased or replaced by fear-inducing stimuli. Montgomery & Monkham (1955) found that fear induced by loud noise or shock in a Y maze led to decreased activity. This finding does not necessarily indicate that there was a supression of exploration, since there may have been a shift from active to passive exploration: thus Birke & Archer (1975) found that after sounding a bell in an open field, rats showed reduced active exploration (walking and sniffing, or rearing) and increased passive explora-tion (sniffing while stationary). Other studies have tried to overcome the difficulty inherent in using ambulation as a measure of exploration by studying the preferences of rats for a novel or a familiar arm of a maze. Generally these have shown that shock given prior to a maze choice reduces the preference for the novel arm and enhances the preference for familiarity (e.g. Aitken, 1972).

Reluctance of a fearful animal to explore or venture into an open area has been used as a basis for measurements of 'emotionality': for example, reduced ambulation in the open field test or reluctance to leave the home cage in a timidity test (Archer, 1973a) are both regarded as indicating a reduced tendency to explore a novel area. However, as I mentioned in Section 1.2, there are difficulties in assuming that ambulation is a measure of exploration (see also Sheldon, 1968a; Archer, 1973a).

Fear-inducing stimuli can also inhibit attack. Although the stimuli which evoke fear and aggression are similar (Archer, 1976a) it appears that as the intensity of noxious stimulation rises, fear behaviour replaces attack. Thus at high intensities of electric shock, fear and escape behaviour suppress the attack which is shown at lower intensities of shock (Archer, 1976a).

Thus, under many conditions, fear behaviour shows dominance over other types of activity such as feeding, drinking, copulation, exploration and attack. This is not always the case since the relative intensities of the two competing types of motivation have also to be taken into account. Thus food-deprived animals may overcome mild fear in order to obtain food. For example, during the acquisition of a running response for food in a runway, chicks first typically show fear and distress behaviour (e.g. peep calls and jumps) in response to the novelty of the test apparatus. When they begin to feed, this fear behaviour is suppressed, but it may reappear during the extinction of the running response (Archer, 1974c). Similarly, in tests where food- or water-deprived animals are given food or water in a novel container (e.g. Andrew, 1956b; Barnett, 1958), the animals eventually overcome their fear sufficiently to feed or drink.

2.3.5 Partial Interruption

Fear-evoking stimuli may also partially interrupt another type of behaviour or affect the way in which it is carried out. Thus, animals feeding in an open space where they could be vulnerable to predators may frequently interrupt their feeding behaviour to look around. In the laboratory, the fear-inducing effects of novelty have been utilised in tests which measure the susceptibility of hungry animals to interruption of a learned feeding response by a novel stimulus. Thus, in a runway, novel patterns introduced into the side walls may prevent or delay running to the end of the runway and feeding (Archer, 1974b), and they may even interrupt feeding once it has begun (Andrew & Klein, personal communication). A novel pattern or colour on the animal's food dish is more likely not to be noticed at first but subsequently to lead to interrupted feeding, both in chicks (Archer, 1974b) and mice (Archer, 1977b). Changing the place of the feeding dish also affects the number of times the chick interrupts its feeding (Archer, 1974b). It appears that a greater degree of novelty (e.g. a changed pattern in the runway walls) is likely to supress feeding altogether whereas a lesser degree of novelty is more likely to produce interrupted feeding.

Generally, there is little evidence available on the effects of mildly fear-evoking stimuli on the manner in which other types of behaviour are carried out. A study by Tugendhat (1960a and b) found that when three-spined sticklebacks were shocked in the food area of their tanks, their rate of feeding was increased but the time spent feeding decreased. Whether such increased vigour but decreased duration of behaviour is a characteristic of fear-inducing stimuli on other types of activity is a question which must await further studies to be answered.

3   Factors Affecting the Type of Fear Behaviour

3.1   Introduction

So far, I have discussed the various types of behaviour described as fear responding, including the expressive social behaviour occurring with the fear responses. I have also considered how fear-evoking stimuli affect other types of behaviour. In this part of the chapter, I shall be concerned with the factors that determine which of these particular fear responses occur. The first part of the discussion concerns a brief consideration of the broad evolutionary context of fear responses, before going on to discuss interspecific differences in fear behaviour in relation to its adaptive significance as an antipredator response. In the third section, I consider the situational determinants of specific fear responses.

3.2   Fear Responses in a Broad Evolutionary Context

All organisms encounter stimuli capable of inflicting physical damage. In responding to these, they have evolved mechanisms of repair and regeneration (see, for example, Young, 1971, Chapter 12). For plants, this remains a major way of counteracting such damage. But animals can move about, and also monitor stimulus change in their environment over short periods of time; hence they are endowed with the potential to respond in ways other than simply repairing tissue damage after it has occurred. Pain

76

perception has evolved to monitor tissue damage, and effector systems taking appropriate action are linked through the nervous system to these receptors, enabling several types of alternative responses to be feasible in such circumstances. One is active withdrawal into a protective enclosure, and is, of course, the only one possible for sedentary animals, e.g. colonial hydrozoa and tubeworms such as *Sabella* and *Branchiomma*. If the pedal disc of a sea anemone is stimulated mechanically, the animal closes up rapidly and completely, and this closure occurs as a result of a through-conducting system (Pantin, 1935). Such a system of faster-transmitting giant fibres occurs in a number of invertebrates where transmission via the normal nervous pathway would prove too slow as a withdrawal or avoidance response.

A more common response to harmful stimuli is active escape, i.e. the animal removes itself from the immediate environment, rather than withdrawing into a protective covering. For free-swimming animals, such a response would have conferred a clear selective advantage over those which were comparatively unresponsive, or slow to respond. It seems that active escape or avoidance reactions must have been among the first functional systems which evolved. *Paramaecium*, for example, shows an avoiding reaction if its forward course is interrupted by a solid object, if the water is hot or cold, and in response to potentially harmful chemical stimuli (Jennings, 1906): in the latter case the repellant power is not necessarily proportional to the injurious effects of the chemical. In their reaction to osmotic pressure, *Paramaecium* demonstrate the consequences of an avoiding reaction being taken too late: in this case, the response is not shown until the animal is seriously damaged.

An alternative response which is more appropriate if the harmful stimulus is a small localised physical object is removal of the stimulus rather than the removal of the animal from near the the stimulus. Such an alternative response would have been the functional prototype for aggressive behaviour (and also for care of the body surface), and would be of selective advantage where removal of the animal (escape) would mean withdrawal to a harmful of suboptimal area in terms of resources.

A later refinement in evolutionary development would have involved the ability to decide in advance of tactile or chemical stimulation whether danger was likely. It is clearly preferable to perceive in advance whether or not a predator or a conspecific attacker is near, and to take the appropriate avoiding action, than to wait for it to be in contact before responding. Thus, as animals evolved more sophisticated sensory and neural equipment, this would have enabled them to monitor the environment for potentially dangerous stimuli, and to avoid these before damage could occur. I have argued (Archer, 1976a) that this monitoring system basically involves a central representation or series of representations of various features of the environment: any large discrepancy between observed and expected stimuli would induce escape or withdrawal responses (or attack if the appropriate stimulus was present). Presumably, with a relatively unsophisticated level of neurosensory development, monitoring for change in the environment is an effective way of avoiding danger, and hence would have conferred a great advantage on animals which could act in this way.

In the majority of species, it is likely that predation is the most important danger to avoid, and thus mechanisms ensuring predator avoidance will have been necessary for survival in most animal groups. This supposition enables us to understand a number of features concerning the range of fear responses in different species. For example, Von Uexkull (1934) argued that many predators only respond to moving prey, particularly in the invertebrate world, and in vertebrates where cryptic colouration occurs; as a consequence there would have been selection for immobility as a response to predation in many animal groups. On some occasions this would have been more successful than actively escaping, since an escaping prey is moving and if the predator is fast it would catch some moving prey, but none of those which remained immobile. Further consequences of viewing fear responses as antipredator adaptations are considered in the next section.

3.3   The Adaptive Significance of Fear Responses as Antipredator Behaviour

From the argument advanced in the previous section, it follows that an animal's most readily emitted type of fear behaviour can be understood functionally in terms of the type of predation pressure that particular species has experienced under natural conditions. It is suggested that the following factors would be important:

(1) predation pressure, i.e. frequency of encounters with predation;
(2) speed and efficiency of the predators and prey;
(3) whether escape to a place not occupied by the predator can occur readily;
(4) whether cryptic colouration is used and whether cryptic cover is available;
(5) whether the predator can see moving prey easily (see above);
(6) whether the prey possesses its own means of protection, e.g. in the form of a hard shell or spines.

The first of these would determine how effective the fear responses were and how readily they would be emitted. In a general sense predation

78

pressure would determine how 'tame' a species is: for example, it is commonly observed that birds and mammals living on isolated islands free from predators typically present elsewhere appear unafraid of man and dogs. On the other hand, animals that actively avoid their predators will be alert and vigilant, looking round and sniffing for signs of danger.

Speed and efficiency of predators will, in general, determine the speed of escape reaction in the prey. In practice, there may be constraints on running speed by other selective forces, such as the structural capabilities of the animal (Alcock, 1975, Chapter 13). The escape behaviour of ungulates, such as the wildebeast, illustrate a fast active escape response. Of course, such responses are of little use without either the animal being able to outrun the predator (and predators are selected for fast locomotion in pursuit of prey), or it having a place to escape to.

Lack of speed may to some extent be compensated for by an erratic direction of running, e.g. in the zig-zag runs of snipe and ptarmigan (Edmunds, 1972, Chapter 6). Driver & Humphries (1970) have called such irregular responses 'protean displays' – a general term for movements which defeat detailed prediction. Protean displays embody irregularities and stimulus variety as basic principles: hence they increase the reaction time of the predator, and are highly resistant to countermeasures.

Another means of slowing down the pursuit of a predator is by what Edmunds (1972, Chapter 7) calls deimatic behaviour, characteristic intimidating postures or startle displays. These may either warn or bluff the predator, but in many cases they are effective antipredator devices in their own right: for example, the sudden appearance of bright colours or simulated eyespots on the wings of certain species of butterfly elicits escape behaviour in many bird predators (Edmunds, 1972, Chapter 7).

In general, if the prey live in places where the predator cannot, it is sufficient for the prey to respond quickly so that it is soon out of the predator's reach. For an animal that can fly, this is clearly the best way to escape from a ground-dwelling predator. Since this is so effective, birds can remain in view of potential mammalian predators with relative impunity and this is why we see so many bird species in our everyday lives, but so few mammals. Semi-acquatic animals, such as frogs, can also avoid land predators by jumping into water. Other species may climb trees, or escape down burrows. Edmunds (1972, Chapter 5) described many examples of animals which live in burrows or holes from which they emerge to feed. Such animals typically respond to predators by rapidly retreating into their hole. One unusual example is the pearl fish, *Carapus acus*, which retreats from predators through the anus of a sea cucumber. One disadvantage of withdrawal into a burrow or hole is that some small predators such as the ferret, polecat and weasel can follow prey down a burrow. This may be counteracted by entrance-blocking devices or second exits.

If an animal is cryptically coloured, or if there is camouflage available in the environment, the predominant form of fear behaviour will be immobility. Often this may be preceded by fleeing for a short distance and then remaining motionless and cryptic so that it cannot be detected by the predator (e.g. in frogs and grasshoppers). If the predator cannot see moving prey, immobility will also tend to be the favoured strategy (see also Section 3.2). Predators are in general very sensitive to movement and Alcock (1975, Chapter 13) has suggested that hiding from a predator by becoming immobile is such a common strategy because it exploits this sensitivity. Often the behavioural response maximises cryptic colouration, and involves more than merely the ability to remain motionless: e.g. the prey may be oriented so that its cryptic colouration matches the surroundings. Some moths have striped wings which resemble grooves in the bark of trees: they orient on the tree trunk with heads pointing up or down if they have vertical stripes or with their bodies at right angles to the trunk if they have horizontal stripes (Alcock, 1975, Chapter 13).

Animals which hide from predators often possess a second line of defence if they are discovered by the predator, e.g. flying off or running, or retreating down a burrow or shell. Alternatively they may surprise the predator with deimatic displays (see above) or direct the predator away from vital areas (an extreme example of this is the lizard's tail which breaks off and continues thrashing wildly while the lizard escapes). Even if an animal is caught by a predator it may have a final antipredator response – the tonic immobility reaction described earlier in this chapter. This response exploits the fact that many predators feed only on freshly caught prey and will attempt to kill and capture only animals that move.

Some animals possess anatomical structures that defend them against predators, e.g. the spines of hedgehogs, the armoured plates of woodlice and the shells of bivalve molluscs and tortoises. In these cases, the antipredator reaction would involve the withdrawal of the soft unprotected parts of the body so as to be protected by the spines, plates or shell. The woodlouse, *Armadillidium*, and millipedes roll into a ball which protects their delicate head and ventral parts by means of horny plates or spines (Edmunds, 1974, Chapter 5; Ratner, 1977). In these animals, the predominant fear response will consist of a withdrawal response followed by immobility.

In practice, a mixture of defensive strategies may occur – a combination of active and passive behaviour, possibly accompanied by antipredator attack. There may, for example, be fast initial dispersal of a group of animals, followed by immobility combined with hiding in the vegetation. Alternatively, as in the case of some ground-dwelling birds, escape may consist of short flights which become progressively shorter until the bird only moves a few yards and becomes immobile wherever it happens to land. Such an escape strategy would make the bird an easy prey for a persistent and intelligent predator such as early man (Pfeiffer, 1969, Chapter 5).

In order to predict the type of fear response typically shown by a species, we should have to ask first whether predation pressure is high. If it is, there will have been selection for either fast escape (depending on the speed and efficiency of the predator and the habitat), or escape to another niche (depending on whether this is possible in terms of the animal's general adaptations and locomotion), or immobility (depending on whether the predator can see moving prey and whether there is suitable camouflage available). For example, animals such as cavies, which live in dense vegetation, show prolonged freezing as their dominant fear response under laboratory conditions. Animals which typically retreat down holes and burrows show a more variable and predominantly active form of escape behaviour.

3.4 Situational Determinants of Fear Responses

I have suggested that the predation to which a species has been subjected will determine the overall intensity and form of its escape responses. This approach to the understanding of fear behaviour extends Bolles's (1970) notion of species-specific avoidance responses: he suggested that different species show characteristic escape and avoidance responses and that the ease of establishing particular avoidance conditioning responses in the laboratory is related to whether the required avoidance response is appropriate in terms of that species' typical escape behaviour.

I am not, however, suggesting that animals have automatic, species-specific avoidance responses, which occur in all fear-evoking situations. In Section 2 of this chapter, I described the range of responses which has been described under the term fear behaviour, and also suggested that these provide a flexible repertoire for the animal to use according to the particular circumstances to which it is responding. We should therefore expect that certain immediate situational factors will influence which of the various types of fear behaviour occurs. For example, if an animal is already moving, it may be advantageous for it to keep moving since there is a greater chance that it will already have been seen by a predator than if it were immobile. If, on the other hand, the animal is immobile, it would be better for it to remain immobile, as there is a lesser chance that it would have been seen by the predator. There is some evidence from experiments with voles and with chicks that this is the case. Fentress (1968) interrupted the ongoing behaviour of two species of vole in a large alley with an overhead moving object. When locomotion preceeded the stimulus presentation, fleeing rather than freezing was found to occur, whereas freezing was more likely to occur following prior immobility. Forrester and Broom (personal communication) interrupted the ongoing behaviour of chicks by illuminating a bulb on their cage wall. The magnitude and duration of the response was found to be related to what the bird had been doing just before the stimulus was presented. When it had been walking or pecking, it was more likely to run and jump, and emit distress calls. When it had been motionless it fixated its gaze on the bulb but showed no active response. The response of birds which had previously been preening was intermediate, immobility and bulb fixation being associated with some activity. Subsequent work by Culshaw and Broom (personal communication) has shown that the response also depends on the point during a bout of activity at which the stimulus is presented. Chicks startled at the end of a bout of preening or feeding showed a greater response than those at the beginning of a bout.

The distance a predator (or other fear-evoking stimulus) is from an animal may also affect the type of fear response. Ratner (1967) has suggested that animals will tend to freeze if the predator is some way off but will show active escape if it is nearer; finally, if cornered, it may show attack and if actually caught may show tonic immobility (see Section 2.1).

The effects of the intensity of a fear-evoking stimulus, such as an electric shock, have been investigated in laboratory rats. Barcik & Collins (1972) found that low to medium shock intensities resulted in immobility whereas higher intensities produced flight. Blanchard & Blanchard (1968, 1970) found that a more localised shock produced active escape behaviour, whereas a more diffuse one evoked immobility. Possibly this indicates a greater tendency to escape from clearly localised stimuli and to become immobile in response to more difuse stimulation. This interpretation would be supported by Andrew's (1956b) observation that freezing in buntings (*Emberiza* spp.) is aroused in particular by unlocated sources of fear.

With the exception of the two studies of interrupting ongoing behaviour described above, there is not much evidence available on how the animal's internal state may affect the form of its fear responding. These two interruption studies investigated the influence of the animal's immediately preceeding state on performance. There is some evidence concerning longer-term internal influences from hormone studies. Archer (1976b) investigated the effects of testosterone on the behaviour of chicks after being placed into an open field containing a bell which was sounded for the first 5 seconds. Testosterone-injected chicks showed more freezing and immobility but fewer active escape and avoidance responses than did control chicks. It was suggested that such differences were an indirect consequence of attentional effects of testosterone found in other studies (e.g. Andrew & Rogers, 1972; Rogers, 1974; Andrew, 1972b; Archer, 1974b and c) rather than a direct effect of testosterone on the type of fear responding – since no comparable effects are found where there is no localised source of fear-inducing stimulation (e.g. Archer, 1973b, c and d; Andrew, 1975).

Other studies on rats have shown a sex difference in the most readily emitted type of fear responding. Beatty & Beatty (1970) showed that, whereas female rats responded to a shuttle-box active avoidance task with active escape behaviour, males more readily showed immobility and defecation (and hence showed poorer learning of the shuttle response). Several studies (Beatty & Beatty, 1970; Savage, 1960; Wilcock, 1968) have also reported more readily emitted running and jumping responses in female than male rats. On the basis of these studies, I suggested (Archer, 1975) that male and female rats show different 'sex-typical fear responses', females being more prone to active escaping and males to immobility. Such a generalisation, based as it is on limited evidence, requires further studies before it is worth speculating further (e.g. on the adaptive significance of such a sex difference).

There is, therefore, some evidence – admittedly from very varied sources and limited in nature – that the types of fear responses an animal shows depend on its immediately preceding behaviour, its longer-term internal state (e.g. its sex hormone make-up) and on the nature of the particular fear-evoking stimulus (e.g. on properties such as intensity and location).

In many cases, the situation is more complex, since fear responses, such as escape and immobility, do not occur as alternatives to one another, but both occur together. For example, in a study which involved interrupting the behaviour of chicks with a loud bell outside an open field (Archer 1973c, 1976b), it was found that the typical response while the bell was sounding was active escape but that this was replaced by immobility when the bell had ceased ringing. This also occurs in rats (Archer, 1974a) and mice (unpublished observations). There are unfortunatley rather few studies of the changes in fear behaviour over time following the presentation of a fear-inducing stimulus.

3.5 Conclusions

In summary, the specific type of fear behaviour an animal shows is influenced by its evolutionary history, long-term and short-term internal factors and the nature of the fear-evoking stimulus, and the time since the fear-evoking stimulus appeared. These factors are best viewed as all contributing to the production of a variety of possible fear responses, of the type described in Section 2 of this chapter, which enable the animal to vary its response according to its internal state and the external conditions.

4 General Conclusions

In this chapter, I have outlined the complex nature of the behaviour associated with 'fear' in animals and man. During this discussion, a number of issues were raised which have implications for the problem of divising measures of fear (see Section 1 of this chapter).

The first issue is a conceptual one – that in many of the tests used in animal research there is the assumption that a single fear state leads to the simultaneous or near-simultaneous activation of the various forms of fear behaviour; it is also assumed that these can be measured and placed along a single intensity dimension. In the earlier parts of this chapter, I showed that these assumptions are unwarranted in view of both the low correlations between different measures of fear, and the complex nature of behavioural fear responses.

Another assumption made in relation to the animal tests is that fear-evoking stimuli provide the sole influence on the behaviour which is measured. This implies an absolute specificity of control by a single motivational system. However, in practice it seems that many of the responses measured as fear behaviour are influenced by factors other than fear-evoking stimuli. The examples of defecation and ambulation in the open field were mentioned earlier (Section 2.2) to illustrate the effects of food intake and general activity on these measures. Similarly, in the case of tests which involve measuring the time taken for an animal to emerge from its home cage into a novel environment, there may be influences on the response measure other than those which are mediated by fear (Archer, 1976c). Measures such as ambulation or latency to move are in fact only indirect indices of fear responding since they rely on the suppression of other types of behaviour by fear-evoking stimuli. They are, therefore, based on the indirect consequences of fear-evoking stimuli on behaviour controlled by another motivational system, such as exploration. Their use as an index of fear responding fails to take into account the influence of factors specific to the other motivational system, and general influences affecting, e.g. activity in a wide range of conditions (see Section 1.2).

Fear-evoking stimuli may affect other types of behaviour in one of several different ways, inhibition being only one possibility (others included facilitation and partial interruption). Such a range of possible indirect effects has not been taken into account in constructing measures of fear responding, where the assumption is simply that fear behaviour suppresses other types of responses.

In this chapter, I have shown that there is a wide range of behaviour associated with the fear state and that many other sorts of behaviour are indirectly affected by fear stimuli. Thus the term 'fear behaviour' can be used to describe various forms of escape and immobility responses together with expressive responses and social signals, and the indirect (e.g. inhibitory) influences of fear stimuli on behaviour such as eating, drinking and ambulation (see pervious paragraph). Many of the tests used in animal research have not made the best use of this wide range of possible responses. The reason for this is that psychologists working in the animal learning tradition have generally sought a few easily recordable measures and have assumed unidimensionality in fear responding: hence a wide range of measures is viewed as unnecessary duplication.

Related to this neglect of the wide range of fear responses is the lack of attention paid to species differences and their possible adaptive significance (see Section 3). Thus although different fear responses are shown by different species of animal, test measures have not generally been adapted accordingly. For example, in using the open field test for animals very different from rats or mice, researchers have tended to continue to use activity and defecation measures (e.g. in monkeys, chickens and cats: Candland and Nagy, 1969). The range of fear responses shown by individuals of the same species also varies with the nature of the fear-evoking conditions and the animals' long and short term internal state (Section 3.4). In measuring fear responses, it has often been assumed that the nature of the fear stimulus and the internal state of the animal affect only the intensity of fear responses and not the form these will take.

In conclusion, the evidence on the diversity of fear responses, summarised in this chapter, suggests that the notion of a similar set of responses occurring to a variety of fear-evoking situations is incorrect; that research based on this assumption, e.g. in attempting to measure the degree of fear, is therefore founded on an inadequate theoretical model. Instead, fear responses should be regarded as arising from a variable response repertoire showing different characteristics in different species (and even within the same species) and which can provide a series of varied but integrated responses appropriate for different situations. The control mechanism for such a flexible system would clearly involve more complex regulation than is implied in simple models involving control by a single central fear state. As Hinde (1970) stated, the need for such intervening variables may be useful at initial stages of analysis but their continued use to imply a simple unidimensional control system prevents further detailed analysis of that system; and such intervening variables may be even more misleading when they appear to correspond to subjective experience (Hinde, 1974). These comments are particularly appropriate in the case of fear behaviour.

CHAPTER 4

Fear-Evoking Stimuli

P. A. Russell

Many different objects, situations and events have been described as fear-evoking in man and other animals: darkness, heights, snakes and other creatures, strange objects, sudden noises, enclosed and open places, injury and pain are a few which spring to mind. Many of these stimuli are species predictable, i.e. they evoke fear in all or most individuals of a species. Some are common to many different vertebrate species. This is largely because responding fearfully to certain types of stimulus is adaptive in many different organisms, a fact which represents one of the unifying themes of vertebrate evolution. This chapter seeks to set out the main general classes of fear-evoking stimuli in vertebrates in the light of their adaptive significance.

Before embarking upon this task, it is necessary to consider some general issues relating to the functional and adaptive aspects of fear. As has been pointed out by various theorists, notably those working within an ethological framework such as Bowlby (1969, 1973), the aspects of behaviour conventionally lumped under the heading of fear are essentially a collection of adaptive whole-body responses serving to protect the organism from potentially harmful stimuli, i.e. stimuli which could be damaging, injurious or fatal. The survival value of these protective responses is usually self evident. Escaping (fleeing) from a stimulus, avoiding (i.e. failing to approach a stimulus or escaping from stimuli associated with it), hiding and wary watching fall into this category. Immobility, freezing, cowering and the cessation of general activity may also be adaptive responses to harmful stimuli. Various aspects of attachment behaviour between individuals including following, clinging and signalling are also protective responses which may be activated or heightened by potential harm. Protective responses may be correlated with physiological changes including the various concomitants of autonomic functioning such as heart rate, defecation and urination, and with subjective reports of feelings of fear in humans,

I am indebted to Professor E. A. Salzen for much helpful discussion during the preparation of this chapter.

though this chapter concentrates mainly on the overt behavioural aspects of fear. The term 'protective behaviour' thus describes behaviour patterns which serve to reduce or avoid contact with, or ameliorate the effects of, a harmful stimulus. Some authors (e.g. Bolles, 1970; Blanchard & Blanchard, 1971) have used the term 'defensive behaviour' to describe these same patterns, though this term also embraces aggressive behaviour which, though it often has much the same general function and often occurs in similar contexts (Archer, 1976a), is not dealt with here.

This is not to say that fear is a simple unitary phenomenon. As Bowlby (1973) and others have argued, fear is not a single form of behaviour but rather a heterogeneous collection of interrelated responses each of which may be elicited by a slightly different set of conditions. The main justification for grouping these diverse responses is that they often tend to occur together or sequentially, are often elicited by the same stimuli, and have the same general protective function. The fact that different responses are not invariably associated, however, complicates the identification of fear stimuli since a given stimulus may be regarded as 'fear-evoking' or not depending on which aspect of behaviour is being measured. For this reason it is clearly essential to specify the behaviour involved in each particular case rather than simply describe a stimulus as fear-evoking. This approach also has the advantage of pointing up the existence of any special associations between particular stimuli and particular behaviour patterns.

There have been relatively few previous attempts at a comprehensive classification of vertebrate fear stimuli, though numerous authors have concerned themselves with one or two specific stimulus dimensions such as novelty (Berlyne, 1960; Bronson, 1968a) and intensity (Schneirla, 1965). More embracing, though still incomplete, reviews have been provided by Hebb (1946), Marks (1969), and Scarr & Salapatek (1970). The scheme adopted in this chapter owes most to the analyses of Gray (1971b), Bowlby (1973) and Archer (1976a).

On the most basic level, species predictable fear stimuli may be distinguished according to whether they originate in the organism's physical environment, from predators, or from conspecifics. Each of these sources is examined in the following sections. Fear stimuli which are not species predictable are considered briefly in the final section.

1 Predator Stimuli

Predation appears to have played a prominent role in the evolution of protective responses in many species. These responses fall into the general category of what Edmunds (1974) calls secondary (or direct) defences against predators, i.e. ones which operate when a predator is encountered, and serve to increase the chances of survival during the encounter. As well as flight and withdrawal, the responses include immobility and freezing, which may reduce the likelihood of detection and attenuate the attack of a predator in close proximity (Ratner, 1967). Protective responses are thus distinct from primary (or indirect) defences such as camouflage and mimicry, which operate regardless of whether a predator is present.

Should an animal actually be caught by a predator, protective responses, as well as retaliatory defensive behaviour, may be elicited by the stimulation of proximal touch and pain receptors. There are usually 'last ditch' measures, however, and the anticipation of a predator attack, with appropriate avoidance behaviour (whether active, or passive such as freezing) is a more effective antipredator strategy. Avoidance entails the use of distal cues stemming from the predator which enable the prey to react while it is still at a distance. The distance at which prey respond to a given predator has been termed the flight distance (Hediger, 1950) or, more generally, the reactive distance (e.g. Dill, 1974). The stimuli involved in 'recognition' of and reaction to a predator may be quite specific to a particular predator or class of predators (see Section 1.2) or they may be much more general. Particularly where a species is preyed upon by a range of predators, the response mechanisms could be triggered by stimulus features which the predators have in common. These are likely to be relatively nonspecific stimuli such as novelty (Section 3.1) and stimuli associated with the predators' attack behaviour.

1.1 Nonspecific Stimuli Associated with Predator Attacks

Some clues to the possible cues generated by a variety of predators can be obtained by examining their attack behaviour. The main common feature is sudden, fast, direct movement towards the prey, starting either in full view or from cover. Lions hunting herd ungulates such as wildebeest and zebra, for example, usually rely on stalking and getting close without being detected or on an ambush technique (Schaller, 1972). In both cases the final attack is a short dash from cover and the ungulate's flight is thus elicited by the sudden appearance of a fast approaching lion at close quarters. Resting lions are usually ignored and lions walking in full view are simply watched and kept at a distance, reflecting the fact that lions seldom indulge in long rushes where they are likely to be outrun. Species which attack in full view show a period of rapid, direct movement which develops suddenly from a slow walk, e.g. cheetah (Kruuk & Turner, 1963) and spotted hyena (Kruuk, 1972). The basic movement features of suddenness of onset, rapidity, directness and closeness of proximity are common to the attacks of most predatory fish, reptiles, birds and mammals. In some cases an attack may also be accompanied by sudden noise (e.g. pounding feet, rushing wings). These basic features are clearly important in the response of many prey species to predators and could in principle mediate protective behaviour without any specific recognition of the predator. Their potency in this respect is illustrated by the fact that *nonpredator stimuli* incorporating one or more of these features frequently elicit protective responses.

1.1.1 *Movement Features*

A moving predator is often more likely to be responded to than a stationary one. For example, Blanchard, Mast & Blanchard (1975) found that dead or anaesthetised cats failed to elicit freezing in laboratory rats in an inescapable situation while a moving cat did, though it was immaterial whether the movement arose from a live cat or a dead one moved by the experimenter. Bronstein & Hirsch (1976) also noted that a moving cat but not a quiescent one elicited escape in young rats, though older ones responded to both (suggesting that other factors are also involved in rats' response to cats: see Sections 1.2.1. and 1.2.2.). Moving predatory hawks and owls and their models are more effective in eliciting various fear responses in some small birds (Nice & Ter Pelkwyk, 1941) though movement is not always essential, a finding confirmed for the mobbing of predator models (see Section 1.2.1.) by chaffinches (Hinde, 1954) and pied flycatchers (Curio, 1975).

The importance of movement is further demonstrated by the fact that moving nonpredatory objects increase the probability of protective behaviour. Haslerud (1938) found that young chimpanzees were less likely to reach outside their cage for food if there was a moving, rather than a still, object near it. In chimps (Menzel, 1964b) and geladas (Hughes & Menzel, 1973) avoidance behaviour increases as a function of the rate and extent of an object's movement. A moving gloved hand, but not a still one, decreases rats' activity in an inescapable environment (Bronstein & Hirsch, 1976).

The effectiveness of movement in general is largely predictable since it is both attention-getting and a reliable (though obviously not infallible) cue to the presence of life. There is evidence, however, that the specific movement features of directness, speed, suddenness, and closeness of approach identified above are especially crucial, though it is often difficult to disentangle the effects of these different aspects. The evidence comes from studies of prey exposed to predators, predator models, nonpredator objects, and shadow projections simulating features of moving objects.

Approach is more likely to elicit protective behaviour than retreat. Schiff, Caviness & Gibson (1962) found that rhesus monkeys sprang back or ducked, sometimes with distress calls (infants), in response to a steady increase in the size of a shadow projected on a screen in front of them. Similar avoidance has been reported in fiddler crabs, frogs and chicks (Schiff, 1965), and turtles (Hayes & Saiff, 1967). A human infant moves its head away and back and brings its arms up to its face (Ball & Tronick, 1971). Human adults do not avoid the shadow but they do report seeing the two-dimensional size increase as an *approaching object*. Avoidance in other species seems to be elicited by this approach feature since a steady reduction in shadow size, indicating retreat, is ineffective (Schiff, 1965; Ball & Tronick, 1971) as is the sudden darkening of a lit screen (Schiff). Further, magnification of a lit area against a dark screen is ineffective in crabs, frogs and chicks (Schiff, 1965), probably correlated with the fact that in nature an approaching object usually reflects less light than its background.

Direct approach of a moving object is particularly crucial, predictably so since even a nonpredatory object is potentially harmful if on a collision course. Walther (1969) reported that Thomson's gazelle showed longer flight distances to a vehicle moving directly towards the herd rather than tangential to it. An asymmetrically growing projected shadow, appearing as an object approaching on a miss path, elicits visual monitoring but not avoidance in human infants (Ball & Tronick, 1971). Two studies reporting negative findings for rats directly approached by a prod (Blanchard & Blanchard, 1969a) and a moving hand (Blanchard & Blanchard, 1971) may indicate a species difference or, more plausibly, the use of suboptimal movement conditions.

An approaching object subtends an increasingly large angle at the retina as it draws closer, and since the angular size increase is geometric a sudden optical 'explosion' or *looming* effect occurs as the object begins to fill the entire visual field, indicating imminent collision. Schiff (1965) found that magnification of the shadow projection below about 25° of visual angle produced little avoidance in chicks and crabs while magnification above about 40° was highly effective. Extrapolating to real objects, this could mean either that avoidance is triggered by a simple increase in visual angle above some threshold, in which case large objects would be avoided when still relatively distant, or that the closeness of approach of an object is crucial more or less irrespective of its size. Both possibilities are consistent, for example, with Walther's (1969) observation that Thomson's gazelle fled at greater distances to a large vehicle than to a small one if it is assumed that gazelle unfamiliar with vehicles see a large one as being closer. Bower, Broughton & Moore (1970), however, found that the avoidance response of human infants, at least, is controlled by closeness of approach, not absolute visual angle, since a 20 cm cube approaching to 8 cm produced strong upset,

90

while a 50 cm cube approaching to 20 cm, and subtending the same visual angle, had much less effect.

Increased speed of approach of a predator or object increases the flight distance or probability of response in a number of species (Eibl-Eibesfeldt, 1965; Schiff, 1965; Hayes & Saiff, 1967; Walther, 1969). Dill (1974) suggested that in some cases the rate of change of the visual angle subtended by the object is crucial, which is supported for zebra danio fish by his finding that the reaction distance to an approaching predator or model was increased with an increase in either its size or velocity. The reactive distance of damselfish, however, appears to be independent of the speed of approach of a given size of predator model, within the limits used by Hurley & Hartline (1974).

1.1.2 Suddenness

Although anecdotal reports, such as Walther's (1969) observation that the sudden appearance of a banded mongoose group from a termite heap elicited flight in Thomson's gazelle while a similar group in full view was ignored, testify to the effectiveness of stimuli with a sudden onset in eliciting protective behaviour, there have been few systematic studies of this variable. Schiff's (1965) failure to elicit avoidance by suddenly darkening a lit screen has been noted in Section 1.1.1. Sudden stimuli in all modalities, however, are capable of eliciting startle patterns in many species (Landis & Hunt, 1939; Bronson, 1968a; Scarr & Salapatek, 1970). Sudden loud noises often produce rapid locomotion which probably represents flight and escape (Collias, 1952 – chicks; Archer, 1974a – rats, 1977a – mice) and may reduce an animal's subsequent tendency to enter a novel area (Haywood & Wachs, 1967 – rats; though see Mottin and Gatehouse, 1975 and Section 3.1.1).

1.1.3 Proximity

Although the triggering of protective behaviour depends on a variety of stimulus features, there is little doubt that in general the closer a threatening stimulus is the more likely it is to be responded to or the stronger the response is. This is implicit in the clinical technique of desensitising phobic patients by exposing them to the feared stimulus at a distance and then bringing it gradually closer (see, for example, Rachman, 1974). Udin, Olswanger & Volger (1974) found that when a tarantula was moved towards human subjects, avoidance (as measured by the frequency with which they pressed a button to halt the stimulus) increased as a function of its proximity. A similar spatial gradient is illustrated by the behaviour of a caged chaffinch placed at various distances from a stuffed owl (Hinde, 1954): the closer the

91

owl is the more avoidance predominates in the alternate approach/ avoidance behaviour involved in chaffinch mobbing (see Section 1.2.1).

1.2 Recognition of Specific Predators

There is evidence that at least some prey species respond to a specific predator or class of predators. The fact that some have different reaction distances to different predators suggests, though it does not prove, that they are able to 'recognise' specific predators. Walther (1969), for example, found that Thomson's gazelle had short flight distances to animals such as jackals which do not prey on them, through intermediate distances to species from which attack is possible but unlikely (e.g. lions, which prefer larger game), to long ones for specialised gazelle predators like the wild dog and the cheetah. Although this implies specific recognition it is possible that discrimination is based upon nonspecific cues such as movement features (Section 1.1.1.) or size. It is difficult to rule out completely the operation of such features when dealing with live predators, though easier with experimental models designed to stimulate one or more features of a predator.

Predator recognition raises two main questions which are related but should not be confused. One is which feature, or features, of the predator elicit protective behaviour. In some cases at least, evidence relevant to this question exists. The second question concerns the origin of the eliciting property of the predator feature. The main issue here is whether it has acquired its property through the prey's experience with the predator (or perhaps with other stimuli) or is an innate releaser which operates independently of experience. This question is usually difficult or impossible to answer on the basis of the existing evidence and is not considered here, though the issue is taken up again in Section 5.

Response to a predator is often mediated by a stimulus compounded of several features, which may involve more than one sense modality. The evidence is most conveniently summarised, however, according to modality. Signals given by animals to warn conspecifics of the presence of a predator are also discussed in this section, since they elicit protective behaviour in much the same way as predator features themselves.

1.2.1 Visual Features

Visual features are presumably involved in fear of snakes, a class of predator to which special significance is often ascribed for various reasons (Morris & Morris, 1965), of which one is that snakes are potentially dangerous to a wide range of animal species. Strong avoidance of snakes is shown by some humans (Jones & Jones, 1928; Mellstrom, Cicala &

92

Zuckerman, 1976) and by many other mammals (Morris & Morris, 1965). The main problem is whether the snake stimulus has special properties over and above the effects expected on the basis of its novelty (Section 3.1) and general movement features (Section 1.1). Any special effectiveness would presumably stem from the snake's thin, elongated appearance, possibly coupled with skin texture and/or some *specific* aspect of its movement (e.g. wriggling and slithering).

Snake fear serves as a convenient model for illustrating the general problems involved in establishing that specific predator features elicit protective responses. Evidence of some special property of the snake configuration would entail the demonstration that a snake elicits more avoidance, say, than some other object which is equally novel and moves in a similar way or in a way which is equally novel (or the movement variable could be eliminated by using still animals or models). Adequate controls are difficult to contrive and no existing studies are entirely satisfactory in this respect. Those incorporating at least partial controls provide little support for the special effectiveness hypothesis. Yerkes & Yerkes (1936) found that chimpanzees avoided a live garter snake but did not respond to novel inanimate objects. Since they avoided a tortoise, however, avoidance may have been mediated by movement. Haslerud (1938) observed that chimps were no more inclined to avoid live or dead garter snakes than other novel animals and objects. Joslin, Fletcher & Emlen's (1964) rhesus macaques avoided snakes and still snake-like objects without responding similarly to food or a wooden block, though these stimuli could have been less novel.

A number of studies have failed to find any avoidance of snakes at all (e.g. in primates: Tinkelpaugh & Hartman, 1932; Wolin, Ordy & Dillman, 1963; Butler, 1964). The apparent discrepancies may stem from various sources including experiential differences between subjects (e.g. the possibility of enhanced responding in wild-caught as against laboratory-reared animals: Joslin, Fletcher & Emlen, 1964), differences in the effectiveness of particular types of snake, and differences in presentation conditions. In the latter connection, one neglected possibility is that a snake which is not too close may simply be visually monitored, and avoided only if it approaches or moves suddenly (see below for other instances of 'wary watching'). Interestingly, the 'snake chutter' vocal warning given by a vervet monkey spotting a snake causes other troop members to look towards the snake without immediately withdrawing (Struhsaker, 1967).

Some investigators have concluded that a specific visual feature is involved in the elicitation of the protective behaviour (including avoidance and running to cover) shown by some birds such as turkeys, geese and ducks to hawks and similar aerial predators. Lorenz (1939) found that turkeys responded to a silhouetted model moved overhead, and that a hawk-shaped model, i.e. a cross with two arms of unequal length and the shorter arm or 'neck' at the front and the longer one or 'tail' at the back, was more effective than a goose model, i.e. the same model moved with the longer arm (neck) leading. This, together with related observations on some other birds which are preyed upon by hawks, led Tinbergen (1951) to conclude that a *short neck* in a moving silhouette mediates protective behaviour in a number of species.

The novelty problem is also encountered here, since for birds reared with the opportunity to experience other birds flying overhead it is possible that real hawks are encountered less often than long necked birds such as ducks and geese, permitting differential habituation. In line with this, Schleidt (1961a and b) found that turkeys with no previous experience of flying objects initially responded equally to hawk and goose models but habituated to frequently presented models while retaining responsiveness to those encountered more rarely. Several other studies using naive birds concur that the hawk model is no more effective (Hirsch, Lindley & Tolman, 1955; Rockett, 1955; Melzack, Penick & Beckett, 1959; Müller, 1961). Of course these negative findings do not preclude the possibility that, even where both models are equally novel, the hawk may be more effective under conditions other than those employed: for example with different movement speeds (see Section 1.1.1). In this connection, Melzack, Penick & Beckett (1959) found that habituated mallards could be dishabituated by increasing the models' speed and that this was more effective with the hawk than the goose. It must also be noted that there are some reports of greater hawk model effectiveness even with naive birds (e.g. Green, Green & Carr, 1966; Green, Carr & Green 1968 with mallards).

A second explanation in terms of general rather than specific features holds that a hawk model could be more effective because its relatively blunt leading edge produces a more abrupt darkening of the visual field than the tapering front end of a goose (Schneirla, 1959). Although suddenness of onset is a potentially important stimulus feature (Section 1.1.2), this explanation is difficult to reconcile with the finding of Green, Green & Carr (1966) that a hawk form was more effective than both a triangle with the broad base leading and a hawk model with the head deleted, both of which should produce more sudden visual darkening.

There is thus considerable dispute over both whether the hawk shape is more effective and if so whether this indicates the operation of a specific predator feature or the operation of more general cues. It may also be noted that there is at least one indication that wild birds with experience of real predatory birds utilise cues other than short-neckedness in recognition. Grubb (1977) observed that wild American coots formed a protective flock huddle when overflown by bald eagles, which are waterfowl predators which attack coots, but not by two other short-necked predatory birds which do not prey on coots, the osprey and the red-shouldered hawk, or by a 'short-necked' aircraft. Since the hawk and the aircraft were less familiar to the coots as inferred from flight frequencies during observation, it appears that novelty was not the crucial factor. Grubb reports that the eagle and the osprey had apparently similar flight characteristics so the operative cue is obscure. Martin & Melvin's (1964) report that a live red-tailed hawk was more effective than a life-sized silhouette of it in inducing freezing in naive bobwhite quail also implicates cues other than short-neckedness.

There is thus some evidence that, at the very least, short-neckedness interacts with other features in eliciting protective behaviour. Another example of protective behaviour released by visual cues which is of interest because the *compound* nature of the releaser has been clearly demonstrated is the mobbing of owls and other predators by various small passerine birds. Mobbing consists of a complex pattern of responses including alternate approach and retreat from the predator, visual fixation, and various stereotyped movements and alarm calls (e.g. Marler, 1956; Curio, 1975). As well as possibly serving to drive the predator away, mobbing may reduce the chances of being caught unawares by the predator and provide the opportunity to learn the characteristics of potential danger (Marler & Hamilton, 1966; Kruuk, 1976: and note the apparently similar monitoring of predators in some ungulates, e.g. Walther, 1969; Schaller, 1972). Mobbing may be shown to ground predators including humans and sometimes to novel objects, as well as to flying and perched avian predators, but there is evidence that the optimal stimulus is often quite specific. Thus, the optimal stimulus for mobbing by chaffinches, as ascertained by experiments with models, is a compound owl configuration with a large head and short neck and tail, a solid contour, a patterned surface with spots, streaks or bars, brown or grey coloration, a beak, and a pair of frontal eyes (Hartley, 1950; Hinde, 1954): suboptimal models elicit less vigorous mobbing.

Curio (1975) has presented a detailed analysis of mobbing in the pied flycatcher to two of its major avian predators, the pigmy owl and the redbacked shrike, which clearly illustrates the compound nature of the cues involved. Movements, vocalisation and novelty are relatively unimportant. For the shrike, the characteristic plumage pattern of the male is crucial and the less striking female elicits less mobbing. Experiments with models show that male plumage features interact with one another in a nonadditive way. Thus, a model with the black facial mask deleted but the rest of the plumage intact and a model with the mask intact but the other plumage omitted, each evoke only about 10% of the response given to a complete plumage model (which is effectively the other two models combined). Plumage also operates in conjunction with body size and correct orientation is important. For the

95

owl the relevant features are less clear, though the feathered plumage texture seems indispensable (a realistically painted model is virtually ineffective), and the eyes, and possibly an owl shape (see above), are important. The effect of the eyes depends on other features in that an eyed model without feathers is ineffective but a feathered model without eyes elicits some responding. Failure to find any mutual enhancement effects with models having combinations of effective shrike and owl features (e.g. a feathered owl model with a shrike facial mask) leads Curio to conclude that the pied flycatcher may possess two quite distinct predator recognition 'channels' tuned to shrikes and to owls.

There is also some evidence that compound cues are involved in the recognition of cats by rats, though here visual form cues probably interact with movement and with olfactory cues. Laboratory rats inescapably exposed to a cat separated from them by mesh attempt to escape if the environment is novel and freeze if it is familiar (Blanchard, Fukunaga & Blanchard, 1976). Movement of the cat is not essential since an immobile cat elicits avoidance, freezing and defecation (Satinder, 1976), and escape where this is possible (Blanchard & Blanchard, 1971). The effects are unlikely to be due to stimulus novelty alone, since a novel object and another animal (rabbit) of comparable size and colour are ineffective (Satinder, 1976). Blanchard, Mast & Blanchard (1975) found that cat vocalisations and odour (an anaesthetised cat concealed by a shroud) failed to increase freezing in an inescapable environment, which implicates visual cues as the primary mediator though interpretation of this result is complicated by the fact that in this case only a moving cat, not an immobile one, proved effective. Since Bronstein & Hirsch (1976) found that rats older than 30 days responded to an immobile cat (though younger ones responded only to a moving cat) it seems probable that a stationary cat is capable of eliciting protective responses in rats and that the effect is increased by movement. Although further data are obviously required, it also appears that, despite the negative odour finding of Blanchard, Mast & Blanchard, the optimal cat compound probably includes olfactory as well as visual cues (see Section 1.2.2).

Further work is also needed to clarify the exact nature of the visual cues eliciting protective responses to cats. The fur texture and the eyes are obvious candidates and indeed these features have been suggested as possible cues to mammalian predators in general. The evidence for the releasing effect of fur texture is slight though Bertrand (1971) noted that a brown, furry teddy bear produced avoidance and other fear behaviour in stumptail macaque monkeys whereas a smooth teddy of the same size, colour and (presumably) novelty did not. A pink furry teddy also elicited fear though a smaller white one and the separated head and body of the pink one did not, which could indicate that a furry texture operates in conjunction with size and, possibly, shape cues. The incorporation of fur texture in a compound with other elements would parallel the evidence that feathered plumage combines with other features to elicit owl mobbing (see above). Kramer & von St. Paul (1951), however, found that models with a hairy or feathered texture elicited fear behaviour in bullfinches even if they did not correspond to any animate shape.

Eyes could also be a predator cue since predators presumably fixate their prey when attacking and many nocturnal predators in particular have conspicuous eyes (e.g. owls and some cats). Special significance of eyes could also derive from the use of a direct stare in some conspecific social signalling systems (see Section 4.2). Mobbing by pied flycatchers seems to be elicited by owl eyes only in conjunction with other features such as feathers and shape, and eyes presented without these other features are ineffective (Curio, 1975 reviewed above). Failure of eyes in general to elicit responding in the absence of other predator features would make some sense in that inappropriate fear responses to the eyes of conspecifics and nonpredators would be obviated (Scaife, 1976a). However, there is evidence that in other species eyes isolated from other cues do release protective responses. Blest (1957) found that yellow buntings, chaffinches and great tits would escape from a feeding table when patterns resembling eyes were illuminated as they alighted. The more similar the pattern was to a vertebrate eye (e.g. incorporating shading to give an impression of solidity) the more effective it was, and non-eye patterns were much less effective. Scaife (1976a) also found evidence of the effectiveness of eyes in the absence of other cues. A stuffed perched kestrel with conspicuous glass eyes having a yellow iris and black pupil produced strong avoidance in naive chickens, which was reduced by covering the kestrel's eyes but not by altering its characteristic hawk beak shape. An equally novel stuffed kiwi with small eyes was approached rather than avoided, but replacing the eyes with the conspicuous ones changed this to strong avoidance, though this effect could, as Scaife notes, be the result of the kiwi being regarded as a sort of chicken and the eyes construed as a conspecific threat (see Section 4.2). Further evidence for the effectiveness of eyes per se, however, comes from studies of immobility following manual restraint in chicks. The immobility response has been interpreted as a fear reaction to predators (e.g. Ratner, 1967; Gallup, 1974) and in chicks it is increased by the experimenter gazing directly at the bird's eyes rather than indirectly at it (Gallup, Cummings & Nash, 1972) and by the presence of a stuffed hawk, covering the eyes of which reduces its effectiveness (Gallup, Nash & Ellison, 1971). The latter study also found that a pair of brown glass eyes suspended above a chick were effective. The possibility that the effectiveness of the eyes in all these studies stems simply from their being novel and particularly conspicuous (e.g. iris/pupil contrast) stimuli

(Coppinger, 1970) cannot be completely ruled out. This explanation is unlikely, however, for Gagliardi, Gallup & Boren's (1976) finding that for chicks the immobility effect is quite specific to eyes with a pupil:size ratio of 11:20, with other ratios being ineffective. Conspicuous novelty also seems unlikely to account for Scaife's (1976b) finding that chicks avoided concentric circle eye patterns more than comparable rectangular ones. This study also provided some evidence that the avoidant properties of eyes is increased if they are moved in a biologically meaningful manner to 'track' the chick's head rather than its feet.

Indirect evidence for the effectiveness of disembodied eyes comes from the fact that a number of animals including some *Lepidoptera* and fish (Edmunds, 1974) have prominent eyespot patterns which constitute or form part of a startle display to a potential predator. Although, as Edmunds points out, small eyespots may have evolved to distract a predator attack away from vulnerable body areas, the evolution of large conspicuous eyespots is more likely to have been a capitalisation on the fact that some predators respond with avoidance to the eyes of species which prey on them. The forewing eyespots of the peacock butterfly, for example, appear to be an important part of the open wing display the insect gives when disturbed. Peacocks with the eyespots rubbed off are much less effective than intact butterflies in eliciting escape in yellow buntings (Blest, 1957). This could be explained, however, on the conspicuousness hypothesis and other butterflies certainly utilise other conspicuous patterns in displays: for example the tortoiseshell has variegated orange over brown patterns, removal of which similarly greatly reduces the display's effectiveness (Blest, 1957). On the other hand, the remarkably accurate mimicry of the vertebrate eye by some eyespots, often including shading giving a vivid impression of three dimensionality and a white dot simulating the real eye's highlight, argues strongly for the predator eye hypothesis of eyespot evolution and for the releasing characteristics of vertebrate predator eyes. Gagliardi, Gallup & Boren (1976) found that the eyespot pupil:size ratio for the one butterfly species they investigated (*Antomeris io*) conformed closely to the 11:20 ratio which was most effective in increasing immobility in chicks.

In summary, there is evidence that some prey species show protective responses to particular predators and classes of predator which imply discrimination that is not based upon novelty or movement characteristics and that this responsiveness involves fairly specific visual 'releasers' such as plumage features and eyes. It seems that these features are most effective in a compound with others, though in some cases at least they are capable of eliciting protective responses in isolation from other cues.

1.2.2 Olfactory Cues

It is widely believed that predator scent provides an important advance warning to some mammalian prey and that predators usually approach from downwind to minimise their chances of detection. Schaller (1972) found that lions hunting Thomson's gazelle actually took no account of wind direction, though hunts were about three times more likely to succeed if conducted from downwind, so it appears that the gazelle do utilise odour cues. Yet Schaller also observed that gazelle and other ungulates often seem to ignore the odour left behind by lions, though they do sometimes avoid it. Possibly lion odour is responded to most strongly in the presence of other cues such as the recent sighting of lions in the area or in places where cover could harbour a lion.

Assessment of the role of predator odours isolated from other cues suffers from the same general problem of separating recognition of a specific predator from reactions mediated by novelty noted in connection with visual cues in Section 1.2.1. Reports that golden hamsters show alarm and defensive posturing to dog and polecat odour (Dieterlen, 1959), that salmon are repelled by various mammalian odours in the water (Brett & MacKinnon, 1954, reported in Pfeiffer, 1962), and that minnows stop swimming and sink slowly to the bottom on encountering water in which a predatory fish has been swimming (Göz, 1941) are suggestive but, in the absence of novelty controls, not conclusive evidence of specific odour-mediated protective responses. Perhaps the best evidence for these comes from the response of rats to cats, since in addition to visual cues (Section 1.2.1) olfactory ones seem to be involved. Although Blanchard, Mast & Blanchard (1975) found that a shrouded anaesthetised cat, which presumably afforded odour cues, failed to elicit increased freezing in rats in an inescapable situation, Sieck, Baumbach, Gordon & Turner (1974) reported that the odour left behind by a cat walked through an alley produced freezing and/or attempted escape and increased urination in rats, while another novel, distinctive odour (trimethylpentane) had little effect. Further studies are needed to compare the effects of cat odour with other predator odours and other biological odours.

1.2.3 Auditory Cues

Since most predators hunt and attack as quietly as possible, auditory cues from this source are unlikely to be of major importance in eliciting protective behaviour, though prey might respond to calls and other noises made by predators which are not actually hunting. Schaller (1972) reports that Serengeti ungulates usually ignore lion roars and other calls unless the lions are very close, which parallels their relative indifference to lion odour (Section 1.2.2.) and slow moving lions (Section 1.1). Although the mobbing behaviour of pied flycatchers is not critically dependent upon auditory stimuli emitted by the predator (Curio, 1975), Miller (1952) maintains that the imitated hoots of several owl species elicit the approach of various small birds and that specific predator recognition is involved since, for example, the smaller birds respond to the calls of the small species of owl which prey on them but ignore the calls of larger owls which do not.

1.2.4 Behavioural Cues

There is evidence that some prey respond to specific behavioural features associated with a predator attack. Pruitt (1965) noted that caribou may not show alarm to wolves moving nearby but will flee at the distant approach of a wolf with head lowered and pointing forward, causing the neck and shoulder hair to become prominent, and attention fixed on its prey. African wild dogs show a similar head lowering which, together with pack bunching, increases the flight distance of various ungulates (Schaller, 1972). Pruitt implies that the lowered head is the crucial releaser, though since this is invariably coupled with direct approach (see Section 1.1.1) and usually (in the wild dog) with bunching this is not a necessary interpretation. Possibly head lowering is one aspect of a complex behavioural cue. Besides bunching, pack hunting animals often offer other cues to their hunting 'mood', particularly increased pack size (Kruuk, 1975 – hyenas and wild dogs). Walther (1969) also noted increased flight distance of Thomson's gazelle to hyena and dog packs in hunting formation.

1.2.5 Predator Signals from Conspecifics

One benefit of a social existence (see also Section 3.4) is the possibility of using cues from conspecifics to release protective responses to predators. In general these cues serve the same 'early warning' function as cues deriving directly from the predator.

Alarm calls are the most obvious example of this and have been reported in a great many birds and mammals. Depending on species and situation, an alarm call given by an individual spotting a predator or other potential danger will elicit alertness or flight (Walther, 1969 – Thomson's gazelle), flight into cover followed by freezing (Marler, 1956 – chaffinches), or freezing in cover (Heinz, 1973 – ring-necked pheasant chicks). Although related species may have rather similar alarm calls, e.g. small birds such as finches, tits and sparrows (Marler, 1956), some gulls' (Frings, Frings, Cox & Peissner, 1955), and some monkeys' (Rowell, 1972), alarm calls generally take a variety of forms, with a relatively short duration being the only universal feature. Small birds like the chaffinch have high-pitched relatively pure tone calls, with a gradual onset and offset which reduces their cue value to the predator (Marler, 1956), while some primates like baboons have a deep bark alarm call (Washburn & DeVore, 1961). The call may be of high intensity, as in herring gulls (Frings, Frings, Cox & Peissner, 1955) or low intensity, as in the soft warning snort of Thomson's gazelle (Walther, 1969).

The evolution of specific alarm calls quite distinct in form and function from other auditory signals almost certainly means that the calls have specific releasing properties independent of any effects due to intensity (Section 2.1) or suddenness of onset (Section 1.1.2) and this is consistent with the fact that recorded calls have effects on behaviour quite different from those of white noise of comparable intensity (Heinz, 1973 – pheasant chicks) and that other conspecific calls played at the same intensity have quite different effects (Frings, Frings, Cox & Peissner, 1955 – herring gulls). Also consistent with a specific releaser hypothesis, many species, including Burmese jungle fowl (Lorenz, 1937), lemurs (Jolly, 1966) and vervet monkeys (Struhsaker, 1967) give quite separate calls to terrestrial predators and to aerial ones such as birds of prey, releasing upward flight into trees and downward flight into low cover respectively. Struhsaker also reports a specific snake warning (the 'snake chutter') given by juvenile and female vervets, which elicits visual monitoring of the snake. Apart from the visual communication of danger by tail movements and/or a distinctive flight pattern in a few species such as Thomson's gazelle (Walther, 1964), other modalities than hearing seem to be little used for alarm signals, though they may be involved in an individual responding to a conspecific which has actually been caught by a predator or met some other undesirable fate. In such cases distress stimuli from the victim can elicit protective behaviour. Screams and other distress calls are an example: many birds in particular make distress calls when caught or restrained and the effectiveness of these calls in eliciting escape and avoidance is testified to by the fact that recordings of them efficiently disperse conspecific flocks (e.g. Bremond, Gramet, Brough & Wright, 1968; Brough, 1969 – starlings) and can act as reinforcers in avoidance learning (Morgan & Howse, 1973 – jackdaws.)

Visual cues from distressed or frightened conspecifics might have a similar effect, though the evidence is limited. Symmes (1969) found that rhesus monkeys responded so as to view a large photograph of a conspecific facially expressing fear less than a blank screen, though a normal live conspecific increased viewing time. This could indicate avoidance mediated by the facial expression of fear but is tentative in the absence of data on the effects of photographs of nonfearful monkeys. The effect did not appear when the picture could be inspected through a peephole and Butler (1964) similarly found that the sight of a live fearful monkey did not suppress peephole viewing. The sight of dead or mutilated individuals could also elicit protective behaviour. Hebb's (1946) chimps showed signs of particularly strong fear and avoidance to a chimp skull, a plaster cast of a chimp visage, a severed chimp head and an anaesthetised chimp, which is consistent with this possibility but also with an object novelty/incongruity explanation (see Section 3.1.2). A similar point could be made about Van Lawick Goodall's (1974) report that a physically disabled chimp produced fear grinning and avoidance in other chimps. Humans report discomfort and show autonomic changes when faced with a physically disabled person (Kleck, 1966). Pictures of mutilated human bodies evoke heart rate acceleration (as opposed to the deceleration associated with orienting and curiosity: Hare, 1972), at least in subjects professing to a strong fear of mutilation in a questionnaire (Klorman, Wiesenfeld & Austin, 1975). Novak & Lerner (1968) suggest that people's fear behaviour in such cases is linked to the thought that the same disability could strike them, though there is some evidence that conflict between motivation to view a strongly novel stimulus and the social inhibitions on staring plays an important part (Langer, Fiske, Taylor & Chanowitz, 1976).

Evidence that some animals respond to odours ('alarm' or 'fright' substances) produced by dead, injured or frightened conspecifics is less equivocal. Minnows and other small fish, particularly schooling species, rapidly flee from an injured (live or dead) member of their own kind and a series of experiments by von Frisch and his associates (reviewed by Pfeiffer, 1962, 1963) have identified the releaser as a chemical discharged into the water from cells in the damaged skin epithelium. Similar protective behaviour has also been observed in various species of toad tadpole (review by Pfeiffer, 1974). The avoidance of an area previously occupied by a conspecific stressed by electroshock or other means in wild and laboratory mice (Müller-Velten, 1966: Carr, Martorano & Krames, 1970) represents a comparable phenomenon in a mammal. Rottman & Snowdon (1972) demonstrated that this avoidance occurred to an odourised airstream and so is not dependent upon the immediate presence of urine or feces from the stressed mouse. Similar effects may be predicted for other species with well developed olfactory communication and rats, at least, can learn a discrimination based upon the odours associated with shocked/unshocked conspecifics (Valenta & Rigby, 1968).

2 Physical Environmental Dangers

All organisms face a variety of inanimate hazards. On the most general level these include the danger of being in an environment offering inadequate supplies of food, water and other resources, or which provides an inappropriate level of temperature or humidity. To some extent these dangers can be guarded against by maintaining a familiar environment (see

Section 3.1), though more specific protective behaviour is also involved. Examples of avoidance of, and escape from, inadequate and inappropriate environments are numerous. Rats, for example, will escape from an environment in which they have previously obtained food when the food source runs out (Adelman & Maatsch, 1956). Various terrestrial species will escape from immersion in water (Wilcock, 1972 – rats; Feunzalida & Ulrich, 1975 – garter snakes) and avoid a situation previously associated with falling into water (Thompson & Galosy, 1969 – rats). High temperatures elicit similar behaviour (Brosgole & Ulatowski, 1973 – gerbils; Brosgole, 1976 – box turtle) and rats will perform an instrumental bar press response to activate a heat lamp in a cold environment (Weiss & Laties, 1961). In the absence of a hen, young chicks show increased distress peeping to a drop in the ambient temperature (Kaufman & Hinde, 1961; Herbert & Sluckin, 1969), probably as a consequence of a temperature drop normally being associated with loss of contact with the hen.

Danger also stems from the possibility of injury by intense stimuli and, for many terrestrial species, by falling from a height, and these factors have been investigated fairly systematically.

2.1 Stimulus Intensity

That an intense stimulus in any sense modality is potentially injurious and likely to elicit reports of pain in humans and protective behaviour in a variety of species scarcely needs documentation. The intense tactile stimulation of electric shock has been studied most frequently, eliciting escape and avoidance of stimuli associated with the shock as a function of its intensity (e.g. review by Mackintosh, 1974). A short inescapable foot-shock elicits agitated running, jumping and hiding in rodents (Baron, 1963; Galef, 1970) and postshock behaviour usually involves increased immobility and freezing and decreased general activity (Blanchard & Blanchard, 1969a; Klare, 1974; Bolles & Collier, 1976). These responses seem to represent protective behaviour elicited by an intense stimulus which is not clearly localised, making it difficult for the animal to avoid the environmental stimuli associated with it. Postshock immobility effects are most marked if the animal is kept in the shock situation rather than shifted to a nonshock environment (Blanchard & Blanchard, 1969a; Bolles & Collier, 1976). This appears to reflect the fact that the new environment elicits escape or exploration responses (see Section 3.1.3) incompatible with immobility since postshock immobility is greater if the nonshock environment is familiar rather than novel (Baron, 1963, 1964 – mice; Sheldon, 1970 – rats).

The inhibitory effects of shock on postshock activity are also demonstrated

103

by the increased duration of the immobility response following restraint in chicks (see Section 1.2.1) caused by prerestraint shock (Gallup, Nash, Potter & Donegan, 1970). Prior exposure to a loud, low-frequency, short-duration sound had a similar effect in the chicks, as it does in leopard frogs (Nash, Gallup & McClure, 1970). Other effects of sudden, short, intense noises have been mentioned in Section 1.1.2. More prolonged, continued exposure to high-intensity noise increases locomotion and defecation in a novel environment in rats (Broadhurst, 1957; Livesey & Egger, 1970) and locomotion in mice (Blizard, 1971), presumably reflecting flight behaviour (see Section 3.1.3).

Other aspects of protective behaviour elicited by prior exposure to shock are a reduction in the tendency of rats to enter a novel area (Sheldon, 1968b; Aitken, 1972), decreased inspection of a novel stimulus in the environment (Gillen, 1973), and increased thigmotactic behaviour (Grossen & Kelley, 1972: see also Section 3.1.3).

2.2 Heights

Falling from a height is obviously potentially disastrous for most terrestrial species. Sudden loss of support elicits catching of the breath and clutching movements with the hands in human infants (Watson & Morgan, 1917) which must be mediated by tactual, vestibular and kinaesthetic stimuli. Once loss of support has occurred it is usually too late to do much about it and it is no surprise to find that animals readily detect and avoid situations where it could happen. This is clearly demonstrated by studies using the visual cliff apparatus (Walk & Gibson, 1961), which consists of a solid centre board bounded on one side by a shallow drop and on the other by a deep one (cliff), both covered with glass to prevent actual falling and with the floor of the drop areas patterned to provide textural cues to depth. Placed on the centre board, a variety of species, including rats, chicks, goats, lambs, pigs, dogs, turtles, cats, monkeys and human infants, prefer to leave via the shallow side, avoiding the cliff. Placed on the glass over the deep side, neonatal monkeys show behavioural signs of fear such as crouching, vocalisation, rocking and self-clasping (Rosenblum & Cross, 1963) and kittens and young goats freeze and tense (Gibson & Walk, 1960). Human infants show less clear-cut behaviour when on the cliff side (Schwartz, Campos & Baisel, 1973). Significantly, nonterrestrial species including ducklings (Walk cited in Gibson, 1969) and aquatic species of turtle (Routtenberg & Glickman, 1964) fail to show avoidance of the cliff.

The effective stimulus for avoidance of heights must be a depth gradient extending vertically with respect to gravity since the corresponding horizontal gradient (e.g. a doorway) is not avoided, and the evidence points

104

to differential motion parallax of textural elements at the edge and the foot of the cliff with head movements as the primary cue to the existence of depth (studies reviewed by Gibson, 1969; Walk & Walters, 1974).

3 Stimuli Associated with Increased Risk of Predation and Other Dangers

Some situations and events that are not necessarily dangerous in themselves are associated with an increased risk of danger from predation and other sources. As such they can act as signals or predictors of danger and may elicit protective behaviour. Some of these situations and events may be specific to one or a few species, such as a particular habitat or region being associated with an increased risk of encountering a certain type of predator. Others are more general: into this category come being in a strange area away from familiar surroundings, in an open area offering little cover (for species which normally make use of cover), in darkness (for diurnal species) and daylight or other strong light (for nocturnal ones), and being alone (for social species).

Bowlby (1973) has pointed out that fearful behaviour is especially likely in situations that compound two or more fear stimuli or situations. Anecdotal evidence suggests we are more likely to be frightened by a sudden noise if we are alone in the house, and much more so if it is also dark and the house is unfamiliar. Evidence on the effectiveness of compound situations in eliciting protective behaviour is also presented below.

3.1 Novelty: Unfamiliar Places and Objects

A familiar environment affords insurance against danger in various ways. It ensures that the organism is aware of the location of food and water sources, shelter, hiding places, sleeping sites, heights and the likely whereabouts of predators. Consequently, many species have evolved mechanisms for keeping the organism within a familiar home range (Jewell, 1966). Most social primates, for example, have a home range which can be defined by tracing the group's movements over a period (Jolly, 1972). Bowlby (1973) sees the home range in the context of a homeostatic system which maintains a steady relationship between the individual and its environment, based on attachment to a familiar area and avoidance of the novel areas encountered at its boundaries.

Novelty may also be encountered as discrete animate or inanimate objects within the home range. Localised novel stimuli of this sort are potential predators (the possible role of novelty in eliciting protective responses to predators has been considered in Section1) or other sources of danger and so may also elicit protective behaviour.

Protective behaviour towards novel areas and objects is by no means universal, however. Novelty frequently elicits *exploratory* behaviour (Berlyne, 1960; Hutt, 1970) and this, too, is obviously adaptive in that exploration of a new object or area may supply useful information. An object may prove to be a food source, a hiding place, or a tool. A new area may yield additional food, fewer predators and so on. Novelty may, therefore, produce some conflict between the largely incompatible responses of approach and exploration on one hand, and escape, avoidance or immobility on the other. Some of the numerous organismic and situational variables on which the behavioural outcome depends are identified below.

Following Berlyne (1960), novelty can be either complete (or absolute), i.e. something never ever experienced before, or short term (or relative), i.e. something not experienced recently or familiar things arranged in a new way. Except for young, inexperienced organisms, any new experience is likely to be relatable in some way to previous ones, and so is strictly simply relatively novel. Stimulus aspects related to novelty include incongruity (the juxtaposition of familiar elements not normally associated) and surprisingness (a stimulus which disagrees with expectation): see also Section 4.1.2.

3.1.1 Free Access to a Novel Area

Of the experimental paradigms which have been used to study response to novelty, permitting an organism free access to a novel area adjacent to a familiar one provides the closest parallel with encountering a novel area at the home range boundary. Reluctance to enter the novel area (neophobia) is often seen initially. For example, when a novel chamber or alley is attached to the front of their home cage, laboratory rats at first avoid the new area but subsequently spend increasing time in it (Montgomery, 1955; Blanchard, Kelly & Blanchard, 1974). A prior period of forced familiarisation with the area reduces avoidance (Blanchard, Kelly & Blanchard, 1974). An apparently similar neophobic effect has been reported by Smith (1974) in 2.5- to 4.5-year-old children who were allowed to play in two thirds of the available area of a room for a time before a partition was removed to make the remaining third available. Although the new area was very similar to the familiar one and contained similar toys, entries into it during an initial 10-minute period were short and infrequent, though there were no overt signs of fear and the area was subsequently occupied normally.

The evidence from these studies is thus that although there may be some avoidance of a novel area initially, this does not last very long, which tallies with other observations that a new area is soon explored. Captive wild rats rapidly enter a new enclosure which is opened up for them (Barnett & Spencer, 1951) and wild and laboratory rats and mice in a residential maze repeatedly enter and investigate a new arm immediately or very soon after it is opened (Barnett & Cowan, 1976). The lack of evidence for permanent avoidance of a novel area suggests that these studies relate more to the extension of a home range artificially compressed by captivity than to avoidance of novel areas at the boundaries of the range.

3.1.2 *Novel Stimuli in a Familiar Area*

Reports on a number of species show that a novel object or other discrete localised stimulus in a familiar area is also often approached and explored only after a period of avoidance. Welker (1956a and b) noted that 3- to 4-year-old chimps rapidly manipulated and inspected novel objects placed in their cages but younger ones first looked at the objects from a distance and only touched them after prolonged exposure. Introduction of further novel objects reinstated watching without touching in the young animals. Similar object neophobia was seen by Menzel, Davenport & Rogers (1961) in isolation reared chimps. Object contact increased with exposure and when the chimps had received considerable experience of novel objects any new object was contacted immediately. Gelada baboons also show object neophobia (Hughes & Menzel, 1973) and free-ranging Japanese macaque monkeys orient to novel objects placed along their trails but more often move away than touch them (Menzel, 1965).

Neophobia is frequently seen in rodents, and rodent studies are important in suggesting some of the factors which promote avoidance over exploration. Susceptibility to predation and the animal's familiarity with its environment appear to be particularly important. Barnett & Cowan (1976) reviewed a number of instances of strong neophobia in several wild commensal *Rattus* species (primarily dependant on man for food) which contrasts with the absence of neophobia in laboratory rats and in wild noncommensal species. Cowan (1977) reports a typical study in which novel objects placed in one arm of a residential maze elicited exploration in noncommensals but persistent avoidance in commensals. Since laboratory rats do show object neophobia under some conditions (Mitchell, Williams & Sutter, 1974; Mitchell, 1976) it appears that the commensal/noncommensal difference is one of degree rather than kind. Barnett & Cowan interpret these findings in terms of commensals having undergone evolutionary selection for object neophobia as a consequence of human predation in the form of trapping and poisoning and there is evidence that susceptibility to predation may be a determinant of object neophobia in general. Glickman & Sroges (1966) suggest that exploration is favoured (by implication over avoidance) in species that have

107

a well organised social structure and/or a habitat offering good cover, both of which minimise predation risks (see Sections 3.4 and 3.2), and low natural predation. Their study of caged animals' responses to novel objects provided some supporting instances. For example, within the primate *Cercopithecinae* subfamily baboons explored more than guenons, which correlates with the baboons' larger size, strength and greater ability to detect and deal with predators (though differences in the species' food-getting habits are probably also relevant).

Object neophobia is rare in humans, which may also correlate with man's relative insusceptibility to predation as well as to probable strong evolutionary selection for the investigation and manipulation of novel objects. Hutt (1970) has argued that selection has eliminated object neophobia in man though, as Smith (1974) suggests, this is probably an overstatement of the fact that the threshold for neophobia is very high. The most striking examples of fear and avoidance of novel objects are seen in infants and children, though even here a combination of novelty and some other factor such as direct or unpredictable movement (see Section 1.1.1.) is usually involved. For example, Scarr & Salapatek (1970) found that about 10–15% of infants showed some sign of fear (such as crying and running to mother) to a mechanical dog walking towards them and to a jack-in-the-box. Hutt (1970) attributes Schaffer & Parry's (1969) finding that one-year-olds initially avoided touching an object moving towards them (though they did fixate it) to the disconcerting experience of an object moving without a detectable agent rather than to object novelty per se. Prima facie evidence of object neophobia in children, however, comes from the studies reviewed in Section 3.4 showing that interaction with novel objects can be facilitated by the presence of a peer or other person, the implication being that some neophobia is present when a child is alone. It is possible, however, that this 'neophobia' stems from reluctance to touch someone else's property (the experimenter's) rather than novelty. In these studies, too, the test environment is not thoroughly familiar and situational novelty (Section 3.1.3) may affect the child's behaviour, so that it remains uncertain whether object neophobia ever occurs in a completely familiar setting such as the home.

With regard to the influence of the organism's familiarity with its environment on object neophobia, wild rats avoid novel objects in a familiar area but show no avoidance if the area is also novel (Cowan, 1976). Mitchell (1976) argues that insufficient habituation to the test situation may underlie some failures to detect object neophobia in laboratory rats. These environmental effects are predictable since not only is novelty avoidance impossible unless there is a relatively familiar area to withdraw to, but it is probably adaptive to rapidly explore a novel environment and any objects in it (see Section 3.1.3) but to approach a novel stimulus in a familiar environment only with caution.

Neophobia also extends to food objects. Potentially edible food or prey which has never, or rarely, been encountered before is often rejected by many animals (review by Curio, 1976). Captive wild rats, for example, may remain in the backs of their cages for some hours before even approaching novel food and show reduced consumption for several days thereafter (Richter, 1953; Rzoska, 1953, 1954). This effect parallels object neophobia in being sometimes undetectable in laboratory rats (Barnett, 1956), though likewise it is actually simply greatly reduced (Carroll, Dine, Levy & Smith, 1975). Novel prey may elicit other fear responses besides avoidance. For example, Burmese junglefowl chicks that refuse a novel mealworm show inhibition of movement and changes in shrill calling (Hogan, 1965) and blue jays that normally eat butterflies may react to novel species of butterfly with avoidance and alarm calls (Coppinger, 1969, 1970). Food neophobia may thus be seen as a specific example of the general tendency to show fear behaviour to a novel object, particularly when mediated by visual and/or olfactory cues before the food is actually sampled. Avoidance of food on the basis of flavour cues, however, is in itself probably protective against the specific danger of poisoning or gastric upset and following sickness consequent on eating a new food animals show an enhanced neophobic response to other new foods (Richter, 1953; Rzoska, 1954; Carroll, Dine, Levy & Smith, 1975).

3.1.3 Confinement to a Novel Area

Novel confining environments with no familiar reference points and no avenue of escape have been used extensively in research on fear behaviour and exploration in animals in the form of the open field apparatus developed by Hall (1934a and b) and various kinds of maze (reviewed by Halliday, 1968). That organisms are relatively unlikely to encounter an inescapable novel environment in nature is probably one reason why data from these situations, particularly the open field (see, for example, Archer, 1973a; Walsh & Cummins, 1976), has proved difficult to interpret. The avoidance behaviour which often characterises an initial encounter with localised novelty (Sections 3.1.1 and 3.1.2) is obviously precluded. Some species, notably rats, often show an initially high level of locomotion in a novel confining environment, which may reflect an attempt to escape, though since the novelty is unlocalised it is difficult to separate escape bahaviour aimed at removing the animal from the environment from exploratory behaviour aimed at increasing contact with it (see, for example, Williams & Russell, 1972; Russell & Williams, 1973). Other species, particularly chicks, seem to respond initially to a novel environment by freezing (Salzen, 1962;

Candland, Nagy & Canklyn, 1963). Interpretation of data from the open field is further complicated by the fact that as well as being novel it comprises a relatively large open space (Section 3.2), is usually brightly lit (Section 3.3), and often exposes the subject to continuous loud noise (e.g. Broadhurst, 1957; and see Section 2.1).

These problems aside, there is no doubt that confinement to a novel area elicits various protective responses. Archer (1976a) has reviewed studies of a number of animal species demonstrating attempted escape behaviour (including locomotion and jumping), immobility and freezing, defecation, and distress calling. Human infants show inhibition of locomotion and increased crying (Rheingold, 1969) though this is primarily a response to a novel environment in the absence of the mother since her presence greatly reduces protective responses and increases exploration (see also Rheingold & Eckerman, 1969 and Section 3.4).

Of particular importance in the ascription of these responses to environmental novelty is the demonstration that they vary with the degree of novelty of the situation. Defecation rate, for example, has been shown to be higher in a novel open field than in the familiar home cage for rats (Candland & Campbell, 1962; Russell, 1973a) and chicks (Candland, Nagy & Conklyn, 1963) and to decrease with repeated exposure to the field in rats but not mice (studies reviewed by Archer, 1973a; and Walsh & Cummins, 1976). Distress peeping in chicks is also higher in the open field than the home pen (Candland, Nagy & Conklyn, 1963) and increases as a function of the degree of environmental novelty (Fullerton, Berryman & Sluckin, 1970).

Also important in showing that a novel environment elicits protective behaviour is the fact that rats will leave an open field when permitted to enter a small enclosed box (Welker, 1957, 1959a; Glickman & Hartz, 1965; Valle, 1972) or the home cage (Blanchard, Kelley & Blanchard, 1974) attached to it. In line with the habituation of avoidance of localised novel stimuli with exposure (Sections 3.1.1 and 3.1.2), this escape behaviour declines with repeated exposure to the field and is replaced by an ambulation in the field which presumably reflects exploration (Valle, 1972).

3.2 Openness

Prey species in which antipredator behaviour depends on cover in the form of vegetation, burrows, etc., may be expected to avoid open, exposed places, since these increase the chance of being spotted and decrease the chances of successful evasion. The behaviour of rodents like the brown rat, which typically inhabits underground tunnels or enclosed places in buildings and sewers (Twigg, 1975), clearly illustrates this. Openness is probably a factor contributing to protective behaviour in rodents in the open field and, as noted in Section 3.1.3, they show various fear responses including attempts to escape, though the relative importance of openness as against novelty is difficult to assess. Where the size, and hence the degree of openness, of the field is increased, ambulation usually increases but defecation shows little systematic change (various studies of rats, mice and gerbils reviewed by Walsh & Cummins, 1976). Increased ambulation is presumably linked with the increased available area for movement and could reflect increased attempts at escape, though the significance of ambulation is not entirely clear (see Section 3.1.3).

One well documented open field effect is the preference for the peripheral areas adjacent to the walls and the avoidance of the centre, reported originally by Hall (1934a) and in several later studies (reviewed by Archer, 1973a). This thigmotactic or 'wall hugging' behaviour is clearly related to the tendency to seek cover and avoid open areas, and declines with familiarisation (Valle, 1971; Williams & Russell, 1972), particularly if the central area contains stimuli to investigate (Russell & Williams, 1973). A related effect is seen in rodent studies comparing behaviour in enclosed mazes (having side walls and, sometimes, a top) with elevated ones (no sides or top and the maze floor raised off the ground). Consistent with the fact that the enclosed variety offers a less open, more burrow-like environment, rats avoid elevated maze arms when enclosed ones are available (Montgomery, 1955). Rats are also less active on first exposure to an elevated maze compared with an enclosed one (Halliday, 1967; Lester, 1967) which could reflect more freezing in an inescapable open area, though Halliday found that repeated exposures to the maze were accompanied by a drop in enclosed but not elevated maze activity so that the initial difference was reversed (see Russell, 1973b, for a more detailed consideration of elevated and enclosed maze studies).

There is little documentation of the behaviour of animals such as plains ungulates which inhabit open areas and base their antipredator behaviour on long range detection and efficient flight, though avoidance of cover, which could harbour a predator and hinder flight, might be predicted.

3.3 Illumination

Diurnal species, adapted for daylight activity, are likely to be seriously disadvantaged if forced to be active in the dark, while nocturnal species are similarly handicapped in the day. Consequently, both types show protective responses designed to maintain them in the illumination conditions in which they function most efficiently. Among nocturnal species this is best

111

documented for rodents, particularly the laboratory rat, which is averse to bright light (review by Lockhard, 1963). For example, rats will escape from a brightly lit chamber into a dark one (Jerome, Moody, Connor & Ryan, 1958). Dim light, however, is less aversive and may indeed have attractant properties since rats and other species will perform instrumental responses in order to illuminate their environment dimly (Lockard, 1963), leading to the suggestion that individuals or species have a preferred illumination level from which both increases and decreases are aversive. Most nocturnal species are probably adapted to dim light rather than total darkness.

Increasing the ambient illumination in the open field (Section 3.1.3) increases defecation and reduces ambulation in rodents (reviews by Archer, 1973a and Russell, 1973a). Valle (1970) found that rats' thigmotactic behaviour (Section 3.2) was increased in bright light compared with darkness, which probably reflects avoidance of a brightly lit open area, though the absence of visual cues to the whereabouts of the walls in the dark could be important. The albedo of the environmental background may also influence behaviour: given a free choice rats spend more time in a black painted area than in an otherwise identical white one (Williams & Kuchta, 1957; Aitken, 1974).

Dark aversion in diurnal species has been studied less often, though fear of the dark is reported by many human children and some adults, and dark escape/avoidance tests have been used in experimental studies of human fear (e.g. Mellstrom, Cicala & Zuckerman, 1976). Jersild (1943; Jersild & Holmes 1935) found that parents reported darkness as one of the situations commonly producing fear in 1–5 year olds (inferred from crying, avoidance etc.) though it was less often reported than some other factors such as noises, strangers and animals. Jersild also used darkness as a fear-evoking situation in a study of 2–5 year olds; asked to enter a dark passage to retrieve a ball about 45% of children refused entirely or would not go unless accompanied. It is difficult to control all the variables in studies of this kind and novelty (Section 3.1) may also have been involved here. That some children entered the passage with an adult is consistent with the expectation that being alone in the dark is a compound which is especially avoided. Darkness may in fact increase the sense of being alone by reducing visual contact and Bowlby (1973) points out that darkness is often associated with strangeness simply because the reduction in visual cues makes even familiar stimuli ambiguous and difficult to recognise.

A social existence has various advantages that are denied the isolated individual, including greater efficiency in detecting and dealing with predators (Treisman, 1975a and b). Consequently, social species have evolved behaviour to promote and maintain contact between individuals and for re-establishing contact once lost. The same is true of the particularly crucial relationship between the infant and its mother (or other caretaker). Contact behaviour comes under the general heading of attachment (Bowlby, 1969, 1973), defined by Ainsworth & Bell (1970) as an affectional tie between individuals involving such behaviour as seeking to gain and maintain proximity (varying from close physical contact to interaction and communication across a distance) by approaching, following, clinging and signalling (crying, smiling, calling etc.). Loss of contact leads to such protective responses as distress calling and searching, which are designed to re-establish contact.

In experimental studies, loss of contact with companions is often coupled with exposure to a novel environment, though there are a few reports of behavioural changes consequent simply on the absence of companions. Removal of companions from a chick which has been reared socially increases distress peeping even though the chick is maintained in a familiar environment (Kaufman & Hinde, 1961; Fullerton, Berryman & Sluckin, 1970). Infant primates, too, show marked behavioural changes, including distress calling, hyperactivity (searching?), followed by 'depression' with reduced activity when their mother is removed leaving them in a familiar environment with familiar conspecifics (Kaufman & Rosenblum, 1969; Hinde, 1974).

Loss of companions coupled with exposure to some other threatening event or situation is particularly likely to evoke strong protective responses. Many of the studies of response to novelty reviewed in Section 3.1 actually involve socially housed animals taken from their companions and tested with novel stimuli. In general, neophobia and related behaviour is increased in the absence of companions. Rowell & Hinde (1963), for example, noted that group-housed monkeys put into individual cages showed more threat and hair raising and less grooming, foraging and sitting still than monkeys maintained in groups when both were exposed to various novel events such as being watched by a person wearing a strange mask and cloak. For chicks, the presence of companions in a novel environment reduces distress calling (Collias, 1952) and searching and escape behaviour (Salzen, 1962). The immobility response which may be induced by manual restraint occurs more readily in socially reared chicks removed from their companions and is attenuated by the sight of other chicks (Salzen, 1963). Socially experienced

113

rats show comparable effects, including less avoidance of an area previously associated with shock, if tested in groups rather than singly (Morrison & Hill, 1967), and reduced defecation (Latane, 1969; Latane & Glass, 1968; Latane & Werner, 1971) as well as increased activity (Hughes, 1969; Latane, 1969) when tested in pairs in an open field. The effect of being alone is also seen in childrens' responses to a novel object. Hutt (1966) found that 3–5 year olds were slower to approach the object when alone than when an adult was present, though subsequently Hutt (1970) suggested that the difference between the conditions might have been due to (incidental) differential familiarity with the test room, rather than heightened neophobia when alone. Rabinowitz, Moely & Finkel (1975), however, found that children played less with a novel toy and more with familiar ones when they were alone than when with a same sex peer.

Besides these peer effects, the absence of the mother increases protective responses to novelty. Arsenian (1943) found that human infants were more disturbed (crying, inhibition of play, etc.) in an unfamiliar room when the mother or a familiar caretaker was absent, a finding since extensively documented (see, for example, Bowlby, 1969, 1973; Rutter, 1972 and Section 3.1.3). Similarly, Harlow & Zimmerman (1959) observed that rhesus monkey infants placed alone in a novel setting with novel objects showed signs of intense fear (including vocalisation, crouching, rocking, sucking and frantic running) which were ameliorated by the presence of a cloth surrogate mother on which the infants had been reared. Chicks reared by a hen, too, show a reduction in distress calling in a novel situation when they can see a hen and a further reduction when they can also hear her (Bermant, 1963).

Being alone is a novel experience for a socially reared organism and novelty per se probably contributes to its fear-evoking qualities. Thus, at least part of the ameliorative effect of the presence of the mother or a companion on an individual's behaviour in a novel environment may stem from the presence of a familiar stimulus (familiar as an individual or as a member of a known class). Several pieces of evidence are consistent with this interpretation. One is that individuals which are unfamiliar with conspecifics as a result of being reared in social isolation are relatively unaffected by the presence of companions. Placed with companions in a novel environment, isolate reared chicks show more searching and escape than their socially reared counterparts and fail to show the approach, nestling and contentment calls that the latter direct at the companions (Salzen, 1962). Kaufman & Hinde (1961) found that putting a mirror in a test box to produce a reflected 'companion' for an individual chick actually *increased* distress peeping in isolates (while decreasing it for socially reared chicks), suggesting that for isolates a conspecific can be a source of novelty giving rise to fear behaviour. Also consistent with the role of novelty in being alone is the fact that the

114

presence of familiar non-conspecific stimuli can have similar ameliorative effects to companions. One demonstration of this comes from studies of imprinting in chicks and other nidifugous birds. In a novel environment, a familiar object (which may be moving or stationary and may or may not bear some resemblance to the bird's parents) may elicit following, nestling and contentment calls, and reduce fear behaviour such as distress calling, freezing and escape (see reviews by Smith, 1969 and Sluckin, 1972). Similar effects are attributable to the presence of a familiar cloth surrogate mother in rhesus monkey infants (Harlow & Zimmerman, 1959 and see above). This is not to say that the effects of being alone are entirely explainable in terms of novelty and that all equally familiar stimuli necessarily have equal ameliorative effects on fear behaviour. Just as some novel stimuli are more effective than others in eliciting approach behaviour and imprinting (Sluckin, 1972) so features of a stimulus besides its familiarity may be important in reducing fear. There is some evidence that, as might be predicted, a familiar conspecific is more effective than a familiar inanimate object. Socially experienced rats in a novel environment are more attracted to another rat than to a metal object and defecate less in the presence of the rat even if the object is familiar through having been kept in the rat's cage prior to testing (Latane, Meltzer, Joy & Lubell, 1972). Similarly, a familiar rat reduces immobility in a novel environment more than a familiar tennis ball (Latane, Poor & Sloan, 1972). These studies are not entirely conclusive since the subjects were prefamiliarised with rats or objects by being confined with them for several days prior to testing, but they probably had earlier experience of rats which may have rendered conspecifics more familiar than the objects.

4   Stimuli Stemming from Conspecifics

Although the presence of companions often reduces fear behaviour (Section 3.4), conspecifics can also be a source of fear stimuli. One reason for this is that they can provide some of the *general* stimulus features which elicit protective responses (Sections 1.1 and 3.1). A second reason has its origins in the tendency of animals to space themselves relative to conspecifics (see, for example, Marler & Hamilton, 1966).

4.1   *Conspecifics as Sources of Novelty and Movement Features*

The possibility that a conspecific can be a source of novelty for an organism reared in isolation, and so produce fear behaviour, has been noted

115

in Section 3.4. Conspecific novelty and movement features may also play a role in eliciting fear even in organisms reared normally. This is obviously most likely to be true for young, inexperienced organisms. Fear of strangers in human infants is an example.

4.1.1 Fear of Strangers

A great many studies have reported that human infants show various protective responses including avoidance, crying and clinging to the mother in the presence of an unfamiliar adult (reviews by Bowlby, 1973; Rheingold & Eckerman, 1973; and various chapters in Lewis & Rosenblum, 1974). Although in many cases the infant is in an unfamiliar environment (Section 3.1.3) and in some its mother is absent (Section 3.4), fear is often seen even in a familiar home setting with the mother present. The effect becomes particularly evident at about 6 months and peaks at about 1 year (Morgan & Ricciuti, 1969; Scarr & Salapatek, 1970). Reports of stranger-fear in other infant primates are infrequent, though Rosenblum & Alpert (1974) found that infant bonnet macaques (but not pigtail macaques) avoided a strange conspecific but approached their mother.

Fear of strangers is usually seen as an aspect of the more general neophobia (Section 3.1) which protects the infant from predators and other hazards (Scarr & Salapatek, 1970; Bowlby, 1973) and this is not incompatible with the idea that it also prevents dilution of the primary attachments the infant has already formed with its mother and, possibly, other group members (Freedman, 1967; Bowlby, 1973). Despite the widespread acceptance of this novelty hypothesis, little is known of how stranger fear varies as a function of the degree of novelty of the stranger. Ross (1975), however, has shown that repeated 4-minute exposures to a stranger decreased stranger-avoidance and time near or in contact with the mother relative to the behaviour of infants experiencing a different stranger on each exposure. It seems unlikely, however, that novelty alone underlies stranger fear, since at the same age infants rarely show comparable behaviour to inanimate novel objects such as toys, and indeed these are often approached and explored (Hutt, 1967; Ross, 1974a and b). When the infant's reactions to a novel toy and a novel person are compared directly (Eckerman & Rheingold, 1974), the toy evokes prompt approach and sustained physical contact while the person evokes little or no contact (but may be visually monitored and smiled at: see also below).

Although Bowlby (1973) argues that fear of strangers and of strange objects appear at about the same time in development, the reports of the latter which he cites actually involve novel objects that *move* in a sudden or unpredictable way or approach directly (see studies reviewed in Section 3.1.2) and this may give a clue to an important feature of strangers: they are

116

novel *and* move in a way which is outside the infant's control (Bretherton & Ainsworth, 1974) and may approach directly and closely (see also Section 1.1.1). In this connection, there is evidence that avoidance, gaze aversion and frowning are elicited not so much by the mere presence of a stranger but by the stranger's approach to the infant, and they increase in frequency with the closeness of her proximity (Lewis & Brooks, 1974; Brooks & Lewis, 1976). Although proximity seems to be important, direct movement towards the infant is not essential for the production of fear behaviour, however, and a seated stranger can be sufficient (e.g. Ross, 1975). Size may also be important, since a stranger is a much larger novel object than a typical toy. Brooks & Lewis (1976) suggest that several reports that male strangers are more fear-evoking than females may reflect the males' greater height, since when height is equated the sex effect disappears. They also found that a child elicited less fear behaviour than an adult and more exploration and attention as indexed by looking behaviour, though this difference seems to be mediated by facial features rather than size, since a child-sized adult midget was about as fear-evoking as a normal adult (though the midget was looked at more). The stranger's behaviour is also important. Eckerman & Rheingold (1974) found that infants avoided less and made more contact with a responsive stranger who smiled and talked to them than to a nonresponsive stranger.

The fact that children are less fear-evoking than adults is inconsistent with a simple novelty interpretation as it is not at all clear that infants are any more familiar with children than with adults. Brooks & Lewis also argue that this fact is also difficult to square with the incongruity theory according to which strangers elicit fear because they are sufficiently similar to an existing schema the infant has of a familiar person (the mother or caretaker) to evoke comparison with that schema, yet incorporate discrepancies from it (Hebb, 1946; Schaffer, 1966, 1974). A child is more discrepant from the mother schema than is another adult. This leads them to conclude that the major schema or referent is the infant's concept of *self*, and that an adult departs more markedly from this than does another child. An alternative possibility is that a child is sufficiently dissimilar from the mother schema not to be compared with it: hence there is no incongruity attaching to children. Ross (1975) suggests that strangers are actually compared with a number of stored schemas established on the basis of prior experience with people.

The incongruity explanation of stranger fear is a specific instance of the more general idea that fear behaviour in infants, and indeed in adults and other animals, can be elicited by a stimulus which violates an expectancy, i.e. is incongruous or surprising rather than simply novel (Berlyne, 1960; Hutt, 1970). Besides anecdotal reports, the evidence includes Berlyne's description of Buhler's finding that children were more afraid of a distorted voice emanating from a familiar face or a familiar voice from a novel mask than of a novel voice or mask alone and Hebb's (1946) report that stimuli which departed from the physical form of a normal chimp (e.g. a severed chimp head) were particularly potent elicitors of chimp avoidance (see Section 1.2.5).

The evidence, then, suggests that fear of strangers is based upon a variety of factors including the infant's categorisation of the stranger as discrepant from existing familiar persons, and the stranger's size, proximity, movement and behaviour.

It has also been pointed out by several authors (e.g. Rheingold & Eckerman, 1973; Ricciuti, 1974; Ross, 1975) that fear responses such as avoidance and crying are by no means universal or persistent features of infants' reactions to strangers and that *looking* behaviour is often the most striking feature. This could parallel the 'wary watching' of a potentially dangerous object by various animals noted in Section 1.2.1. If looking is equated with exploration, there appear to be important parallels between strangers and inanimate sources of novelty inasmuch as they are both capable of eliciting either exploration or fear behaviour (see Section 3.1).

4.2   Stimuli Associated with Spacing Behaviour

Spacing entails the maintenance of an area around the individual which is either free of conspecifics or which places limitations on how conspecifics can behave in it. Spacing also operates at the group level when a similar space is maintained by a group with respect to other groups. A variety of functions have been suggested for spacing, including the efficient utilisation of food and other resources and the regulation of population size (Wynne-Edwards, 1962; McBride, 1971).

The most obvious example of spacing is the active defence of a fixed territory against intruders, though a variety of more subtle types of spacing exist such as adherance to a home range coupled with mutual avoidance by neighbouring individuals or groups mediated by long-range signals (see, for example, Esser, 1971; Hinde, 1974, Chapter 25). Spacing of the individuals within a group may involve a system of ranking or dominance with respect to access to food, mates, etc. (see Hinde, 1974 Chapter 22, and 1977 for discussions of the meaning and validity of the concept of dominance in intragroup interactions).

The importance of spacing and dominance in the present context is that they are established and maintained largely by actual or ritualised aggression between individuals which can lead to protective behaviour. An individual that comes too close to others or that violates a dominance relationship may be subject to physical aggression (behaviour directed at causing physical injury), e.g. dominant male wild and laboratory rats attack and bite a strange intruding male (Barnett, 1975; Blanchard, Fukunaga, Blanchard & Kelley, 1975) and established rhesus monkey groups react similarly to an unfamiliar conspecific (Bernstein, 1964; Southwick, Siddiqi, Farooqui & Pal, 1974). Such aggression produces flight, though pain-mediated escape of this sort is less common than avoidance or spacing elicited by conspecific *threat*, particularly where the 'aggressor' and the threatened are familiar with one another. Rather as animals often anticipate a predator attack on the basis of distal cues and take avoiding action (Section 1) so they utilise distal cues in anticipation and avoidance of a conspecific attack. The cues involved are usually threat signals which form an element in a threat/flight or submission system which obviates the need for actual attack by the 'aggressor'.

4.2.1 *Conspecific Threat Stimuli*

Conspecific threats take many forms in different species, though they are linked by a few underlying principles. As threat signals are seen as having evolved for the express purpose of communication, it is generally assumed that they have specific eliciting properties independent of the more general features of fear stimuli discussed in Section 1. Some signals, however, fairly obviously involve some of these general features, particularly intensity and movement. The derivation of conspecific signals in general is discussed by Tinbergen (1953), Marler (1959, 1965, 1968), Andrew (1972a) and Hinde (1974), among others. Their evolution usually involves ritualisation (Blest, 1961, pp. 102–124) of responses derived from intention movements and other sources. Conspecific threats are most conveniently summarised in terms of the modality through which they communicate.

Communication of threat in the visual modality often involves one or both of two general principles (Marler, 1968): an increase in apparent size of the 'aggressor' (head held high, legs extended, bristling/erection of hair or feathers) and the display of fighting weapons (teeth, horns and feet). Both are clearly related to actual attack behaviour. The upright posture of a threatening herring gull, with downward pointing bill and raised wings preparatory to pecking and striking an opponent, is an obvious example (Hinde, 1974). Other threat features seen in many species which may be regarded as intention behaviour derived from actual attack (e.g. primates, van Hooff, 1962, 1967; Andrew, 1972a) include a forward-directed body posture, which may be coupled with responses associated with charging (e.g. pawing the ground, repeated jerky head movements), actual lunging forward, cuffing the ground or branches, various open-mouth faces (intention biting), and a direct fixed stare (fixation prior to attack).

119

Threat often has a vocal component and sounds are most often used to emphasise or draw attention to a visual threat (Rowell, 1962; Andrew, 1963b). Harsh, intense sounds such as the bark and roar of many mammals, including primates, occur in conjunction with intention biting and forward and downward head movements. Nonvocal noises may also accompany visual threats, e.g. dominant male chimpanzees generate noise by stamping on the ground or on tree trunks as an element in threat displays (Van Lawick Goodall, 1968; Pitcairn, 1974).

It can be seen, then, that in many cases threat signals are a relatively complex mix of postural, movement and auditory stimuli. As Cullen (1972) pointed out for animal signals generally, the complex, and frequently subtle, behaviour comprising a signal is usually very difficult to analyse. The individual components are not easily separable from one another in the total matrix of behaviour, and yet unless they are separated the contribution of the various components to the whole cannot be evaluated. This makes it difficult to identify the fear-evoking aspects of threat signals with any precision.

The visual and auditory signals discussed so far represent short-range communication, but long-range signals may also elicit protective behaviour and these are often easier to analyse. Visual signalling is obviously precluded when the participants are unable to see one another, but auditory and olfactory communication is still possible. An example of the former is provided by the howling of howler monkeys, which increases as two groups approach one another in dense vegetation (which prevents visual sighting) and causes them to move apart again, facilitating spacing (Chivers, 1969).

The importance of olfactory signals is that, unlike visual and auditory ones, they can continue to operate in the absence of the animal emitting them. Scent marking forms the basis of territorial marking behaviour in many species (Myktowycz, 1974; Stoddart, 1976), where a scent signal becomes a substitute for the animal itself and is designed to prevent the intrusion of conspecifics by eliciting escape and avoidance. Scent marking is particularly important in some rodents, and the males of several species will avoid an area which has previously been occupied by another male. In the mouse, this is mediated by an androgen-dependent pheromone originating in the coagulating gland and secreted in combination with urine (Jones & Powell, 1973a and b). A similar effect of voided male urine has been reported in rats (Gawienowski, DeNicola & Stacewicz-Sapuntzakis, 1976) and the flank glands have been implicated in territorial marking in male golden hamsters (Alderson & Johnston, 1975).

5 Species-Predictable Fear Stimuli and Experience

It is often assumed that if a fear response to a stimulus is species predictable then it must be innate in the sense of being shown independent of any specific prior experience with the stimulus. It can be argued that the evolution of a mechanism which provided appropriate behaviour on first encounter with a dangerous stimulus such as a predator would be favoured over mechanisms where the behaviour awaits experience with the stimulus. An example is Tinbergen's (1951) suggestion that, in some birds, protection against hawk predators is achieved by the innate releasing of escape by short-neckedness in a moving overhead silhouette. Leaving aside the well known controversy concerning the validity and usefulness of innateness as a concept (Lehrman, 1953, 1970; Lorenz, 1965), studies demonstrating the greater effectiveness of a short-neck model over others in birds lacking in experience of objects moving overhead (Section 1.2.1) lend support to the innateness hypothesis in this particular case. It must be said, however, that the evidence is conflicting. In the case of most of the other fear stimuli discussed in the preceeding sections, evidence on their innateness or otherwise is either even more contentious or lacking altogether and it is for this reason that no attempt has been made to identify innate fear stimuli in this chapter.

Although the evolutionary argument for eyes, fur and other predator features (Section 1.2) and nonspecific stimuli like movement features (Section 1.1) being innate releasers of fear behaviour is quite persuasive, the hypothesis is very largely untested. Experience with a particular stimulus, or with other stimuli, could be a prerequisite for the appearance of fear behaviour to it (see Section 6) though it must then be the case that all individuals are exposed to the same (or equivalent) experience or the behaviour would not be species predictable. This might explain why there are marked individual differences in responsiveness to some fear stimuli. Avoidance of snakes, for example, may be strong in some individuals or groups but weak or even absent (and therefore not strictly species predictable) in others of the same species (Joslin, Fletcher & Emlen, 1964; Morris & Morris, 1965). In the case of social species, learning from conspecifics may be important. It is known that food preferences and feeding habits, for example, can be transmitted through social learning in primate groups (review by Hinde, 1974, pp. 243–245) and responsiveness to fear stimuli could be learned and/or modified in a similar way.

As well as leading to the development of responsiveness, experience with a fear stimulus could also result in a reduction or extinction of responding. Short-term, reversible changes are frequently found with repeated presentations of a stimulus. For example, habituation effects have been reported for chaffinch mobbing of models (Hinde, 1954) and turtles' avoidance of a looming shadow (Hayes & Saiff, 1967). Although the value of habituation to biologically irrelevant stimuli is obvious, it is less immediately clear why organisms habituate to biologically important stimuli such as these predator cues. Part of the explanation is probably that the massed or continuous exposure to a fear stimulus given in experimental studies is uncommon in nature, where habituation will rarely have time to occur. Also, reports of habituation usually involve stimuli (e.g. models) which incorporate only one or a few of the cues which normally signal a predator and these 'sub-optimal' stimuli are likely to be habituated to relatively rapidly. Some marine worms that withdraw into a burrow when disturbed habituate quickly to a moving shadow or a vibration but much more slowly to the shadow and vibration together (Wells, 1968) and similar effects may occur in vertebrates. The use of multiple cues in responding to predators and the occurrence of habituation to suboptimal complexes is probably adaptive in ensuring that prey do not waste time responding to natural 'false alarms' which incorporate one or a few, but not all, of the cues which signal a predator.

Long-term, more permanent loss of responsiveness with experience (whether of a specific or general kind) is also to be predicted, especially for suboptimal cues. This is presumably what is involved in the attenuation of the avoidance response to a 'looming' shadow projection in humans, which is shown by infants but not adults (Section 1.1.1). The disappearance of the human infant's fear of strangers (Section 4.1.2) may be another example.

6 Fear Stimuli that are Not Species Predictable

Many stimuli obviously elicit protective behaviour in only some individuals of a species. In the main, these stimuli derive their fear-evoking property from having been associated with a species-predictable stimulus. The ability to associate stimuli in this way is clearly a fundamental feature of vertebrate behaviour and permits protective responses to be tailored to the specific requirements of the individual's environment. Studies of signalled avoidance learning in animals (reviewed by Mackintosh, 1974) provide a good demonstration of this: subjects will escape from, or show other protective responses to, stimuli which have previously been associated with (and so come to signal) an aversive stimulus such as electric shock (which is thereby avoided). Conditioned fear in humans, as exemplified by the classic study of the 11-month infant 'Little Albert' by Watson & Rayner (1920) provides a further example. Watson & Rayner found that when a sudden loud noise, which caused the boy to cry and show other fear behaviour, was paired with a white rat, the rat acquired fear-evoking qualities.

It is also clear that some stimulus associations are formed more readily than others. Seligman (1970; Seligman & Hager, 1972) has pointed out that organisms are 'prepared' by evolution to form some associations and 'contraprepared' to form others. An example comes from Garcia & Koelling's (1966) demonstration that rats associated sickness with an earlier encounter with a distinctive taste stimulus but not with an audiovisual stimulus, and subsequently avoided the former but not the latter. The audiovisual stimulus, however, was more readily associated with a painful shock. Further constraints on association are shown by the fact that associations between sickness and food taste are formed much more readily if the taste is novel rather than familiar (Revusky & Bedarf, 1967) and that although the food itself is avoided the place in which it was eaten usually is not (Garcia, McGowan & Green, 1972). This preparedness is explainable on the assumption that in nature sickness is much more likely to stem from novel food or drink than from an exteroceptive stimulus, while pain is more likely to stem from the latter, and organisms are 'tuned' accordingly.

Man's particular ability to form associations between stimuli probably accounts in large measure for the range and diversity of stimuli which can be fear-evoking for humans. Idiosyncratic fears of objects, people and situations can be established through association*. The most striking evidence of this comes from the data assembled in support of the conditioning theory of phobias (strong, traumatic fears) developed by various workers (e.g. Wolpe & Rachman, 1960; Eysenck & Rachman 1965; Rachman, 1968), which proposes that phobias are essentially conditioned fear reactions of the general type exemplified by the case of 'Little Albert'. A specific example is the sample of people with an extremely strong fear of visiting the dentist reported by Lautch (1971), all of whom were found to have previously experienced a traumatic dental experience such as pain or fear of suffocation.

Here too, associations are more likely to be formed between some stimuli than others. In particular, phobias involve a relatively limited set of stimuli. Marks (1969), for example, classified phobias of external stimuli into four main groups which covered all the phobias seen at the Maudsley Hospital, London over a 10-year period. These were agoraphobia (fear of going out into public places), social phobias (fear of eating, speaking, etc., in the presence of strangers), animal phobias (usually of a specific animal type, such as birds or spiders), and miscellaneous specific phobias covering a limited number of stimuli (e.g. fear of heights, thunder, darkness, enclosed

*See fuller discussion pertaining to this in Chapter 7 by A. T. Carr.

places, etc.). Seligman (1971) has pointed out that phobias of such things as knives, hammers and electrical appliances are very rare or nonexistent, despite the fact that they are quite likely to be associated with pain or other trauma. This leads to the suggestion that certain stimuli and stimulus features are more readily associated with fear-evoking stimuli than are others as a result of preparedness through human evolution. It is certainly true that the objects of many phobias are stimuli which: (a) evoke fear to a lesser degree in all, or many, nonphobic human beings (e.g. heights, spiders, speaking in public); (b) also evoke fear in animals (e.g. heights, thunder, open places); and (c) have a reasonable claim to being important dangers to human survival (e.g. heights, open and enclosed places, darkness, animals and strangers). Some evidence that there are important constraints on human associations comes from follow-up studies of the 'Little Albert' experiment, which show that it is extremely difficult to condition infants to fear familiar, everyday objects such as toys (English, 1929; Bregman, 1934). Watson & Rayner's rat was probably *prepotent* by virtue of its novelty (Section 3.1), movement (Section 1.1.1) and possibly its animal features such as fur and eyes (Section 1.2.2).

CHAPTER 5

The Ontogeny of Fear in Animals

Eric A. Salzen

1 Fear and Fear Behaviour

This consideration of the development of fear in young animals will be restricted to vertebrates. It is difficult enough to reach a consensus on the phenomena that constitute fear in vertebrates. Its existence as a homologous entity in invertebrates is controversial and is of doubtful moment except in the context of the evolution of protective movements and responses cf. Eibl-Eibesfeldt (1975). Within the subphylum Vertebrata this evolution has operated on a common genetic foundation for a common anatomophysiologic framework (cf. Romer, 1962; Smith, H. M., 1960). It is reasonable, therefore, to seek and attempt to construct a common description of the development of fear in vertebrates. In order to arrive at such a description the phenomena that constitute fear in vertebrates must be made explicit and their common foundational nature must be substantiated. No citation of authorities is needed to support the view that the term 'fear' adumbrates two distinct concepts, namely 'fear behaviour' and 'fear state'. These two concepts are reasonably clearly identifiable and understandable in man. In other vertebrates we can certainly recognise behaviours, such as fleeing, escaping, crouching, freezing, hiding, calling and autonomic discharge patterns, that are comparable and even clearly homologous with our own fear behaviour (cf. Hinde, 1970; Marler & Hamilton, 1966) but we can only infer whether they might be accompanied by internal bodily and neural states comparable with the feeling or emotion of fear in ourselves. Whether or not accompanied by a 'fear state' all 'fear behaviour' can be seen to have the function, either immediate or subsequent, of protecting the individual from immediate or potential physicochemical damage arising from physicochemical or animate agencies in the environment. Since any change in the normal 'safe'

I should like to thank Alison Williamson for help with the bibliographic work.

125

environment is more likely to be detrimental than otherwise, I have suggested (1978) that the vertebrate is organised to respond so as to remove any change in stimulation and restore the familiar status quo (*sensory homeostasis*) and I have outlined an orientation mechanism that would do this. This sensory homeostatic system is the basis of self-protective behaviour which includes not only fear orientation behaviour (cf. Salzen, 1962, 1970) but also infantile and social care-soliciting behaviour, shelter seeking and investigative behaviour (cf. Scott, 1958). All other categories of vertebrate behaviour can be grouped into either *physiological homeostatic* behaviour systems operating through metabolic imbalances or *reproductive* behaviour systems operating through hormonal states (cf. Salzen, 1978).

What then are the self-protective behaviour patterns in vertebrates? I suggest they fall into three classes of behaviour as follows:

(1) protective contact-responses;
(2) avoidant distance-responses;
(3) signalling thwarting-responses.

Protective contact-responses are Sherringtonian flexor responses (cf. Sherrington, 1947) to stimulation of skin receptors and especially nociceptors which produce *withdrawal* of the stimulated limb or body-region, and, if stimulation is repeated or sufficiently strong, the whole body. These contact-receptor protective mechanisms might be expected to develop 'in embryo' and to show little change in the young animal (cf. Carmichael & Smith, 1939; Schneirla, 1959). It is a matter of taste (a contact-receptor system that can also give the protective reflex of *rejection*) whether protective reflexes are regarded as fear behaviour since they are associated with internal and central neural states that correspond with distinctive feelings in man which are unpleasant or unbearable rather than fearful. In fact nociceptive reflexes and pain are commonly considered to give rise to the state and emotion of fear (cf. Gray, J. A., 1971b; Miller, N.E., 1948; Mowrer, 1960a) and so will be included in this review. Avoidant distance-responses are movements of body-parts or of the whole body in response to stimulation of the distance-receptors (olfactory, auditory, visual) which prevent the contact nociceptive stimulation that might otherwise ensue. These are in fact the 'precurrent' actions of Sherrington. The simplest of these orientations are comparable with the protective contact-responses in being reflex-like withdrawal responses of body-parts which serve to protect specific body parts, e.g. *auditory startle*, the *eye-blink response*, *visual looming response* and perhaps protective *crouching* and *grimacing*. They differ in that they require distance-receptor stimulation. Whole-body responses in this class are clearly orientation behaviour which serves to keep the individual away from the

126

stimulus source. They include the more obvious fear responses of *withdrawal*, *flight, escape* and *avoidance* movements. Where the source of stimulation is unlocalised there can be no directional component for this orientation and the behaviours of *inhibition* and *freezing* prevail until the stimulus field becomes polarized (cf. Salzen, 1970, 1978). Where the stimulus source is also the only available direction of withdrawal or escape, *defensive aggression* may occur. Because these avoidant responses are elicited by distance-stimuli operating on the distance-receptors their development in young animals will be related to the state of development of the distance-senses and their interactions with the environment. These avoidant distance-responses are all accompanied by supporting autonomic activity and clearly have associated neural states. So they may also be associated with or accompanied by distinctive feelings or emotions of 'fear'. When these responses are performed quickly and effectively the associated states are short-lived or absent. This is well shown in avoidance learning, cf. Church (1972).

It is the persistent autonomic patterns and somatic motor patterns which occur in the thwarting or conflict of avoidant responses that give the characteristic appearance of 'fear' and it is these patterns which have been selected in evolution for their signalling value and effectiveness in eliciting protective or assistance behaviour from social partners or parents (etepimeletic behaviour for eliciting epimeletic behaviour in the terminology of Scott, 1958, 1969). Thwarting and conflict responses that can give rise to social signals in vertebrates have been summarised by Morris (1956) and I have elsewhere shown how these responses can be considered synonymous with emotional behaviour and emotion (Salzen, 1978). Leyhausen (1967a) has written on emotion in a broadly similar way. Morris distinguished two classes of thwarting response. *Primary thwarting responses* are the immediate patterns of intention movements of the aroused behaviours and their autonomic accompaniments. Many social signals and agonistic displays involve combinations and alternations of elements of protective, attacking and mating movements and postures. These form the various displays of courtship and status of which scared-threat, submission, appeasement and greeting behaviours might be regarded as fear behaviours (cf. Andrew, 1956b, 1963a; Baerends, 1975; Hinde, 1970, 1974; van Hooff, 1962). The autonomic changes that may accompany thwarting may also form distinctive chemical, auditory and visual displays (cf. Andrew, 1956a, 1972a; Eibl-Eibesfeldt, 1975; Leyhausen, 1967a and b). Fearful displays include urination and defecation (alimentary changes), pallor (circulatory changes) vocalisations (respiratory changes) and sleeking and sweating (thermoregulatory changes). The *secondary thwarting responses* distinguished by Morris (1956) are certain types of behaviour that tend to occur when the primary responses fail to change the situation or the social partners so as to

127

remove the conflict or thwarting. These secondary responses include displacement activities, redirected activity, regressive behaviour and neurotic inactivity. I would also include an additional response – aggressive behaviour. Fearful secondary thwarting responses, therefore, include grooming (displacement), panic escape (redirection), convulsive struggling and infantile distress calling (regression), tonic immobility and sleep (neurotic inactivity) and fearful or defensive aggression (cf. Andrew, 1956b, 1972a; Leyhausen, 1967a and b). As has already been made clear these behaviours may be associated with prolonged or even chronic autonomic and central neural states of 'fear' or 'anxiety'.

The protective behaviours outlined above are dependent on appropriate stimulation. There is now something approaching a consensus in the grouping by Gray, J. A. (1971b, p. 20) of fear stimuli into the categories of *intensity*, *novelty*, *'special evolutionary danger'* and *'social interaction with conspecifics'*. Gray has also made the point, on the basis of data on children's fears reported by Jersild & Holmes (1935), that fear responses to 'intense' and 'novel' stimuli such as noise, strange objects and persons, pain, falling and loss of support, and sudden unexpected movement, tend to decline with age. He suggests that this is due to 'adaptation' and 'habituation' to intensity and novelty respectively. On the other hand the 'special fears' of predators and conspecifics tend to appear with age. Gray notes that the maturation of these behaviours makes biological sense since they have no selective advantage in infancy when parental care is effective. In view of the importance of frequency and context in the occurrence of responses to these kinds of stimuli, the likelihood that they also involve familiarity and learning seems high. Clearly then the influence of experience and learning must be considered carefully for all types of fear stimulation when looking at the development of fear in young animals. The following account of the ontogeny of fear in young vertebrates will therefore consider the three classes of fear behaviour which I have defined and then the roles of maturation and experience in their development. Bronson (1968a) has reviewed the development of fear in humans and other primates and in dogs especially in relation to novelty, familiarisation and maternal stimulation. There seems to be no other review source for data on the ontogeny of fear in vertebrates. The excellent review of the ontogeny of emotional behaviour by Candland (1971) includes fear and provides a useful bibliography.

2 Protective Contact Responses

The somaesthetic and motor systems become operative 'in embryo' and so the earliest protective contact responses might be expected to be present before birth. Their state of development and significance after birth will depend on whether the young are precocial, i.e. born with functioning distance receptors and locomotory systems, or altricial, i.e. born with closed eyes and inadequate locomotor abilities. Altricial young are characterised by being dependent on a nest environment which they cannot normally leave. The young of fish, amphibia and reptiles (poikilothermic vertebrates) typically hatch as free swimming/moving forms, i.e. they are precocial. Precocial birds, although hatched in a nest, are soon able to leave, i.e. are nidifugous. Altricial birds stay in the nest until vision and locomotion are adequately developed. Precocial mammals are not born in nests while altricial ones are. Primates span the categories, prosimians but not simians being born in nests. I have classed the simian primates as precocial because their vision functions soon after birth and their precocial active clinging and climbing are appropriate and adequate motor abilities. The protective contact responses may therefore be examined in embryos and in precocial and altricial neonates.

2.1 Embryonic Responses

In a recent review Gottlieb (1971a) has marshalled evidence to the effect that there is a sequence of sensory development in mammals, i.e. somaesthetic – vestibular – auditory – visual, which corresponds with that in birds as determined in the chick embryo (Gottlieb, 1968). It is the contact receptor responses which appear first in embryonic development throughout the vertebrate classes. The evidence has been assembled and reviewed by Carmichael (1970) and two generalisations can be made. There is a cephalocaudal development in tactile sensitivity and the reflex motor response is typically a lateral C-shaped body-flexion leading into S-shaped swimming movements. This response pattern was first described for fish and amphibia by Preyer (1885, translated by Coghill & Legner, 1937) and has been confirmed at or soon after hatching in fish (e.g. in the toadfish by Tracy, 1926, and in the zebra fish by Kimmel, Patterson & Kimmel, 1974), and in amphibia (e.g. in anurans by Youngstrom, 1938, and Wang & Lu, 1943) and before hatching in reptiles (e.g. in loggerhead turtles by Smith, K. U. & Daniel, 1946). The initial flexion takes the body away from the stimulus (cf. Coghill, 1929) and repeated stimulation leads to swimming movements which serve the same function in the larva. The cephalocaudal development of responsiveness is typical but not invariable (cf. Tracy, 1926).

In birds and mammals the initial tactile response is again usually elicited from the head and shoulder regions and develops caudally (cf. Gottlieb, 1968, 1971a; Barron, 1941), although again this pattern is not always so

129

simple (cf. Carmichael, 1970). The response is usually a flexion which takes the head and neck away from the stimulus, e.g. in the 5-day carrier-pigeon embryo (Tuge, 1934). In the domestic chick and Pekin duck embryos the head is effectively withdrawn from stimulation of the oral region according to Gottlieb (1968) who notes that these tactile reflexes appear at 1/3 of the incubation period in both species. Gottlieb & Kuo (1965) earlier reported that in the 10-day duck embryo the head turned away when the wing-tip or toes contacted the bill or chin region but if the touch was light then bill clapping occurred. This is consistent with the notion of a high threshold flexor withdrawal system which I have outlined elsewhere (Salzen, 1978). Flexion of limbs in response to distal mechanical stimulation has been demonstrated as early as 7 days in chick embryos (Orr & Windle, 1934).

The evidence for head flexion to anterior tactile stimulation in mammalian embryos is considerable and Barron (1941) has listed the data for the rat (16 days), rabbit (15–16 days), cat (28 days), guinea pig (31 days) and man (8 weeks). Only the sheep (34 days) shows head extension rather than flexion and the human foetus shows body flexion. Since Barron's review this picture has been generally confirmed (cf. Carmichael, 1970). In the rat, Narayanan, Fox & Hamburger (1971) reported a cephalocaudal development of sensitivity which was complete by 20 days with head turning away and limbs withdrawing from local stimulation. Carmichael (1970) cites the rat study of Straus and Weddell (1940) as showing that limb extensor muscles were more readily stimulated than flexor muscles. This suggests once again a possible higher threshold for flexor responses. In the rabbit, lateral flexion of neck and trunk to touch has been described (cf. Gottlieb, 1971a). In the guinea pig, Carmichael & Smith (1939) obtained local responses to light touch and more general movements to heavy touch, with a general cephalocaudal development in this sensitivity from 35 days. The responses included neck flexion and forelimb movements towards the stimulated body region. Avery (1928) describes kicking and withdrawal of the foot to pinching in the 58-day foetal guinea pig. Carmichael's (1970) review of cat embryo development again indicates a general cephalocaudal sequence of tactile responsiveness with a C-flexion appearing by 31 days and with a proximodistal sequence in the limbs. Hind-limb flexion appeared at 38 days and forepaw flexion at 40 days. Pain responses also appeared in the late foetus.

2.2 Precocial Neonates

When the young vertebrate emerges from the egg or uterus the embryonic protective tactile reflexes are free to operate. In addition extensor-based feeding approach movements appear, especially to moderate stimulation of head and oral regions. This is true from the fish larval biting response to the human neonatal rooting response (cf. Carmichael, 1970). But the basic withdrawal and swimming response to strong tactile stimulation of the body remains and is clearly important in fish and amphibian larvae (e.g. Kimmel, Patterson & Kimmel, 1974; Youngstrom, 1938). In the amniote vertebrates (reptiles, birds and mammals) the swimming movements are transformed into locomotory limb movements of creeping, crawling, walking and running, e.g. 8–12 days before hatching in loggerhead turtles (Smith, K. U. & Daniel, 1946).

In precocial birds, such as gallinaceous fowl, the newly hatched young may show simple limb or head withdrawal to strong tactile stimulation such as pinching. Kruijt (1964) has reported that 1-day chicks will give fear trills and an alert posture when stepped on by another chick or when seized by hand. He also describes withdrawal running and jumping when his chicks crossed hot sand. Newly-hatched chicks may give momentary withdrawal responses to painful stimulation but increase their approach towards an object that can provide continuous contact (cf. Hess, 1959a; Kovach & Hess, 1963). Inhibition of approach behaviour by strong electric shock may develop after the first day (Kovach & Hess, 1963; Brown, C. P., 1977). I have previously (Salzen, 1967, 1969) discussed the effects of providing the neonate with continuous body-contact and it is clear that the newly hatched chick will be active and distress call until such contact is achieved. Thus a deficiency of contact may stimulate protective responses as well as too intense contact stimulation. The same is true for temperature and the neonate will show withdrawal and locomotor movements until contact and temperature stimulation resembling the foetal condition is achieved or until adaptation to a new steady state of stimulation occurs (cf. Salzen, 1962, 1970, 1978).

In precocial mammals the same protective contact-responses are available but detailed study is lacking. New-born guinea pigs clearly show limb reflexes to contact stimuli (Avery, 1928) and also seek bodily contact with others (e.g. Harper, 1970, 1976; Rood, 1972). The rhesus monkey infant has been studied although not always specifically for protective responses. A report by Foley (1934) of one infant also includes a summary of data for four other infants from two earlier studies by Lashley & Watson, and Hartman & Tinklepaugh. Unspecified motor responses and crying in response to painful stimulation were seen at 1–3 days of age. In the absence of contact stimulation the infants showed climbing and clinging behaviour. A more systematic study by Mowbray & Cadell (1962) still only examined the clasping response to contact stimulation. This response is prepotent in the new-born and tests showed that it is 7–8 days before it can be inhibited by the righting response and 10–18 days before it is inhibited by inadequate or unsuitable contact stimulation. Mowbray & Cadell also noted a tendency to maintain nose contact by 'following' movements at 4 days of age, and of course the rooting response to facial touch is present from birth.

2.3 Altricial Neonates

Obviously protective contact responses will remain the prime protective behaviour in the early neonatal period and until pre-empted by the distance responses that follow maturation of the distance receptors, especially the eyes. In passerine birds typically the first response to any touch or vibration such as jarring the nest is head and neck extension with gaping, i.e. the feeding response. This has been well described by Kuhlmann (1909) for passerine birds 1–3 days old. But later this stimulation comes to give inhibition of gaping and finally crouching. Rand (1941) has described earlier protective responses to nest-jarring in the curve-billed thrasher. At 1 day the nestling turns and crawls, by 5 days the response is foot extension and gripping of the nest, at 7 days bodily shrinking develops, and from the 12th day the handled bird runs and crouches under cover. The final directed response involves visual orientation and guidance. There is probably an interaction between drive state (hunger) and stimulus strength (vibration of nest) in the logistics of the nest-jarring response alternatives of gaping and crouching, until the contact response system is pre-empted by distance receptor systems (cf. Tinbergen, 1951, for development of the begging response in the thrush).

In altricial mammals protective contact responses are evident in general limb flexion and C-flexion or S (sigmoid) movements of the trunk which occur to strong stimulation of these body parts and of the head region respectively. However moderate tactile stimulation of the face and head appears to give forward movement and turning to the stimulus source (cf. Schneirla, 1965). This pattern is typical of the opossum at birth where the marsupium functions as a 'nest' and the neonate is clearly 'altricial' (cf. Carmichael, 1970). In the mouse, limb flexion to toe pinching and struggling body movements to pain increase in vigour from 1 to 3 days after birth to be replaced by more specific responses by 9 days (Fox, 1965). Squealing and leg waving to tail-pinch are described for 0- to 4-day-old mice by Williams & Scott (1953) who also noted that by 4 days the mice would move back into the nesting litter if more than half the body became exposed. This suggests that a deficit in tactile and thermal stimulation may also give flexion and withdrawal responses. Fox (1965) has also reported tactile avoidance of a cliff edge as present in mice at 1 day and strongly developed at 7 days, while Oliverio, Castellano & Allegra (1975) report the same response at 3 days. In

132

the white rat, Anderson & Patrick (1934) could elicit limb withdrawal by foot tickle and pressure, and body flexion towards a body prick at 2 days. At 4 days, prick in the nose region gave nose withdrawal while in the body region it produced movement of the limbs towards the stimulated site. As in the mouse, a touch-mediated cliff-edge withdrawal is present and develops from 1 to 7 days (Altman & Sudarshan, 1975). At 5 days Anderson & Patrick (1934) were able to elicit a general flexion of a startle pattern with an air-puff. Also, as in the mouse, temperature responses are evident, for Fowler & Kellogg (1975) got increased movement in rat pups placed in a cold (23 °C) compartment and after 5 days of age the pups were able to move to a warm compartment. Increasing their mobility by injecting laevodopa did not give differential choices before 4–5 days of age. This is the time when creeping locomotion develops (Blanck, Hård & Larsson, 1967).

For the cat, Fox (1970) has reported limb withdrawal and distress cries at birth in response to a pinch. By 10–12 days the response had developed into crawling away and by 17 days there was marked limb withdrawal, struggling, escape movements and vocalisation. Fox noted that from 0 to 9 days the neonatal kitten is positively thermo- and thigmotaxic and there is active orientation and crawling in the absence of adequate thermal and contact stimulation. Earlier work by Tilney & Casamajor (1924) also indicated general contraction and cries to painful stimulation 2–3 days after birth, with contact orienting and temperature avoidance responses from the first day. Fox records that in the period 10–17 days after birth these contact responses are replaced by auditory and visual orientations. In his comparable study of neonatal dogs, Fox (1964) obtained perinatal head turning away from touch, reflex limb withdrawal from touch, and distress struggling and vocalizing to pain. By 5–18 days avoidance and escape behaviour in response to pain had developed. Scott & Fuller (1965) describe crawling movements and vocalisations to pain and cold in 2- to 3-day-old puppies. Unconditioned reflex rejection responses to quinine were earlier described by Scott & Fuller (1965); see also Fox (1970). The presence of protective orientation responses to tactile deficit has been noted by James (1952) who showed that in puppies it produced activity directed by tactile stimuli provided by the mother or by other objects. This is how positive approach and attachment behaviour could arise from orientation behaviour instigated by deficient stimulation and is probably comparable with later separation distress and searching (cf. Davis, Gurski & Scott, 1977). Similar relationships apply to temperature, for Fredericson, Gurney & Dubois (1956) showed that a warm surface elicited relaxation while a cold one gave increased vocalisation and attempts to move even in 1-day-old puppies. Welker (1959b) has shown that neonatal puppies vocalised and made pivoting movements (struggling locomotory movements) on an open surface lacking normal contact and if too warm or too cold (see also Blanck, Hård & Larsson, 1967). Surface contact with the snout produced forward movements or turning if laterally placed. A cold neonate turned away from a cold contact while a hot neonate turned away from any contact. Thus again there seems evidence that the neonate is activated into orientation movements by changes from its customary tactile and thermal state. At its most intense level such orientation behaviour has the appearance of, and is frequently labelled as, 'distress'.

3 Avoidant Distance Responses

In general in the larval or infant vertebrate the functional distance receptors (olfactory, auditory and visual) soon come to give rise to orientation behaviour that largely pre-empts the contact receptor-mediated protective responses (touch, temperature, pain and taste). The order of functional distance receptor ontogeny appears to be olfactory, auditory and visual and there is a comparable ontogeny in locomotor ability which gives a trend from local turning or pivoting movements to bodily translocations in relation to the stimulus source and features of the environment, i.e. approach/withdrawal, avoidance and escape paths. The different kinds of avoidant distance responses will be described roughly in their order of development.

3.1 Olfactory Avoidance

There are few studies of olfactory avoidance responses in neonates. Gard, Hård, Larsson & Petersson (1976) observed movement and pivoting by newborn rat pups in response to ammonia vapour. Altman & Sudarshan (1975) report orienting to the home cage through pivoting movements by 3- to 8-day rat pups and Bolles & Woods (1964) describe orientation to the nest and mother as early as 2–4 days. These early orientation movements were probably guided by olfactory cues. In the Syrian golden hamster avoidance of certain organic odours may occur as early as 3–4 days after birth according to Cornwell (1975). In the 2-day-old dog, Fox (1970) produced cessation of rooting and strong head and body turning away from strong olfactory stimuli such as clove oil, anise, benzene, xylene and acetic acid. Earlier, Scott & Fuller (1965) got withdrawal movements in response to dog-repellant odour in neonatal puppies. In the precocial guinea pig turning away from anise and asafoetida occurs at birth or even in the premature foetus (Avery, 1928). In the rhesus monkey responses to camphor and ether vapour were present when first tested at 2–3 days (Foley, 1934). What

134

evidence there is, therefore, would suggest that olfactory-elicited avoidant turning and withdrawal movements do indeed occur in the very young neonate.

3.2   Auditory Startle Response

The evidence on auditory responses confirms that they appear next, at least in altricial neonates, and are prepotent over any visually mediated responses in the very young infant. The elementary protective response to intense and sudden sound is the startle response (originally described in man by Strauss, 1929, and Landis & Hunt, 1939). This response involves general body and limb flexion and abduction along with eye-closure and a facial grin-like protective 'grimace'. Any general massive body flexion in mammals, or indeed in almost any animal, in response to sudden intense stimulation now seems to be called 'startle'. Landis & Hunt (1939) considered the startle response to be distinct from the Moro reflex (extension of trunks and limbs, cf. Goldstein, Landis, Hunt & Clarke, 1938) which it replaces developmentally. They also considered it to occur in mammals but not in amphibia and reptiles. Since then Fleshler (1965) has shown that auditory startle in the rat depends on an adequate peak intensity of sound being reached within 12 ms. Auditory startle responses of this kind appear in neonatal mice at 7–15 days (Williams & Scott, 1953; Fox, 1965; Oliverio, Castellano & Allegra, 1975), in the opossum at 50 days and deermouse by 10–18 days (cf. Gottlieb, 1971a) and in the rat from 11–13 days (Anderson & Patrick, 1934; Bolles & Woods, 1964) where according to Friedrich, Pickenhain & Klingberg (1967) the amplitude of the response increases while its latency falls in the succeeding period of 13–28 days. In the altricial carnivores the response appears from 8–10 days in the cat (Fox, 1970) and from 18–25 days in the dog (Fox, 1964; Scott & Fuller, 1965). In the precocial guinea pig the startle response can be obtained from 60- to 62-day embryos (cf. Avery, 1928; Gottlieb, 1971a). In the rhesus monkey it has been recorded from 7–18 days (Tinklepaugh & Hartman, 1932; Mowbray & Cadell, 1962).

The term startle has also been used for a tail-flip response to a vibrating stimulus in the zebra fish by Kimmel, Patterson & Kimmel (1974). This response appears in the larva at hatching (4–5 days) and at 7 days the same response occurs to a tactile stimulus and finally, in the adult, to a shadow.

The interesting point about the auditory startle response is that Strauss (1929) recognised that the primary startle response, the immediate protective flexion reflex, is followed by a secondary 'emotional' response pattern including spying, defence and flight. Landis & Hunt (1939)

135

described this pattern as including autonomic changes, curiosity, fear, annoyance and overflow. This secondary pattern is clearly emotional behaviour with an emotional state and it appears and increases as the infant develops. Simple orienting of head to auditory stimuli of lesser intensity and suddenness (the orienting reflex of Sokolov, 1963) seems to occur later than the startle response, at least in altricial mammals. According to Volokhov (1970) the times of appearance are 10–12 days for rats (19–21 days according to Bolles & Woods, 1964), 12–15 days for rabbits; 13–16 days for cats (12–14 days according to Fox, 1970), 16–24 days for dogs, 1–2 days for guinea pigs, and 40–45 days for hamadryas baboons. In rhesus monkeys the response is very early, 1–7 days (Foley, 1934; Mowbray & Cadell, 1964) and apparently precedes startle. Clearly these responses will be very dependent on the intensity and quality of the sounds used.

3.3 Inhibition, Freezing and Crouching

Typically these are the responses to sounds which are intermediate between those that will elicit the startle and orienting reflexes. Volokhov (1970) describes 'freezing' or immobility with slowed breathing and heart rates as the 'primitive orienting reaction'. Here the term inhibition is used for this cessation of ongoing activity in response to an unlocalized or unlocated stimulus. It is commonly given to sudden noises; it may follow a startle response; or it may be given to alarm calls or to the cessation of noises, i.e. to a sudden silence (cf. Andrew, 1956b). Alarm calls are characteristically calls that are difficult to localise (cf. Marler, 1965; Marler & Hamilton, 1966). Briefly or poorly localised visual stimuli such as distant movements, 'aerial predators' and sudden shadows may also produce inhibition. It is probably part of the 'primitive orienting reaction' as described by Volokhov (1970). At high intensity and duration it becomes 'freezing'. Thus freezing is maintained inhibition. It may also involve eye and slight head movements to locate the stimulus source (cf. Andrew, 1956). Crouching occurs to the same stimuli and is probably a general flexion response followed by freezing (cf. Andrew, 1956b), although I have seen birds that freeze in the standing position and slowly subside into a crouch. In any event the crouch represents a protective pattern characteristic of the early embryonic contact flexion responses. Recently Blanchard, Dielman & Blanchard (1968a) have noticed that crouching is the response given by rats to a single footshock. Obviously the rats are unsure of the source of the shock, i.e. it is an unlocated stimulus. When shocked with a prod the response is avoidance of the located stimulus (Blanchard & Blanchard, 1969b). Finally, as should be expected, Blanchard & Blanchard (1969a) found that the crouching response becomes associated with the situation and that previous familiarity with the situation reduces the response (Blanchard, Dielman & Blanchard, 1968b).

When the 'fear' stimulus has been located and is localised the animal is able to make orientation movements so as to remove the stimulus presence by withdrawal, flight or avoidance behaviour. But as Leyhausen (1967b) has pointed out in relation to what he calls 'fright paralysis' in response to a strong 'unclassified' stimulus, when the stimulus is located and classified the fright can change to any appropriate behaviour, '. . . escape, attack, . . . or dancing for joy!' When the classified stimulus leads to fleeing the escape movements may result in renewed uncertainty of the locus of the fear source and so again freezing and crouching may occur. This is common when the flight has taken the animal into cover giving the 'hiding' response (cf. Andrew, 1956b). Rakover (1975) has also given evidence that in the rat freezing is not a conflict response and that withdrawal occurs when a way of escape has been found. Freezing and crouching may also occur when the whole perceptual field is fearful, e.g. in a strange or unfamiliar environment or to overwhelming stimulation. The latter fits an early description by Duerden (1906) of 'death-feigning' by ostrich chicks suddenly come upon by man. The characteristic crouching of isolate-reared rhesus and chimpanzees (Mitchell, 1970) and dogs (Scott & Fuller, 1965) in strange environments is perhaps understandable in this way too.

In ontogeny these responses appear early. The initial response of young larval African cichlid fish studied by Myrberg (1965) to slight disturbance of the environment was inhibition of movement and settling on the bottom. Similar responses are common in fish and amphibian larvae but systematic ontogenetic studies seem lacking.

In precocial birds, Borchelt & Ratner (1973) have studied the developing bobwhite quail and found that freezing was minimal until after 10 days and reached a median duration of 10 seconds by 29 days of age. The incidence of the response increased steadily from 20% at 4 days to a maximum of about 80% by 19 days. Usually freezing ended with the development of distress calling leading to locomotion. This is similar to the domestic chick (cf. Salzen, 1970) and seems to be typical where the chick is separated from familiar places or companions. In the case of the junglefowl, Kruijt (1964) reports alerting with monocular fixation, i.e. arrest and 'inhibition' in day-old chicks. Shortening the neck and bending the legs begins at the same time and develops into 'squatting' by the 3rd day (see also Hunt, 1897) when it may be preceded by running. This type of response is given to loud sounds and may be incipient crouching, but Kruijt says that it is replaced after 2 weeks by 'freezing'. Candland, Nagy & Conklyn (1963) have recorded the incidence of freezing by domestic chicks in an open-field test from 1 to 90 days of age. There appeared to be a fall in its incidence from 1 to 8 days, followed by a recovery to

137

a maintained 50% level from 20 to 45 days, after which the incidence declined to nearly zero by 60–90 days. This pattern might correspond with Kruijt's distinction of two types of freezing response in ontogeny. In the blackheaded gull, the first signs of crouching – a shrinking of the head and body – appear on the 2nd day (Kirkman, 1937) in response to hand waving, clapping, alarm calls, disturbance take-offs by parents, and colony disturbance flights. Crouching is commonly preceded by a short run during the first few days and this gives 'fleeing the nest'. In precocial mammals inhibition, freezing and crouching have not been well studied. In general they seem to develop with the startle response and are evident especially in the absence of the parent to whom approach and contacting are directed following a disturbing stimulus. In the rhesus, the neonate is in continuous contact with the mother and sudden disturbances give clinging. When separated from the mother or raised in isolation crouching may occur, especially in a novel environment (cf. Harlow, 1960), but this response may also be providing some self-contacting stimulation (cf. Salzen, 1967, 1978). The initial arrest and orienting response (Volokhov, 1970) is present soon after birth in precocial birds and mammals.

In altricial birds these responses have been studied by a number of workers, e.g. Kuhlmann (1909), Rand (1941), Nice (1943), Barraud (1961) and Schaller & Emlen (1961). In nestling grackles studied by Schaller & Emlen, the first signs of tensing (inhibition) appeared after 3–4 days in response to strong shaking of the nest. After 5–6 days intense crouching had developed, and after 10–11 days partial bill opening sometimes appeared also. Crouching to visual stimuli occurred only after 9 days, i.e. 2–3 days after the appearance of optomotor responses. The initial response during these 2–3 days was indiscriminate gaping; so crouching to a visual stimulus involves a learned discrimination. Barraud (1961) reported that at 6 days of age young chaffinches showed no fear of nest movement or of whistles. At 8 days the alarm call for a flying predator gave a begging response; by 12 days there was crest-raising, crouching and sleeking to any marked change in the environment; and by 18 days crouching, sleeking and scanning occurred to any strange or sudden movement. In his careful study of the curve-billed thrasher, Rand (1941) noted freezing at 6 days when removed from the nest, and slight shrinking to jarring of the nest at 7 days. Crouching in the nest or under cover had developed by 12 days. In the song-sparrow, studied by Nice (1943), cowering to a scream or loud hiss occurred at 7–9 days. At 9–10 days the nestlings responded to alarm and fear calls by 'freezing', 'cowering' or 'hiding'. Bill opening as in gaping sometimes accompanied these responses. Kuhlmann (1909), from his study of a number of passerines, concluded that after 1–3 days the first sign of 'fear', cessation of food begging, appeared and developed into a slight shrink or shiver (2–5 days) and into crouching with eyes closed (6–7 days). This development was dependent on the extent to which the stimulation differed from that provided by the parent alighting at the nest. For the first two days any sound gave the food begging response (cf. Tinbergen, 1951) and fear to nest-jarring and clucking sounds appeared last. By 8–10 days a hand waved over the nest also gave cessation of begging. From 10–12 days the response changed to alert watching, and from 12–17 days the nestlings were likely to jump out of the nest, run to cover and crouch ('hide'). It is clear that the development of inhibition, freezing and crouching follows a standard pattern in altricial birds and involves developing discrimination first of auditory and then of visual stimulation provided by the parents.

In altricial mammals specific studies of the ontogeny of this form of fear response are lacking. In the rat, Bolles & Woods (1964) observed freezing to a sudden noise at 23 days of age. Bronstein & Hirsch (1976) presented young rats with a caged domestic cat, a footshock, or a suddenly moving object and found that freezing was common at 30 days of age but not at 20 days. They note that this is about the age at which the young feral rat would first leave the burrow. In the cat, Fox (1970) saw freezing following auditory startle from 13 days. In dogs, Scott & Fuller (1965) noted that from 12 weeks of age puppies placed in a strange pen became quiet. Crouching when being weighed developed after 3 weeks and reached a peak at 5 weeks in Basenjis and 7 weeks in Cocker spaniels.

3.4   Visual Looming Response

The most elementary protective visual responses are eye-blink and flinching to a rapidly approaching object or to a rapidly expanding retinal image – the visual looming response. In prematurely hatched chicks, Fishman & Tallarico (1961a and b) failed to elicit eye-blink with a feigned poke at the eye but chicks, whether light- or dark-reared, three hours after hatching did show head and neck movements to an approaching object although not to an expanding fan presented to one eye. Schiff (1965) obtained flinching, crouching, turning and jumping or stepping back to a rapidly expanding shadow in 3- to 10-day chicks. He also obtained these responses in nine 1-day and nine 3-day dark-reared chicks. In younger chicks the head was pulled back and down, or they fell backwards, while the older chicks would step back or dart around in a circle. Salzen (1970) found that these flight responses appeared after one hour of undisturbed visual experience in day-old chicks. Schiff also tested kittens which showed weak responses at 26 days of age reared either with or without experience of approaching objects. Schiff, Caviness & Gibson (1962) had previously tested

5- to 8-month-old rhesus infants and obtained head ducking and jumping back comparable with adult responses. Scott & Fuller (1965) mention looming responses in dogs after 2 weeks of age. So the looming response seems to be an unlearned primary withdrawal response pattern appearing with functional vision.

3.5   Avoidance, Withdrawal, Flight and Escape

All these behaviours involve locomotion of the young animal away from the source of fear. The requirements are therefore functional distance receptors, locomotor ability, and the perceptual ability to differentiate sources of fear and sources of security or relative safety. Vision enables more precise orientation than sound but also involves more restricted scanning or attention. Thus in most vertebrates sound is the primary alerting stimulus and tends to give the less directed fear responses already described. Vision tends to mediate the active directed locomotory orientation movements of avoidance, withdrawal, flight and escape. In adults, locomotion is away from the fear source or situation and towards safety which may be open sites for fast moving species, hiding places for slow moving cryptic species, or social companions for group living species (cf. Eibl-Eibesfeldt, 1975; Markgren, 1960; Marler & Hamilton, 1966). It is clear, therefore, that these behaviours are polarised movements and so are inseparable from their opposites – approach, searching and sheltering. Flight may not occur if sources of safety are lacking or have never been established. Thus cage-reared gerbils described by Clark & Galef (1977) would approach a strange visual stimulus but after 24 hours of experience of a tunnel system they showed flight and concealment instead. In many instances, then, the development of fear and fear behaviour is inseparable from the development of security and security-seeking behaviour (cf. Bowlby, 1969, 1973). I have elsewhere described an orientation system which can operate in gradient fields of familiarity/unfamiliarity or danger/safety that can encompass these two related states and behaviour patterns (Salzen, 1978). The present treatment of avoidance and flight will be better appreciated in the light of this theoretical approach. In the sense used here *avoidance* involves a small turning movement with continued locomotion to give a path around a focal fear stimulus. *Withdrawal* involves moving back and away from the fear source, the degree of turning depending on the relationship between the fear and security sources in the perceptual field. *Flight* usually involves the highest degree of both turning (180°) and locomotion while still directed by the fear/security gradient fields. *Escape* tends to involve varied turning movements and locomotion in a poorly polarised situation; at lower intensity it might well be described as *searching*.

140

The ontogeny of these behaviours has been intensively studied in selected precocial birds. As early as 1873 Spalding conducted careful observations and experiments on newly hatched chicks and found that their initial response to moving objects was to approach and follow. He also noted fleeing and hiding at 1 week on first seeing a sparrow-hawk overhead. In 1899 Thorndike was studying newly hatched chicks and noting that they showed only momentary avoidance of objects thrown at them at 4–5 days, but would chirr, run and crouch for 5–10 seconds at 25 days of age. He decided that this latter behaviour developed from 10–20 days, and in the same period the chicks came to avoid open places. Jaynes (1957), while studying imprinting in chicks, noted that flight from a moving object was absent in the first 30 hours after hatching but had developed by 54–60 hours. Hess (1959b) studied the development of avoidance movements and distress calling to a sound-emitting imprinting object and found that these responses appeared at 13–16 hours and were universal by 33–36 hours after hatching. He also showed that the ability to locomote developed from 5–8 hours and that most chicks could move adequately by 21–24 hours. Thorndike's results of much later fear development are not to be discounted however, for Kruijt (1964), in his study of the ontogeny of behaviour of junglefowl, records that waving a hand or paper gave no withdrawal at 1 day, slight withdrawal at 2 days, and shrill calling at 3 days; but strong withdrawal did not appear until 1 week. However, Kruijt also commented that if the chicks were not used to the experimenter strong escape occurred at 3–4 days. He also claimed that isolated chicks showed fear of other chicks at 12 days. Clearly the nature of the test stimulus and situation in relation to the chick's experience is critical for the fear responses shown at any age and more systematic study is required. Such a study was provided by Schaller & Emlen (1962). They used varieties of domestic chick, pheasant, turkey, duckling and Chinese goose. The chicks were reared in isolation and tested in their rearing boxes by inserting a rod-mounted rectangular-shaped card which was moved systematically, or in a directed manner to the bird, or was held still. Schaller & Emlen were then able to plot the development of avoidance behaviour which they scaled to give a composite rating from zero to panic escape. Some repeated testing was involved, but in general in domestic chicks low avoidance (intent watching) appeared within 10 hours and developed into a peak response of flight by 50–80 hours and then increased again to escape behaviour at 100 hours. A similar pattern with similar responses and slightly different developmental rates held for the other precocial species studied. Escape behaviour after the third day was also seen in socially reared chicks by Guhl (1958). Bateson (1964a) also found that domestic chicks began avoiding a moving object after the first day of isolation rearing, with 80% showing initial avoidance behaviour at 2 days. In a cross-sectional study of

141

the first 5 days he found strongest initial avoidance at 5 days, but these chicks ceased avoiding after about 4 minutes and approach behaviour appeared about 8.5 minutes after testing. On the other hand at 3 days, when approach and following were strongest, approaching only began after 13 minutes because the preceding initial avoidance had lasted about 11 minutes. Thus, in terms of persistence, avoidance was greatest at 3 days. In ducklings fear seems to develop rapidly. In incubator-reared tufted ducklings escape from man occurs by 12–48 hours (Fabricius, 1951) and goldeneye ducklings show fear by 12–20 hours (Bjerke, T. & Bjerke, L. G., 1970). However Boyd & Fabricius (1965) describe avoidance to a moving object as occurring in all their mallard ducklings only after 80 hours. It is interesting to note here also that black-headed gull chicks showed running to cover by 4–7 days of age (Kirkman, 1937). It is clear that the full range of avoidance responses develops within the first week of life of precocial birds.

In precocial mammals similar rapid development of avoidance responses must occur but experimental evidence is scanty. Guinea pigs make short excursions from the homesite at 2 days of age and retreat to the parent or sibling can occur (cf. Rood, 1972). After 10 hours of experience of littermates and mother they may show withdrawal to man (cf. Harper, 1976). Yet in the laboratory young guinea pigs have been induced to follow a small moving object as late as 7 days of age (Sluckin, 1972). In the rhesus monkey, Harlow & Harlow (1965) have found that after 20 days infants reared with mother surrogates will flee from a strange mechanical 'animal' and cling to the 'mother'. Macaques in general may depart short distances (2 feet) from the mother after 1–3 days and are walking steadily by 2–4 weeks (Hinde, 1971). Retreat to the mother presumably develops in this period.

For altricial birds, Kuhlmann (1909), from a study of passerine young, concluded that flight and escape from the nest into cover was the culmination of fear development and was complete by 12–17 days. These responses occurred to the unusual and strange; so that the experience of the young bird during this period of development was important for the subsequent fear responsiveness. In the curve-billed thrasher studied by Rand (1941) fleeing to a rapidly approaching object first occurred at 17–18 days. Rand reared some birds in captivity and they showed a similar ontogeny of this fear response. He also noted that towards the 18th day they showed 'fits of wildness' (escape?) in their small cages. If taken from the nest at 15–16 days nestlings would feed from people, but if taken at 18 days they fled. Hand-reared birds tended to become shy at about 30 days and avoided man by 35 days. In the song sparrow (Nice, 1943) fleeing and escape appear at 10–17 days in response to movement in the immediate environment, threatened capture and rarely to sound. By three weeks of age fleeing is followed by freezing. Chaffinches can fly in escape by 15–23 days and great

142

tits by 30 days (Barraud, 1961). The grackle can flee the nest after 12 days and Schaller & Emlen (1961) experimented with blindfolding and with artificial objects to determine the responsiveness to visual stimuli. The experiments indicated that visual experience was necessary for parent recognition and discrimination to develop. Several days of pattern vision were needed before differential avoidance responses were obtained.

In altricial mammals the data again are somewhat limited. In the mouse, running in escape occurs at 11–12 days (Williams & Scott, 1953) just after the eyes open. A period follows (12–25 days) in which the young overreact to sounds, movements or shadows, making frantic dashes with hiding or intense freezing. There are also flurries of vigorous hopping and dashing – like exaggerated escape movements. Mutants of the kinky-tail type show maximum tail kinks at this 'hoppy stage' (15–25 days) and are extremely nervous, darting madly and jumping in the air at the slightest provocation. The kinks in the tail may disappear with further development but tend to reappear in the adult at times of excitement. Yerkes' waltzing mouse shows jerky movements preceding the development of startle responses by 1–2 days and leading to the 'hoppy stage'. Williams & Scott (1953) after discussing these data conclude 'The nature of this 'hoppy stage' suggests strong and uncontrolled emotional reactions which might be the result of an inability to discriminate between dangerous and harmless stimuli'. It is interesting that the deermouse shows a similar jumpiness from 15–20 days – again shortly after the eyes open (King, J. A., 1958). In one subspecies of deermouse (*Peromyscus maniculatus bairdii*) this response is maintained and becomes directed after 22 days. The subspecies *gracilis* is slower to mature and loses this nervousness if handled before 30 days of age. These two subspecies also show different tonic immobility responses in ontogeny which appear related to these differences in jumpiness. The white rats studied by Bolles & Woods (1964) oriented to sounds at 19–21 days, to vision by 14–18 days and ran towards anything novel for several weeks thereafter. Jumpiness appeared on day 14 and continued to day 20. Cringing and fleeing to opening of the cage door was seen to appear in the period 22–29 days. The cat develops escape running from 26 days of age according to Tilney & Casamajor (1924) and by 17 days according to Fox (1970) who also reports the defensive fear pattern of arching back, hair raising and hissing at this same time. Dogs showed escape and avoidance to humans at 5 weeks when reared in a field out of contact with man (Scott & Fuller, 1965). The period of 3–12 weeks seems to be one in which dogs develop social attachments (Scott, 1967) and, as in the case of precocial birds, avoidance to unfamiliar stimuli seems to follow closely the period in which the social partner is learned. In fact Scott finds that puppies begin to show fear of the strange at 7 weeks of age and this development is completed by 12 weeks.

143

Scott (1962) was early to point out the comparability of periods of socialisation in precocial birds (domestic chick) and mammals (rhesus monkey) and in altricial birds (song sparrow) and mammals (dog). In all four there seems to be a period of visual learning following eye-opening, which is succeeded by development of orientation responses away from stimuli not experienced in the socialisation period and towards familiar stimuli especially the social partner. This orientation behaviour is avoidance and fleeing from strange stimuli and approach and searching for familiar stimuli. Thus searching behaviour and its associated state of loss and insecurity may equally be regarded as fear since it is unsuccessful, blocked or thwarted orientation away from unfamiliar/dangerous stimulation and towards familiar/safe stimulus sources (cf. Bowlby, 1969, 1973; Scott & Senay, 1973; Davis, K. L., Gurski & Scott, 1977; Salzen, 1978).

4 Signalling Thwarting Responses

The fear responses of this third class can be understood as the results of the thwarting of aroused fear responses of the first two classes. Data on the ontogeny of these fearful signalling thwarting responses are fragmentary. An attempt will be made to consider some of the better studied behaviours. These are of three kinds – tonic immobility, distress calls and agonistic displays, where the latter includes both aggressive and submissive displays.

4.1 Tonic Immobility

The nature of this response in adult animals has been well reviewed by Gallup (1974, 1977) and its relationship to fear behaviour and state seems well attested. In an interesting contribution to the subject Ratner (1975) has made it clear that 'defensive immobility' or 'death feigning' is a response to *being held* by a predator. It is therefore a contact receptor response according to the present classification and occurs when normal withdrawal and struggling escape movements from strong contact stimulation have failed, i.e. it is a thwarting response. It is probably an ambivalent posture brought about by tonic action of both extensors and flexors involved in the struggling escape movements – hence tonic immobility is the appropriate term. It is distinct from inhibition and freezing behaviours which are distance receptor responses and are preparatory or intention movements of flight – hence the tendency to crouch in preparation for locomotory takeoff. The term 'immobility' is sometimes used to mean 'freezing' especially in open-field studies of emotionality. Vestal (1975) has given a good description of these two distinct behaviours for the deermouse.

144

The ontogeny of the tonic immobility response has been studied in a few species. In the domestic chick, Ratner & Thompson (1960) found that the response developed after 7 days, reached a maximum duration by 12 days, and was maintained at this level until 59 days of age. Salzen (1963) also got a strong response at 8 days in socially reared chicks. However a subsequent study by Rovee & Kleinman (1974) showed that the response could be obtained within 12 hours of hatching and increased in strength up to 10 days if the chicks were immobilised with the head down in a crouched position. The incidence of eye-closure followed the same development. Braud & Ginsberg (1973) also obtained responses from the first day by supporting the inverted chick in a cloth trough. Recently Prestrude (1977) has reported a somewhat shorter maturation period of 5 days. It is important to note that the immobility response in chicks is affected by the rearing conditions, and their relationships. Thus Salzen (1963) found that no isolate-reared chicks showed any strong (5 minute) immobility response by 14–16 days of age compared with 43% of socially reared chicks. A rearing/testing or familiar/unfamiliar testing environment effect has since been confirmed by Rovee & Luciano (1973), Rovee, Agnello & Smith (1973) and Ginsberg, Braud & Taylor (1974). A state of fear induced immediately before the holding treatment will also enhance tonic immobility (Gallup, 1977) and this has also been shown when escape responding has preceded the immobility response in bobwhite quail (Tortora & Borchelt, 1972). Borchelt & Ratner (1973) have followed the ontogeny of both tonic immobility and freezing in the latter species in response to handling and the visual presence of the experimenter respectively as the fear stimuli. The first strong responses appeared by 15 days with a medium duration of 60 seconds for tonic immobility and 10 seconds for freezing. Freezing was more common than immobility at 9–10 days and characteristically was ended by distress calling followed by locomotion. Immobility ended variably, either in locomotion or in escape but usually without calling. The same patterns of these two behaviours hold for the domestic chick.

A good ontogenetic study has also been made in the deermouse by Vestal (1975). In *Peromyscus maniculatus* the tonic immobility response developed from 13 to 20 days, i.e. 4–8 days after eye-opening. In *P. leucopus*, however, the response was present only in the period 3–5 days after eye-opening (days 15–18), although it is present in the adults. It is interesting that the 'jumpy' phase in *P. maniculatus* peaks at 15 days and that this phase does not occur in *P. leucopus*. A very different picture appears in rats. Svorad (1957) obtained a decline in response duration from 10 minutes at day 1 to zero at 15 days. Klemm (1971) describes a similar decline to a short duration response by 15 days with a further decline in susceptibility and duration to $3\frac{1}{2}$ weeks. More recently Prestrude (1977) has described a decline from a high incidence at 1

145

day to zero at 9 days in hooded rats and a similar decline in albinos following an initial rise from 1 to 3 days. Prestrude supposed this rise and fall indicated development of an immobility system followed by development of an inhibitory system. Klemm (1971) and Gallup (1974) have also discussed the possible interaction with an inhibitory system especially in mammals. However the occurrence of tonic immobility in adults seems to be typical of prey species — both bird and mammalian — rather than predator species (cf. Gilman & Marcuse, 1949; Ratner, 1967). The rat seems intermediate in that according to Klemm (1971) it shows immobility only in infancy and old age. Typically, then, in prey species immobility responses might be expected to develop, as in the chick or deermouse, early in infancy and to remain in the adult.

4.2   Distress Calls

Distress and fear vocalisations have been well studied in precocial birds, particularly in the domestic chick and the duckling for which they have been described by Collias & Joos (1952) and Rajecki & Eichenbaum (1973). In principle any change in contact stimulation from the pre-hatch condition precipitates struggling and distress calling (Collias, 1952; Salzen, 1962) in the newly hatched chick, so that the effective stimuli are usually cold and lack of body contact. As Collias (1952) showed, restoration of temperature and contact inhibits the distress calling. Temperature effects in distress calling have since been confirmed and studied in some detail (e.g. Fischer, 1970; Rajecki, Eichenbaum & Heilweil, 1973). Collias (1952) also showed that distance stimulation would also affect the distress calling of chicks. In particular it was reduced by clucking-hen sounds or by intermittent low-frequency sounds and also by the sight of moving objects. This has been studied in more detail subsequently (e.g. Fischer & Gilman, 1969; Fischer, 1972) for sounds and Rajecki et al. (1973) for intermittent visual stimulation. Rajecki (1974) has also shown that if chick embryos are stimulated by light or sound from 13 to 18 days of incubation the distress calling following hatching is significantly more effectively reduced by stimuli of the modality that was experienced before hatching. The role of experience in the control of distress calling was again clearly noted by Collias (1952), who found that social experience resulted in increased distress calling during subsequent periods of social isolation. Kaufman, I. C. & Hinde (1961) made a study of this and found that, when alone in a strange pen, socially reared chicks showed increased distress calling, especially at 3–6 days of age, while isolate-reared chicks showed no change in calling. Following this work Bermant (1963) showed that 7- to 9-day hen-reared chicks, when separated from the hen, reduced their distress calling on hearing, and especially on hearing and seeing, the hen. More recently Zajonc, Markus & Wilson (1974) have made a careful study of the distress calling given to objects of different degrees of familiarity and have confirmed that reduction of calling is related to the degree of familiarity of the object. Clearly, then, the ontogeny of distress calling cannot be considered without reference to the neonate's experience or even the embryonic experience. Thus Hess & Schaefer (1959) have shown that chick distress calling in response to a male mallard model which emitted a rhythmically spoken 'gock' sound developed in the period 13–32 hours. However, these chicks could hear each other in the incubator where they were kept and so Hess' curve for development of fear may simply represent the increasing discrimination of the 'gock' sound from chick vocalisations, i.e. represent a group learning curve. Unfortunately most of Hess' studies of imprinting (1973) have used vision and sound in testing while keeping the birds in visual isolation only and this may account for the well defined critical period which his work seems to indicate. The importance of controlling the auditory experience or of avoiding it in the imprinting situation is indeed well shown by Hess' own work on the natural vocal interactions between duck and foetal ducklings (Hess, 1973). Studies of distress calling by ducklings in an unfamiliar environment (Hoffman, Eiserer, Ratner & Pickering, 1974) also show how it can be stopped by presenting a moving object and subsequently come to be emitted whenever that object is absent. These results replicate those of numerous imprinting studies of domestic chicks and ducklings (cf. Hess, 1973). Gaioni, Hoffman, Klein & DePaulo (1977) have recently made the interesting finding that socially reared ducklings become accustomed to their group size and will distress call when the group is substantially reduced.

The character of distress calling as arising from thwarting of orientation behaviour is well shown by the work of Hoffman, Searle, Toffey & Kozma (1966). They trained 6- to 8-hour ducklings to key-peck to produce an imprinting object. Distress calling became rare when pecking was effective in this way. But when the key-peck was made inoperative (extinction procedure) the initial effect was to increase the key-pecking rate and only subsequently did this give place to distress calling. Of course thwarting can occur at any level of intensity of the aroused behaviour. The distress call of chicks is an intermediate level response. The highest level of fear call is the squawk of a hen held in the hand, for Collias & Joos (1952) have described the dropping frequencies near the end of the squawk as similar to those of the distress call. The lowest level of calling is the twitter or contentment call, as has been suggested by Andrew (1964) who considers that it is given to low levels of contrasting stimulation. Thus there is an intensity continuum of calling from the twitter, through distress peeping to squawking in response to

147

increasing change in stimulus novelty or unfamiliarity (cf. Salzen, 1970) Initial inhibition and freezing to intense stimulus change such as a loud noise or electric shock (Montevecchi, Gallup & Dunlop, 1973) or the open-field (Ginsburg, Braud & Taylor, 1974) is followed by distress calling and then by locomotory orientation as the degree of environmental unfamiliarity or stimulus contrast declines through adaptation. Candland, Nagy & Conklyn (1963) studied the ontogeny of distress calling in the open-field in chickens. All chicks distress called until 10 days of age but by 15 days few called and from 15–19 days the incidence remained below 20%. The incidence of freezing indicated fear during most of this period so the distress calling appears to be an infantile behaviour which is replaced by active locomotory searching in older birds.

In precocial mammals there seems no detailed study of infant fear calling. Rood (1972) mentions 'whistling' occurring in new-born guinea pigs and declining in frequency of occurrence in the following 4 weeks. Harper (1976) describes the 'whistle' as a separation call at 3 days of age. In the rhesus infant, Hinde, Rowell & Spencer-Booth (1964) recorded that 'geckering' occurred as a discomfort or insecurity call from the first day. Short high squeaking calls appeared in the next 3 weeks as an accompaniment to looking around and, on one occasion, on being dropped. A 'coo' or 'whoo' call accompanying a 'pout' face is seen in a number of primate infants in response to discomfort or temporary feeding frustration (cf. van Hooff, 1962) and appears to be distress calling. This distress pattern can reappear in adults but normally the frequency of coo vocalisations decreases with age (cf. Redican, 1975). A 'scream' call (Chevalier-Skolnikoff, 1974) may be higher intensity distress calling. Like chick distress calling, it brings the mother to the infant. Bernstein & Mason (1962), working with isolate rhesus infants, report that vocalisations were given to sudden movement, loss of support, or loss of contact from 0–2 months and that from 2–6 months there was a shift to vocalising to moving unfamiliar visual stimuli. So experience of distance stimulation determines fear responses of rhesus infants to objects. In the first 3 months unfamiliar objects produce, in the absence of a mother or mother surrogate (cf. Harlow & Harlow, 1965), fear vocalisations and crouching. After 3 months these responses are replaced by barks and withdrawal locomotion. Where the mother is present retreat and clinging to her occur as early as 20 days. Also, as in precocial birds, a stage in ontogeny is reached when separation from the familiar mother object leads to searching and 'coo' or 'whoo' calling and screaming (cf. Brandt, Baysinger & Mitchell, 1972; Hinde & Spencer-Booth, 1971; Salzen, 1978).

In altricial forms, where the young are confined to a nest until capable of independent movement and hiding, fear calling might be expected to be less evident. In birds, gaping for feeding is accompanied by vocalisations but the

148

fear response is a silent crouch. On leaving the nest the flight response takes the infant into silent crouching or hiding. However, Nice (1943) reports a location call appearing in the song sparrow from 9 days and a fear note appearing at 19–21 days. Vocalisations accompanying mobbing behaviour in passerines and its development will be considered as an agonistic display. Recently, too, attention has been given to high frequency (ultrasonic) calls made by newborn rodents. In the rat (Noirot, 1968; Okon, 1971; Allin & Banks, 1971; Oswalt & Meier, 1975; Nitschke, Bell, Bell & Zachman, 1975) the calls occur in the first 3 weeks with some variation in achieving maximal frequency and intensity (3–9 days to 11–13 days peak, according to strain, test temperature and experimenter). What is agreed is that they are given when the neonate is cold and the development mirrors the development of homoiothermy (Okon, 1971). They also occur to any touch or olfactory stimulation which differs from the customary input (Oswalt & Meier, 1975). Noirot (1972) has claimed that there are two types of call; one given to temperature loss elicits maternal approach, and the other given to touch (response to being stepped on) elicits maternal withdrawal. Bell (1974) has challenged this claim and suggested that there is a single call of two intensities. Similar calls have been recorded in mice (Okon, 1970a and b) also with strain differences over a 12-day period (Nitschke, Bell & Zachman, 1972). In the deermouse (Hart & King, 1966) the frequency of calling at a given temperature declines after 8–11 days in *Peromyscus maniculatus bairdii* and somewhat later, 11–15 days, in the *gracilis* subspecies; in either case this is 1–2 days before homoiothermy is complete. The squeak calls of the infant deermouse have a sonographic appearance (King, J. A., 1963) that is similar to the distress calls of chicks, and the isolation call of the infant squirrel monkey (Salzen, 1978). As in these species, when the infant deermouse is separated from the mother or nest, the distress or isolation calls elicit maternal retrieval responses. In the carnivores, infants in distress have characteristic calls. In the cat, Rosenblatt & Schneirla (1962) described loud high-pitched wails from kittens placed on a floor that was olfactorily strange. In dogs yelping to pain, cold and hunger occurs at birth and declines over 4 weeks (Scott & Fuller, 1965). There is a growth in calling in response to unfamiliar visual and auditory stimulation, as when isolated in a strange pen. This appears at 3–4 weeks, is fully developed at 6–7 weeks, and declines again from 8 to 12 weeks (Elliot & Scott, 1961). As in chicks and rhesus monkeys, distress calling is increased in the absence of the social partner and this is followed in ontogeny by fear of strangers and objects which appears after 7 weeks (Freedman, King & Elliot, 1961). Davis, Gurski & Scott (1977) have pointed out that puppies are den-living predators and their responses to focal fear stimuli tend to be avoidance or investigation rather than retreat to the mother. These workers have recently shown that tail-carriage in 6–8

149

week puppies reflects fear of an object while vocalisations reflect 'separation fear'. This is consistent with the obvious function of distress calling as a social isolation signal attracting the mother or the social partner to provide safety. It also highlights the point of the present approach to reviewing fear in young animals, i.e. of considering each type of fear response separately. As far as the ontogeny of infantile distress calling is concerned it seems that calling is primarily to loss of contact requirements, then to loss of the familiar distance-stimulation and especially the social partner (cf. Bronson, 1968b). Calling declines as locomotory and orientation ability develops but reappears subsequently in the older infant or adult when orientation behaviour fails to restore the familiar social world.

4.3 Agonistic Displays

The displays that will be considered here will be those understandable as blocked escape responses and as conflict between flight and approach. Aggressive displays are the most obvious but there are others such as marking displays (e.g. defecation), mobbing displays, and other 'predator' and 'social' fear displays. The defensive aggressive pattern in cats described by Leyhausen (1967a) is a good example of an agonistic signalling thwarting response. If, as Leyhausen believes, and some ethological studies indicate (cf. Eibl-Eibesfeldt, 1975), aggression is a behaviour pattern in its own right, then its occurrence as a thwarting response could be classed as a displacement behaviour. It is possible, however, that defensive aggression is peculiar to thwarted escape and there is some evidence that it appears earlier in ontogeny than offensive aggression. This consideration of the ontogeny of fearful aggression may be put in the context of the recent review of aggression and fear by Archer (1976a). Where defensive aggression results from approach/withdrawal conflict, it should be in response to a narrow range in the familiarity/unfamiliarity stimulus dimension. The same should be true for other conflict displays. The occurrence and nature of such agonistic displays in ontogeny has not been systematically studied and the following review can only be fragmentary.

Early aggressive responses have received some study in precocial birds. Both Guhl (1958) for the domestic chick and Kruijt (1964) for the junglefowl describe aggression and fighting as developing from frolicking (1st week) and hopping movements which lead to sparring (2nd week), to which pecking and kicking are added after the 3rd week. Yet Miller, D. E. (1966), in a well controlled study of the response of isolate and social chicks to a moving object, observed aggressive responses as early as the 1st day with a peak at 35–38 hours in isolates. The response was rare in socials and in both types of

150

chick the aggressive pecking tended to accompany approach responses given immediately following a period of escape behaviour. It also occurred in chicks that were late in showing initial approach responses to a moving object. This has also been reported in imprinting exposure of chicks by Bateson (1964a), and Fabricius (1962) had earlier commented on the aggressive responses of mallard ducklings to small imprinting objects. Evans, R. M. (1970) looked at aggressive behaviour in chicks from $\frac{1}{2}$ to $4\frac{1}{2}$ days in response to a small moving object. Initial threat was clearly present at $1\frac{1}{2}$ days and increased thereafter. Both threat and aggressive pecking declined with repeated presentation of the object, as did withdrawal responses, but nonaggressive exploratory pecking increased. Evans thought that social experience must similarly reduce the aggressive responses and that this could account for the later development of fighting in social chicks. However, this later aggression may be offensive and not conflict aggression. More recently Rajecki, Ivins & Rein (1976) have studied the early vigorous pecking in chicks and shown that it occurs as early as the 1st day in social groups, is increased to strange chicks added to the groups, and is much more frequent and exaggerated in isolates. This pecking is accompanied by distress calling and so Rajecki et al. argue that it cannot be exploratory pecking which is incompatible with fear. In a previous review of approach behaviour development I have suggested (1978) that exploration of novel stimuli could be fearful approach. The results of Evans, R. M. (1970), who clearly distinguished between aggressive and exploratory pecking, are consistent with the view that aggressive pecking is a conflict response at the change-point from withdrawal to approach and the succeeding exploratory pecking is low-level fearful approach behaviour. There is comparable evidence for ducklings. Hoffman & Boskoff (1972) showed that imprinted isolate ducklings would 'attack', i.e. peck vigorously, at a socially reared duckling presented along with their imprinting object but in the absence of the object they would flee and distress call. In a further study Hoffman, Ratner, Eiserer & Grossman (1974) went on to show that previously imprinted ducklings would respond to a new moving object showing first escape, then aggressive pecking and finally following. The amount of aggressive pecking of 2-day and 5-day birds was determined with or without their imprinting object present. The younger birds were less aggressive with their imprinting object present and showed more approach to the new object (i.e. fear below aggressive threshold) while the older birds showed more aggression (i.e. fear below escape level but in aggressive range). Hoffman et al. argue that their data fit the view that aggression appears at lower levels of fear than escape. In the same study aggressive behaviour was greatly enhanced when the 5-day ducklings were confined close to a new object. This would support a conflict/thwarting explanation of the aggression.

151

Further fearful conflict displays are shown by chicks in their feeding behaviour. Hogan (1965) has studied the chick's feeding responses to mealworms and his results can be analysed in terms of thwarting responses. Thus he was able to show that the approach to a mealworm is checked by a tendency to withdraw from the novel stimulus, so that the chick stops and fixates and may then show head shaking or sleep (displacement and neurotic inactivity). Hogan in discussing his results recognises fear responses to the whole situation (inhibition and shrill calling) but does not regard withdrawal from the focal stimulus (mealworm) as a fear response. This leads him to a special definition of fear and a rejection of an approach/withdrawal conflict interpretation. When the chick picks up the mealworm (Hogan, 1966) it shows 'food-running' (Kruijt, 1964). Hogan's data can be understood if 'food-running' is in fact 'flight' behaviour that has been in conflict with food approach. This conflict is ended when the mealworm is seized; approach ceases and the residual thwarted flight tendency is released. Experience might well result in increased food-running, because the seizing becomes a conditioned operant for the flight behaviour. The food-running behaviour occurs as early as the 2nd day in junglefowl according to Kruijt (1964). Finally it is worth noting that chicks show elimination following inhibition and freezing and during the subsequent searching locomotion. Candland & Nagy (1969) have reviewed their studies of open-field elimination (autonomic thwarting response) during ontogeny and in the chicken elimination frequency rose to a maximal level by 15 days and was maintained to the end of testing.

Studies of primate infants have given some data comparable with those for the chick (Salzen, 1967), especially showing how isolation rearing may result in abnormally aggressive behaviour when subsequently placed in a social environment (cf. Mitchell, 1970). McCulloch & Haslerud (1939) reported avoidance and some aggression by their isolate-reared chimpanzee, especially to moving objects, at 7 months of age. At 15 months there was more aggression especially to objects that gave moderate levels of avoidance. They concluded '. . . aggression tends to occur when there is approximate balance between tendency to approach food and tendency for an incompatible activity when that activity is avoidance'. In a study of macaque responses to food with a strange object present, P. C. Green (1965) found that feral juveniles ($1\frac{1}{2}$–2 years) would threat-bark especially to the more realistic 'animal' or 'animal part' objects, as well as approach or crouch and screech. Dark-reared ones were indifferent to the objects and isolates simply crouched. In a study of isolate-reared rhesus exposed to various 'animal' objects Bernstein & Mason (1962) also got fear grimaces, barks, lipsmacking and ear retracting (mixtures of fear and attack patterns) in juveniles 3 months to 2 years of age. Hinde, Rowell & Spencer-Booth (1964) record the appearance of lipsmacking in alarm at 6 weeks in the rhesus, and the fear grimace (intention protective face cf. Andrew, 1972a) at 10–22 weeks. Redican (1975) in reviewing the ontogeny of facial expressions in primates puts the first grimace at 2–3 months for rhesus. The first signs of threat (composites of attack and protective faces cf. van Hooff, 1962) were seen by Hinde et al. no earlier than 5 months in their rhesus colony. The observational evidence (Redican, 1975) is that the infant has to learn the significance of adult aggressive social signals (cf. Leyhausen, 1967a, who makes a similar point), although Sackett (1966, 1973) has claimed that his isolate-reared rhesus infants showed disturbance behaviour (fear-rocking, huddling and withdrawal) to projected pictures of threatening monkeys from 2.5 to 4 months of age and also showed a lower operant rate for obtaining these pictures. These threat pictures elicited play and climbing-up before and after the 'disturbed' period, as did also pictures of infants. Although isolate-reared monkeys may develop species fearful threat and aggressive patterns they are inappropriately directed and controlled and may occur to their own body parts (cf. Redican, 1974; Mitchell, 1970). Similar results have been described in the chicken by Kruijt (1964).

In altricial birds the best studied fearful agonistic display is the 'mobbing' response, a conflict of approach and flight. The adult behaviour has been well studied by Markgren (1960), Nice (1943), Hinde (1954, 1970) and more recently by Curio (1975). In the curve-billed thrasher, Rand (1941) described a stereotyped 'snake display' not unlike a mobbing display. It appeared at 24–30 days and was given to a variety of animals and objects that seemed to have in common features of size, movement and strangeness or incongruity, all very evident in snakes. In the chaffinch, mobbing appears from 30 days while offensive intragroup aggressive threat and chasing appear later at 47 days (Barraud, 1961). In the pied flycatcher the first sign of the response is at 5 weeks (Curio, 1975) and it seems that novel stimuli as well as specific predators can elicit the behaviour. In many respects these mobbing displays have the properties of Protean displays (Chance & Russell, 1959; Driver & Humphries, 1970). Somewhat similar behaviour to 'mobbing' is described by Myrberg (1965) in juvenile African cichlids. The interesting point, however, is that these fish become pale grey and the eyes fully black and this is a sign of 'fright'. Small novel objects produce approach without this 'fright' pattern. When chased by a predator the juveniles show a slow jerky swimming movement suggesting a conflict state and producing a Protean type of display.

In altricial mammals data are not readily available. Candland & Nagy (1969) describe the development of defecation in open-field tests of rats and mice. In rats (Candland & Campbell, 1962) there is an increase from 18 days to an asymptote frequency at 40–50 days which is unchanged in the oldest tested at 200 days. A similar increase is shown by mice from 18–21 days to an asymptote at 30 days with relatively little change to 100–103 days. Richardson (1942) has described the development of an interesting conflict display of 'foot thumping' to snakes in the wood rat. For the first 5 days after eye-opening young wood rats treated snakes as inanimate objects. After 9 days they simply squeaked when struck by snakes. The first alarm thump occurred at 26 days (11 days after eye-opening). It occurred in older young without previous experience of snakes; and movement, sound and odour of the snake were required. Defensive biting and paw raising appear in mice by 12 days of age (Scott, 1958). Affective defence in cats (back arching, pilo-erection and hissing) appears at 17 days (Fox, 1970) and may occur to sudden stimulation. Kolb & Nonneman (1975) were able to elicit the same response with a two-dimensional black-and-white cat model from 6- to 8-week kittens. In dogs agonistic reactions to handling develop at 5–15 weeks and a tendency to attack strangers also appears in this period; but social aggression begins slightly later at 7 weeks and its relation to defensive aggression is unclear. Urine marking, another possible autonomic conflict response, in dogs starts at 5–8 months. It is clear from this fragmentary account that specific studies of fear responses in the ontogeny of vertebrates are needed.

5 Maturation and Fear

It is evident from the foregoing analysis and review of the ontogeny of fear behaviour that maturing receptor and effector systems increase the intensity and variety of fear responses. It is not clear whether there is a maturing fear state system contributing to this development. Experimental studies of domestic chicks and ducklings provide some of the evidence on this question of the maturation of fear. In ducklings, fear development appears to involve a complex interaction with experience. Thus Moltz and Stettner (1961) reared their ducklings in nonpatterned diffuse light and got less avoidance of a silent moving object at 1 to 3 days than in light-reared isolates. Asdourian (1967) also found that ducklings could show approach and attachment to a silent moving object after 18 days especially if subjected to extended social isolation or darkness. R. T. Brown (1975) has reported similar findings for isolate-reared ducklings from 1–5 days old although there was a tendency for longer latencies to respond positively owing to initial crouching and avoidance of the silent moving object. More recently Weiss, J., Köhler & Landsberg (1977) have found that there is a corticosterone increase in Pekin ducklings 12–28 hours after hatching and they have suggested that this may be the basis of any increase in fear. Landsberg & Weiss (1976) have also claimed that the corticosterone level can be raised by cold stress or by ACTH (adrenocorticotrophic hormone) injections followed by exposure to a moving calling object. In either case the birds fail to show discrimination of the object in subsequent tests. Clearly there seems to be an experiential effect on the corticosterone release and Landsberg & Weiss estimate the age contribution at only 8%. This also seems consistent with the isolate and experiential deprivation studies previously cited.

Experimental studies of imprinting in domestic chicks have noted fear responses to moving objects becoming strong at 3–5 days whether reared socially, e.g. Jaynes (1957), or in the dark, e.g. Spalding (1873). Spalding reared chicks with translucent or opaque hoods or with their ears sealed. When unhooded at 4 days three chicks showed fleeing from him to a window or into hiding. Spalding declared that a day earlier these chicks would have shown approach to him. P. H. Gray, (1962) has since replicated Spalding's hooding experiment and found that at 5 and 6 days half his unhooded chicks ran away from him into a window. He was able to show that if an overhead light was used and there was no window, directed fleeing did not occur. This is a good example of the role of a polarised environment in directed flight responses. P. H. Gray & Howard (1957) also noticed a fearfulness or 'flightiness' both in 4-day chicks taken from a dark incubator and in ones imprinted to the experimenters. However, Guiton & Sluckin (1969) found that after 24 hours dark-reared chicks showed less calling and avoidance of a silent moving object than did light-reared isolates. Fujita & Hara (1971) have also reported reduced fear responses in open-field testing of 4-day dark-reared isolate chicks. These dark-rearing studies seem to disagree with those of Spalding and Gray. In the study of the ontogeny of fear responses of isolate chicks to an intruding moving object by Schaller & Emlen (1962) the three groups that were reared in darkness for 1–3 days showed the same level of fear responding as the light-reared isolates and this suggests a maturation effect. However these birds became hyperresponsive for 2–3 days after their initial testing at 1 and 2 days respectively and this suggests a puzzling experiential interaction since it was not shown in the group tested first at 3 days. However the evidence of initial fear responding would support the claims of Spalding and Gray and indicate a maturation of fear responses with a possible early peak at 4–5 days. Schaller & Emlen also allowed some of their isolates to view the laboratory and these birds had somewhat reduced levels of fear after 5 days. Simple social isolation-rearing does not stop fear developing to silent moving objects within 35–38 hours according to D. E. Miller, (1966). Miller also found that socially reared birds were earlier in this respect (30–38 hours) and that if the object made tapping sounds the avoidance changed to approach, suggesting that visual experience had contributed to the fear development. Earlier Guiton (1958) had noted that although 3–day isolate chicks would show approach behaviour to a moving object they would start 'nervous', even in a state of 'acute terror'. In contrast some socially reared chicks showed no initial fear. This later fear in isolates could have been stronger simply because a moving object was totally novel to them, unlike socials who had seen different but nonetheless moving bodies. Salzen (1962) also noted initial fear responses in isolate-reared chicks exposed to a silent moving object at 3 days, although they soon began to show approach responses. In another specific study of fear development in chicks (Phillips & Siegel, 1966) two lines of white Plymouth rocks were tested with a sudden loud sound (bell) in an open-field, and subsequently with an approaching hand. In one genetic line the isolates and socials had a similar running response with maximum responses at 2–4 days. In the other genetic line the isolates had a running response which peaked over 2–5 days while the socials showed a steady increase in their running response. These data imply a maturation interacting with experience. The general picture of fear development in chicks is thus one of freezing, flight and escape behaviour developing to a high level by 3–5 days in isolates and possibly earlier in socials. Guhl (1958) in a description of social development in domestic chicks records the emergence of frolicking by the end of the first week. This frolicking also suggests a maturation of excitability. Bateson (1964b) checked the general activity of his chicks to compare with their responses to moving objects and he found a minimum at 5 days. However Broom (1968) found a maximum in activity at 6 days but related it to feeding activity and the chick's use of its food reserves. So there is no evidence of a general increase in motor excitability to explain fear development in chicks. There is some evidence for nonspecific visual facilitation of some behaviours however. Simon (1954) has shown that nonspecific patterned visual experience is necessary for the development of some optomotor responses in chicks. Vince & Chinn (1972) have also shown that light stimulation both before and after hatching speeds the development of standing and walking.

Precocial mammals have a similar initial period of approach responses mediated by distance receptors with the development of avoidant fear responses following. There is no evidence for any physiological maturation rather than an experiential basis for this development. Campbell & Mabry (1972) found no activity changes in guinea pigs over the period 5–100 days. Harper (1976) has cited reports that the young guinea pig is hopping within 1 hour and leaping within 12 hours postpartum. It is a commonplace that young ungulates go through a 'frisky' period such as the 'gambolling' of lambs. Interestingly, Hinde, Rowell & Spencer-Booth (1964) describe 'gambolling' appearing in the 7th week of development of rhesus infants, or even as early as 3–4 weeks.

156

In altricial birds the overall description of fear ontogeny given by Kuhlmann (1909) for passerines remains valid, i.e. first cessation of food begging, then alert watching and finally panic flight and escape followed by crouching and freezing. Schaller & Emlen (1961) have shown that this development depends on the maturation of vision but only because it allows appropriate experience. They isolated young grackles for 1–2 days before eye-opening and found that the appearance of crouching was delayed by the same time. By blindfolding nestlings they showed that crouching to nest-jarring appeared normally while visual discrimination was delayed for at least 24 hours after release from blindfolding. This change in visual responses, whether through maturation or learning, must be rapid, for Rand (1941) also found that curve-billed thrashers taken from their nest at 15–16 hours would take food from people but if taken at 18 hours they would flee. Clearly visual experience is necessary for avoidance of novelty but the sensory and motor development must be appropriate. It is not clear whether there is a maturation of excitability or activity in altricial birds although Rand (1941) did notice that his caged birds showed 'fits of wildness' by 18 days. Such a peak of excitability would certainly result in fleeing the nest to even moderate stimulation.

In altricial mammals the evidence already reviewed suggests that withdrawal and flight responses develop within a short period following eye-opening. This suggests an interaction of maturation and experience. There is some evidence of a phase of heightened excitability following this period which, of course, could be the consequence of the experience itself. In the deermouse the period of 'jumpiness' peaks at 15–20 days (King, J. A., 1958), in the mouse between 10 and 26 days (Williams & Scott, 1953) or 8–28 days for 'overgeneralised emotional reactions' (Fox, 1965). Bolles & Woods (1964) noted a hyperactivity in rats at 17–20 days and Baenninger (1967) describes running and jumping at 18–36 days. Randall & Campbell (1976) note that despite a series of earlier studies showing a peak in activity of rats and mice at about 15 days, when such measures are taken in the home nest or in the presence of siblings or anaesthetised adults no such peak occurs; rather there is steady rise in activity after 15 days. In the Siamese cat, Meier & Stuart (1959) found that kittens showed 'spiraling' or 'spinning' behaviour when being photographed at the end of the first month. Kittens that had been handled daily did not show this, so it too is probably an experiential effect. In dogs the only comparable phenomenon is the failure of field-reared puppies to respond positively to man after 14 weeks (cf. Scott & Fuller, 1965). Fentress (1967) noticed that his home-reared wolf became especially 'nervous' at 20 weeks. But in both dog and wolf experiential effects cannot be excluded.

Until the 1976 paper (Randall & Campbell, 1976) Campbell and coworkers were giving serious consideration to the role of the development of cortical inhibition in ending the rising excitability of developing brain-stem systems. They identified serotonin and acetylcholine systems in this inhibition. Other physiological hypotheses have involved the development of adrenocorticotrophic activity in developing fearfulness and emotionality. Bousfield & Orbison (1952) noted that adrenal growth and adrenal levels in human infants may parallel emotional development. It is interesting to note that Meier & Stuart's handled Siamese kittens showed earlier pigment development. Pigmentation and emotionality have been correlated for a number of mammals by Keeler (1947). Fuller (1967a) has suggested that albino mice appear to be more stressed than pigmented ones in testing procedures and that their deficiency in tyrosinase might mean different catecholamine levels in the brain. In the cichlid fish studied by Myrberg (1965) juveniles showed pigment changes i.e. went pale, in response to a large predator and only recovered on its removal. Certainly in adult rats there is evidence that adrenalin can improve avoidance learning (Latané & Schachter, 1962) and increase avoidance of unfamiliar stimuli (Leventhal & Killackey, 1968). The corticosteroids could also be involved in view of the effects of handling and early stress on emotionality in rodents (cf. Levine, 1970; Denenberg & Zarrow, 1971). Weiss, J. M., McEwen, Silva & Kalkut (1969) found that adrenalectomised rats showed more passive avoidance, i.e. 'inhibition'-type fear responding. It may be significant that according to Moog (1959) the maximum relative size of the rat adrenal cortex is reached at 18 days and there is heightened secretion from 10 days peaking at 18 days. But the early stress and handling studies in rodents indicate an interaction between experience and the developing adrenocortico-pituitary system.

It would seem that fear orientation behaviour develops from embryonic withdrawal and swimming movements into juvenile locomotory running and turning in oriented stimulus fields, and into inhibition and crouching to unlocalised stimuli or undifferentiated stimulus fields. At the same time the effective stimulation changes from somaesthetic and taste, through olfaction and auditory to visual as these receptor systems mature and come into operation. Experience of stimulation may affect this development through physiological mechanisms such as the adrenocortical system (cf. Levine, 1970; Zarrow, Philpott, Denenberg & O'Connor, 1968) but the development cannot be stopped. The major effects of experience however are via the elicitation and performance of the orientation responses and these will now be considered.

6 Experience and Fear

Some fear responses seem independent of experience in that they occur to intense stimulation (cf. Schneirla, 1965). The work of Ewert (1970, 1974) and Ingle (1976) has shown how size, brightness and velocity of objects can determine feeding or flight responses in amphibia and how separate brain mechanisms may be involved. In newly hatched chicks it is difficult to arouse any withdrawal to visual stimulation apart perhaps from looming (Salzen, 1970). Loud sounds may produce inhibition or crouching (Kruijt, 1964) especially if of long duration and low frequency (Collias, 1952). There is some evidence of an optimal range of stimulation, both sound (taps and tones, Fischer, 1972, and Fischer & Gilman, 1969; clucking, Evans, R. M., 1975) and visual (flicker, Simner, 1976; size, Smith, F. V., 1962, and Schulman, Hale & Graves, 1970) for approach behaviour. There is now considerable evidence that the late embryo or foetus is responsive to auditory and visual stimulation and that the stimulation experienced may affect the 'optimal' or preferred stimuli for approach behaviour of the neonate. This evidence has been reviewed in detail by Gottlieb (1971b, 1973), Impekoven & Gold (1973), Impekoven (1976a) and Hess (1973). The character of such optimal stimulation may well affect the range of stimulation that will elicit fear responses in the neonate. In the case of sounds Impekoven & Gold (1973) have some evidence that in the laughing gull parental calls may directly affect embryonic movements, with the 'crooning' nest-relief call increasing motility. In another paper, Impekoven (1976b) reported that in day-old gull chicks both the 'uk-uk' and 'kow' alarm calls give freezing and crouching. If the embryos are regularly exposed to the 'kow' call, the chicks show somewhat less inhibition or freezing to this call. Interestingly, incubator-hatched chicks, to whom the 'crooning' call is novel, developed increasing mobility. In another paper, Impekoven (1976b) reported that in young birds and mammals to alarm calls may involve elementary intrinsically effective stimulus qualities such as intensity and frequency. Alley & Boyd (1950) felt that any loud harsh call gave the concealment response in young coots and Collias (1952) and Kruijt (1964) found that similar stimuli gave inhibition and freezing in day-old domestic chicks or junglefowl. Heinz (1973) found the same for pheasants 10–20 hours old but white noise did not produce a response. In the turkey, Hale & Schein (1962) have described a segmented alarm call to potential ground predators which elicits slow dispersal of young, and a flying predator call which at its lower pitch elicits running for cover (see also Collias, 1960, for other specific alarm calls). These responses occur from 2 weeks of age, but by 8 weeks they have given place to attentive responses to the source of the alarm. In a study of the cease-begging response to alarm calls in great tits, Ryden (1972, 1973, 1974a and b) showed that this response developed after 10 days and that it could not be attributed to the infrequency of such an intense call or to its conditioning to predator attacks. Exposing 11- to 14-day-old nestlings to intermittent alarm calls for 2 hours did not prevent the fear response developing. Although conditioning to feeding, to the absence of parents, or to predator attacks did affect the response, the effects were only temporary. The probability that alarm calls function because of their intrinsic stimulus quality cannot be dismissed.

In the case of prenatal light experience it is possible that neonatal orientation movements would be affected so that comparable or contrasting stimulation would elicit approach or avoidance respectively. Dimond (1968) reported that illumination of eggs resulted in 36-hour domestic chicks showing more freezing and avoidance to a moving object than did dark-incubated chicks. Unfortunately Adam & Dimond (1971) subsequently found the opposite, for chicks from eggs illuminated late in incubation (19 days) were less fearful (less freezing and less intense distress calls) than chicks from eggs illuminated at 15 or 17 days when tested in the presence of a rotating black/white disc. Rajecki (1974) has found that after intermittent light exposure at 13–18 days of incubation similar stimulation or a moving object produced reduced distress calling in the chicks compared with controls. But there is little evidence of fear responses to specific visual stimuli in the neonate. Guyomarch (1974) has recorded alarm trills in 2-day chicks in response to a hawk silhouette moved above them. The hawk/goose silhouette differential fear effect (Tinbergen, 1951, 1957) was not obtained by Hirsch, Lindley & Tolman (1955) or by McNiven (1960) for young chickens, ducks or pheasants. It has been explained as a stimulus intensity difference by Schneirla (1965). This has been challenged by Green, M., Green & Carr (1966) and a specific effect claimed for naive mallard ducklings. Martin & Melvin (1964) found that a real hawk was distinguished from a silhouette by adult bobwhite quail. Melzack, Penick & Beckett (1959) have also obtained some evidence in favour of at least an initial stronger effect from a hawk silhouette in young mallards. Later Melzack (1961) noted that after many presentations the responses remained as attentive orientations which could be selective for a particular model but according to where the model was presented (i.e. to the hawk above but to the goose at a lower angle) rather than simply to the hawk shape. Schleidt (1961) concluded that in 11-week turkeys the critical stimulus aspects were relative speed and size interacting with relative amount of previous experience.

For visually elicited fear responses then, the influence of experience largely begins when the neonate begins to view its environment. The function of auditory responsiveness, whether through prenatal or previsual experience or intrinsic character, is to direct this visual experience. This early visual

160

experience establishes the neonate's social and physical environmental norms, (cf. Salzen 1962, 1970, 1978). This has been elegantly demonstrated by Broom (1969a) who kept domestic chicks in isolation and observed their responses to changes in the customary illumination of the cage and of a small light-bulb fitted in each cage. Fear responses of freezing, distress calling and escape jumping developed over the tests at 2, 6 and 10 days of age. Broom (1969b) went on to show that at 6 days chicks that had been reared with a moving object or with a mirror in their cages reacted to illumination of their light-bulb with less distress calling and freezing than chicks with experience only of stationary objects. This may have been due either to the visual change being less unfamiliar in the chicks with experience of independently changing visual images or to the availability of the alternative fear response of fleeing to the familiar object or mirror. However, these visually experienced birds also resumed their normal activities more quickly, so there is evidence of less intense effects of the stimulus change. The retreat to the familiar focal object, by restoring the familiar environment, necessarily ends fearful orientation behaviour and consequently the fear state. This operates in open-field tests where a familiar object is present and Candland, Nagy & Conklyn (1963) showed that chicks reared socially or with manipulable objects would go to a chick or object in the open-field and were less emotional, showing less freezing and less elimination than isolates. Rubel (1970) has demonstrated that exposing quail to an imprinting stimulus at 5–9 hours resulted in less distress calling and escape to the same stimulus at 36 and 48 hours than if first exposed at 10–14 hours. This supports the view that the first visual experiences are establishing perceptual 'norms' for the individual. In establishing these visual norms or environmental models the distinction between static and independently moving objects is important (cf. Salzen, 1962, 1970) and is often overlooked when studying the responses of chicks in test situations. I have suggested that there may be a special system for modelling animate stimuli, distinct from that for the static environment (Salzen, 1970). At very least it will differ in involving movement detectors of the visual system (cf. Tolhurst, 1973). This could explain why ducklings imprinted by Hoffman & Ratner (1973) passed through a stage where a familiar and a strange object would be treated differently when static yet not so discriminated when in motion. These ducklings had yet to refine the model of their familiar object in motion. The special nature of the moving species partner as a potent provider of distance and contact stimulation is also indicated by its power to reduce fear responses elicited by strange static focal stimuli or unlocalised stimuli, e.g. electric shock in rats (Morrison & Hill, 1967) and ducklings (Moltz, Rosenblum & Halikas, 1959), or novel environment or object in chicks (Candland, Nagy & Conklyn, 1963), ducklings (Stettner & Tilds, 1966), rats (Thompson & McElroy, 1962), dogs

(Scott & Fuller, 1965) and rhesus monkeys (Mason, 1960). Fear responses may also occur to differences between the test situation and the home environment (cf. Bateson, 1964c) and separately to the moving objects in the test in comparison with the familiar moving social partner. R. T. Brown & Hamilton (1977) have recently taken up this point and shown the effects of rearing compared with testing situations on the responses of chicks to their familiar imprinting object. Of course novelty of environment is extreme in isolate-reared young when taken into testing situations which are usually more complex (cf. Fuller, 1967b). Where moving objects are also encountered a second and wholly new class of stimulus is involved, for isolates have no experience of independently moving objects. The more established and restricted the neonate's familiar environment, both social and physical, the less likely that foreign stimuli will be treated as 'novel', i.e. psychologically mildly different, rather than 'strange', i.e. psychologically grossly different. Thus restricted isolation rearing will induce gross fearfulness while varied social rearing in 'complex' environments will predispose to exploratory and investigatory responses to foreign stimuli. The former seems to be the case for isolate-reared chickens (Kruijt, 1964), cats (Konrad & Bagshaw, 1970), dogs (Fuller, 1967b; Fuller & Clark, 1966), rhesus monkeys (Sackett & Ruppenthal, 1973; Salzen, 1978) and chimpanzees (Menzel, Davenport & Rogers, 1963a and b); see also Konrad & Melzack (1975) for a recent review.

In his review of the fear of novelty, Bronson (1968a) marshalled some of the evidence for the development of fear in response to novelty in birds and mammals. He has indicated how such novelty is dependent on previous familiarisation processes and concludes that the ontogeny from immobility to retreat and to aggression is a function of endogenous changes as well as the quality of experience. The present review indicates that the early appearance of inhibition and freezing seems to be associated with the early auditory responsiveness and unlocalised stimulation. Retreat seems to appear along with visual responsiveness and localised differential stimulation. The later development of aggression could be associated with endogenous changes such as the development of nonfearful offensive aggression and perhaps increased androgen levels. However the early occurrences of aggression are probably associated with conflict states of approach and withdrawal, and the change from retreat to aggression is a result of experience reducing the stimulus novelty to a level that leads to approach responding. Evidence has also been cited in the present review suggesting a possible peak of excitability, emotionality or fearful responsiveness in both bird and mammals. This too suggests endogenous changes especially in view of the differences in the ontogeny of this behaviour state between genetic forms of mouse already described and discussed. However, this period of hyperexcitability also

162

seems to occur a short time after visual experience of the environment has begun, i.e. after birth in precocial and after eye-opening in altricial forms, and when locomotory activity brings the neonate into a wider field of experience in which novelty can be encountered. An experiential explanation then is that the neonate learns its limited local environment when visually capable (the imprinting phase); further experience in a larger environment (spatially and temporally) will bring new stimulation which is responded to as strange (the excitable phase) until it too becomes incorporated in the neonate's familiar perceptual world (the juvenile sophisticate).

CHAPTER 6

The Ontogeny of Fear in Children

Peter K. Smith

This chapter will review the research on fear and its development in infants and young children up to about the middle school years. Research in this area has been most intensive with very young children. We can now say quite a lot about how fear develops in babies in the first year or so of life. There is also considerable research material on fear in preschool children, aged say 2–4 years. Some of the research on babies and preschool children has been laboratory work, using carefully controlled conditions, but there have also been observations of fairly natural behaviour in the homes of young children. A considerable variety of methods and measures have been used. For older school-age children the picture is different. Generally, research has been by questionnaire, and the detailed observational and experimental procedures used with younger age groups have not often been carried out.

Mention of the different measures used as indices of fear raises the question of what we count as fear and what we do not. There is no generally accepted answer to this. Indeed, so far as terminology is concerned, it is tempting to say there is generally accepted confusion!

Fear, like other emotions, can be taken to be an internal state of the organism, but this must be operationalised into some kind of observable act or response for investigation and research to proceed. The most usual class of observables are avoidance or withdrawal behaviours, or freezing and perhaps inhibition of approach. Such behaviours suggest a perception of a potentially or actually dangerous situation that could cause harm, together with an attempt to avoid it. Some behaviours seem to serve more as signals to others rather than direct coping responses – crying in babies, for example. Gaze aversion is a behaviour which may have both a direct coping function as an avoidance behaviour (cutting off an over-arousing stimulus) and also a signalling function (of appeasement, or desire not to interact).

Besides directly observable acts, indirectly observable behaviours such as physiological responses have been used. For example, heart rate (HR) has been monitored in babies, and heart acceleration used as a possible fear index.

Finally, with older children it is possible to ask them directly what they are afraid of – the interview or questionnaire approach.

All these methods have difficulties, especially if used in isolation. As Mary Ainsworth has commented, an act such as 'moving away' from a stranger may be fear, while 'moving away' from a mother could be exploration. Signalling behaviours such as crying can also have different causes; for example, pain rather than fear. Signals may also be deceptive; as Trivers and other sociobiologists have pointed out, signals generally are for the benefit of the organism giving the signal, and may not always be strictly 'accurate' from the point of view of others receiving it. A physiological response such as HR acceleration could occur with fear, but also with general arousal, or even laughter. Finally, interview or questionnaire replies can be inaccurate, misleading or incomplete by virtue of memory distortion and loss, as well as any conscious unwillingness to admit to fearful behaviours.

We can have more confidence when two different classes of index covary; for example Waters, Matas & Sroufe (1975) found a close correspondence between gaze aversion and HR acceleration in the response of infants to a stranger approaching. In many studies however only one kind of index is used, and its indication of fear rather than some other emotional state is inferred from the more general context (such as stranger approach, or presentation of an incongruous stimulus).

Another problem is that fear motivation may be simultaneously aroused with other motivational systems, such as exploration, affiliation or aggression. One might then find indices of fear combined with indices of approach. Marvin & Mossler (1976) have described 'coy' behaviour in young children, in which simultaneous intention movements of approach and withdrawal are observed; for example, turning the head to one side or lowering it to the shoulder, while maintaining eye contact. They found that this kind of operational definition of coyness agreed quite well with adults' usage of the term.

Other researchers have tried to operationalise not only 'fear', but also other everyday terms such as 'distress', 'anxiety', 'alarm' and 'wariness', often on the basis of a particular theoretical perspective. Thus Bowlby (1969, 1973) distinguishes between 'anxiety' as the desire for closer proximity to an attachment figure, and 'alarm' as the desire to withdraw or avoid danger, both being examples of 'fear' or 'feeling afraid'. Bronson (1972) distinguishes between 'distress' in babies at sudden changes in the physical environment, 'wariness' of perceptually discrepant stimuli, and 'fear' based on learnt associations or contingencies (earlier, Bronson 1971, these were labelled 'distress', 'fear' and 'anxiety' respectively). Others use 'wariness' differently.

165

Schaffer, Greenwood and Parry (1972) use it to refer to inhibition of approach or manipulation when the infant is alerted, which may or may not culminate in some fearful response. Sroufe (1977) uses the term to refer to presumed low-intensity fear, such as indicated by gaze avoidance. These different approaches will be discussed in more detail subsequently.

Precisely what we call fear, and how we define other terms such as wariness, will thus depend on how we envisage the causation of fear and its ontogenetic development. However the overall 'umbrella' definition of fear is best kept in functional terms. Fearful behaviour serves to protect the individual from potentially harmful situations. From a sociobiological perspective, fear might be expected when there is a perceived threat to inclusive fitness (Hamilton, 1964). (This would also imply feeling some fear when a close relative is threatened – which may well be the case.) The resultant behaviour should then be to remove the threat, perhaps by avoiding it, or calling for help. The maximisation of inclusive fitness can be expected to apply to the behaviour of nonhuman species, but not necessarily to humans, where cultural evolution or change is of such great importance relative to biological evolution. This point will be considered again at the end of the chapter.

1   Résumé of Research Perspectives

One of the earliest researches on fear in children is now a classic (and often a misquoted one, Cornwell & Hobbs, 1976). This is the study of Watson & Rayner (1920) on 11-month old Albert. Albert was a stolid, unemotional baby, who hardly ever cried (before Watson's experiments commenced!). Watson (1924) believed that two kinds of stimulation – loud noises and sudden loss of support – were the innate bases of fear, and that other fear-producing stimuli or situations were so only by reason of association or conditioning with one of these (or possibly with painful stimuli such as hot or cold objects, pricking, etc.). He succeeded in conditioning a fear of a white rat in Albert by associating the rat with a loud sound produced by striking a hammer on a suspended steel bar. After seven such pairings, Albert was afraid of the rat, and this fear generalised to other stimuli such as a rabbit, a dog, a fur coat, cotton wool and Watson's hair (Albert didn't object, however, to the hair of two other observers present!).

Watson's conditioning results were confirmed by others such as Mary Cover Jones who worked with him on subsequent research. Jones (1924) also worked on the elimination of fears. She found that a deconditioning procedure worked well – Peter, a 3-year-old who was afraid of rabbits and other furry things, was shown the rabbit at a distance while having his crackers and milk. In other, similar cases she reported that social imitation – seeing other children approach a rabbit, for example – could also be effective in fear reduction.

However Jones & Jones (1928) and Valentine (1930) criticised the idea that all fears were learnt in the way Watson suggested. Valentine tried an experiment with one of his own daughters when she was 11 months old. He blew a loud whistle each time she touched a pair of opera glasses, but all she did was look round to see where the noise came from. Later he blew the whistle when she was shown a woolly caterpillar on her brother's hand. She screamed and turned away. Clearly there was a pre-existing difference between the caterpillar and the opera glasses, as to how easily fear could be associated with them. Valentine thought that other fears, such as of animals, the sea, and perhaps darkness, seemed to have 'maturational' components and were not just feared by suggestion or conditioning.

Valentine also noted instances when his daughter, playing happily, saw her brother with a brown paper bag over his head; she cried suddenly with a high scream and hurried away. She was also afraid of her doll when it was broken, with its eyes popping out on springs. These are examples of fear of strange or incongruous stimuli.

As Hebb (1946, 1949) subsequently pointed out, fear of the strange implies some prior learning of what is familiar. This could be a very general kind of learning, so the fear could appear to be a maturational phenomenon. Hebb found that chimpanzees showed 'spontaneous' fears of skulls, plaster casts of chimpanzee faces, and so on. He suggested that fear could be produced both by strange or incongruous sensory stimulation, and also by sensory deficit such as loss of support, darkness, solitude. Fear then originated in the disruption of temporally and spatially organised cerebral activities, ameliorated by withdrawal or avoidance.

Hebb's hypothesis was taken further by Hunt (1965), who proposed a preference for an optimum degree of incongruity between sensory input and some internal standard or engram. This general approach – the 'discrepancy' or 'incongruity' hypothesis – has been elaborated further by Schaffer, Kagan, Bronson, Sroufe and others, and will be discussed subsequently.

Returning to the 1920's and 1930's, other work on emotional development in infancy was being carried out by Bridges (1932), Gesell (1929), Buhler (1930), Shirley (1933) and others, in the context of laying out the general norms of development in infancy. In particular the development during the first year of fear of separation from the mother ('separation anxiety'), and fear of strange persons was noted – a theme taken up in many more recent investigations. In older children, Jersild and his coworkers (Jersild &

167

Holmes, 1935) were carrying out laboratory and questionnaire studies of fear.

Two other streams of thought prominent in the 1940's and 1950's were from psychoanalysis and ethology. In the psychoanalytic tradition, Spitz (1950) saw separation anxiety and fear of strangers as fear of loss of a loved object. Benjamin (1961), however, saw fear of the strange, per se, to be an additional causal factor in fear of strangers.

Bowlby (1958, 1969, 1973), while starting from a clinical and indeed psychoanalytic orientation, has gone much further in modifying these earlier concepts, and also incorporating ideas from ethological and psychological work, such as goal-corrected mechanisms of instinctive behaviour. His theory of attachment, to be discussed later, incorporated a theory of fear and anxiety which is perhaps the most embracing currently available. It has influenced experimental work such as that of Ainsworth and her coworkers (Ainsworth, 1973), and theoretical formulations in systems terms such as that of Bischof (1975).

Much other experimental and observational work has gone on without such obvious historical or theoretical links; for example, research by Rheingold, Eckerman, Corter, Ross and others on the balance between exploration and fear in young children. Decarie and coworkers have investigated fear of strangers, and its relation to cognitive development, from a Piagetian framework. Indeed several researchers have attempted to link the development of the object concept in infants, at around 8 months, to the separation anxiety and fear of strangers which also often seem to appear then.

The following sections consider the ontogenesis of fear in more detail. In the first six months of life, sudden changes in physical stimulation, together with a simple discrepancy hypothesis, may be largely sufficient to explain fearful behaviour. The first section considers this period. The next section covers the period from about 6 months to 2 or 3 years. Here we must take account of cognitive changes with the acquisition of sensorimotor intelligence, and social changes with the establishment of affectional bonds to the mother and/or other adults and caretakers. Explanations of fear will now involve discrepancy in a more complex sense, such as disruption of hypotheses, as well as specifically learnt associations, and also difficulties or frustrations in proximity maintenance to attachment figures. Fear of strangers, separation anxiety and the relation of these to cognitive development are considered in some detail.

The following section considers fear in preschool and younger school-age children. By now, the proximity-maintaining phase of attachment behaviour has waned; fear of perceptual incongruity, noises, strange persons or events declines. Fears related to social or conflict relations with peers, animal fears, and fears of imagination such as of monsters or darkness are more salient. Learnt cultural fears, and incongruities among beliefs or between beliefs and behaviour, may assume more importance in older childhood and adolescence.

This ontogenetic sequence is followed by brief discussions of sex differences in fear, and temporal stability of individual differences in fearfulness. Bowlby's general approach to fear is then discussed, and Bischof's systems model is considered. Finally, the adaptive significance of fearful behaviour is returned to.

2   Fear in the First Six Months of Life

Since Bridges (1932) early monograph, researchers have often used the term 'distress' rather than 'fear' to describe negative emotions in the first few weeks of life. This is also Bronson's (1972) usage of the term; in this first ontogenetic stage, the baby has no wariness of visual novelty (everything is novel) and has no learnt fearful associations, but it does respond in a largely reflexive way, either by defensive actions or by crying, to certain stimulus situations. Bronson, and Kagan (1970), cite rapidly changing physical stimulation, such as loud noises, or sudden loss of support, as examples. Another example would be 'looming' – an object rapidly approaching the face. Bower (1974) has shown that infants as young as one week will widen their eyes, retract their heads and raise up their hands in a defensive movement against such an approach.

Wolff (1969) and Dunn (1977) have described in detail the situations which cause crying in early infancy. These include hunger, cold, lack of contact with clothes or caretaker, pain, colic, and violent or sudden stimulation. To some extent parents can distinguish cries from different causes – a hunger cry and a cry of pain, for instance. During the third week, some mothers identify a low-intensity 'fake' cry, which seems to mean that the baby simply wants attention or stimulation.

Soon babies will tend to cry to situations of frustration or teasing. In the first few weeks, stage one of sensorimotor development, frustration is generally the immediate removal of a gratifying object. In the second week infants may cry if feeding is interrupted (even in the first week, repeated removal of a pacifier can cause crying). At two or three months, the baby has reached Piaget's second stage of sensorimotor development, an important aspect of which is achievement of eye-hand coordination. Now a baby will tolerate feeding interruption but will cry if a toy such as a rattle is removed from its hands, frustrating its attempts at assimilation. Later on, other events

169

will become frustrating, influenced presumably by the cognitive level the infant is currently at.

In the third week, Wolff reports that infants may smile at human voices and faces, or at a 'pat-a-cake' game, if they are alert, but cry if they are tired or fussy. This would indicate that these stimulus situations are arousing and moderately difficult to assimilate (see Kagan's theory later). By the fifth week, the human voice or face will instead soothe a crying baby. A person leaving a baby may also cause crying, but only for a short time; as yet, the baby does not have a concept of person permanence sufficient to cry at someone's continued absence.

Until recently it was assumed that the baby could not distinguish between individual persons until about 4 months or later. Wolff describes a $5\frac{1}{2}$-month-old infant encountering his grandmother for the first time. She fed, diapered and played with him, and he smiled and cooed as he would to his mother. Grossly observable differences in reactions to familiar and unfamiliar persons are not seen before 4 months. However, it does seem as though more sensitive differences in baby's reactions can be detected much earlier than this. Mills & Melhuish (1974) found experimentally that at 3 weeks infants would suck a teat more if it resulted in hearing the mother's voice than if it resulted in the voice of a female stranger equated for loudness. Yarrow (1967) observed that at one month, many babies showed positive reactions to their mother but not towards a stranger. And Carpenter (1975) looked at visual attention in an experimental situation, in babies aged 2–7 weeks. They looked more at the mother's face than the stranger's face. Moreover a mismatch of mother's voice with stranger's face caused turning away. This latter finding suggests an already learnt association between faces and voices; though other experimental work fails to support this – Cohen (1974) found evidence for face-voice expectations in 8-month-olds but not in 5-month-olds.

Carpenter's findings that the babies looked more at the mother's face than the stranger's could be explained by the 'incongruity' or 'discrepancy' hypothesis. This suggests that the infants are seeking an optimal level of arousal, as mediated by sensory (primary visual) discrepancy or incongruity. Discrepancy here is assessed against engrams or schemata being established in the infant's memory; it thus depends on previous perceptual learning, although the actual reactions to discrepancy may be largely determined by quite nonspecific developmental processes.

Kagan (1970) summarises research suggesting that whereas in the first few weeks infants pay attention to rapidly changing stimuli (moving, talking faces being a good example!), after this and for the next several months the longest attention is paid to stimuli moderately discrepant from established schemata; less attention is paid to very familiar stimuli (boring) and very

170

discrepant stimuli (fear-provoking; or in Bronson's terminology, leading to wariness). There is therefore an inverted U function of magnitude of discrepancy to degree of arousal or attention.

In its fully developed form, Kagan's (1974) version of the discrepancy hypothesis is that a discrepant event in the environment will lead to alerting and (visual) attention. (Sudden or intense change in physical stimulation will also lead to alerting and attention, followed by rapid adaptation.) The infant attempts to assimilate the discrepant event – to find a suitable coping response. Successful assimilation will lead to loss of attention or, if the assimilation is moderately difficult, to smiling, vocalising and repetition. Failure to assimilate will lead to avoidance, wariness or crying.

Carpenter's findings suggest that 2- and 3-week-old infants find a stranger's face more difficult to assimilate than the mother's. As they get older, presumably the schema for human faces will become more sophisticated, and stranger's faces will be more attractive. This seems to be true, in that older infants look a lot at strangers – more than at the mother (e.g. Bernard & Ramey, 1977, at 4 and 6 months), though they still may find it difficult to assimilate a stranger's sudden approach and initiation of interaction (so-called stranger anxiety).

The actual optimum for discrepancy will vary from one baby to another because of what we might call temperamental differences. Thomas, Chess, Birch, Hertzig & Korn (1964) have documented behavioural differences in infants; from the earliest days of life there are variations in activity level, approach and withdrawal, adaptability, intensity of reaction and other dimensions or characteristics. These might well relate to a temperamental 'threshold' for optimum stimulation. Scarr & Salapatek (1970) provide some supportive evidence for this, although Paradise & Curcio (1974) only found evidence of the approach scale relating to fear of strangers at 9 months. Serafica & Cicchetti (1976) and Cicchetti & Sroufe (1976) provide evidence that Down's syndrome children have a low 'threshold' for fear and emotional reactivity generally.

In the short term, a baby's mood may influence its threshold at any particular time; compare Wolff's observations on 3-week-old babies when alert, or tired and fussy, mentioned above.

The inverted-U prediction of the discrepancy hypothesis has received support from studies of how infants up to 7 or 8 months attended to visual patterns differing in novelty and complexity (Zelazo & Komer, 1971; McCall, Kennedy & Appelbaum, 1977). However, one problem is that we have no prior knowledge of what schema the infant has, and therefore what is discrepant to it and to what extent. Instead, researchers have generally used some metric such as complexity, or novelty (change from previous stimulus), assuming this is related to discrepancy.

171

Others have suggested that arousal might be a linear, rather than a curvilinear, function of discrepancy. However, some support for the curvilinear model in relation to social stimuli comes from Bernard & Ramey (1977). At 4 and 6 months, they found infants preferred slides of an adult female stranger (moderately discrepant) to that of the mother (familiar), but looked and vocalised least at slides of a 5-month-old infant (most discrepant).

In summary, the newborn infant shows distress at painful, or rapidly changing, physical stimulation. Soon, wariness or crying occurs at events that are difficult to cognitively assimilate. This is taken by discrepancy theorists to include wariness at perceptual incongruity, as well as crying in response to frustration or teasing, as described by Wolff.

3 Later Infancy: from Six Months to Two or Three Years

From about 8 months onward, Kagan (1970, 1974) feels that the discrepancy hypothesis still applies, but that attempts at assimilation are now best described in terms of the activation of hypotheses or expectancies of the baby, rather than in terms of static stimulus discrepancy. As by now the baby is roughly at stage 4 of Piaget's sensorimotor period, it has expectancies of cause-effect relations in the environment, irrespective of its own actions, and is also beginning to show search abilities for hidden objects or missing persons. It thus appears to make sense to start talking about hypotheses the baby has. However expectancies of a sort by the baby about its own actions may be violated even at stage 2 – crying when a rattle is removed from the hands, for example, as noted earlier. The terms 'hypothesis' and 'expectancy' are not too precise; nor is it entirely clear that the two earlier kinds of fear – wariness at perceptual incongruity and crying at frustrated assimilation – can be as closely conjoined as discrepancy theorists would imply. Talking about discrepancies in hypotheses or expectancies does however allow a broad approach to the causal explanation of fears in this age range, including separation anxiety and stranger fear.

An alternative to Kagan's theory, for children older than 6 months, has been put forward by Sroufe, Waters & Matas (1974). In this model a novel or incongruous situation leads to attention or 'tension', but whether this tension results in pleasure (e.g. laughing) or fear/wariness (e.g. crying) depends on the evaluation of the context. The inverted-U governs attention but not affect.

Sroufe et al. argue that the same stimulus situation can lead to laughter or crying depending on context. For example a mother picking up her 15-month-old baby by the heels produced laughter; but when a stranger

172

appeared, the baby cried when the mother repeated the action. Similarly, 10-month-old babies laughed at mother wearing a mask at home, but were more wary when in a laboratory, or after they had seen a stranger wearing the mask. Such context and order effects were not seen for 6-month-old children.

This implies that the older children can 'evaluate' the context in a way that the younger children cannot; and that this evaluation, rather than arousal level, determines affect. Even very high arousal levels – such as a mother playing very vigorously with her baby – can lead to pleasure and (it is claimed) hardly ever to fear.

Although Sroufe et al. predictably criticise the discrepancy hypothesis for being difficult to define operationally, their own concepts of 'context' and 'evaluation' seem no more precise – especially when they concede that context and fatigue can influence tension as well as affect. Kagan uses the term 'event' to cover 'stimulus in context'. Whereas Sroufe's babies would seem to be separately and sequentially evaluating stimulus and context. Kagan's babies evaluate an event as a whole and try to assimilate it.

One main distinction between Sroufe's and Kagan's approach seems to be how predictably stimulation with a very large discrepancy leads to fear. Kagan would say that it would lead to fear because it will be difficult to assimilate. Sroufe would say that this would depend on context. Kagan would reply that the context is part of the overall familiarity or novelty of the stimulus event involved in the discrepancy. Both would agree that, after an initial alerting, affect will depend on evaluation (Sroufe) or success at assimilation (Kagan).

Schaffer (1971, 1974) describes a similar process in different terminology. He distinguishes between a 'perceptual learning mechanism' and a 'response selection mechanism'. Before 8 or 9 months of age, an infant can distinguish a novel object, paying it greater visual attention, and will also reach out to manipulate it as fast as it would to a familiar object. Rather than any fear or wariness, we have here what Schaffer calls impulsiveness. Only after 8 or 9 months does manipulative latency to a novel object show an increase (Schaffer, Greenwood & Parry, 1972). This ability to inhibit an approach response Schaffer calls a change from impulsiveness to wariness (as noted earlier, this usage of wariness is different from others). He links it developmentally with a change from sequential to simultaneous consideration of stimuli, and with recall as well as recognition memory.

Recall memory should be linked to object and person permanence. Once the baby has an enduring memory or engram of its mother (or other attachment figure) as a specific person, for example, it could be anxious at her absence, and fearful of a stranger. Hence the new wariness to novel objects, and the new social fears typically held to become prominent at this time, have similar cognitive roots.

173

However, some kind of comparison with a stored memory or engram would seem to be possible before 8 months, if work such as that of Carpenter's is to be believed. Bronson (1972), too, found that some infants were wary of strangers as early as 3 or 4 months. They followed a behaviour sequence that simple discrepancy theory might predict as the stranger approached – a fleeting smile (assimilation of general face schema), a stare for 16–30 seconds (attention to details of face) and, in some cases, frowning, breathing heavily and crying (failure to assimilate specific face). About half of Bronson's sample of 32 babies showed wariness of strangers this early, at least once.

However such wariness perhaps does not imply true concepts or engrams of 'mother' or 'familiar person' as such, in the sense that an older Piaget stage 4 baby might have these; indeed the presence of the mother did not affect wariness of strangers at the younger age, which suggests some lack of a generalised 'mother' concept. It may well be more specific aspects of the mother or the stranger which the infant is recognising, or failing to recognise, at this age; perhaps particular facial expressions, or familiar associations or temporal contingencies. (Such an interpretation could apply a fortiori to studies such as Carpenter's.)

It remains the case that fear of strangers as such seems to be generally noticeable in the second half of the first year, often from about 8 months onward, whatever more subtle effects may be detected at earlier ages. Certainly, infant testers generally expect an easy time with babies below six months, and again after about 3 years, but perhaps some difficulty within these age limits. As an example, research by Schwartz, Campos & Baisel (1975) on the visual cliff may be considered. They tested 20 five-month-old and 20 nine-month-old babies; they had no trouble with the 5-month-olds. However, in the course of the project 16 other 9-month-olds had to be dropped because of 'inconsolable distress' in the experimental situation when they were required to separate from the mother and accompany the (strange) experimenter. The experimenters, incidentally, found that the older infants showed HR acceleration and limb movement when placed on the deep side of the visual cliff, taken as indicative of fear; the younger ones showed HR deceleration, taken as indicative of interest. This is another example of the difference in fearfulness between babies younger or older than 6–8 months, and suggests that fear of the visual cliff may also be linked to cognitive evaluation processes.

4   The Fear of Strangers Phenomenon

A number of studies agree in finding an accentuation of negative responses to strangers in babies between 7 to 9 months, including longitudinal studies by Schaffer & Emerson (1964) and Emde, Gaensbauer & Harmon (1976). This is supported by several cross-sectional studies; for example, Waters, Matas & Sroufe (1975) found both increased gaze aversion and HR acceleration to strangers after 7 months. Skarin (1977) and Campos, Emde, Gaensbauer & Henderson (1975) also used both HR and behavioural measures, and also found a similar age difference. Sroufe (1977) has summarised such studies. Not all infants show fear of strangers by any means, but if low-intensity fear (gaze aversion, HR acceleration) is monitored as well as frank fear (overt crying or flight), many infants – say around 60% – may be expected to show signs of fear they would not have shown in a similar situation a few months earlier.

The 'fear of strangers' concept has however been sharply criticised by writers such as Rheingold & Eckerman (1973) and DeCarie (1974). In part, their criticisms are that different and sometimes unvalidated indices of fear were used in different studies, and also that inconsistencies in reports of age of onset and likelihood of fear were prevalent. These two criticisms may well be related – the more careful and objective studies summarised by Sroufe (1977) give a more consistent picture.

Rheingold & Eckerman (1973) and Solomon & DeCarie (1974) also point out that in many situations infants do not fear strangers but instead respond positively and affiliatively (Solomon & DeCarie's further suggestion that negative responses are less stable than positive ones is effectively criticised by Sroufe). They go on to suggest that the fear seen in stranger-fear situations may be due to the unnatural circumstances typically involved, for instance a laboratory setting with unusual stranger behaviour.

There is certainly a point here, and it illustrates the costs as well as benefits of controlled laboratory studies. Following Schaffer (1966), many investigators have standardised stranger approach to a 'stepwise' sequence (thus ensuring that different subjects experience the same phenomenon). The stranger enters and stands 5 or 6 feet away from the infant, and (i) calls to the infant, (ii) smiles, (iii) approaches, (iv) offers to pick up, (v) touches, and (vi) picks up the infant. This could appear unnatural, and certainly leaves little scope for allowing contingency of response between infant and stranger. Even more atypical is the procedure used by Greenberg, Hillman & Grice (1973). After a loud knock on the door, 'the stranger entered the room and stood on a marked spot approximately 5.4 meters away from and directly facing the infant. After standing on the 5.4 meter spot for 10 seconds, a light behind the mother signalled and the stranger walked slowly towards the infant and stopped at a marked spot 2.7 meters away from the infant. The stranger then kneeled down, took the infant's hands and gently shook them. Throughout the experimental session the stranger had a somber expression and looked directly at the infant. This concluded the experimental session, and the stranger then got up and left the room'!

175

Shaffran (1974), by contrast, observed how strangers would approach an infant in more ordinary circumstances. Soliciting friends (of hers) and acquaintances in a park, she asked them to approach 12-month-old Stephané. 15 adults approached Stephané in turn. Fortunately Stephané, like Albert, was a phlegmatic soul. 'Basically friendly, she never showed fear or sullenness, displaying at most what seemed to be occasional fatigue'! The observed approaches were richer, more random and fluid than the stepwise approach. (Based on this study, Solomon-Shaffran & DeCarie (1976) have suggested a semistructured approach as a more natural alternative for experimental purposes.)

However, while the stranger's unnatural approach may accentuate fear, the important point is that an action which by the mother will cause pleasure, by a stranger will cause wariness or fear. Klein & Durfee (1976) asked mother and stranger to approach 1-year-olds, in a laboratory, in a similar, structured fashion; infants were more negative to the stranger at the pickup phase of the approach.

In reviewing the fear of stranger literature, Sroufe (1977) points out that any wariness of strangers is consistently ameliorated if the stranger approaches gradually, if the child feels some control of the situation (i.e. stranger is responsive to child's signals), if the mother is present and if the overall context or setting is familiar. There are also individual differences in wariness of strangers, which show some stability across time.

Even in a very natural situation, stranger fear may not be avoided. Monahan (1975) carried out a study in which the stranger, an 'attractive, vivacious young woman' visited mothers and their 8- or 13-month-old infants at home. The stranger behaved perfectly naturally. As noted above, we would expect wariness to be minimised in such circumstances, and exploratory and affiliative behaviours to predominate. Monahan indeed found such results, and argued that fear of the stranger was an unjustified construct. Nevertheless, three of her sample of 24 children cried so hard, on one visit at least, that observations had to be terminated.

Sroufe (1977) seems justified in stating that 'the construct of wariness of strangers is sufficiently viable to withstand recent critiques'. This in no way gainsays the fact that often – more often than not, usually – infants show exploratory and affiliative reactions to strangers. In general, it appears that infants up to 1 year will look a great deal at strangers, and often smile, perhaps more than at the mother; though they less often vocalise to strangers or approach them (Monahan, 1975; Bretherton & Ainsworth, 1974). In the second year, as well, infants may direct affiliative behaviours (smile, look) to strangers as much as or more than to parents, although attachment behaviours (touch, proximity) are directed primarily to parents (Lamb, 1977; Bretherton, 1978). This would be consistent with the idea that strangers are moderately difficult to assimilate – somewhat unpredictable – but that this will generally bring about exploratory responses from the infant given that other contextual factors are reassuring. Eckerman & Rheingold (1974) explicitly compare reactions to unfamiliar persons with reactions to unfamiliar toys, and rooms. A considerable body of literature (e.g. Ross, 1974b) shows that 1-year-old babies prefer investigating novel toys to familiar ones, and also novel to familiar rooms, by locomotion and manipulation. Similarly infants like investigating strangers, and will even look more at a 'new' stranger than at an 'old' one introduced 5 minutes earlier (Eckerman & Whatley, 1975), but this exploration is usually from a distance – looking and smiling. Actual approaches are often ambivalent (Bretherton & Ainsworth, 1974), being followed sometimes by retreat; but approach is facilitated if the stranger offers to play with a toy (Ross & Goldman, 1977).

So far I have hinted at an incongruity hypothesis explanation of stranger wariness, when it does occur. The stranger is increasingly perceived as discrepant from the mother or other familiar adults, this ability crystallising at around 8 months. This could explain the importance of stranger behaviour, mediation with a toy, familiarity of surroundings – especially if coupled with the assumption that presence of mother, or familiar surroundings, either influences arousal level (Kagan, 1974), or evaluation of context (Sroufe, Waters & Matas, 1974). It would also explain why a moderately discrepant stranger – such as one in reassuring surroundings behaving naturally – should elicit more exploratory or approach responses than the mother.

However, there are difficulties with the incongruity explanation as such. For instance, it is not too clear why a baby may look and smile at a distance, but become wary or cry when picked up, or if a stranger stands close and tries to communicate (Klein & Durfee, 1976; Gaensbauer, Emde & Campos, 1976). Bower (1977) suggests that it is the inability to communicate with the stranger which is frightening for the baby. Bower puts the emphasis on verbal communication – hence the decline in stranger anxiety after 2 or 3 years as the child is able to talk. However, his hypothesis might be strengthened if 'communication' was generalised to 'able to maintain contingent behaviour sequences'. A stranger standing close and picking up or talking provides a highly salient event for the baby over which it has little control – things are happening which are quite non-contingent on the baby's own actions. The aspect of contingency or control is probably very important. For example, if the baby can approach the stranger in its own time it doesn't usually show fear (though still some ambivalence – Bretherton & Ainsworth, 1974). We would also expect on this hypothesis that if a stranger imitates characteristic and familiar

177

behaviours of the mother, this would be less frightening. Rafman (1974) found some evidence that this was so.

This would also explain why children hardly ever show wariness or fear of strange objects, or rooms, however incongruous they may be (Bronson, 1972; Ross, 1974b). The only important exceptions to this generalisation seem to be moving or mechanical toys. Stern (1924) reported 'G (1:10) was given a little metal dog that ran about gaily when wound up. The boy set up a terrible cry and ran from the animal; on the other hand, when it was still he liked to pick it up'. Similar fears of a mechanical dog, and a jack-in-the-box, have been reported by Meili (1959), and Scarr & Salapatek (1970). In such cases, the toy's actions are unexpectedly noncontingent on the child's behaviour (until the child can master the action of winding up the dog, for example). Generally, though, toys and other objects are predictable, their proximity can be paced by the infant, and they react contingently or consistently to exploratory manipulations.

This emphasis on communication, or contingency of response, may not be incompatible with a discrepancy-type theory. Perhaps the infant has developed hypotheses (Kagan, 1970) about how familiar persons will act, and how to influence their behaviour. Thus assimilation is more difficult when the stranger behaves unpredictably or in a noncontingent way. Again the point is made that terms such as 'difficulty in assimilation', 'schema' or 'hypothesis' need defining precisely, probably in relation to a specific theory of cognitive and social development, for the theory to be scientifically useful.

Another difficulty for discrepancy theory is raised by Greenberg, Hillman & Grice (1973) and Lewis & Brooks (1974). These researchers found that 7- to 19-month-old infants generally showed some negative reactions to approach of a strange adult, but neutral or slightly positive reactions to the approach of a strange child. If the mother (or familiar adult) is the referent in discrepancy theory terms, the strange child should be the most discrepant and therefore responded to most negatively (this does seem to happen at earlier ages, Bernard & Ramey, 1977). Lewis & Brooks (1974) suggest that the infant by now also has a concept of self, to which others may be referred – though concept of self as defined by mirror recognition is not found till about 19 months (see also Amsterdam, 1972). They also suggest an early sense of gender identity (usually placed at about 3 years, Thompson, 1975). Lewis & Brooks suggest that this could explain why their female more than male infants were frightened of a male adult stranger (though the trend was nonsignificant). Greenberg, Hillman & Grice (1973) found that 12-month-old male infants were more fearful of male strangers. This is the opposite of the Lewis & Brooks result and would appear to contradict their hypothesis so far as gender identity is concerned. However, both

178

investigators agree on the primary phenomenon – less fear of unfamiliar child than of unfamiliar adult.

What features of the unfamiliar child are relevant to this distinction? Brooks & Lewis (1974) attempted to find out by using a small adult (dwarf) in comparison with a normal-height adult and 5-year-old children. The infants (7–24 months) smiled most at the 5-year-olds, frowned more at all the adults, but gaze averted only from the normal height adult. The small adult thus seemed to be intermediate in provoking wariness. Perhaps both height and facial characteristics are important relevant aspects of the stranger. Given the differences reported to male and female strangers (see Morgan & Ricciuti, 1969; Skarin, 1977; as well as the above), other features such as voice pitch may be important. To what extent particular stimulus features such as these can lead to an explanation of the findings, or whether more general cognitive concepts of self- and even gender-identity need to be invoked, remains controversial.

Perhaps, alternatively, the lesser wariness to children could be based on experience or social expectancies that children are less powerful, less likely to impinge abruptly on them, than strange adults. The idea that expectations based on earlier social interactions or learnt associations becomes important as a cause of fear after 8–12 months has been put by Bronson (1972, 1978) and Bronson & Pankey (1977). Indeed, it is to such causes that Bronson feels the term 'fear' can be applied. Bronson feels that although discrepancy or incongruity may be the main cause of wariness of strange adults up to around 8 months, cumulative social experience will increasingly be a determinant of fearful (or nonfearful) responses later in the first year, and onwards.

Levy (1951) described reactions of babies to a doctor about to give a similar injection to one given a few weeks earlier. Before 11 months, few reacted anxiously the second time, but one quarter of the sample did so by 11 and 12 months. This suggests a specifically learnt and recalled fear association becoming possible at about this age.

Bronson & Pankey (1977) carried out a longitudinal study of children's responses to new play situations in the second year of life. A factor analysis of temporal correlations over situations suggested a two-factor model of fearfulness. Factor one was operative at the beginning of the second year, and was ascribed to individual differences in 'wariness'. This was unrelated to factor two, which was responsible for individual differences later in the second year, and (unlike factor one) predicted also fearful behaviour at $3\frac{1}{2}$ years. This was ascribed to individual differences in learnt 'fearfulness' after exposure to a mildly difficult situation.

To what extent could learnt fear associations explain fear of strangers generally? The incongruity theory has the advantage that wariness appears

179

gradually, and usually only becomes marked after the familiar (mother, caretaker) is discriminated. However, at 9 months Bronson (1972) reports that infants show fear very quickly – compared to the delayed onset at 4 and 6 months as discrepancy is assimilated.

Bronson (1978) has re-analysed these 1972 data for temporal correlations. Again a dual factor model was suggested. The first factor explained individual differences at 4 and 6 months, and correlated with reactivity to a looming stimulus – suggesting a 'wariness' factor again. At 9 months, individual differences were due to a separate factor ascribed to learnt aversion. Bronson cites some more anecdotal evidence from his own and other studies indicating that a previous unhappy experience with a stranger can predict subsequent stronger stranger aversion.

It is possible that initial experiences of a baby with a stranger could often be aversive, if (as Bower suggests) the baby finds communication or contingent interaction with the stranger difficult. This might be especially the case if the stranger behaves in a stereotyped way typical of many psychological experiments, as described earlier. Trause (1977) examined stranger fear in 1-year-olds at two successive short visits; children were *more* fearful at the second visit. This would be surprising if one viewed the stranger as becoming more familiar (cf. Bretherton, 1978; Ross & Goldman, 1977). But, as this experiment involved the mother leaving the baby with the stranger, and subsequent distress, this finding is well explained on Bronson's learnt fearfulness theory.

Greenberg, Hillman & Grice (1975) attempted to test between the incongruity theory and social learning theory explanations of stranger fear, by comparing its onset and intensity at 8 and 12 months in first- and later-born infants. Their 'somber stranger' (see earlier) produced fewer positive reactions in the later born children – they were, if anything, the more fearful. Now on the incongruity theory, it is argued, the later-born children would have more variety of stimulation and hence a more generalised internal schema for human figures; thus novel persons should be less incongruent and less fear-provoking. This is the opposite to what was found. On the other hand, the results are explicable on a social learning theory, if it is assumed that parents and other siblings are less uniformly positive to later-born than first-born infants.

However both Schaffer (1966) and Collard (1968) found that first-born children are more fearful of novel persons (or developed this fear response earlier). This is precisely the opposite result, and could support incongruity theory. This issue is not finally resolved. However, it is likely that both incongruity theory and social learning theory have a contribution to make to understanding stranger wariness, either as overlapping sequential but largely independent explanations (Bronson, 1972; 1978), or in a more

180

interactive sense. Remembering Valentine's experiment with the opera glasses and the woolly caterpillar, it may well be that infants readily learn specific fears of strangers or aspects of strangers, and retain and generalise them, because of their initial discrepancy in visual appearance, and/or noncontingent or unpredictable sequencing of behaviour. Bronson's work may indicate that individual differences in learnt fearfulness are largely independent of individual differences in wariness, but this does not mean that the types of situation typically giving rise to wariness may not also be likely to give rise to learnt fear associations in children generally.

5   Stranger Fear and Separation Anxiety

Most approaches to stranger fear also provide a similar explanation of separation anxiety. Schaffer & Emerson (1964) took (reported) separation protest as an operational definition of attachment, and found it to be first present from an age range of 22 weeks to 15 months in their longitudinal sample. It is observed of course to other attachment figures as well as the mother – for example to fathers, grandparents, siblings. Freud & Dann (1951) reported strong separation protests among the six refugee babies brought to England from a concentration camp when 3 years old. A great deal of evidence (Schaffer, 1977) shows that attachments, and hence separation protest, are primarily to other persons who react positively and contingently to the infant (for example, playfully), rather than to persons who just do physical caretaking or satisfy primary need states. Ricciuti (1974) found caretakers of children in a daycare centre to be intermediate between mother and stranger, so far as attachment and fear behaviours were concerned.

From the psychoanalytic viewpoint, Spitz (1950) saw both separation anxiety and stranger fear as being caused by the child fearing the loss of a love object (the mother). Thus separation anxiety is primary. Spitz's explanation of stranger fear in this way is unsatisfactory, since it is still clearly seen when mother is present, sometimes even when the baby is seated on mother's lap (Morgan & Ricciuti, 1969).

Bower (1977) also links separation anxiety and stranger fear, but rather on the basis of communication skills. I suggested earlier this might be generalised to the ability to maintain contingent interaction sequences. Having built up such expected contingencies with one or a few persons, the baby is distressed when such expectancies are removed (separation, baby alone), or violated (stranger interaction). So far as separation anxiety is concerned, this fits in with the increase up to 2 years, and then the general decline in separation anxiety through the 2- to 4-year age range, as the child becomes more able to communicate and interact with others, including relative strangers, as well as with a few attachment figures (Cox & Campbell, 1968; Maccoby & Feldman, 1972; Kagan, Kearsley & Zelazo, 1975; Marvin, 1977).

This would imply the importance of social communication skills in separation anxiety. There seem to be more cognitive components too. Littenberg, Tulkin & Kagan (1971) observed 11-month-olds at home, and found that more infants cried if mother left by an unusual exit, rather than the more usual one. Monahan (1975) found that 8- and 13-month-olds fussed or cried at 50% or more of programmed mother separations, when observed at home, but only at 14% of natural, nonprogrammed separations, when the mother left the room to answer the doorbell or see to the cooking. This suggests that the infant perceived certain modes of separation as being incongruous relative to a schema, or hypothesis, about their mother's normal separation behaviour – depending perhaps on quite subtle cues such as facial expression or abruptness of separation, though this remains to be elucidated. Litteenberg et al. (1971) thus suggest an incongruity theory explanation of separation anxiety, though it is clear that specific social learning about mother's behaviour might well be influential and could provide an apparently different explanation; infants could be upset at mother's abrupt departure because it was incongruous (unusual) or because they had expectations (based on previous experience) that she would subsequently be less accessible.

The latter explanation is perhaps supported by the fact that infants, even when in a strange laboratory, are often *not* distressed if the mother is out of sight. Corter, Rheingold & Eckerman (1972) asked mothers to put their 10-month-old infants in a large room, then sit in an adjoining room out of sight. The babies often played a while with their toys in the larger room before searching for the mother. Even when placed in an unfamiliar playpen, with the mother out of sight, some babies did not cry straight away – though most did by 3 or 4 minutes. Again crying was delayed by putting toys in the playpen. Corter (1976) showed that having mother in sight prolonged infant's exploratory behaviour, but, surprisingly, that it made no difference if the mother left the infant (with toys) or if the infant left the mother (to go to toys). It may be relevant in this experiment that the infants had seen both rooms, so could know the mother was available even if out of sight. If, in contrast, mother leaves and closes a door behind her, as in the 'strange situation' experiment of Ainsworth & Wittig (1969), crying is a very predictable response (Corter, 1976). Closing a door seems to make a very considerable difference as to how a 10- or 12-month-old infant 'evaluates the context' of a separation. A closed door is surely not very incongruous, but an infant might well have a learnt association of closed doors with subsequent inaccessibility of mother and relative powerlessness to bring her back speedily, or follow her.

Ainsworth's 'strange situation' experiment involves a sequence of events. It starts with mother and baby being shown into an experimental room, containing toys: mother puts baby down and sits in a chair (3 minutes); a female stranger enters, sits, converses, and approaches the baby (3 minutes); mother leaves unobtrusively, leaving the stranger with the baby (3 minutes, unless distressed); mother returns, stranger leaves unobtrusively; after baby is settled again, mother leaves, baby is alone (3 minutes, unless distressed); stranger enters, sits, converses, approaches baby (3 minutes, unless distressed); mother returns, stranger leaves; situation terminated after reunion (Ainsworth & Wittig, 1969; Ainsworth & Bell, 1970).

As indicated, crying was most likely in episodes 4, 6 and 7 – involving both separation anxiety and stranger fear. Ainsworth's 'strange situation' yields a rich harvest of behaviour in separation and reunion situations to mother, as well as exploration and affiliation to stranger (e.g. Bretherton & Ainsworth, 1974). However, cumulative sequential effects may be an important factor in the impact of different episodes. Thus, it is difficult to obtain a measure of separation anxiety 'uncontaminated' by stranger fear. This is also the case with most studies of separation anxiety, which have either used even more complicated sequential procedures (e.g. Spelke, Zelazo, Kagan & Kotelchuck, 1973), or have had a (strange) observer present to watch the 'separation anxiety' as the mother exits (e.g. Tennes & Lampl, 1964; Littenberg, Tulkin & Kagan, 1971).

The relation between these two kinds of anxiety or fear is important theoretically (see discussion of Bischof's systems model later). Sroufe, Waters & Matas (1974), using HR acceleration, found a significant correlation of 0.38 over 10-month-old babies between reaction to stranger approach and reaction to mother separation – but again, mother left baby with the stranger.

Tennes & Lampl (1964) stated that the onset and age range of these two kinds of reaction were different, with stranger fear coming first, chronologically (they also suggested that girls showed more stranger fear, boys more separation anxiety). Schaffer (1966), however, found stranger fear to be later. As we have seen, much depends on the precise indices used, context, and so on. Schaffer (1966) supposed that object permanence was a prerequisite for both kinds of fear (not including the signs of wariness seen at earlier ages, presumably). Some research has been done to test this assumption, with mixed results.

6 Separation Anxiety, Stranger Fear and Cognitive Development

Bell (1970) looked explicitly for a relationship between person or object permanence, and strength of attachment of infant to the mother. The latter was measured using Ainsworth & Wittig's (1969) 'strange situation', in which the infant's response to separation and reunion is a major diagnostic feature. Bell tested 33 infants for person and object permanence levels, from $8\frac{1}{2}$ to $11\frac{1}{2}$ months of age. She found that babies with secure, unambivalent attachment to the mother were more advanced than the other babies on levels of person permanence. The results for object permanence were not so clear cut. Cook (1972) also failed to find any relation between object permanence (Uzgiris-Hunt scale) and differential behaviour of 8-, 9- and 10-month-old infants to mother and stranger in separations and reunions.

Other researchers have tried to relate object concept measures to wariness of strangers. Scarr & Salapatek (1970), however, found only slight correlations between intensity of stranger fear in the age range 2–23 months, and performance on the object permanence and means-ends Uzgiris–Hunt scales; the correlations were essentially zero when age was partialled out. Paradise & Curcio (1974) also failed to relate stranger reaction to object permanence, but did relate it to person permanence. 15 out of 30 9- to 10-month-old boys showed negative stranger reactions; 13 out of the 15 were in stage 6 for person permanence, compared to only 5 of the 15 who did not fear strangers (most of these latter being in stage 5). This suggests a threshold of stage 6 person permanence for stranger fear, for *most* infants.

Brossard (1974) and Goulet (1974) measured person and object permanence, and causality, in 8- to 13-month-old infants. No clear relationships were found to stranger reaction, except that there was a tendency for infants who changed from being positive when stranger was distant to being negative when stranger was close to be at least at stage 5 of person permanence, or causality.

Fraiberg (1975) has carried out a longitudinal study of infants blind from birth, compared to sighted children. The blind infants first showed stranger avoidance or fear between 7 and 15 months, usually when held by the stranger. This was a similar range to the sighted children. However, both stage 4 of person permanence and mother separation protest were delayed from around 6–8 months in the sighted children to 10–16 months in the blind children. Fraiberg concludes a connection between stage 4 of person permanence and separation protest, but no direct connection to stranger activity.

These results are confusing. From a theoretical viewpoint, one would expect both separation anxiety and stranger fear to be linked to person or object permanence (Schaffer, 1966), although, as Flavell (1977) points out, it is not so clear which level or stage of person permanence is the likely

184

candidate for a threshold effect. Stage 3 already implies some recognitive ability, while stage 4 implies some search ability when a person disappears; But only stage 6 brings a general internal representation with successful search strategies. The obvious empirical disagreements do nothing to resolve this question.

The significant findings which have been obtained all relate to person permanence or causality (rather than object permanence). The person permanence norms reported by the above investigators, while not in exact accordance, are all well ahead of the usual object permanence norms, in which stage 4 is typically achieved around 8–12 months, and stage 6 at around 18 months (Flavell, 1977). Bell (1970) did report earlier object permanence achievement than this, but still 23 of her 33 subjects showed positive decalage for person permanence, and only 7 the opposite effect.

The very substantial species decalage generally inferrable from these studies needs to be explained. In part, differences in detailed task requirements may be responsible. Jackson, Campos & Fischer (1978) found that looking behind screens is an easier task than looking under a cloth. The usual person permanence task has used the former method, the usual object permanence task the latter. Person permanence tasks have usually involved the mother *or* the experimenter hiding behind chairs or doors and getting the infant to search for or point to them. Clearly the infant's emotional state may well affect its performance here, thus confounding the relationship which is being investigated. Perhaps Bell's (1970) poorly attached infants did less well at the person permanence tasks because they were less motivated to search for the mother. Similar problems might affect the comparisons of stranger fear and test achievement. Thus Goulet (1974) found her 40-week-olds did better than her 48-week-olds on the causality scale, as 'good rapport with the examiner favoured this group on the causality test'!

Further progress in this area will probably depend on more careful and sophisticated techniques being used, in longitudinal studies. Cicchetti & Sroufe (1976), in a longitudinal study of Down's syndrome infants, succeeded in obtaining impressively high correlations between cognitive measures, and general measures of affect including first negative reactions. The Bayley and Uzgiris–Hunt scales were used, and in this study relations of affect to object permanence *were* obtained. A wider range of items, but of a more precise nature, were used to assess emotional state in this than in the earlier studies.

7 Summary of Different Theoretical Approaches

The most prominent kinds of fear in this age range are stranger fear and separation anxiety. The incongruity hypothesis, fairly successful in terms of purely static stimulus discrepancy for infants below 6 months, needs modification for the age span in which these fears are most manifest. Although wariness of strangers and distress at separation can be seen at younger ages in certain circumstances, context and order effects, such as pointed out by Kagan and Sroufe, are only apparent after 6 months. This necessitates that the incongruity theory be made more cognitively complex. Kagan attempts this by introducing the ability of the infant to activate hypotheses; the success or failure of hypotheses to relate discrepant events to established schema determines whether fear occurs. Sroufe considers that the infant evaluates the context in which a discrepant event occurs, and that this evaluation decides positive or negative affect.

But what sorts of hypothesis or evaluation are being made? To be really satisfactory any theory of this type must relate to a developmental theory embracing not only cognitive, but also social and communicative skills. It is unlikely that a predominantly cognitive approach such as that of Piaget's will be wholly sufficient. This is not just because most attempts to relate fear development to Piagetian stages have been questionable or unsuccessful. The empirical work summarised above suggests other relevant aspects which must be accounted for. Firstly, the possible importance of self-concept, as proposed by Lewis & Brooks, must be considered. Secondly, the predictability or contingency of adult behaviour seems especially important to the infant's emotional state (whether the adult is mother or stranger). I take this to be a generalisation of Bower's viewpoint; that the infant feels secure if communication, in the sense of manageable interaction sequences (verbal or nonverbal or preverbal) can be established, and distressed if this is not the case. Thus, the violation of certain kinds of hypotheses, or the evaluation of certain kinds of context, relating to salient but unpredictable behaviour, seem especially to predispose to fear.

Incongruity per se requires only perceptual learning; fear follows from discrepancy irrespective of whether the discrepant stimulus actually has had any aversive consequences previously or not. This is clearly different from an associative learning approach. But as the incongruity theory becomes more cognitively complex, this distinction becomes blurred. If an infant has hypotheses about mother separating via an unusual exit, or in an abrupt manner, or by closing the door, which are particularly difficult to assimilate successfully, it is more difficult to separate out general or perceptual learning (mother doesn't usually behave like this) from specific learning (when mother behaves like this, it's difficult to get her back again). Indeed, are the hypotheses activated about incongruity, or about consequences? If the latter, as some evidence certainly points to, then we move towards an associative learning viewpoint, and the importance of incongruity declines (though still perhaps important in facilitating learning specific fear associations). As

186

noted before, incongruous stimuli (strange toys) may cause no fear, while a more familiar stimulus (doctor giving injection) may cause fear, by the end of the first year. As a more sophisticated cognitive network is established in the infant's brain, we would indeed expect 'discrepancy' as such to be a less meaningful measure, as well as a less reliable guide to affect and action. Bronson's recent work strongly supports the idea of a transition from wariness of discrepancy to learnt fears of situations or events during the stage of later infancy.

8   The Preschool and Early School Years

After the first year, other children (peers) become an increasingly important part of a young child's experience. This is so as the close proximity-maintaining phase of adult (mother) attachment wanes (Marvin, 1977), and as the child's cognitive development allows more successful and productive peer interactions to be coped with (Mueller & Lucas, 1975).

Generally, one-year-olds are interested in peers, and exploration and tentative affiliation, often toy-mediated, are predominant over negative affect (Lewis, Young, Brooks & Michalson, 1975). If one child takes a toy off another this is not often apparently constructed as 'aggressive' (Bronson, 1975). One-year-olds look more at unfamiliar peers than at unfamiliar adults such as unfamiliar peers' mothers (Bronson, 1975; Kagan, Kearsley & Zelazo, 1975).

Kagan et al. (1975) found that there was more inhibition of play when with a strange peer at age 20 months, than at either $13\frac{1}{2}$ or 29 months. They suggest that it is only by 20 months that children are developing schemas about unfamiliar peers and how they behave, but that at that age, unlike later, they are often unable to resolve hypotheses that may be activated; that is, they are uncertain how to cope. This suggestion parallels Kagan's explanation of separation anxiety (see earlier). However, the data are not conclusive; Lewis & Brooks (1974) found special interest in peers at 12 months, suggesting schemas already being developed; while Kagan et al. (1975) themselves found mother proximity in peer presence to be greatest at 29 months, suggesting apprehension at the later age.

In peer relationships, as perhaps in early social relations with adults, there may be some distinction between fear due to uncertainty as to what to expect, and fear due to specific expectations as to what to expect; of which Kagan's explanation ostensibly refers to the former, whereas Bronson's 'fear' refers to the latter. With regard to the former, children of 3 or 4 years show some signs of fear when introduced to unfamiliar peers or to a new playgroup. Schwartz (1972) found less mobility and less positive affect in

187

4-year-olds with a strange compared to a familiar peer. McGrew (1972) and Smith (1974) have documented reactions of preschool children, aged 3 and 4 years, to introduction to nursery or playgroup. There are great individual variations, but some children do cry and scream, and generally there is some settling-in period during which inhibition of motor activity declines. At 6 and 7 years of age, Jormakka (1976) found that unacquainted peers when introduced showed more signs of gaze avoidance, immobility and automanipulation than were seen in acquainted peers. In all these studies, signs of wariness or fear rapidly declined with time, suggesting initial uncertainty of expectation was being resolved; this does not discount some influence of prior experiences on individual differences and intensity of reaction, of course.

Prior experience may be the main determinant of fear response in normal ongoing social interactions among acquainted children; for example where there is a conflict over a mutually desired resource such as a toy or play apparatus (Smith, 1974). The outcome of disputes in a group of children can often be summarised by a fairly linear dominance hierarchy, and this also seems to be an emergent concept in 3- and 4-year-old children (Sluckin & Smith, 1977). This implies that a child has expectancies or hypotheses about who will win, or lose, a conflict. Children expecting to lose may show signs of fear, some of which can function as appeasement or submission gestures. Strayer & Strayer (1976) include cry-scream, rapid flight, cringe, hand cover, flinch, withdraw and request cessation, as behaviours shown by losers in conflict situations.

Stern & Bender (1974) observed appeasement signs in 3- to 5-year-old children asked to approach three unsmiling adults who fixated the child. Girls tended to show signs of appeasement mixed with affiliation (coy behaviour, cf. Marvin & Mossler, 1976). Boys tended to show appeasement mixed with aggression. In more natural situations, where the child approaches under his or her own volition (Connolly & Smith, 1972), or where the adult is friendly and initiates interaction with toys (Haskett, 1977), such appeasement signals are not so noticeable.

Most of the information on fears in older preschool and school age children is from interviews and questionnaires, either with mothers or with the children themselves. This work was pioneered by Jersild (see Jersild, 1933, 1946, for summaries).

Jersild & Holmes (1935) obtained information from parents and teachers on children's fears, based on observations over a 21-day period. For the under-two's, most commonly reported fears were of noise and agents of noise, and of strange objects, persons and situations, as well as of pain, loss of support, and sudden unexpected movements accompanied by lights or shadows. These all fit in with fear as being due to sudden changes in physical stimulation (Bronson's 'distress'), or to incongruous events (Bronson's 'wariness'), discussed earlier (with some reservations about how broadly 'incongruity' is being stretched). These fears declined with age, being still present but relatively infrequent by 4 years. Other types of fear increased; at 4–6 years the most common fears were of imaginary creatures, being in the dark or alone, animals, threat or danger of harm from traffic, drowning, fire, jail, etc.

Jersild, Markey & Jersild (1933) interviewed children aged 5–12 years. They also named fears such as of ghosts, witches, being in dark or alone, danger of attack by animals, bodily injury or illness. Some of these fears seem to be reality based, perhaps from prior experience. Over 70% of the sample described traffic accidents or illness as being 'actual worst happenings', for example. Other fears, such as witches or ghosts, are imaginary or fantasy in nature though perhaps learnt from adults.

Hagman (1932) interviewed mothers of 2- to 6-year-olds. She asked about things which their children had directly shown fear of or attempted to avoid. The most commonly reported were dogs, doctors, storms, deep water, vacuum cleaners, loud sounds and darkness. The original situations in which the fears were shown often involved seeing a strange object or being in a strange situation, and sudden approach was often implicated as well. Thus even for these learnt fears of middle childhood, factors of strangeness or sudden physical change may still predispose to the acquisition of a fearful response.

It is noticeable how fear of animals is prominent from 2 years on. It seems unlikely that many children have had direct hurtful experience with an animal such as a dog; only 1.8% of Jersild et al.'s (1933) sample described this as an 'actual worst happening'. Unfamiliar animals might, like unfamiliar humans, be discrepant stimuli whose behaviour is unpredictable and difficult to influence – even more so than unfamiliar humans, hence fear peaking later. On the other hand, many supposedly feared animals would not have been encountered. Pratt (1945) found that rural children aged 4–16 years reported many animal fears, such as of bears, snakes, lions, dogs, bulls and tigers; he regarded these as largely stereotyped – bears, snakes, lions and tigers were not found in the area concerned, and the fears could have been passed on by cultural tradition.

The studies by Jersild, Hagman and Pratt were all carried out in the USA some 30 or 40 years ago. More recent work by the Newsons in Britain (Newson & Newson, 1968) comes up with a similar picture, however. Their data are based on interviews with mothers of 4-year-olds. Two thirds of the children were reported as having definite recurrent fears of which mother was aware. Many of these were fantasy fears, such as of tigers or ghosts, though perhaps brought out by actual circumstances such as

189

animal-patterned wallpaper on a child's bedroom. Other fears were of incongruous stimuli – 'funny' masks, or people with physical defects – or of insects, night-time, mud, water. Children who had earlier experienced marked separation anxiety were reported as being more fearful generally (a theme developed by Bowlby, 1973).

Beyond the primary school age, typical fear-eliciting situations change again. Angelino, Dollins & Mech (1956), questioning 9- to 18-year-olds, found fears or worries about school to be prominent, while worries about safety, and animals, declined with age. Worries about social relations, and economic or political matters, tended to increase. Croake (1969) also found worries about safety, and school, to be important in 12-year-olds. Bauer (1976), using questionnaire data, found fantasy fears (monsters, ghosts) to decrease from 4 to 12 years, but worries about injury and physical danger to increase. Miller, Barrett, Hampe & Noble (1973) reported a factor analytic study of a fear inventory filled in by parents of children aged 6 to 16. Three main factors were obtained. Fear of 'natural events' declined over the age period, while fear of 'physical injury' and 'psychic stress' were maintained.

There are severe methodological problems with some of these studies. Questionnaires are a crude measure to use; Hagman (1932) found that interviews produced much more detailed results. Data from mothers on children's fears may be biassed or incomplete; Lapouse & Monk (1959) found many disagreements in reports of fear between 8- to 12-year-old children and their mothers, the latter often under-reporting compared to the former. Finally, rationalisation, misattribution and projection may all lead to inaccurate data being obtained by verbal report (Bowlby, 1973). Croake (1969) in a review pointed out inconsistencies in the results of different studies such as those above, probably due to these methodological problems as well as to the different times and places in which they were carried out.

9 Sex Differences in Fear

It has been held that girls are generally more fearful than boys (Gray, 1971b; Bowlby, 1973) but this is by no means consistently supported by the evidence. In their general review of sex differences, Maccoby & Jacklin (1974) conclude that observational studies usually do not show significant sex differences in fear, although studies based on self-reports or teachers' ratings do tend to do so.

Sex differences might vary of course with the type of fear being considered; Tennes & Lampl (1964) reported separation anxiety to be greater in boys, but stranger fear to be greater in girls. However, sex differences, even 'significant' ones, seem to be very difficult to replicate consistently. Corter

(1976) summarised sex differences in separation anxiety (see also Maccoby & Jacklin's Table 6.1). Corter's own studies were inconsistent in this way — some suggested boys followed mother more quickly on departure, but his 1976 study showed that boys stayed away longer when leaving on their own initiative. Possibly sex differences interact with who initiates the separation, boys being both more distressed if mother leaves, but more exploratory if they leave mother; but this is far from a firm conclusion at present. It could tie in though with evidence from several studies, summarised in Smith (1974), that boys are more likely than girls to experience difficulty in first settling to a nursery or playgroup.

Sex differences in fear of strangers have been summarised by Lewis & Brooks (1974) (see also Maccoby & Jacklin's Tables 5.3 and 6.2). Several studies do suggest that girls are either earlier, or more intense, in their fear of strangers, but other studies find no difference, while Bronson (1971) and Maccoby & Feldman (1972) found the opposite result.

10 Temporal Stability in Fears

Not many studies have looked to see if consistencies can be found in individual differences in fear across an appreciable time span. Those that have generally come up with moderate correlations.

Robson, Pedersen & Moss (1969) found that the frequency of mother-infant gazing at 1 and 3 months correlated positively to gazing at stranger, and negatively to fearfulness, at 8 and $9\frac{1}{2}$ months. The correlations were strongest for boys.

Bronson (1969a), using data from the Berkeley Growth Study, found consistencies in individual levels of fearfulness (observed or rated) from 1 month to $8\frac{1}{2}$ years for both sexes, but much more substantially for boys. Bronson (1969b), using data from Ainsworth's short-term longitudinal sample, found as in his previous study that age of onset of fear of strangers correlated with intensity of fear at one year, for boys but not for girls.

It is possible, however, that girls tend to show a different pattern of continuity in development. Kagan (1971) found that boys who were irritable and fearful at 4 or 8 months grew up to be quiet and inhibited 2-year-olds; whereas girls fearful at the earlier ages grew up to be restless, active and talkative 2-year-olds. Kagan suggests this is due to different parental reactions to fears in boys and girls.

Maccoby & Feldman (1972) found moderate stabilities from 2 to $2\frac{1}{2}$ and 3 years in both separation protest, and stranger interaction and fear. Bronson and Pankey (1977) would presumably ascribe these stabilities to learnt associations, in line with the stability they found from 2 to $3\frac{1}{2}$ years in

191

response to novel play situations. Bronson's two-factor model predicts some stability from about 1 year onwards, but not before, in apparent contrast to Kagan's results.

11   Bowlby's Theory of Attachment and Explanation of Anxiety

The most comprehensive theory of the origin and development of fear in childhood is that of Bowlby (1969, 1973). Bowlby places the development of fear in an evolutionary perspective, in terms of the kinds of behaviour likely to further survival. He links fear in childhood with the development of attachment relationships, seen as primarily serving a protective function while the infant is helpless. This in turn leads to a unitary theory of anxiety in terms of insecure attachment.

Bowlby defines attachment behaviours as those that tend to maintain proximity to particular individuals. He sees the process of attachment between infant and mother (or caretaker) as developing through four phases. In Phase II, the baby orientates and signals to persons, without discrimination. In Phase II, the baby orientates and signals preferentially to one or a few specific individuals. In Phase III (one year onwards) the baby can locomote as well as signal, and acts to maintain proximity by means of both types of behaviour. This is conceived of as a plan with a set goal. At this stage, however, the baby can take little if any account of the mother's plans or objectives. By 2 or 3 years, though, the young child can do so, and Bowlby talks then of a goal-corrected 'partnership' between mother and child, this being Phase IV.

Marvin (1977) has extended Bowlby's scheme. As an example of taking account of mother's plans, he devised a 'cookie' test. Children were asked to wait while mother finished a letter, before being given a cookie. 2-year-olds could not wait, but most 3- and 4-year-olds could. While this situation is not specifically an attachment one, Marvin argues that this kind of skill – integration of mother's plans to one's own – would generalise to different contexts. The 3- and 4-year-olds would thus be in Bowlby's Phase IV. Marvin extends the scheme to Phase V (four years on), in which actual physical proximity or contact with mother are no longer major goals of the child. Rather, concordance with mother's attitudes or plans is aimed for. This implies a greater degree of nonegocentrism or perspective-taking, for which Marvin and others have found evidence at 4 years and onwards. The relationship is now a more abstract one, related to understanding and approval.

Bowlby and Marvin see the main function of attachment behaviour, in evolutionary terms, as being the protection of the relatively helpless infant from danger. On the infant's side, it can best achieve this at first by signalling and locomoting to maintain proximity. It would normally be safest when with a mother or other familiar adult. Its signalling and locomoting should be especially strongly activated if it can detect signs of danger or clues to danger – stimuli which would normally or often indicate danger. Such signs would lead to fear, which would be allayed by proximity or contact with the attachment figure. Failure to make satisfactory contact would maintain a state of anxiety. (Bowlby uses anxiety in this specific sense to mean inadequately fulfilled attachment behaviour, or goals; alarm in contrast means recognition of a specific danger; fear includes anxiety and alarm.)

The situation in which children experience anxiety will thus depend on the particular phase of attachment they are in. Separation anxiety will emerge in Phase II, but will become more contingent on detailed circumstances – such as what mother's plans are, or how she explains them – by Phases IV and V. Marvin gives details of the behaviour of 2-, 3- and 4-year-olds in response to Ainsworth & Wittig's (1969) strange situation experiment, which he feels supports the distinctions above.

In considering the kinds of situation or stimulus leading to fear, and to the activation of attachment, Bowlby reviews much of the work considered earlier in this chapter. The early fear stimuli – pain, loud noises, loss of support, rapidly changing physical stimulation, looming, visual cliff, strange/discrepant persons or objects – are considered natural clues to danger. Additional fears prevalent in the second and third year, such as fears of animals, being alone or in darkness, are considered to be readily learnt derivatives of natural clues. By 'natural', Bowlby is referring to the environment of evolutionary adaptedness (a hunter-gatherer existence) in which human biological evolution primarily occurred. It would be to the advantage of the baby if it responded fearfully to 'natural' clues to danger from very early on; the responses would thus be virtually innate, or depending only on maturational or nonspecific learning processes. The development of fear in the first two or three years is thus seen as environmentally stable, or relatively unsusceptible to different rearing environments. For example, fear of strangers at a similar age and in similar form to British and American children has been observed among the Kung Bushmen (Konner, 1972), Hopi Indians (Dennis, 1940), Guatemalans (Lester, Kotelchuck, Spelke, Sellers & Klein, 1974), Ganda infants (Ainsworth, 1963) and Zambian infants (Goldberg, 1972).

As the child gets older it responds fearfully more and more to what Bowlby calls 'cultural' clues, of which he distinguishes two varieties. Some cultural clues are learnt by observation of others being fearful in certain situations; for example, fear of dentists, dogs, thunderstorms, might be learnt in this way. Others are learnt from adults more indirectly, as ways of assessing and avoiding danger. These are typically characteristic of later childhood and adolescence; for example, fears of natural disasters, murder or kidnapping, political instability.

Some fearful responses to natural and cultural clues will appear sensible, but others (e.g. darkness, thunderstorms) may appear irrational. Clues to danger may be misleading, especially if environmentsl circumstances have changed from when the clues were useful predictors of danger. Nevertheless such 'irrational' fears are a normal, expected part of development. The child is also of course developing its own directly made evaluations of what is or is not dangerous, based on its own experiences (learnt associations, at the simplest level), and these will be developing parallel with (or in combination with) response to the natural and cultural clues outlined above; Bowlby puts most emphasis on the latter, however.

The most controversial part of Bowlby's view concerns the long-term and pervasive effects of secure or insecure attachment on anxiety and fear. Evidently, attachment figures do provide security in early childhood. Bowlby suggests that this provision of security can be more or less effective, depending on the general success of the attachment relationship. Children whose attachment figures are not consistently available, who behave unpredictably or rejectingly, will develop 'anxious attachment'. Not only will they be less secure in the short term, they will also be more prone to either intense or chronic fear later in life. Confidence in the availability of attachment figures is built up slowly through childhood, which therefore constitutes a sensitive period for the development of the ability to cope with problems in a self-reliant, or alternatively anxious, way.

Bowlby's model of fear development stands as a considerable achievement in drawing together a great deal of empirical work, and his emphasis on the adaptive value of fear deserves further consideration from a modern sociobiological perspective. There are however some objections and reservations to be made.

Firstly, Bowlby's arguments concerning the evolutionary functions of attachment and fear are phrased in group selection terms. It is now widely accepted that individual selection is almost always much more important than group selection, and that inclusive fitness is the metric for the adaptive value of behaviour. This does not greatly affect Bowlby's argument; avoiding danger is generally beneficial for the individual as well as for the group, or species. Some more subtle aspects of Bowlby's views are affected, however – in particular the use of signals, and possible conflict situations between mother (caretaker) and child.

Briefly, Trivers (1974) has indicated that some degree of conflict can be expected between mother and child, since the child should value itself (relative to, for example, siblings) more than its mother does. This could

194

affect Bowlby's arguments that, for example, spoiling a child is not a meaningful term in early childhood. In particular, we should bear in mind that signals – such as crying – are designed to maximise the fitness of the sender and not the receiver (contrary to what a group selection model would predict). This makes exaggeration or faking of messages seem more plausible. Perhaps the 'fake' cries referred to by Wolff (1969) are an example of this – it could be to the advantage of the child to encourage more care from its mother, using cry signals, provided that by so doing it does not jeopardise its protection in times of more urgent need.

It would also be possible to take issue with Bowlby as to whether fear is best seen as one system or several (Bronson, 1974; Dunn, 1977). In fact Bowlby does not seem to be tied to one mechanism for fear (as opposed to one primary adaptive function), so some of these criticisms may miss the point. However, Bowlby does tie the predisposition to many fears, and also specific phobias in later life such as school phobia or agoraphobia, to secure versus insecure attachment in childhood. Although he marshals much evidence in support, this is clearly a very bold claim which will need more empirical validation, including specific attempts to disconfirm it, before it can be generally accepted. It should be borne in mind that some theorists, such as Harré (1974), regard peer relations in later childhood as an autonomous world bearing little direct relationship to the earlier attachment phase with adults. Also, the evidence for very early social interest in peers (e.g. Lewis, Young, Brooks & Michalson, 1975) suggests realms of social interaction developing outside the mother or adult-child bond.

Related to this, Bowlby might be said to underestimate the importance of contingency of responsiveness in affiliation or positive motivation, and noncontingency as a possible cause of fear. He does indeed point its importance, in terms of sensitivity, for the mother-child bond. However, he does not consider contingency outside the attachment relationship – contingency of peers, objects or events. A more general 'effectance' model might put the undoubted importance of adult-child attachment realtionships in a broader perspective (Weinraub, Brooks & Lewis, 1977). Such a model might be better related to cognitive assimilation models such as those of Sroufe, Waters & Matas (1974) and Kagan (1974).

For further progress, the cognitive models will need to be more precisely specified in terms of developmental theory (what is a hypothesis, at a particular point in development? why is it difficult to assimilate? what perspectives can be understood, and plans constructed?). However a cognitive model, even one taking account of social and communicative competence, must also take account of, and ultimately be unified with, a model of the motivational bases to behaviour. A systems theory model of fear motivation has been proposed by Bischof (1975). His specific model is based

195

partly on Bowlby's theory, also on research and concepts from animal ethology.

12   Bischof's Systems Model of Fear Motivation

Bischof's model incorporates two set-goal systems. First is a 'security' system. Depending on its level of 'dependency', the infant has a need for 'security', which it seeks by signalling and locomoting to the mother. Proximity to mother is monitored to reach the set goal at which security is sufficient to match dependency. Bischof differs mainly from Bowlby here in surmising that the dependency level could fall much lower as puberty is reached, for example, that this would lead to a negative need for security, or 'aversion' (note that this is primarily a motivational explanation for an age change in attachment, rather than a cognitive one).

Superimposed on the 'security' system, though maturing somewhat later, is an 'arousal system'. Depending on its level of 'enterprise', the infant has a need for 'arousal' which it seeks to moderate by either exploration (enterprise greater than arousal), or fear (enterprise less than arousal). The set goal here is reached by monitoring the relevance and novelty of stimuli (which affect arousal) and taking appropriate approach or avoidance measures relative to the level of enterprise appertaining at the time.

Bischof's model is unelaborated cognitively, for example as concerns the specification of his cognitive detectors which determine proximity, relevance and novelty. It does not incorporate any delay between alert and affect, or a continuing attempt to assimilate a situation, as incongruity type theorists suggest. Proximity is seen in physical terms, so the later cognitive phases in Bowlby's and Marvin's attachment model (partnership in terms of plans) is not explicitly accommodated in Bischof's model. However, the model is quite complex motivationally. It supposes separate systems of attachment or surfeit (moderated by dependency), and exploration or fear (moderated by enterprise). It is supposed that the 'security' system matures before the 'arousal' system, so that the infant does not initially fear the (novel) mother – this would interfere with the attachment process. Prior to the maturation of the 'arousal' system, the main cause of fear would be distress when the need for security is unsatisfied. When the 'arousal' system matures (after primary attachments are formed at, say, 8 months), fear of novelty or incongruity will appear. This might agree with Schaffer's (1974) shift at 8 months 'from impulsiveness to wariness', though not so well with evidence suggesting earlier wariness to strange or incongruous persons or events which other investigators have noted. It would appear to indicate a greater distinction between separation anxiety and fear of incongruity than some cognitive theorists would admit to.

Bischof does state that the 'security' and 'arousal' systems become interconnected to a certain extent. The proximity of the mother, as a familiar and relevant stimulus, will inhibit arousal, and thus facilitate exploration (as well as promoting security, as before). Clearly this could be true of other attachment figures. Bischof assumes an 'imprinting' model of attachment formation, but given a more cognitive emphasis on contingency of responsiveness, the model could perhaps be adapted to give a broader reference frame for attachment than Bowlby's model possesses.

Following Bowlby, Bischof supposes a long-term damping effect of security on dependency; according to Bowlby's view there should also be a long-term damping effect of security on enterprise. (Indeed it could be questioned whether 'dependency' and 'enterprise' should really be considered as separate entities – compare the discussion as to whether separation anxiety and fear of strangers are closely related.) However, the details of what leads to 'insecure attachment' are not elaborated in Bischof's model. It almost certainly is not just the mother's familiarity, but includes aspects such as contingency and sensitivity of her behavioural meshing with the infant's demands, and how well the infant can begin to understand and assimilate her plans (compare Marvin's discussion).

While motivationally elaborate, Bischof's model is cognitively simple. Nevertheless, flow diagrams or systems models such as his have the advantage of making assumptions clear, and of generating predictions (even if sometimes it seems all to easy to adapt a model to cope with any disconfirmation). Attempts to integrate a motivational systems model with a sophisticated cognitive model, perhaps on the lines of those in the artificial intelligence field but with a firm developmental basis, would be a useful next step.

13   The Adaptiveness of Fearful Behaviour

Bowlby has suggested that the early development of fear follows largely preprogrammed lines, even in the human infant. If this is the case, it makes sense to consider the adaptiveness of such fearful behaviour from the standpoint of biological evolution and inclusive fitness. As mentioned earlier, Bowlby makes out a case for the early fear-provoking events being natural clues to danger. This seems clear enough for pain, sudden change in physical stimulation, darkness, being alone.

Why, wariness of strangers? In terms of inclusive fitness, it makes sense for the attachment bond to develop between an infant and closely related adults, as it is closely related persons who are most likely to behave altruistically. Closely related adults are therefore the best bet to protect an infant from danger (as in doing so they will help to preserve their own genes in future generations). Normally, related adults will be those familiar to the infant and interacting contingently to it, so the infant uses these as actual criteria as to whom to form bonds with. Strangers are unlikely to be closely related (in the environment of evolutionary adaptedness), and are therefore a less safe bet in terms of likely positive responses to the infant. It would pay an infant to 'sound out' the intentions and disposition of a strange adult before approaching or making affiliative gestures too readily. An initial wariness (mixed with exploration and affiliation) could be a suitable means of doing this.

Since present-day environments for most children differ very considerably from the environment of evolutionary adaptedness, the adaptiveness of early fearful behaviour may not always now be clear. In many respects the child's world of today is much more protected. Strangers, and animals, are not usually a danger; though there are new dangers, such as stairs, electric sockets, motor cars. The young child may seem insufficiently afraid of some circumstances, while other aspects of shyness or fear — the new child to a playgroup, for example — may seem more of a problem than an asset.

Later fear development depends more on cognitive factors than on sudden physical changes, or incongruity. The more that fearful responses are determined by specific learning experiences of the child, rather than general learning or maturational processes, the more directly relevant and adaptive they might be expected to be to the child's actual present environment. The problem in considering adaptiveness is now a different one. What is the metric against which adaptiveness is to be measured? With later development, there is increasing emphasis on cultural factors and demands, and consistency with beliefs and ideas. Kagan (1974) suggests that the recognition of inconsistency between beliefs and behaviour, or of dissonance between or among beliefs, can be causes of distress in older children, adolescents and adults. In such cases, behaviour which furthers the survival of the individual, or of the individual's genes (inclusive fitness) seems to be becoming subordinate to behaviour, mediated by complex cognitive processes and cultural transmission, which furthers the maintainence of cultural ideas or instructions, or 'memes' (Cloak, 1975; Dawkins, 1976). The degree of intermeshing between biological and cultural evolution is still very debatable (Barkow, 1978), and some argue that inclusive fitness may still be a useful criterion for human behaviour in settled communities (Durham, 1976). However, it wuld be dangerous to assume that fearful behaviour in middle and later childhood, and even more in adults, is adaptive in the same way that fear in early childhood has probably been selected to be.

CHAPTER 7

The Psychopathology of Fear

A. T. Carr

The context within which this chapter is set is one that illustrates the essential normality of fear and its associated behaviours. Inevitably, this raises the question of what differentiates pathological fear from normal fear. The first point is that the differentiating characteristics are not properties of the emotional experience itself: there are no grounds for supposing that the subjective experiences of the agoraphobic individual swept up in a melee of football supporters are qualitatively or quantitatively different from those of a normal person on the tenth floor of a building during a violent earthquake. Both would describe their experiences in terms of apprehension, a tendency to panic and a desire to get away. It is insufficient to confine this comparison to subjective experience alone for, as Rachman and Hodgson (1974) have pointed out, the various measures and indices of fear correlate so poorly that a satisfactory description requires assessment on behavioural and physiological dimensions as well as on the dimension of subjective emotional experience.

As described elsewhere in this volume, the behavioural and physiological concomitants of normal fear are typically immobility or flight and heightened sympathetic autonomic activity. The unfortunate individuals mentioned above will respond similarly with some permutation of freezing or flight, tachycardia, sweating, trembling, nausea, giddiness or fainting. This is not to say that there are no individual differences in susceptibility to fear or in the patterning of autonomic responses, but rather that once a state of fear exists, whether it would be labelled normal or pathological, the distinction between normal and pathological fear is not apparent in the dimensions normally used to measure and describe that state.

It could be argued that there is a dimension of this state, although not commonly used, which would help us to make the discrimination between normal and pathological fear. It appears from the limited evidence currently available (e.g. Carr, 1974; Marks, 1977) that individuals whose fears could be described as pathological make interpretations or cognitive appraisals of their emotional experience which differ from those made by people whose fear we would describe as normal. In phobic and obsessional disorders the afflicted persons recognise the irrationality of their fears, or more precisely they are aware of the lack of correspondence between the nature and extent of their reaction and the characteristics and implications of the situation which provokes that reaction. In normal fear, however, such as that experienced during an earthquake, the person is not aware of this discrepancy between his reaction and the nature of the precipitating stimuli or events; however disruptive or maladaptive it might be, it is recognised as not unreasonable under the prevailing circumstances.

So despite the lack of behavioural, physiological and experiental criteria that might differentiate pathological fear from normal fear, the cognitive appraisals made by a fearful person provide one dimension along which such differentiation could be achieved. However, an individual's appraisal of his own state of fear as reasonable or not is hardly sufficient for there are many situations in relation to which a fearful response would be regarded as reasonable and also regarded as pathological. The pathology lies in the degree to which the fear disrupts, directly or indirectly, behaviours or other processes which are functionally important to the individual. An intense fear of heights is unlikely to merit description as pathological for the typical farmer or shop assistant, but certainly would do so for a window cleaner or construction worker. Intense fears of social situations could hardly fail to disrupt the lives of people in crowded urban environments but would have much less impact upon those who live in sparsely populated rural settings. The point is well illustrated by the case of a height-phobic male who presented for treatment at the age of 56. He reported that he had been intensely fearful of heights all his life but that this fear had been largely irrelevant to his life-style. He had been able to walk to work, thus obviating the possibility of having to sit on the upper deck of a bus, and his office was situated in a single-storey complex. However, one month before he sought treatment his employers had moved to a purpose-built tower block in the centre of the city. His new office was on the seventh floor and he found it impossible to face the daily prospect of sitting at his desk beside a large picture window looking out over the town. While in his office he was continually nauseated, giddy and quite unable to work. He experienced feelings of panic and an overwhelming desire to get down to ground level. Within two weeks of the move he began to avoid going to work and rapidly sought help for his problem. However unreasonable one might consider this man's fear, it had not constituted a problem at any time during the many years prior to his employers' change of premises and thus could not be considered pathological during that period. Subsequent to the move, which was a purely situational change, the fear assumed pathological proportions because of its disruption of behaviour which fulfilled a highly valued and necessary function for this particular individual.

Clearly, the degree and nature of the disruption consequent upon the fear will influence the cognitive appraisal an individual will make of the fear in terms of how reasonable or appropriate it is. The greater the disruption and the more valued or functionally necessary the behaviour or process that is disrupted, the more likely it is that the person will see the fear as unreasonable.

In this brief discussion we have argued that fear is pathological to the extent that it is appraised as unreasonable and disrupts valued or functionally important behaviours and other individual processes. The term disruption implies interference with ongoing activity of some kind but there are instances in which the anticipation of fear and its consequences prevents the development of new behaviours or involvement in new activities for the individual. In such cases the person does not typically experience fear or clearly demonstrate the behavioural and autonomic correlates of the experience. There is not the readily observable behavioural deficit which occurs when a person becomes unable, through fear, to continue to exercise or to perform some activity which had previously occurred with some frequency. Rather than a loss of function there is a restriction of the range and diversity of activities available to the person: the highly proficient amateur musician who performs only in private despite a personal desire to perform in public, and who does not do so for fear of the anticipated consequences of such an extension of his activities, could be regarded as being afflicted with a pathological fear. It is hardly likely that a fear of this kind would be sufficient to bring the person into a clinical situation if he is otherwise undisturbed and coping. However, it has been argued (e.g. Maslow, 1973) that the mere absence of distress and the presence of adequate coping are insufficient criteria of psychological wellbeing: psychological health requires the active process of fulfilment or actualisation, the realisation of one's potential as a human being with certain abilities and needs. We might therefore extend our definition of pathological fear to include those fearful anticipations which preclude the desired adoption of new behaviours as well as those fears which disrupt ongoing behaviours and processes which are highly valued or functionally important. Although the former type of fear may lead to psychological disturbances under certain circumstances, e.g. depression, the major clinical problem arises from the distress and functional deficit resulting from the latter type of fear, those which disrupt ongoing behaviours and processes that fulfil an important function for the individual.

Clearly, the criteria of pathological fear that have been discussed

201

correspond closely to the criteria commonly used to identify clinical phobias. For example Marks (1977) defines a phobia as 'a special kind of fear that is out of proportion to the reality of the situation, can neither be explained nor reasoned away, is largely beyond voluntary control, and leads to avoidance of the feared situation (p.177)'. In view of what has been said earlier, this definition appears to stress unduly the significance of avoidance behaviour for this is not an inevitable consequence of intense fear. Although avoidance is usually disruptive, provided that it prevents the person from exercising some functionally important behaviour, disruption can result from disturbances in such functions as attention, recall or motor coordination. Thus it seems appropriate to emphasise disruption resulting from fear, whether or not the disruption is consequent upon avoidance.

1 Phobic and Obsessional States

Although chronic and acute states of fear may lead to a large number of diverse problems, phobias and obsessions constitute clear examples of unreasonable fears which severely disrupt individual functioning. The former have already been defined and an obsession or compulsion may be defined as 'a recurrent or persistent thought, image, impulse or action that is accompanied by a sense of subjective compulsion and a desire to resist it (Carr, 1974, p.311).' The disruption in obsessional states results from the person's feeling compelled to behave in certain ways or to repeatedly contemplate certain thoughts, even though these are recognised as unreasonable and antithetical to normal functioning.

1.1 Classification

Marks (1969) divides phobias into two main classes, fears of external stimuli and fears of internal stimuli, the former category accounting for about 85% of all clinical phobias. Illness phobias are the only examples cited under fears of internal stimuli and these account for the remaining 15% of clinical cases. Chronic and intense fears of illness appear to have as much in common with obsessional states as with phobias, in that the individual typically experiences repeated intrusive thoughts about the illness and checks for its presence or absence by seeking confirmatory information. This seems entirely consistent with the cognitive experiences and checking behaviours of obsessional patients. If a categorical classification system is to be retained, and fears of illness were to be included with obsessional phenomena, another dimension becomes discernable which, although related to

202

externality/internality, may prove to be more heuristic. The dimension is the avoidability of stimuli, the extent to which the person can avoid the source of fear. This point is discussed in some detail later in the chapter in relation to phobic and obsessional symptoms as alternative 'solutions' to fear, determined in part by the avoidability of stimuli.

Obsessional states may be divided into those that contain overt compulsive behaviour and those that are primarily cognitive with little or no overt manifestation. However, relevant cognitions appear to be a necessary antecedent of ritual behaviour, at least in the acute stages of the disorder, and the development of such behaviours seems to be a function of the availability of appropriate action. For example, ritualised washing is an appropriate response to fears of contamination but there is no similarly appropriate response to fears that one's children might lose their sight or that they might be killed in a road accident. Carr (1974) argued that in the absence of appropriate, available behaviour, the primary symptoms are those of repeated intrusive thoughts and anxiety, with the possibility of apparently 'superstitious' behaviours aimed at averting these feared events. So, both phobic and obsessional symptoms may be determined, at least in part, by the nature of the feared stimuli and the availability of appropriate behavioural responses.

1.2   Temporal Aspects

It is clear that the peak incidence of nonpathological fears is related to the age of the subjects studied (see Chapter 6). Similarly, phobic and obsessional states vary in their incidence and content as a function of age. Animal phobias typically start in early childhood and persist fairly continuously thereafter. As Marks (1969) points out, since fears of animals are common in childhood we must presume that animal phobias in adulthood represent the few instances in which these early fears do not extinguish. In contrast, agoraphobias and social phobias typically start after puberty with peak incidence in the late teenage years, although agoraphobias may occasionally develop after the age of 30 which is rare in the case of social phobias. The remaining major group of phobias, those which are related to specific environmental stimuli, show yet a further pattern of incidence over time. Rather than the skewed distributions of animal, social and agoraphobias, specific phobias follow a square distribution of incidence at different ages. In other words, phobias of heights, thunderstorms, lifts, etc., may occur at any age and persist fairly continuously thereafter.

Where these specific phobias originate in childhood, their persistence runs counter to the general trend. Angelino & Shedd (1953) and MacFarlane et al. (1954) found that for specific fears the frequency showed a definite downward trend with age for both boys and girls. These authors also reported a marked increase in frequency at about 11 years of age. This late peak in incidence coincides with the observations of other authors (e.g. Chazan, 1962; Morgan, 1959) of the peak age for school phobias at about 11 years. The term school phobia is itself problematical for as several authors have pointed out (e.g. Johnson, 1957; Radin, 1967; Vaughan, 1968) it emphasises a common symptom which has a number of diverse underlying antecedents, such as the fear of school, the fear of leaving home or of leaving mother, or no fear at all. Berecz (1969) provides a good discussion of school phobia, and Hersov (1960) and Herbert (1978) carefully delineate the several emotional and behavioural components of persistent nonattendance at school.

Such clear differences in incidence at different ages may reflect the importance of different learning processes at different ages, e.g. classical conditioning in early years and vicarious learning in later years, and/or the different ages at which people are exposed to the stimuli which appear as the phobic stimuli in the several groups of phobias.

In true obsessional disorders the first symptoms typically occur in the early twenties (Ingram, 1961; Lo, 1967; Pollitt, 1957). However, it seems likely that these symptoms represent the start of the disorder which brings the person into a clinical situation, for Pollitt (1957) emphasises the need to distinguish between the onset of the main disorder and the onset of previous 'attacks'. In his study of 150 cases Pollitt demonstrated that early occurrences of obsessional symptoms are common, particularly during adolescence, with up to three such occurrences before the onset of the main disorder. Also, Black (1974), on the basis of cumulative data derived from eight studies, showed that the highest incidence of first symptoms occurs between the ages of 10 and 15 years, by which time almost a third of the cases studied had started. Over 50% of the disorders had begun by the age of 25 years and only about 25% started after the age of 30 years.

Just as there is difficulty in determining the onset of a childhood phobia due to the generally high incidence of fears in childhood (Scarr & Salapatek, 1970), so behaviour with obsessional qualities is sufficiently common in childhood to make the diagnosis of an early obsessional state extremely problematical. Berman (1942) studied 62 children initially diagnosed as suffering from obsessional disorders and found, on closer scrutiny, that only six could be regarded as showing true obsessional symptoms. In summary, the course and age-incidence distribution of obsessional states are similar to the patterns found in social phobias and agoraphobia.

The remainder of this chapter will be devoted largely to a consideration of the theoretical aspects of phobic and obsessional states. In keeping with the theme of this volume, the emphasis will be upon the development of the fear and anxiety which is assumed to underlie the emergence and maintenance of phobic and obsessional symptoms. Because the acquisition of fear and avoidance behaviours readily lend themselves to empirical investigation, the bulk of the discussion is inevitably weighted towards these phenomena. Since fear and avoidance are typical of phobic states, though the criterial significance of avoidance has already been questioned, the discussion is most obviously relevant to phobic states. Consequently, before embarking upon the main theme some preliminary consideration of obsessional states is necessary.

Although several authors have questioned the relationship between fear and obsessions (e.g. Krafft-Ebbing, 1897; Westphal, 1877), the more contemporary view is that compulsive behaviours take place at high levels of anxiety and reduce this anxiety to a tolerable level (e.g. Carr, 1974; Meyer, 1966; Pollitt, 1957; Walton & Mather, 1964). Therefore the discussion of the acquisition of fear which follows this section is of clear relevance to an understanding of obsessional disorders. Theoretical models of obsessional states have been reviewed in detail quite recently (Carr, 1974; Teasdale, 1974), so only brief mention will be made here of points which are relevant and which are not covered in the main discussion.

Apart from the model proposed by Carr (1974), each of the attempts to explain the development of obsessional symptoms has concentrated upon behaviour, and cognitive symptoms have been ignored. Also, the ritualistic nature of obsessional behaviours has not been explained. Since specific cognitions and ritualised behaviours are common features of obsessional states, and it has been pointed out above that appropriate cognitions are necessary precursors of obsessional behaviours, any adequate model must be able to incorporate these phenomena. This point is considered in some detail later.

There is no evidence to support an assumption that traumatic learning is a common factor in the development of the majority of obsessional states. Not only does this assumption receive scant support, but there are clinical data that are contradictory. It is clear from the descriptions of obsessional symptoms given by Pollitt (1957) and by Carr (1970) that the simultaneous occurrence of several different obsessions in the same individual is extremely common. Any theory that is based upon assumptions of traumatic learning can account for a multiplicity of symptoms only by further assumptions of several traumatic learning experiences, or by invoking the principle of generalisation. If generalisation were an important factor, then the several

205

symptoms should be concerned with stimuli that are related in some way. Clearly, the very diversity of obsessional symptoms that can occur simultaneously in the same individual contradicts this expectation and raises more doubts about the role of traumatic learning in the aetiology of obsessional states.

The only theoretical proposals which were not reviewed by either Carr (1974) or Teasdale (1974) are those of Beech & Perigault (1974). These authors proposed that 'obsessionals are characterised by a tendency to exaggerated arousal and that such states may reach critical levels at which, instead of decrement being observed, additional stimulation may produce increased arousal (p.115)'. They go on to argue that resulting spontaneous fluctuations of arousal lead to conditioning in which 'the exceptional state of the organism becomes attached to discriminable environmental cues (p. 116)'. Their emphasis upon the role of arousal arises from their equating 'the pathology of mood states' with 'aberrations of the arousal system (p.116)'. This is somewhat puzzling since the best researched pathology of mood, i.e. depression, has not been explained as an abnormality of arousal per se (e.g. Akiskal & McKinney, 1975). Moreover, the data upon which they argue for the importance of mood states (Walker & Beech, 1969) were not in accord with their prediction. For example, the mood states of obsessional patients did not deteriorate during an expanded judgement task and the initial mood state of the patients did not correlate significantly with the number of additional observations required during the task. However, there seems little doubt that Walker's early experiments pointed to abnormalities of decision processes in obsessional patients and, as other work showed (Carr, 1970), it is possible to provide a viable and comprehensive account of obsessional symptoms in terms of decision processes.

Beech & Perigault go on to demonstrate the existence, in general, of such processes as habituation, sensitisation, one-trial learning, etc., but the relevance of these phenomena to obsessional states is not demonstrated nor argued in detail. Also, they recognise that their proposals regarding the basic abnormality of arousal do not differentiate obsessional patients from other groups such as social phobics and agoraphobics. They point out that 'We would not feel that the failure to differentiate obsessionals from other abnormal groups affects our theory (p.137)'. It seems that this failure is damaging to their theory since the principal symptomatology of these groups is quite different, e.g. neither social phobics nor agoraphobics experience the subjective sense of compulsion which is of criterial significance in obsessional disorders, nor do they typically show the ritualised behaviours that are so common in obsessional states. If their major proposals regarding abnormalities of arousal do not relate specifically to obsessional problems then the important issue concerns the processes by which disparate

206

symptomatologies develop from a common underlying state. Beech & Perigault do not address themselves to this question. As mentioned earlier, it is possible that obsessional and phobic symptoms represent alternative responses to fear although the basic processes of fear acquisition may be common to both types of disorders. Let us now turn to the fundamental issue of the acquisition of fear and its associated behaviours.

2   The Acquisition of Fear and Avoidance

Although it is recognised that conceptual distinctions have often been made between the terms fear and anxiety (see Chapters 1 and 2) there are no clearly persuasive grounds for regarding the respective states as qualitatively different. Even the most traditional distinction has attached criterial significance to a factor which is not a component of the emotional state of the individual, that is, the presence or absence of an observable focus for the emotion; fear has a focal object and anxiety does not. However, there is now growing evidence that the clearest illustration of the objectlessness of anxiety, so-called free-floating anxiety, occurs in response to identifiable stimuli. Beck et al. (1974), Beck & Rush (1975) and Mathews & Shaw (1977) among others, have shown that almost all patients suffering from free-floating anxiety are able to identify thoughts or visual images which regularly precede or accompany anxiety reactions. In this context it is worth noting the study by May (1977) who showed that when subjects intentionally generated thoughts about phobic stimuli, the consequent subjective and autonomic measures of anxiety were as great as those elicited by presentation of the actual stimuli. Other conventional distinctions, such as fear being the emotion elicited in the presence of the feared object or situation and anxiety being anticipatory, appear to reduce to differences of degree with fear being the more intense emotion of the two.

For the purposes of this discussion it is proposed that fear and anxiety are regarded as synonymous, the only differences being differences of degree. It is accepted that because anxiety has consequences for overt behaviour, attentional processes, etc., quantitative changes in anxiety will lead to qualitative changes in dependent functions. For example, avoidance behaviour may only occur when anxiety is sufficiently intense, and this discontinuity clearly constitutes a qualitative change. Such discontinuities in the relationship between anxiety and associated functions were mentioned earlier and have been called desynchronies by Rachman & Hodgson (1974). The question of desynchrony and possible underlying processes will be discussed later. Clinical observation and empirical work suggest that differences in the intensity of anxiety depend largely upon the proximity of

207

the feared object, situation or event, although other factors such as perceived control and predictability of aversive events (Seligman, 1975; Weiss, 1970) will interact with proximity.

It is necessary to distinguish between at least three types of proximity: spatial, temporal and functional. In other words, the closer an anxiety-provoking object, event or situation is in space, or time, or functionally, the greater is the elicited anxiety. It is an everyday observation that as the physical distance between an individual and a feared stimulus is decreased the more anxious he becomes. This relationship between physical distance and the intensity of anxiety is the basis of the behavioural avoidance test (Lang & Lazovik, 1963) and the therapeutic technique of in vivo de-sensitisation by graduated exposure. The effects of temporal proximity are readily observed in undergraduates as the date of final examination draws closer and readily experienced in symposia as the time for presenting one's own paper becomes imminent. They are observed clinically in school-phobic children who may be quite free of anxiety from Friday evening until late on Sunday morning, but who becomes increasingly anxious as Sunday wears on and Monday morning approaches (Berecz, 1968; Hersov, 1960). Similarly, surgery patients show increasing anxiety as the time for their operation approaches (Chapman & Cox, 1977). The countdown to electric shock procedure employed by Epstein (e.g. Epstein, 1971; Epstein & Roupenian, 1970) clearly reveals the effects of temporal proximity upon anxiety as reflected in skin conductance responses.

Examples of functional proximity and its effects are perhaps less obvious than the above illustrations of spatial and temporal proximity. Functional proximity may be defined as the degree to which an event which is integral to a sequence of events guarantees that the sequence will operate to its conclusion, where this conclusion is an aversive event or situation. Everyday examples can be found in such situations as conveying an unwilling infant to a day nursery or an unwilling child to the dentist. Anxiety, with consequent protest and resistance, peaks at the start of the journey and then declines before rising again as a function of increasing spatial and temporal proximity. Clinical observation reveals a similar effect in therapeutic strategies which involve sequential events which lead to an aversive conclusion. The in vivo treatment of school phobia, for example, often falters at the first stage of getting the child to leave the house. Attempts to encourage or persuade the child provoke anxiety and active resistance. However, an agreed change in the end point of the sequence such as a walk up to the school gates and back, or a walk round the school grounds, usually alleviates the anxiety and the child leaves the house without protest. Once again, the countdown to shock procedure used by Epstein and his colleagues (e.g. Epstein & Roupenian, 1970) reveals the role of functional proximity with skin conductance activity peaking as the countdown begins, then declining and finally rising again as temporal proximity to the shock increases. Clearly, functional proximity has the effect of displacing anxiety in time and space. The crucial event will assume aversive qualities through its sequential implications and the factors of temporal and spatial proximity will operate in relation to the event. Also, the judgement of which event constitutes the first irreversible step in a sequence leading to an aversive outcome will sometimes be highly idiosyncratic but there will be many instances of consensus because of the shared realities of the world in which we live.

To summarise: it is proposed that fear and anxiety are essentially similar states, differing only in intensity, and the terms may be regarded as synonymous. Also, it has been argued briefly that the intensity of an anxiety response is a positive function of proximity to the aversive object, event or situation and that proximity operates along spatial, temporal and functional dimensions. The processes through which proximity may exert its effects will be discussed later.

2.1 Theoretical Models of Fear and Avoidance

There can be little doubt that for the past three or four decades the most influential theory of the acquisition of fear and the development of avoidance behaviour has been the two-stage theory, in which classically conditioned fear maintains the operant response of avoidance (Eysenck & Rachman, 1965; Maier, Seligman & Solomon, 1969; Miller, 1948; Mowrer, 1939, 1947, 1960b; Rescorla & Solomon, 1967; Solomon & Brush, 1954). Mowrer (1939) argued that fear develops as a classically conditioned response (CR) through the pairing of an aversive or painful unconditioned stimulus (UCS) with an initially neutral conditioned stimulus (CS). He went on to argue that the conditioned fear motivates avoidance behaviour which, when executed, reduces fear and this reduction in fear reinforces the effective behaviour. Despite modifications and shifts of emphasis (e.g. Miller, 1948; Mowrer, 1960b; Rescorla & Solomon, 1967) the theory continued to survive more or less intact in its essentials until 1969. At the turn of the decade a number of papers appeared that clearly revealed the weaknesses of the theory in the face of accumulating contradictory data (e.g. Bolles, 1970; Herrnstein, 1969; Seligman & Johnston, 1973) and this trend has continued (e.g. Eysenck, 1976; Rachman, 1976).

Many telling points have been made, some of which will be discussed below, but perhaps the most damaging to the two-stage theory has been the demonstration that established, successful avoidance behaviour appears to

209

be independent of any mediating state of anxiety. This conclusion has arisen from two separate, but inevitably related, areas of investigation. First, the attempt to verify independently the existence of fear during persistent and effective avoidance and secondly, the investigation of extinction phenomena for both Pavlovian CR's and instrumental avoidance behaviours.

The measurement of autonomic indices of fear or arousal, such as skin conductance or cardiac activity, during the interval between CS presentation and the onset of avoidance behaviour clearly is the most direct method of investigating the mediating role of fear in avoidance. Such peripheral CR's should be readily observable if, as two-stage theory maintains, avoidance activity is maintained by a state of fear which is elicited by the CS. The considerable data on this issue were reviewed in detail by Rescorla & Solomon (1967) who concluded that there had been a signal failure to identify any peripheral CR's as necessary precursors of avoidance behaviour, and this failure was reiterated by Seligman & Johnston (1973). Additionally, there are numerous reports that successful avoidance responding occurs in the absence of any overt signs of distress or anxiety (e.g. Maier, Seligman & Solomon, 1969; Solomon & Wynne, 1954) and clinical observation reveals that phobic patients do not have to be anxious while avoiding their phobic stimulus, e.g. the school-phobic child typically is not anxious while performing his avoidance behaviour of staying at home, the socially phobic person does not have to experience anxiety in order to avoid going to social gatherings. Similarly, chronic compulsive behaviours do not require an antecedent state of anxiety for their performance; Walton & Mather (1964) and Beech & Perigault (1974) reported this lack of concordance between anxiety and chronic compulsive behaviour and Carr (1974) likened such activity to the performance of 'successful avoidance behaviours (p. 315)'.

The essential point, then, is that there is no firm evidence to support the notion that fear is a necessary antecedent of successful avoidance behaviour. Indeed, there are many instances of everyday avoidance that are not mediated by fear which have been largely overlooked by avoidance theorists, e.g. children avoid eating green vegetables, travellers avoid rush-hour traffic, people without coats or umbrellas avoid walking in heavy rain, etc. This is not to say that fear is not important in the emergence of avoidance behaviour, but rather that it is not a necessary cause and perhaps may be most usefully regarded as a sufficient cause under certain circumstances.

Although this failure to demonstrate the necessity of fear for the maintenance of avoidance behaviour appears to be extremely damaging to two-stage theory, Rescorla & Solomon (1967) suggested that fear might be a central state and thus unavailable to confirmation by measurement of peripheral autonomic parameters. If this proposition is to rescue two-stage theory, an explanation must be found for the disappearance of the peripheral concomitants of fear as successful avoidance develops. Also, it has to be demonstrated that this central fear state has the characteristics of a Pavlovian CR, for two-stage theory maintains that it arises through a process of classical conditioning. Because it is suggested that the fear is a central state without peripheral CR's such characteristics can only be inferred from the features of the supposedly dependent variable, i.e. avoidance behaviour.

It was the lack of concordance between the extinction characteristics of instrumental avoidance responses and classically conditioned responses which first prompted serious doubts about the validity of two-stage theory (Ritchie, 1951; Solomon & Wynne, 1954). Typically, classically conditioned responses extinguish within 30 or 40 nonreinforced trials (Church & Black, 1958; Kimmel, 1965; Silver & Kimmel, 1969) whereas avoidance responses survive for hundreds of trials which similarly are not reinforced by UCS occurrence (Baum, 1970; Brush, 1957; Solomon, Kamin & Wynne, 1953). As Seligman & Johnston (1973) and Rachman (1976) point out, if avoidance behaviour were maintained by a classically conditioned fear state, the time course of extinction for the two classes of response should be similar. The extreme dissimilarity of extinction rates shows that the maintenance of successful avoidance behaviour cannot be due to a Pavlovian conditioned fear response. Eysenck (1968, 1976) has drawn attention to some instances in which CR's continue to gain strength through repeated nonreinforced presentations of the CS. However, these data do not affect the present consideration of the relationship between anxiety and avoidance for we would expect such 'incubated' fear to be subject to the objection already raised in terms of the failure to demonstrate independently the presence of a mediating state of fear by the measurement of peripheral autonomic CR's. The independence of fear and established avoidance suggests that further discussion will be helped by separate consideration of their acquisition and maintenance.

2.2 The Acquisition and Maintenance of Fear

Watson's early demonstration (1920) of the development of a lasting (4 months) fear reaction through a process of classical conditioning, laid the foundation for a theory of fear acquisition which, with refinement and amendment (Eysenck & Rachman, 1965; Mowrer, 1939; Rachman, 1968; Wolpe, 1958; Wolpe & Rachman, 1960), has held the centre of the theoretical stage for half a century. Although clinical and naturalistic observation and empirical studies (e.g. Bregman, 1934; Costello, 1970; English, 1929; Hallam & Rachman, 1976; Marks, 1969; Solyom et al., 1974; Valentine, 1942) have often identified exceptions to the conditioning theory of fear acquisition, detailed consideration of the general theoretical adequacy

211

of this approach has occurred only recently (e.g. Rachman, 1974, 1977). This apparent robustness probably derived from three principal sources: first, the perpetuation of the two-stage theory of fear and avoidance which subsumed the acquisition of fear through classical conditioning, second, the frequent confirmation of classical conditioning as a means by which persistent fear responses could be developed despite the exceptions noted above, and third, the development of successful and efficient therapeutic techniques for anxiety (e.g. desensitisation, flooding) which were based upon the concept of fear as a conditioned response.

The classical conditioning model of fear acquisition is too well known to bear detailed repetition but the essential features may be summarised as follows. Persistent fears are assumed to be acquired and this acquisition takes place through a process of classical conditioning. In this process, a previously neutral stimulus acquires the capacity to elicit fear through one or more pairings with an unconditioned response of fear or pain. The probability that this conditioned response will develop and the intensity of the conditioned fear depend upon the number of pairings of CS and UCS, the intensity of the UCS and the confinement of the subject. The fear CR generalises to stimuli which resemble the CS and the conditioned fear acts as a secondary drive for fear reducing behaviours, these behaviours being reinforced by the fear reduction that is achieved.

Much of the impetus and support for this theory of fear acquisition was derived from a plethora of animal studies. These have been well reviewed several times (e.g. Broadhurst, 1972; Wolpe, 1958) and will not be discussed in detail here. There can be no doubt that fear responses can be conditioned with relative ease, especially in laboratory animals under controlled conditions. Typically the unconditioned stimuli that have been used in these studies have been electric shocks, but conflict and frustration have also been used successfully. The common feature underlying these UCS's would seem to be the aversiveness of the UCR's they elicit, with conditioned anxiety occurring in the presence of a signal (CS) which predicts the aversive state. Gray (1971b) has shown that frustration, in the form of frustrative nonreward, can have physiological and behavioural effects which are indistinguishable from those of pain.

Rachman (1977) argues, with some reservations, that relatively recent work on the acquisition of taste aversions (Garcia & Koelling, 1966; Seligman & Hager, 1972) 'can be used to provide buttressing for the conditioning theory (p.378)'. Although this work is clearly relevant to the persistence of avoidance behaviours, its relevance to the acquisition and maintenance of fear is not clear. The studies to which Rachman refers in order to illustrate the relevance of taste aversion phenomena (Adams & Rothstein, 1971; Wallen, 1945) suggest a common susceptibility in some individuals to

212

develop both fears and taste aversions rather than a common process of acquisition through classical conditioning. Such a susceptibility was proposed by Gray (1970, 1976) in terms of sensitivity or reactivity to signals of aversion or punishment. Also Bitterman (1975), in a useful review of the literature on taste aversion studies, recommends caution in interpreting the data because of deficiencies in experimental design. Amongst other points he illustrates the problems of controls for pseudoconditioning and the problem of after-taste when conditioning occurs with long CS-UCS intervals. However, these studies have given rise to the concept of preparedness which goes some way towards accounting for the unequal distribution of human fears across the range of available stimuli (Seligman, 1971; Seligman & Hager, 1972). This point will be discussed in more detail below.

Perhaps not surprisingly, there have been fewer studies of fear acquisition through classical conditioning in human subjects. Also, a large proportion of the studies have investigated the acquisition of autonomic CR's such as skin conductance responses and, as Lang (1970) pointed out, such physiological changes constitute only one component of the anxiety response. Apart from many clinical and observational studies, investigations of combat (e.g. Grinker & Spiegel, 1945; Lewis & Engle, 1954) internment in concentration camps (Matussek, 1975) and empirical studies (e.g. Sanderson et al., 1962) reveal the relative ease with which conditioned fear responses may be induced in human subjects. On the whole, with significant exceptions to which we will return, the early demonstration by Watson & Rayner (1920) of a persistent fear response in a human infant being developed by simple classical conditioning procedures has been confirmed by subsequent investigators. As in the case of animal studies, there can be little doubt that persistent fear responses in humans can be acquired through the process of classical conditioning.

If classical conditioning is to provide a sufficiently comprehensive model of the acquisition of human fears and phobias, several corollaries should follow. Let us examine these in turn.

2.2.1 Precipitating Events

Retrospective investigation of the development of human fears should reveal one or more instances of appropriate conditioning, in which the currently feared stimulus has been paired with aversive experience of a painful or fearful nature. It is frequently observed that certain phobias, particularly those which are monosymptomatic, often arise from identifiable conditioning experiences and the content of the phobia is clearly determined by the stimulus characteristics of the event. A painful and frightening bee sting may precipitate an insect phobia (Solyom et al., 1974) or frightening experiences during dental treatment may precipitate a dental phobia. In a

213

study of 34 cases of dental phobia (Lautch, 1971) each patient reported suffering at least one traumatic experience at the hands of a dentist during childhood. Four of these patients subsequently avoided any further dental treatment and each of the remaining 30 patients reported a second traumatic experience during subsequent treatment. The subjects described their experiences as painful, frightening or as a feeling of impending disaster. Some were disturbed by having an anaesthetic mask placed over the face without explanation or warning, experiencing a sense of suffocation and fear of the unexpected. Four patients fainted upon recovery and nine felt unwell with nausea and vomiting. These data exemplify the role of classical conditioning in the acquisition of some chronic fears.

However, such examples may be exceptions rather than the rule, particularly in the more common types of phobia such as agoraphobia and social phobias. Many authors (e.g. Eysenck, 1976; Marks, 1969, 1977; Rachman, 1974) have commented upon the difficulty of identifying traumatic learning experiences as precipitants of clinical phobias. In a study of 47 clinical phobias, of which 43 were agrophobias, Solyom et al. (1974) concluded from an inspection of the identified precipitating factors that there was no direct relationship between these factors and the content of the phobias in the vast majority of cases. Fright was identified as a precipitating factor in only 16% of cases, other major precipitants being serious illness, the death of a relative or friend, domestic crisis and unavoidable conflict. It is worth noting that in the absence of a theoretical model which predicts the development of a phobia from such experiences as illness or the death of a friend, these events are more appropriately regarded as precursors or antecedents of the phobia rather than precipitants. We do not know which features or characteristics of these events are functionally important in the genesis of the phobic state and it is conceivable that fear and anxiety were secondary consequences of the events, thus providing an appropriately aversive experience for conditioning to take place. Nevertheless, the paucity of clear conditioning experiences demonstrated by Solyom et al. is in accord with the data of Goorney & O'Connor (1971) who were able to relate the excessive fears of air crews to specific precipitants such as frights or accidents in only one quarter of cases. Similar results were obtained by Grinker & Spiegel (1945) in their study of wartime air crews. Despite the obvious difficulties associated with retrospective enquiries and the apparent tendency to seek traumatic *incidents*, rather than the mere contiguity of fear or pain and some initially neutral stimulus which is the minimum requirement of the conditioning model, the weight of evidence indicates that classical conditioning provides an insufficiently comprehensive account of the development of chronic human fears.

Rachman (1977) points out that there are many reported instances of

214

humans failing to develop persistent fears despite unambiguous and extended conditioning experiences (e.g. Bancroft, 1969; Hallam & Rachman, 1976; Marks & Gelder, 1967). Such instances are not as damaging to the conditioning model as the failure to identify conditioning experiences in the development of established fears. Rather they underline the need to specify more closely the parameters that influence the efficacy of classical conditioning procedures in the acquisition of fear. Current conceptions of such parameters are preparedness (Seligman & Hager, 1972) in relation to stimulus characteristics, introversion and neuroticism (Eysenck, 1975; Eysenck & Rachman, 1965), and fearfulness and sensitivity to signals of punishment (Gray, 1976) in relation to subject characteristics.

Rachman (1974) points out another potential difficulty for the conditioning model in that 'a genuine fear of snakes is often reported by people who have had no contact with the reptiles. Consequently, one is forced to conclude that the fear of snakes can be acquired in the absence of direct contact (p.81)'. However this does not, in itself, appear to pose a real problem for the conditioning model since symbolic representations of stimuli have long been accepted as viable for the purposes of conditioning and, although it is now recognised as inefficient, systematic desensitisation using imaginal representations of stimuli has a long record of therapeutic efficacy. The problem lies more in the high incidence of snake fears in the general population compared with the incidence of other fears and it seems unlikely that the urban populations of Europe and the USA have been incidentally fearful more often in the presence of pictures or other symbolic representations of snakes than in the presence of stimuli such as foxes, bears or big-bad-wolves.

2.2.2 Stimulus Equivalence

The assumption of classical conditioning that *any* neutral stimulus will serve as an effective CS when paired with an appropriate UCS implies that human fears, if acquired through classical conditioning, should occur with frequencies that reflect the probabilities of the feared stimuli occurring contiguously with experiences of fear or pain. The picture will be complicated by the effects of latent inhibition, i.e. unreinforced exposures to the CS will retard subsequent conditioning to that CS. So we would expect the frequency of occurrence of different fears to reflect the ratio of reinforced to unreinforced exposures to the appropriate CS's. Accordingly, many of the examples commonly cited to illustrate the extremely unequal distribution of human fears, e.g. the virtual absence of pyjama phobias (Rachman, 1974), grass phobias or hammer phobias (Seligman, 1971) are understandable and do not appear to damage the conditioning model of fear acquisition.

Nevertheless, there is a growing body of data which illustrates that the

215

concept of stimulus equivalence, or equipotentiality, is untenable (e.g. Garcia et al., 1971; Seligman & Hager, 1972). Although most of the relevant work has been concerned with the acquisition of taste aversions through classical conditioning and there have been several cautionary statements about the methodology of the studies (e.g. Bitterman, 1975) and the relevance of the data to clinical phenomena (e.g. Evans & Busch, 1974), the concept of preparedness which Seligman (1971) and Seligman & Hager (1972) proposed to replace that of equipotentiality has aroused a good deal of interest. Seligman (1971) argued that 'phobias are highly prepared to be learned by humans, and, like other highly prepared relationships, they are selective and resistant to extinction, learned even with degraded input, and probably are noncognitive (p.312)'. He contended that prepared stimuli, to which fear responses are most readily conditioned, have been significant in the evolution of the species in that they have constituted a specific danger to the species. It is assumed that through the process of natural selection the species has developed an innate readiness to acquire conditioned fear to these dangerous stimuli, the survival value lying in the drive properties of the fear response. Clearly, the survival value is maximised when conditioning occurs readily, even with degraded input such as one trial and lengthy CS-UCS intervals, when the conditioned response generalises easily and is highly resistant to extinction.

The frequency with which certain fears occur, particularly specific fears of animals and other restricted stimuli, offers a degree of face validity for the role of preparedness in the development of human fears. For example, the epidemiological study conducted by Agras et al. (1969) revealed that fears of snakes were twice as frequent as dental fears, despite the probability, as pointed out by Rachman (1977), that contact with dentists was more frequent and more often associated with painful experiences. On the other hand the agoraphobic syndrome, which accounts for approximately two-thirds of clinical phobias (Marks, 1969), does not obviously consist of fears which are conditioned to the most frequently occurring, highly prepared stimuli. Of course, this may reflect only the role of conditioning in the development of agoraphobia for Seligman argued that preparedness is an important variable in the conditioning process and if conditioning is unimportant in the acquisition of the fears which constitute the syndrome, the influence of preparedness would be restricted to the relatively few cases (Marks, 1969; Solyom et al., 1974) that originate in conditioning experiences. Also, a refusal to leave the house is, in a sense, the ultimate avoidance behaviour for a wide range of feared stimuli and would be expected where eliciting stimuli cannot be identified or predicted by the afflicted person. On this latter point, many agoraphobic patients describe the apparent spontaneity and autonomous quality of their early feelings of dread and apprehension (Marks, 1969).

Preparedness could help to explain the variable success of attempts to replicate Watson's (1920) demonstration of fear acquisition in a human infant by classical conditioning. English (1929) failed to produce conditioned fear in a 14-month-old child after 50 conditioning trials. It is clear that the CS used by English, a toy wooden duck, is not only an unprepared stimulus but one which may well have reflected the effects of latent inhibition. Also, interpretation of this particular study is complicated by the characteristics of the child who did not appear to respond to the UCS with fear or distress, thus eliminating the possibility of fear conditioning. However, the same UCS was sufficient to produce conditioned fear in a second child when paired with a stuffed black cat as the CS. Valentine (1942, 1946) reported similar variability in the effectiveness of fear conditioning in young children which led him to suggest that fears are more readily conditioned to stimuli with animate characteristics, such as leather or fur, than to stimuli strongly characterised by inanimation such as opera glasses.

The study by Bregman (1934), in which she failed to produce conditioned fear in a group of 15 infants, is frequently cited (e.g. Eysenck, 1976; Rachman, 1977) as providing evidence of the importance of preparedness in fear conditioning. Although this experiment was not directed at the issue of equipotentiality, its relevance to the role of preparedness arises from the use of CS's which are clearly insignificant in the biological sense. Bregman used geometrical wooden shapes and coloured cloths as CS's and failed completely to produce conditioned fear or distress using an electric bell as the UCS. At first sight the data do lend support to the preparedness hypothesis but several points are worth noting. First, we cannot be sure that the UCS elicited fear. Bregman states that the bell, which was an 'electric iron box cow bell (p.171)', elicited the startle response but four subjects who failed to show this response were not included in the experiment. Also, one subject 'developed complete adaptation to S (the bell) (p.176)'. It cannot be doubted that the CS was unpleasant for most subjects cried during its presentation, especially during the early stages of the experiment, but there is no mention of fear in Bregman's description and no information is provided about the frequency or intensity of the sound produced by the bell. Secondly, although a change in the infants' behaviour was produced it was attentional rather than fearful, 'The most frequent change was that of increase in interest (p.190)'.

Thirdly, and perhaps most importantly, there are grounds for doubting the likely efficacy of the conditioning procedure used in the experiment. By the end of the first cycle of training, and most subjects (11) were subjected to two cycles, a typical CS had been presented five times in the course of 4 days, or 8 hours of training. The CS was presented for 90 seconds on each occasion and the UCS, when presented, was sounded four times, for 1 second, at 20-second intervals starting 15 seconds after CS onset. However, of the five CS occurrences only two were paired with the UCS in this way. So on 60% of occasions the CS was not reinforced. Without a reasonably intense CS, a partial reinforcement schedule of this nature would not be expected to result in a conditioned response within the number of trials used and the procedures do not constitute 'thorough attempts to condition a group of 15 infants to fear a range of simple and biologically insignificant stimuli' (Rachman, 1977, p.381). Bregman's study does not provide good evidence that humans are unprepared or contraprepared to develop conditioned fear responses to stimuli of apparent evolutionary insignificance. Nevertheless, the successes and failures of the earlier attempts to confirm Watson's result are in accord with the concept of preparedness, despite the fact that it is often difficult to disentangle the possibly confounding effects of familiarity and latent inhibition. The likely effects of prior unreinforced exposures also complicate inferences about biological insignificance and preparedness from the common observation that it is exceedingly difficult to make children afraid of genuine sources of harm such as knives, glass objects, motor cars and the like.

Marks (1977) cites two serendipitous occurrences that appear to reflect the role of preparedness in human fear conditioning. In the first, a 4-year-old girl was playing in the park and thought she saw a snake. She ran to her parents' car and jumped inside. As she slammed the door she trapped her hand. This caused severe pain and subsequently necessitated several visits to the doctor. 'After this experience a phobia developed, not of cars or car doors, but of snakes (p.192).' However, as Marks points out, the fact that the girl ran away indicates that she was probably fearful of snakes before the incident occurred. In the second example, originally reported by Larsen (1965), a woman was involved in a motor accident while she happened to be examining a photograph of a snake. The elicited fear became associated with the snake and not with any other stimulus which was present during the incident. Restrospective reports such as these, interesting and useful as they are, do not tell us very much about preparedness and ease of acquisition. The same picture would emerge, after some time, if the fear responses were initially conditioned to an array of stimuli, including car doors, cars, snakes, etc., but the responses to the prepared stimuli were highly resistant to extinction and survived long after the other conditioned responses had extinguished. This point does not detract from the preparedness argument per se, since it proposes resistance to extinction as well as ease of acquisition. However, we might expect common, everyday stimuli such as cars, car doors, etc., to be poor CS's for fear conditioning due to their frequency of occurrence without reinforcement.

In a recent series of studies Ohman and colleagues have provided data of more direct relevance to the role of preparedness in human fear conditioning.

Using prepared or fear-relevant stimuli, such as snakes or spiders, and electric shock as the UCS, they have shown that conditioned electrodermal responses are resistant to extinction (Hugdahl et al., 1977; Ohman et al., 1976), are noncognitive in the sense that they cannot be explained away (Hugdahl & Ohman, 1977; Ohman et al., 1975a), and are readily acquired (Hugdahl & Ohman, 1977; Ohman et al., 1975b). The strongest and most consistent effect observed in these experiments, when comparing prepared and neutral stimuli, has been the resistance to extinction of the responses conditioned to the prepared stimuli rather than their ready acquisition. Although this useful work is confirming the inequality of stimuli as CS's for human fear conditioning, at least in its autonomic components, the implications for biological significance and preparedness are somewhat tenuous. The types of stimuli that Ohman and his colleagues have used, for example, snakes and spiders compared with flowers and mushrooms, differ in several respects other than their likely biological or evolutionary significance which could produce similar effects to those predicated on an assumption of preparedness. For example, snakes and flowers are drawn from two quite disparate classes of stimuli, namely animate and inanimate, and they differ greatly in terms of familiarity and likely frequency of previous unreinforced exposures.

Although there can be little doubt that the notion of stimulus equivalence is untenable in its wider sense, the role of preparedness in the conditioning of human fears with its evolutionary implications must await the results of further research. Eysenck (1976) argues that 'the preparedness model suffers from the fact that it postulates, in terms of innate propensities, what requires to be explained (p. 263)'. The charge of circularity would appear to be premature for there seems no a priori reason why a rank ordering of stimuli, in terms of their evolutionary significance, could not be produced independently. The frequency of occurrence of these stimuli as sources of human fears could then be compared and their relative effectiveness as fear CS's could be examined. However, there are inevitable doubts about the feasibility of such a procedure.

2.2.3 Conditioning Experiences

It follows from the conditioning model of fear acquisition that appropriate exposure to conditioning experiences should lead to persistent fears or phobias. There are several sources of data which indicate that this prediction is only partially correct. It is clear from studies of exposure to combat (e.g. Grinker & Spiegel, 1945), internment (e.g. Matussek, 1975), natural disaster (e.g. Parker, 1977) and torpedoing (e.g. Margolin et al., 1943) that only a proportion of individuals who are exposed to traumatic conditioning experiences acquire persistent fear reactions. In the course of their investigations of the reactions of merchant seamen to torpedoing and bombing, Margolin et al. (1943) observed that only 25% of the survivors exhibited severe, persisting reactions. These data are relevant to the conditioning argument only to the extent that people in whom the traumatic event actually elicited fear did not develop subsequent conditioned fears. There can be no doubt that people differ greatly in the readiness with which they respond with fear to traumatic events. Parker (1977) studied 68 evacuees who passed through an evacuation centre within a week of a cyclone. He found that the acutely anxious individuals were not differentiated by the nature of the events that they had experienced but by their appraisals of the events. 'Individuals who appraised the cyclone as a salient threat to their mortality developed physiological arousal and/or anxiety' and 'Initial psychological morbidity was most clearly associated with the experience of thinking that one might die or be seriously injured during the cyclone (p.553)'. However, Parker's study and those of Janis (1951) and Lewis (1942), which examined the effects of air-raids, showed that the vast majority of affected individuals recovered within a matter of weeks and displayed no lasting effects. The role of individual differences is illustrated in the study of dental phobia by Lautch (1971). Although each of his phobic subjects (34) recalled a traumatic incident at the hands of a dentist during childhood, the number of his matched nonphobic controls who recalled similar incidents (10) was not significantly different. Individual differences, rather than ill luck, probably are responsible for the finding that following one traumatic experience the probability of undergoing another within the next two or three visits was about ten times greater for the phobic group ($p = 1.0$) than for the control group ($p = 0.1$). Individual differences in susceptibility to fear and in the tendency to develop persistent fear responses have long been accepted as important moderators of fear conditioning procedures (Eysenck & Rachman, 1965; Gray, 1971b). These have been discussed in detail recently (e.g. Eysenck, 1975; Gray, 1976) and space precludes further discussion of individual differences in the present context.

Notwithstanding the variable influence of individual differences and stimulus characteristics upon the outcome of conditioning experiences, it might be expected that a sufficiently large number of exposures to any CS, when paired with a sufficiently intense UCS, should result in a conditioned fear response in any individual. There is some evidence that this is indeed the case, even with only one trial, when the UCS is particularly frightening. Sanderson et al. (1962) administered scoline to a group of 10 subjects without any warning, 'in no case did a subject know from extraneous stimuli that any drug had been given (p.1235)'. The resulting temporary paralysis, with its total suppression of muscular movement including respiration, must have been 'harrowing to a degree (p.1235)'. The CS, a tone of 600 Hz at 70 db, can reasonably be regarded as an unprepared stimulus. Yet each of the ten subjects showed clear evidence of a conditioned response, in terms of electrodermal activity, when tested with the CS three weeks later.

The clinical application of aversion therapy procedures typically involves many pairings of the relevant CS with electric shock as the UCS, but the outcome is usually one of indifference to the CS (Hallam et al., 1972; Marks & Gelder, 1967) or distaste (Hallam & Rachman, 1976) rather than fear or anxiety. However, the CS's had necessarily been associated with a good deal of positive reinforcement prior to the instigation of aversive conditioning procedures. Also, it has been argued (Seligman & Hager, 1972) that shock is an inappropriate and ineffective UCS when taste cues constitute the CS, which is the case when aversive techniques are used in the treatment of alcoholic patients. In contrast to the effectiveness of the traumatic procedures used by Sanderson et al., Hallam & Rachman (1976) failed to produce conditioned responses, as indexed by cardiac, electrodermal and respiratory parameters, even after 205 trials when the UCS was an electric shock.

Without more information about individuals' subjective reactions to, and appraisals of, apparently traumatic events, it would be premature to regard failures of fear conditioning as particularly damaging to a conditioning model of fear acquisition. However, there are good grounds for believing that although conditioning experiences may be sufficient to generate persistent human fears, under certain circumstances, such experiences are not necessary. It would appear that fears may be acquired through processes which are difficult to construe in conditioning terms.

Rachman (1968, 1974, 1977) and Eysenck (1976) have argued that the clear demonstrations by Bandura and colleagues (e.g. Bandura, 1971; Bandura et al., 1967) that behavioural and emotional responses may be acquired through processes of observational learning and modelling, indicate that fear responses may similarly be acquired vicariously. The same point is made by Marks (1969), 'It is clear that fears can be acquired by modelling (p.65)'. Although there have been occasional excursions into empirical demonstrations of fear acquisition through modelling (e.g. Bandura & Rosenthal, 1966), the main thrust of Bandura's work has been towards the effectiveness of observational learning in the reduction of fears. As Rachman (1977) pointed out: 'It has to be conceded however that, at this stage, the evidence in support of vicarious acquisition of fear in humans is indirect and largely anecdotal (p.382)'. Yet the effectiveness of exposure to a relevant, nonfearful model in the reduction of fear clearly argues for the possibility of fear acquisition by exposure to fearful models.

Solyom et al. (1974), in their study of 47 phobic patients and their families, pointed out that fear transmission from parents to children by verbal or

221

nonverbal means was quite obvious in a number of cases. Hagman (1932) studied 70 children ranging in age from 23 months to 6 years and interviewed their mothers. Amongst other conclusions he reported that there was a real tendency for the children to exhibit fears corresponding to those of their mothers, and there was a correlation of 0.67 between the gross number of children's fears and the gross number of their mothers' fears. Jersild et al. (1933) interviewed 398 children aged 5–12 years and found that the most frequent fear was that of supernatural agents such as ghosts and witches. Although there are some difficulties in interpreting Hagman's data because of the unknown influence of the mothers' fears upon the ratings they gave for their children and the possibility of shared learning experience, the frequency of supernatural fears in the data of Jersild et al. can be accounted for only by some process which does not involve direct exposure to the CS. However, as discussed earlier, this does not necessarily preclude the possibility of conditioning occurring through the contiguity of a state of fear and symbolic representations of stimuli.

Whether or not conditioning is the effective process underlying observational learning of this kind, examples such as these and others cited by Rachman (1974), together with everyday examples of parent-child interactions, leave very little doubt that fears can be acquired indirectly, i.e. without actual exposure to a CS. Indeed, since the possible role of propensities determined by evolution has already been introduced into theories of fear acquisition, it could be argued that a readiness to acquire fear through indirect processes is of greater survival value than ready conditioning through direct exposure. For natural selection to operate, the latter process requires that the individual survives the early exposures to the dangerous stimuli. Sufficiently frequent survival to ensure conditioning implies that the stimuli were not so dangerous that ready development of fear and avoidance would be particularly advantageous. Although Seligman's (1970) concept of stimulus preparedness was proposed in the context of classical conditioning, there seems no a priori reason why this characteristic of stimuli should not facilitate selectively the acquisition of fears through indirect processes. This might help to account for the frequency with which specific fears of spiders, snakes, etc., occur in Western urban populations.

Rachman (1977) identifies a possible indirect process of fear acquisition other than observational learning. 'It is probable that informational and instructional processes provide the basis for most of our commonly encountered fears of everyday life (p.384).' Everyday experience suggests that this is probably true, but, as mentioned earlier, it is notoriously difficult to make children afraid of genuinely dangerous stimuli such as knives and motor cars by instruction and information. However, there is good evidence that merely informing a subject that a painful event will follow a signal is sufficient to elicit fear. Bridger & Mandel (1964) showed that the acquisition of a skin conductance CR was similar when the subjects received shock as the UCS or simply threat of shock. Threat of shock is frequently used in studies of fear and fear acquisition (e.g. Epstein, 1973; Epstein & Clarke, 1970; Hugdahl & Ohman, 1977). Although threat of shock has been shown to be effective most commonly in studies involving classical conditioning, the essential point is that this threat reliably elicits sufficient fear for conditioning to occur. It follows that for as long as the subject holds the belief or expectation that shock will occur in the presence of a certain signal, he will exhibit persistent fear responses to that stimulus. There is little doubt that the transmission of certain types of information, particularly about pain or harm, can produce persistent fears. Perhaps it would be more appropriate to emphasise the subject's acceptance of the information in order to illustrate once more the likely effects of individual differences.

2.2.4 Extinction

If Pavlovian conditioning were the effective process underlying the acquisition of human fears then, like other conditioned responses, fear CR's should extinguish as a result of repeated exposure to unreinforced occurrences of the CS. In general, this corollary is upheld by the data and the rapidity of extinction of fear CR's was discussed earlier in comparison to the persistence of avoidance responses in the absence of reinforcement. However, several authors have commented upon the extreme resistance to extinction shown by some fear responses. Eysenck (1976) refers to this paradoxical persistence of fear CR's, in the face of repeated unreinforced occurrences of the CS, as the 'neurotic paradox'. It seems unlikely that this phenomenon constitutes the essence of neurotic fears for, as we have seen, most phobic patients avoid their feared stimuli and a more common paradox is the persistence of avoidance in the absence of a continued fear response which might maintain the behaviour. However, not all phobic individuals are able completely to avoid their feared stimuli, e.g. spiders, yet the total lack of an external, contiguous, painful or frightening UCS does not lead to extinction of the fear. Solyom et al. (1974) comment on two train- and tunnel-phobic males whose fears persist despite repeated and uneventful exposures to these stimuli. Also, clinical experience suggests that phobic patients typically do not avoid their feared stimuli completely after only one unpleasant experience and the conditioning model allows for a number of 'subtraumatic' exposures to the CS. As Eysenck (1976) and Evans (1976) point out, several authors have commented upon empirical demonstrations of exceptions to the Pavlovian law of extinction (e.g. Marukhanyan, 1961; Razran, 1956). However, Marukhanyan's example is hardly relevant in that the response was a conditioned motor response rather than a fear CR.

223

There are grounds for believing that resistance to extinction of a conditioned fear response may be a function of individual differences in habituation and arousal level (Lader & Mathews, 1968). Physiological aspects of fear have been discussed in Chapter 2 and will not be considered further here. Without more information it is impossible to ascertain the relevance of the examples given by Solyom et al. (1974). For example, if the anxiety which had become conditioned to stimuli of trains and tunnels was elicited by anticipation of situations or events which were consequent upon completion of the journey then, unless that source of fear had been removed, the repeated exposures to the stimuli of travelling were not unreinforced and extinction would not be expected.

Eysenck (1968, 1976) argues that unreinforced exposures to a fear CS not only fail to produce extinction in some cases but also that they may lead to increases in CR magnitude. A similar point was made by Wolpe (1958). The term incubation is used to describe this process but it might be more meaningfully described as 'paradoxical enhancement' (Rohrbaugh & Riccio, 1970). Eysenck (1976) proposed that 'the CS (after conditioning) produces fear/anxiety, i.e. the UCR, even though the UCS may now be absent. This process should set up a positive feedback cycle, with each presentation of the CS-only reinforcing itself, and thus continuing to increment the CR (p.257).' He argues that this process is a characteristic of CS's which are drive producing, whereas the classical law of extinction applies to CS's which are not drive producing. It is possible that enhancement effects, when they occur, may be confined to drive producing CS's, but it seems unlikely that all such stimuli, including fear CS's will obey a law of enhancement. As discussed earlier, most fear CR's extinguish readily and studies which have examined paradoxical enhancement have produced variable results.

Rohrbaugh & Riccio (1970, 1972) failed to demonstrate a significant increase in fear, as indexed by approach to food and drink, after 300 seconds unreinforced exposure to the CS when compared to a group who had experienced no unreinforced exposure following conditioning. However, shorter exposure times of 30 and 60 seconds produced more fear than nonexposure. These experiments used static apparatus cues as the CS and it is possible that the consequent difficulty in discriminating a discrete signal for UCS occurrence makes extinction less likely. The possibility that enhancement effects are more likely when unreinforced exposures to the CS are of short duration would help to explain why fear CR's do not extinguish even when the individual cannot avoid the CS completely. Typically, and understandably, fearful individuals remove themselves from sources of distress relatively quickly. Also, the successful application of in vivo exposure techniques in the treatment of phobias, which was mentioned earlier, usually involves long exposure to the CS.

Eysenck (1976) cites the study by Campbell et al. (1964) of traumatic fear conditioning in humans as providing evidence in support of the incubation hypothesis: 'despite repeated extinction trials, 30 administered 5 minutes after conditioning, 30 one week later, and 40 two weeks after that, GSR continued to gain strength over time (p.259)'. However, some caution should be exercised in interpreting these data as supporting the incubation hypothesis. Firstly, this experiment confounds the possible effects of the number of unreinforced CS exposures with the effects of passage of time, for there was no appropriate control for the passage of time per se. Secondly, whatever enhancement effects were shown occurred between the first and second blocks of extinction trials, at 5 minutes and one week, with apparently insignificant changes between one week and three weeks. Although Campbell et al. do not test for changes between the several pairs of blocked extinction trials, the GSR's do not appear to gain strength between weeks 1 and 3. Thirdly, and perhaps most importantly, no significant effects upon GSR latency or amplitude were demonstrated over trials: significant effects were demonstrated for subjects and blocks of trials. In other words, enhancement effects were not associated with number of unreinforced exposures to the CS but with the passage of time between blocks of extinction trials, and this factor interacted with individual differences. As Campbell et al. conclude: 'If both latency and amplitude are taken as indices of the strength of a CR one may conclude that the conditioned GSR response in the experimental group increases in strength, *as time passes*, following a single traumatic conditioning trial (p.637, italics added)'. However, the incubation hypothesis requires that 'the more frequently the CS-only is presented, the greater will be the CR (Eysenck, 1976, p.264)'.

Eysenck (1976) refers to a number of other studies which, directly and indirectly, attest to the existence of enhancement effects but, in the main, these illustrate extinction characteristics of avoidance and escape responses rather than the enhancement of fear (e.g. Maatsch, 1959; Miller & Levis, 1971; Reynierse, 1966; Sartory & Eysenck, 1976). As Evans (1976) points out, 'Paradoxical enhancement will need more supporting data before it can be considered a replicable phenomenon (p.92)'. The general use of apparatus cues as CS (e.g. Rohrbaugh et al., 1972; Sartory & Eysenck, 1976), together with varying durations of exposure to these cues, does not appear to be an entirely appropriate means of investigating the incubation hypothesis. The hypothetical data which Eysenck uses to illustrate the way in which a CR might incubate through reinforcing itself are based upon repeated instances of exposure to the CS. The equivalence of long duration exposure to a static CS and frequent, separate instances of exposure to that CS is not clear. Also, it is not clear to what extent unreinforced CS exposure times of $\frac{1}{2}$, 1 or 3 minutes constitute extinction trials when, during conditioning, the UCS was presented 5 times during 5 minutes continuous exposure to the CS (Sartory & Eysenck, 1976). This might account for the greater efficacy of long exposure times during extinction, as mentioned above. However, the notion of a CR acting as an effective reinforcer makes sense and, although the possibility of enhancement or incubation must await further empirical confirmation, it seems likely that any theory of fear acquisition must be able to account for CR effects.

The simple classical conditioning model clearly does not allow for possible enhancement effects, but the incubation model proposed by Eysenck (1976) is a simple extension of a conditioning approach in which the infant CR substitutes for the absent UCR and reinforces itself. Of course this contains a potential paradox in assuming that the very minimal CR's whose enhancement the model seeks to explain, are sufficiently intense to act as effective reinforcers. It is possible that a CR intensity threshold exists which must be exceeded before enhancement becomes a possibility.

A positive feedback model to account for the development of debilitating anxiety in the absence of an external aversive UCS was proposed by Evans (1972). He restricted the applicability of the model to those complaints in which the following apply: the presence of an overt manifestation of an autonomic response, or the inhibition of overt behaviour as a result of autonomic activity. Secondly, that this overt manifestation is aversive to the individual so that its appearance represents an unconditioned stimulus for anxiety. The sequence then requires that the manifestation of the elicited anxiety should contain that response which originally acted as an unconditioned stimulus for anxiety. In this way a positive feedback cycle is created: an initial response provokes contextual anxiety, one of the consequences of this anxiety is the response which initially provoked it, and so on. Evans describes several clinical examples which are persuasive and the model helps to explain the gradual development of situational anxieties in the absence of external aversive stimuli which, in the form of social phobias, otherwise are difficult to account for within the conditioning model of fear acquisition.

2.2.5 Generalisation

The generalisation of fear responses to stimuli which resemble the CS is so commonly observed in clinical settings and in empirical work that a detailed consideration of this phenomenon is not necessary. However, it is worth emphasising the role of symbolic processes in the spread of human fears. The point is well illustrated by the following case. For reasons which are too detailed to describe here, a young man (17 years) developed a phobic response to the Beatles group and their music. Subsequently, this response generalised to Volkswagen motor cars, insect beetles, rings worn on fingers, octane ratings displayed on petrol pumps in the form of stars, and the colour yellow. It is assumed that the names of the members of this group of entertainers and of their numbers are so widely known that the above examples of generalisation require no clarification.

2.2.6 Summary

The traditional conditioning model of human fear acquisition is inadequate. As summarised at the beginning of this section, it cannot account for the frequent failure to identify conditioning experiences in the development of phobias, the relative frequencies with which different fears occur, the persistence of some fears in the apparent absence of appropriate reinforcement and the failure to develop persistent fears following exposure to seemingly traumatic conditioning experiences. Also, there are good grounds for believing that persistent fears may be acquired through processes which are not readily described in conditioning terms, i.e. observational learning and information transmission. Apart from these alternative acquisition processes, the obvious weaknesses of the conditioning model appear to derive from the influence of laboratory and other empirical demonstrations of classical conditioning and the consequent emphasis upon unconditioned, aversive stimuli. A greater emphasis upon subjective aversive states, whether or not these are elicited directly by external stimuli, might well have hastened understanding of those instances in which fears develop in the absence of painful or fearful external stimuli. However, the proposals which have been put forward to account for such instances (e.g. Evans, 1972; Eysenck, 1976) are expressed in conditioning terms and, together with preparedness, serve to extend and refine the conditioning model in such a way as to render it a more viable explanation of human fear acquisition.

Nevertheless, indirect processes of fear acquisition are not readily encompassed within this approach and unless we are to regard the several acquisition processes, including conditioning, as intrinsically different, each might be considered as a specific example of a more general principle. In other words, the acquisition of fear through classical conditioning, observational learning and information transmission each might be illustrative of a superordinate principle. In the following section it is argued that such a general principle exists and it is cognitive in nature.

2.3 Cognitive Factors

It is an everyday experience that most transitory fears are anticipatory. It is proposed that such fears occur in response to an anticipation of harm, where

227

harm includes all states of the individual, whether physical or psychological, which are subjectively assessed as endangering continued functioning in a physical, individual psychological or social sense, where such functioning is valued by the individual. So it is proposed that situations evoke anxiety to the extent that they imply harm to the individual. We are anxious in anticipation of an interview to the extent that poor performance, or not getting the post, are appraised as harmful. People are fearful of public speaking, social gatherings, etc., according to their judgements of the harmful potential of such events, e.g. to be regarded by others as incompetent, foolish, boring, ill mannered, etc. Anxiety is obviated either when being regarded as competent, interesting, etc., is not valued, or when the converse negative evaluations are judged as only remotely possible. Clearly, the appraisal of the harmful potential of any situation is a probabilistic judgement, i.e. it depends upon subjective appraisals of the likelihood of harmful states occurring as a result of involvement in the situation or activity under consideration. To the extent that such appraisals of potential harm are consistent over time then persistent fears will result, i.e. repeated occurrences of the stimuli will evoke fear. According to the discussion early in this chapter, in which it was argued that no qualitative differentiation can be made between normal and pathological fear, such persistent fears may readily satisfy the criteria necessary for description as pathological.

It is proposed that the anticipation of harm is a hypothetical construct which represents contingencies between stimuli and states of harm. Also, it is proposed that the anticipation of harm evokes fear. Harm has already been defined as states of the individual, whether physical or psychological, that are subjectively assessed as endangering continued functioning in a physical, individual psychological or social sense, where such functioning is valued by the individual.

Similar points were made by Carr (1974) in arguing that anxiety is a multiplicative function of the subjective probability of outcomes and their subjective costs, although without the same explicit emphasis upon harm as a subjective state. Anticipations are strengthened when they are confirmed and weakened when disconfirmed. In short, it is proposed that the anticipation of harm, and its consequent anxiety, are positive functions of contingencies between stimuli and outcomes and the degree of harm associated with the outcomes, both being subjectively assessed. It should be emphasised that these appraisals of contingencies and degrees of harm are seen as no more deliberate or contemplative than the judgements of whether or not to run through a gap in the traffic when crossing the road, or whether to catch a sharp knife as it falls from the table. Appraisals of contingencies between stimuli and outcome states, and the values of these states, are seen as continuous, ongoing processes of the individual.

228

Since the anticipation of harm is dependent upon subjective assessments of both contingency and harmfulness, any experience which provides acceptable information which demonstrates that a given outcome state is both harmful and probable in a given situation, will give rise to an anticipation of harm and provoke anxiety. It is proposed that classical conditioning, observation learning and information transmission may each provide acceptable information about contingencies and the harmfulness of outcome states and, accordingly, that the development of an anticipation of harm is common to each of these superficially diverse processes of fear acquisition. It is likely that the varying degrees of experiential involvement associated with these processes will influence certain characteristics of the resulting fears, e.g. resistance to extinction, synchrony and desynchrony of the autonomic and subjective components of fear and response to treatments which differ in their emphasis upon experience, such as verbal psychotherapy and in vivo exposure. Of course, there is no reason to suppose that classical conditioning, observational learning and information transmission are mutually exclusive processes.

The possible role of cognitive processes in classical conditioning is not a new concept (e.g. Rescorla, 1969; Spence, 1966; Zener, 1934) yet there have been few ramifications for theories of fear except for Seligman's (1975) use of probabilistic concepts in his useful discussions of the predictability and controllability of aversive events. Evans (1976) reviews a number of studies that have examined the role of contingencies in classical conditioning and concluded that when subjects are categorised according to success or failure in describing contingencies, only the successful show differential conditioning (e.g. Baer & Fuhrer, 1968, 1970; Morgensen & Martin, 1969). Dawson & Furedy (1973) argued that awareness of the CS-UCS relationship is necessary but not sufficient for conditioning to occur. As Evans (1976) noted, the use of any task concurrent with the conditioning procedure, which reduces the cognitive activity of the subject or diverts his attention from the conditioning procedure, has dramatic effects upon various conditioning phenomena. For example, the usually rapid extinction of human CR's is retarded to resemble animal extinction curves when a masking task is used to interfere with the subject's knowledge of contingencies (Spence, 1966). Nelson & Ross (1974) concluded that the effect of masking tasks was achieved through interfering with the subject's attention to CS-UCS relationships and his knowledge of the contingencies involved.

This approach also seems adequate to deal with other phenomena of classically conditioned fear responses such as Pavlovian extinction, partial reinforcement effects, latent inhibition, etc. Standard extinction trials constitute disconfirmations of the anticipation of harm which is based on the contingency acquired during conditioning. During extinction a competing anticipation develops based upon the contingency between the CS and an outcome state of no harm. The relatively slow rate of acquisition of fear CR's on partial reinforcement schedules is similarly accounted for on the basis of competing anticipations. The resistance to extinction of partially reinforced responses would be expected, in that any single extinction trial constitutes an ineffective disconfirmation since CS-only occurrences during conditioning did not preclude harmful outcome states contingent upon CS presentation in subsequent trials. Latent inhibition effects may be interpreted as due to an anticipation of no harm, following unreinforced CS exposures, which will compete with the development of an anticipation of harm during subsequent conditioning and thus retard fear acquisition. The possible effects of CR-only, in the absence of external traumatic events, such as those proposed by Evans (1976) are also readily incorporated. The examples which Evans gives to illustrate his model clearly revolve around anticipations of harm, e.g. 'What if my mouth should go dry when I am singing the solo? (p.239)'. If the autonomic consequences of the anxiety elicited by such an anticipation of harm include dryness of the mouth, then the anticipation is confirmed and a positive feedback cycle is created as proposed by Evans. Also, an anticipation of this type could develop through observational learning or information transmission as well as by fortuitous experience.

As mentioned earlier, when discussing information transmission as a means of fear acquisition, there are numerous reports of the effectiveness of threat of shock in producing conditioned fear responses (e.g. Bridger & Mandel, 1964; Epstein & Clarke, 1970; Hugdahl & Ohman, 1977). Informing the subject that shock will follow a signal clearly provides him with knowledge of the relevant contingency. This point has been shown more directly in studies which have informed subjects of differing probabilities of shock (e.g. Epstein & Roupenian, 1970; Ohman et al., 1973). High shock probabilities elicit more fear than low probabilities. However, the results are less clear cut for medium probability levels (e.g. Epstein, 1972). This may well be due to the reliance, in this study, on statistical probability rather than its subjective counterpart. There is no reason to suppose that subjective probabilities, although related, should maintain a constant relationship to statistical probabilities and data in the middle ranges of probability should be clarified by assessments of subjective probability. Of relevance here is the finding by Grings & Sukoneck (1971) of monotonically increasing CR's with increasing shock probabilities as learned through direct experience.

Clearly, the objective counterpart of subjective harm in empirical studies of fear acquisition is shock intensity, although individual differences in pain thresholds, etc., will make it only a crude index. It is generally recognised that UCS intensity augments all characteristics of fear acquisition such as speed of development, CR magnitude, resistance to extinction, etc., and space precludes a detailed consideration of the relevant data. By way of illustration, Annau & Kamin (1961) showed that resistance to extinction of a conditioned emotional response was ordinally related to the shock intensity used during conditioning. For example, the CER acquired with a shock intensity of 0.28 mA required 12 extinction trials whereas that acquired with a shock intensity of 1.55 mA required 40 extinction trials. Similar effects are obtained when the subject is merely informed of shock intensity (e.g. Ohman et al., 1973) although, as one might expect, the relationship between elicited fear as indexed by skin conductance responses and stated shock intensity is less regular. As with subjective probability, assessments of subjective intensity ratings should clarify the data.

The role of cognitive processes in observational learning appears, in principle, to be straightforward. Observation of a harmful state being induced in the model, upon exposure to certain stimuli, creates the anticipation of harm in the observer contingent upon exposure to the same stimuli. Clearly, if the observer is to infer that stimuli which elicit a harmful state in the model will also elicit a similar state in himself, he must perceive the model and himself as similar in essential respects. Bandura (1969) presents a good deal of data which point to the importance of the similarity between observer and model and successful modelling techniques used in the reduction of fears typically employ peers as models (e.g. Bandura et al., 1967). Also, Stotland (1969) found that perceived similarity between observer and model enhances vicarious arousal.

In summary, it appears that fear acquisition through classical conditioning, observational learning and information transmission may readily be construed in cognitive terms, the common factor in each being the development of an anticipation of a harmful outcome state contingent upon the occurrence of certain stimuli.

Before concluding this section on cognitive factors of anxiety, let us reconsider briefly the topics of proximity and desynchrony which were discussed previously. According to the above argument, in which anxiety is seen as dependent upon an anticipation of harm, any factor that increases the likelihood or severity of the harmful outcome state will provoke greater anxiety. Consequently, it is suggested that the anxiety-elevating effects of proximity, whether spatial, temporal or functional, are due to consequent increases in the subjectively assessed likelihood or severity of the harmful outcome. It is self-evident that, in the absence of any events which might mitigate its harmful potential, increasing spatial proximity to a source of harm increases the likelihood of the harmful outcome. Functional proximity, in guaranteeing the end point of a sequence of events, also acts through an increase in the subjective likelihood of the harmful outcome. The case of temporal proximity appears less straightforward. It was proposed earlier that the anticipation of harm is a continuous, ongoing process, a constant

231

evaluation of the future in terms of its harmful potential. It seems inconceivable that such a process would normally operate over anything other than a relatively limited time base. To extend the processes of anticipation over an indefinite future would be extremely maladaptive and the adaptive features of anxiety, which is consequent upon the anticipation of harm, are indisputable. To take an obvious example: we will all die, the vast majority of us will be anxious when this event is imminent, yet we spend most of our lives with little or no fear of the event. It would appear that imminence provokes active cognitive elaboration of events and outcomes, as a necessary precursor to possible adaptive functioning, which may increase the subjective likelihood and/or severity of the harmful outcome state. Also, as mentioned earlier, the cognitive representation of harmful stimuli elicits autonomic responses and subjective experiences which are indistinguishable from those elicited by the stimuli themselves (May, 1977).

The relatively poor concordance between measures of anxiety (e.g. Morrow & Labrum, 1978) is well known and the general lack of correlation between the subjective, autonomic and behavioural aspects of anxiety constitutes desynchrony (Rachman & Hodgson, 1974). In the light of the earlier discussion in this chapter of the relation between fear and avoidance, and the conclusion that fear is not a necessary antecedent of avoidance behaviour, the lack of correlation between these responses is not surprising. Of more interest is the poor concordance between autonomic indices of anxiety and subjective reports. In the previous discussion of the development of an anticipation of harm, there was no necessity for the individual to experience directly any painful or frightening events. Consequently, autonomic activity is not necessarily involved in, or associated with, the development of such an anticipation. However, conditioning experiences, in which CS exposures are paired with painful or frightening UCS's, are inevitably accompanied by autonomic responses. At the start of conditioning these autonomic responses are elicited by the UCS and will themselves become conditioned to the CS. It is suggested therefore that during classical fear conditioning two separate processes occur: the development of an anticipation of harm through an awareness of contingency and of the nature of the outcome, and the classical conditioning of autonomic responses.

Where the anticipation of harm has been acquired indirectly, the degree of autonomic response to a stimulus will be a function of the number of prior contiguous occurrences of the stimulus and the autonomic activity, in addition to the autonomic concomitants of the anticipation of harm. In the case of information transmission, such contiguous occurrences will depend largely upon the number of actual, short exposures to the feared CS. That is, the anticipation of harm may be acquired through information transmission and actual, short exposure to the relevant stimulus will then elicit fear with

232

autonomic consequences which, according to normal Pavlovian law, will become conditioned to that stimulus. The same argument would apply to observational learning with the additional consideration that autonomic responses may be elicited during instances of observational learning (Stotland, 1969).

Bridger & Mandel (1964, 1965) showed that although conditioning was similar whether subjects received shock or threat of shock as the UCS, when the electrodes were removed the group that had received only threat of shock displayed almost immediate extinction whereas the group that had experienced the shock showed a gradual extinction of the CR. In this experiment the mode of acquisition clearly influenced the synchrony between autonomic and subjective components of the response. When the anticipation of harm was eliminated, by removing all electrodes, the indirect acquisition group exhibited synchronous reduction of autonomic activity but the direct acquisition group showed a desynchronous persistence of such activity. Although the analysis presented above must await further empirical investigation, the implications for the relationship between the behavioural, autonomic and subjective aspects of fear clearly are those of potential desynchrony.

2.4   Avoidance Behaviours

The relationship between fear and avoidance has already been discussed in some detail. Although it was concluded that fear may be regarded most appropriately as only a sufficient precursor to the development of avoidance behaviours the crucial issue, in both a clinical and theoretical sense, is the persistence of avoidance in the absence of any indication of concurrent fear. In that it has been proposed that the anticipation of harm, upon which fear depends, is a function of the subjective likelihood of a harmful outcome state and the severity of that state, any action or circumstantial change which reduces either of these variables will reduce the anticipation of harm. It is proposed that avoidance behaviour is dependent upon an anticipation of no harm. Clearly, successful physical avoidance of the stimulus with harmful potential reduces the likelihood of the harmful outcome state to zero. For as long as the resulting anticipation 'behaviour ———➤ no harm' persists in contrast to the anticipation 'other behaviour ———➤ harm', the appropriate (avoidance) behaviour will also persist. Additionally, since there is no anticipation of a harmful outcome while avoidance behaviour is performed, there will be no concurrent anxiety. Also, successful avoidance obviates any possible disconfirmation of the anticipation of harm, so this anticipation will persist. Strictly speaking, the above argument requires the assumption of a preference for no harm over harm. Seligman & Johnston (1973) have presented a well argued model of general avoidance behaviour based upon an organism's preferences between outcomes.

It is apparent that physical avoidance, whether active or passive, is only one specific means by which an anticipation of no harm may develop by reducing the likelihood of the harmful outcome. As above, any circumstantial change or action which reduces the likelihood or severity of the harmful outcome will have similar effects. Public speaking anxiety may be obviated by not engaging in the activity (avoidance) or by developing a high degree of proficiency which similarly minimises the likelihood of a harmful outcome. The 'choice' of behaviour will depend upon such factors as the nature of the potentially harmful stimuli, the idiosyncratic implications of any particular action for a specific individual, the characteristic response style of the individual to difficulties, etc. For example, Haslam (1965) described a female patient who developed an obsessional behaviour of cutting her food into minute pieces before eating. This followed upon a fear of ingesting broken glass with her food. It is clear that this girl could not reduce the likelihood of the harmful outcome by avoiding food completely, so she adopted the alternative strategy of ensuring that her food was free of broken glass. Carr (1974) has argued that the stimuli which typically precipitate obsessional behaviours, e.g. toilets, switches, dressing, intrusive thoughts, are characterised by their unavoidability. Consequently, obsessional behaviours are seen as attempts by the individual to reduce the anticipation of harm by reducing the likelihood of the harmful outcome, e.g. washing, checking, behavioural interruption, etc. As discussed earlier, avoidance behaviour is a commonly used criterion of a phobic state and it seems probable that, given an initial anticipation of harm through direct or indirect acquisition processes, the emergence of either a phobic or an obsessional state will be determined partly by the availability to the individual of appropriate avoidance behaviours. Where avoidance is possible, both physically and in terms of the value system of the individual, a phobic state will be more likely to emerge. Where avoidance is not possible, an obsessional state is more likely to develop with ritualised compulsive behaviours being the best strategy for minimising the subjective likelihood of the harmful outcome. Carr (1970, 1974) proposed a model of obsessional states based upon subjective appraisals of the probabilities of harmful outcomes in which this point is discussed in some detail.

2.5   Summary

It has been argued that traditional conditioning models of fear acquisition provide an inadequate account of the relevant empirical data and clinical phenomena. Recent developments in terms of stimulus salience, incubation, etc., revitalise this approach to some extent but alternative, indirect modes of fear acquisition cannot be encompassed easily within the concepts of conditioning. It was proposed that a cognitive anticipation of harm, based upon a subjective appraisal of the likelihood and severity of a harmful outcome, is a common factor in both direct and indirect modes of fear acquisition. Finally a rapprochement between phobic and obsessional states was sought by suggesting that the symptoms of these disorders constitute alternative responses to the anticipation of harm which are determined, at least in part, by the nature of the potentially harmful stimulus and its avoidability.

CHAPTER 8

Fear Development: a Brief Overview

W. Sluckin

Fear patterns vary from species to species. The phylogenetic development of fear is largely a matter of intelligent surmise. Individuals within a species also show differences in fear behaviour – often only sight but sometimes considerable. The ontogenetic development of fear, unlike its phylogeny, is amenable to direct empirical study. Fear in one and the same individual will vary from occasion to occasion in the speed of onset, in the composition of the total pattern, in its duration and so on; and the development of fear on various occasions may be subjected to investigation. The present chapter considers very briefly the *development* of fear in each of these senses in an attempt to pull some threads together. It begins with some thoughts on fear phylogeny and ends with reflections on fear learning.

1   Fear Phylogeny: Adaptation to Environment

When observing behaviour of any kind, biologists often wish to know what the adaptive consequences are of the behaviour in question. Fear provides, of course, for the safety of the individual. It may additionally provide for the safety of the rearing group in gregarious species, or at least in primates (Suomi & Harlow, 1976). For it is through fear that an orderly and stable group hierarchy is established; and this appears to make the group as a whole less exposed to external dangers.

Early on in the book Mayes refers to the value of fear in promoting individual and species survival and, more specifically, to the value of the sequence of responses – freezing, fleeing, fight and tonic immobility – displayed by some prey species while facing predators (Ratner, 1967).

Archer returns to the theme of protective value of fear in Chapter 3 when he advocates the use of functional criteria for defining fear behaviour. In pronouncing whether an animal shows fear we may rely on recognising behaviour which we ourselves associate with subjective fear. But running fast, for instance, does not always indicate fright and flight. It is, therefore, more reliable to judge fear responses by the stimuli and situations which evoke them. But, better still, is to adopt the functional approach whereby the appropriateness of the particular behaviour to the given situation is fully taken into account. As Archer points out, freezing is regarded as fear behaviour only if it appears to make the prey animal generally inconspicuous and thereby more likely to survive. Fear responses are thus seen as modes of behaviour which protect the animal from noxious stimuli and anticipated sources of harm. It may be added parenthetically that the latter includes anticipated frustration (Wagner, 1969; McAllister & McAllister, 1971).

In Chapter 4 Russell mentions protective behaviour which may show itself as attachment behaviour. Here the fearful young approach and follow the mother figure, or cling to her. Fear binds the infant closer to the parent(s), thereby providing the former with a safe base for the exploration of the environment. This facilitates learning generally, and social learning in particular.

The proper biological perspective needed to examine the protective function of fear is given special attention in Chapters 3 and 5. In the latter, Salzen points out that in vertebrates the evolution of fear patterns is bound up with the high level of safety inherent in the status quo ante. In other words, some degree of fear must be associated with any exposure to a change of stimulation because of its potentially harmful consequences. And yet, such a change of stimulation is itself often a sine qua non of survival. Fear, then, is a necessary feature of orientation behaviour, of exploratory behaviour, shelter-seeking behaviour and, as said in the previous paragraph, of infantile and social care-soliciting behaviour. Fear is complex self-protective behaviour which has evolved from simple protective contact-responses. Because of the increase in the learning abilities at the higher levels of the evolutionary scale, fear responses are apt to become associated with many kinds of stimuli. This is, of course, generally advantageous, but the side effect is an increased risk of maladaptive fears.

As far as human beings are concerned, the mode of existence has so radically changed since the dawn of civilisation that one may wonder how much adaptive value fear still has in the human species. Smith gives this some consideration towards the end of Chapter 6 and refers to the views of Bowlby (1973), whose focal interests are in infantile attachments and anxiety. Biologically, the tendency of infants to form attachments to adults is, of course, highly protective. By the same token, young children's wariness of strangers is a protective mechanism. In today's world it is relatively safe not to fear unfamiliar persons, or animals, or objects. Therefore whenever such

237

fears are strong and persistent they tend to be maladaptive; although moderate fear of the unfamiliar is certainly as useful as ever. The evolutionary development of the ability to learn fast has been of the greatest value; and learning ensures that fear of novelty is reduced whenever novel experience results in no harm. The child learns readily what not to fear, e.g. darkness and new faces; it also learns quite quickly to become fearful of danger spots in the home, road traffic and the like.

We may well ask whether consideration of phylogeny shed some light on maladaptive fears. There might conceivably be cases where habituation processes are insufficiently effective to eradicate such strong spontaneous fears as, for example, those of heights. Then, some of the readily acquired fears, those for which we appear to have some 'preparedness' (Seligman & Hager, 1972) – for instance, the fear of snakes and 'creepy, crawly things' – could become too firmly established and too resistant to extinction. Sometimes human beings and animals become literally 'scared to death' (Barker, 1968). Apparently, a very high degree of fright can be associated with such hyperactivity of the adrenal system, and such attendant fall in blood pressure, that death is the outcome. This may perhaps be regarded as fear at its most maladaptive.

2   The Arousal of Fear in the Individual

The states of fright, anxiety, nervousness, alarm – to mention some of the words signifying fear – have an onset, reach a peak or a plateau, and then fade away. Descriptions of the development of fear states in the individual may be given at the experiential, physiological and behavioural levels. Perhaps the most vivid and appealing descriptions of the emotion of fear are to be found in novels and poetry. Physiological accounts have proved to be less straightforward than originally thought. A threat appraisal, as Mayes puts it in Chapter 2, is associated with 'a complex set of activations of autonomic, endocrine and cortical systems'. Anomalous occurrences of threat perception without physiological concomitants, or physiological signs of fear without a sense of threat, are fairly rare, but certainly not unknown. Apart from a degree of dissociation between feeling and physiological arousal, there can be imperfect couplings between feelings and modes of behaviour and between physiological fear arousal and fear behaviour patterns.

Fear behaviour, denoting a variety of 'adaptive whole-body responses serving to protect the organism from potentially harmful stimuli' – to quote Russell in Chapter 4 – can be evoked by many kinds of stimulation. These are placed by Russell into several main classes, such as predator stimuli, physical environmental dangers, etc. Man's general learning ability being very high, it is, of course, not surprising that very many different types of stimuli can be fear-evoking for human beings. As Thomson points out in Chapter 1, fears can be very powerful even when fear objects are imaginary rather than palpable. In some cultures the fear of God, the fear of hell and the like are very potent. In others, people may greatly fear apparitions, or dead persons, or witches and wizards; and such fears are often made use of by mothers to discipline their children (Uka, 1966).

Once the stimulus has been perceived or cognized, fear will develop slowly or fast, according to the perception, or subjective assessment, of the imminence of harm. A frightening experience may have more profound repercussions at all levels – experiential, physiological and behavioural – at some phases of the circadian rhythm than at others (Stroebel, 1967).

Very broadly speaking, there are two main types of fear behaviour: flight and immobility. A low level of fear, which is sometimes only the first stage of fear, may show itself, as noted by Archer in Chapter 3, in the avoidance of proximity. Neophobia, or shunning the unfamiliar, may be regarded as an exemplar of this behaviour. As fear develops further, avoidance may turn into flight. But, as mentioned earlier, flight is sometimes preceded by freezing. Flight itself can grow in intensity and then decline; but it is well known that a cornered, terrified individual – animal or human – may stand up and fight.

Activities such as eating, drinking and exploration are somewhat inhibited by low-level fear but, as fear rises, they become fully suppressed. Such actions, as well as sexual behaviour, are simply incompatible with immobility and fleeing. Other activities, however, are positively correlated with flight or freezing – defecation, for instance, and 'distress' vocalisations; and occasionally bouts of aggression may actually accompany flight. Human beings can, of course, experience intense fear without any proximity avoidance, or immobility, or flight, while at the same time showing unmistakable features of autonomic arousal which are characteristic of fear states.

3   The Ontogenetic Development of Fear

Modern accounts of the ontogeny of behaviour do not draw a sharp – and potentially misleading – distinction between 'innate' and 'learned' patterns (Hinde, 1970, 1974). At the same time it is clear that behaviour in the process of development is influenced by genetic/maturational and experiential factors. The unravelling of the intimate interaction between

239

these two sets of factors is of central importance in the study of the development of behaviour, including the development of fear patterns in the individual.

We can distinguish, though not always with ease, two classes of stimuli which evoke fear. These are described by Suomi & Harlow (1976) as those which are 'innately fearful' and as those which elicit 'fear behaviour only after associative learning'. In rhesus monkeys, for instance, frightening stimuli that do not require learning may include such visual and auditory events as lightning, thunder, fire and high wind (perhaps all 'innately fearful' because of their high intensity). To these might be added looming stimuli and heights. Other stimuli are frightening only after some experience; these include 'incongruous' stimuli. Whether threat postures of members of the individual's own species belong to this category is somewhat uncertain. Fear of snakes and the like probably requires observational learning. And many fears are undoubtedly conditioned responses to pain.

Salzen, towards the end of Chapter 5, has sections on 'maturation and fear' and 'experience and fear'; such a separation, although difficult, is convenient in practice. As the receptor and effector systems mature, so the fear responses grow in intensity and variety. Right from the start, however, from birth or even before, the course of fear development is influenced by experience, for instance by the elicitation and performance of orientation responses and by imprinting and exploration.

In his résumé of research perspective early in Chapter 6, Smith reviews the history of the environmentalist and nativist explanations of the origins of fear in young children. Some early-day studies reported cases of fear in children which clearly showed fear to be the result of conditioning. Other studies, however, seemed to suggest strongly that some, at least,of the children's fears had come about with maturation. Somewhat later an 'incongruity' view of the origin of fear in animals and man was advanced (Hebb, 1946; Hunt, 1965). There are different versions of it, but, roughly, fear goes with the perception of a mismatch between the new and the familiar. This explanation of 'spontaneous' fears does not invoke conditioning, i.e. associating the discrepant stimulus with an aversive one. However, the incongruity account does presuppose prior exposure learning, or a process of familiarisation by the young individual with its environment. Fear of novelty, as such, may well be inborn (and associated with the disturbance of status quo), but what actually *is* novel (and feared) depends on earlier learning as to what is familiar. In some sense, therefore, the incongruity hypothesis of fear represented a movement away from the tradition of the nature-nurture controversy.

Numerous empirical studies of the development of fear in young children carried out more recently, together with theory-building to account for the findings, are very fully reviewed by Smith in Chapter 6. The incongruity view of fear development, in its simple form, now appears in general to be more applicable to younger infants than to those above 6 months of age. Thereafter, the incongruity hypothesis begins to require various refinements if it is to be retained (its complete abandonment would probably create more problems than it would solve). The modifications of the theory need to take into account the advancement with age in the cognitive and social functioning of children. Perceived incongruity in the environment has to do with the child's expectations. These expectations depend on perceptual exposure learning as well as on specific associative learning; and, what is more, the two are not necessarily clearly separable. It is possible that as the infant grows older fear based on forms of associative learning increases in importance in relation to fear which is rooted in incongruity. In the end, accounts of fear ontogeny, stressing the roles of maturation, exposure learning and associative learning, which earlier often seemed to be in conflict with one another, nowadays appear more complementary than contradictory.

However, despite everything that has been accomplished by learning theorists since early this century, the mechanisms of fear learning cannot be said to be fully understood. They are almost certainly more varied than used to be thought at one time. Conditioning in the narrow sense of the term is probably not the most important mechanism of fear acquisition in human beings. As Carr points out in Chapter 7, if conditioning is to operate, the individual must survive early encounters with painful and potentially lethal stimuli. For conditioning to be widespread and effective, such encounters would have to be frequent and rarely end in death. Considering the potential mortal danger of exposure to noxious stimuli, it is unlikely that people most frequently learn fear 'the hard way'. It is therefore probable that in human beings learning processes free from direct risk to life, such as observational learning and learning by word of mouth – learning 'the easy way' as it were – are very strongly implicated in the ontogeny of fear.

Such a view of fear acquisition, while partly in the behaviourist tradition, is also cognitivist in outlook (Hintzman, 1978). It appears to be consistent with empirical findings. It is also in tune with the new directions in the study of learning. These point to diverse evolutionary specialisations in learning, such as, for example, imprinting, song learning in certain bird species, star-orientation learning in some migratory birds, food aversion learning in birds and mammals, native language acquisition by children, etc. (Bolles, 1975; Revusky, 1977). This is not to say that the traditional account of fear acquisition in animals and man in terms of classical conditioning (e.g. Mowrer, 1939) should be regarded as incorrect. It should, however, be seen as of limited applicability. It should also be seen in the wider biological

241

perspective. In so far as fear is learned, its acquisition is certainly subject to certain constraints, but it is also governed by built-in preparedness (Seligman & Hager, 1972; Hinde & Stevenson-Hinde, 1973). In the present climate of diminished regard for global, general-process theories of learning, and of heightened interest in hitherto unrecognised or unemphasised learning phenomena, conditions are conducive to a burgeoning of wide-ranging empirical studies concerning the ontogeny of fear both in animals and in human beings.

Bibliography

ADAM, J. & DIMOND, S. J. (1971) The effect of visual stimulation at different stages of embryonic development on approach behaviour, *Animal Behaviour*, **19**, 51–54.

ADAMS, J. & ROTHSTEIN, W. (1971) The relationship between 16 fear factors and psychiatric status, *Behaviour Research and Therapy*, **9**, 361–365.

ADELMAN, H. M. & MAATSCH J. L. (1956) Learning and extinction based upon frustration, food reward and exploratory tendency, *Journal of Experimental Psychology*, **52**, 311–315.

AGRAS, S., SYLVESTER, D. & OLIVEAU, D. (1969) The epidemiology of common fears and phobias, *Comparative Psychiatry*, **10**, 151–156.

AINSWORTH, M. D. S. (1963) The development of infant-mother interaction among the Ganda. In: *Determinants of Infant Behaviour, Vol. 2* (Ed.: B. M. Foss). London: Methuen.

AINSWORTH, M. D. S. (1973) The development of infant-mother attachment. In: *Review of Child Development Research, Vol. 3* (Ed.: B. M. Caldwell & H. N. Ricciuti). Chicago: University of Chicago Press.

AINSWORTH, M. D. S. & BELL, S. M. (1970) Attachment, exploration and separation: illustrated by the behavior of one-year-olds in a strange situation, *Child Development*, **41**, 49–67.

AINSWORTH, M. D. S. & WITTIG, B. A. (1969) Attachment and exploratory behaviour of one-year-olds in a strange situation. In: *Determinants of Infant Behaviour, Vol. 4* (Ed.: B. M. Foss). London: Methuen.

AITKEN, P. P. (1972) Aversive stimulation and rats' preference for familiarity, *Psychonomic Science*, **28**, 281–282.

AITKEN, P. P. (1974) Aversive stimulation and rat's preference for areas differing in novelty value and brightness, *Animal Behaviour*, **22**, 731–734.

AKISKAL, H. S. & McKINNEY, W. T. (1975) An overview of recent research in depression, *Archives of General Psychiatry*, **32**, 285–305.

ALCOCK, J. (1975) *Animal Behavior: an evolutionary approach.* Sunderland, Mass.: Sinauer.

ALDERSON, J. & JOHNSTON, R. E. (1975) Responses of male golden hamsters (*Mesocricetus auratus*) to clean and male scented area, *Behavioural Biology*, **15**, 505–510.

ALLEY, R. & BOYD, H. (1950) Parent-young recognition in the coot *Fulica atra*, *Ibis*, **92**, 46–51.

ALLIN, J. T. & BANKS, E. M. (1971) Effects of temperature on ultrasound production by infant albino rats, *Developmental Psychobiology*, **4**, 149–156.

ALTMAN, J. & SUDARSHAN, K. (1975) Postnatal development of locomotion in the laboratory rat, *Animal Behaviour*, **23**, 896–920.

AMSTERDAM, B. (1972) Mirror self image reactions before age two, *Developmental Psychology*, **5**, 297–305.

ANDERSON, A. C. & PATRICK, J. R. (1934) Some early behavior patterns in the white rat, *Psychological Review*, **41**, 480–496.

ANDREW, R. J. (1956a) Some remarks on behaviour in conflict situations, with special reference to *Emberiza* spp., *British Journal of Animal Behaviour*, **4**, 41–45.

ANDREW, R. J. (1956b) Fear responses in *Emberiza* spp., *British Journal of Animal Behaviour*, **4**, 125–132.

ANDREW, R. J. (1962) The situations that evoke vocalisations in primates, *Annals of the New York Academy of Science*, **102**, 296–315.

ANDREW, R. J. (1963a) The origins and evolution of the calls and facial expressions of the primates, *Behaviour*, **20**, 1–109.

ANDREW, R. J. (1963b) Evolution of facial expression, *Science*, **142**, 1034–1041.

ANDREW, R. J. (1964) Vocalization in chicks, and the concept of 'stimulus contrast', *Animal Behaviour*, **12**, 64–76.

ANDREW, R. J. (1972a) The information potentially available in mammal displays, In: *Non-verbal Communication* (ed.: R. A. Hinde). London: Cambridge University Press.

ANDREW, R. J. (1972b) Changes in search behaviour in male and female chicks, following different doses of testosterone, *Animal Behaviour*, **20**, 741–750.

ANDREW, R. J. (1975) Effects of testosterone on the calling of the domestic chick in a strange environment, *Animal Behaviour*, **23**, 169–178.

ANDREW, R. J. & ROGERS, L. J. (1972) Testosterone, search behaviour and persistence, *Nature*, **237**, 343–346.

ANGELINO, H., DOLLINS, J. & MECH, V. (1956) Trends in the fears and worries of school children as related to socioeconomic status and age, *Journal of Genetic Psychology*, **89**, 263–276.

ANGELINO, H. & SHEDD, C. (1953) Shifts in the content of fears and worries relative to chronological age, *Proceedings of the Oklahoma Academy of Science*, **34**, 180–186.

ANNAU, Z. & KAMIN, L. J. (1961) The conditioned emotional response as a function of intensity of the US, *Journal of Comparative and Physiological Psychology*, **54**, 428–432.

ARCHER, J. (1971) Sex differences in emotional behaviour: a reply to Gray and Buffery, *Acta Psychologica*, **35**, 415–429.

ARCHER, J. (1973a) Tests for emotionality in rats and mice: a review, *Animal Behaviour*, **21**, 205–235.

ARCHER, J. (1973b) The influence of testosterone on chick behavior in novel environments, *Behavioral Biology*, **8**, 93–108.

ARCHER, J. (1973c) Effects of testosterone on immobility responses in the young male chick, *Behavioral Biology*, **8**, 551–556.

ARCHER, J. (1973d) A further analysis of responses to a novel environment by testosterone-treated chicks, *Behavioral Biology*, **9**, 389–396.

ARCHER, J. (1974a) Sex differences in the emotional behavior of three strains of laboratory rat, *Animal Learning and Behavior*, **2**, 43–48.

ARCHER, J. (1974b) The effects of testosterone on the distractability of chicks by irrelevant and relevant novel stimuli, *Animal Behaviour*, **22**, 397–404.

ARCHER, J. (1974c) Testosterone and behaviour during extinction in chicks, *Animal Behaviour*, **22**, 650–655.

ARCHER, J. (1975) Rodent sex differences in emotional and related behavior, *Behavioral Biology*, **14**, 451–479.

ARCHER, J. (1976a) The organization of aggression and fear in vertebrates. In: *Perspectives in Ethology, Vol 2* (Ed.: P. P. G. Bateson & P. Klopfer). New York & London: Plenum Press.

ARCHER, J. (1976b) Testosterone and fear behavior in male chicks, *Physiology and Behavior*, **17**, 561–564.

ARCHER, J. (1976c) Emergence tests in testosterone-treated chicks, *Physiology and Behavior*, **16**, 513–514.

ARCHER, J. (1977a) Sex differences in the emotional behaviour of laboratory mice, *British Journal of Psychology*, **68**, 125–131.

ARCHER, J. (1977b) Testosterone and persistence in mice, *Animal Behaviour*, **25**, 479–488.

ARSENIAN, J. M. (1943) Young children in an insecure situation, *Journal of Abnormal and Social Psychology*, **38**, 225–249.

ASDOURIAN, D. (1967) Object attachment and the critical period, *Psychonomic Science*, **7**, 235–236.

AVERY, G. T. (1928) Responses of foetal guinea pigs prematurely delivered, *Genetic Psychology Monographs*, **3**, 248–331.

AX, A. F. (1953) The physiological differentiation between fear and anger in humans, *Psychosomatic Medicine*, **15**, 433–442.

BAENNINGER, L. P. (1967) Comparison of behavioural development in socially isolated and grouped rats, *Animal Behaviour*, **15**, 312–323.

BAER, P. E. & FUHRER, M. J. (1968) Cognitive processes during differential trace and delayed conditioning of the GSR, *Journal of Experimental Psychology*, **78**, 81–88.

BAER, P. E. & FUHRER, M. J. (1970) Cognitive processes in the differential trace conditioning of electrodermal and vasomotor activity, *Journal of Experimental Psychology*, **84**, 176–178.

BAERENDS, G. P. (1975) An evaluation of the conflict hypothesis as an explanatory principle for the evolution of displays. In: *Function and Evolution in Behaviour* (Ed.: G. Baerends, C. Beer & A Manning). London: Oxford University Press.

245

BALL, W. & TRONICK, E. (1971) Infant responses to impending collision: optical and real, *Science*, **171**, 818–820.

BANCROFT, J. (1969) Aversion therapy of homosexuality, *British Journal of Psychiatry*, **115**, 1417–1431.

BANDURA, A. (1969) *Principles of Behavior Modification*. New York: Holt, Rinehart & Winston.

BANDURA, A. (Ed.) (1971) *Psychological Modeling*. Chicago: Atherton.

BANDURA, A., GRUSEC, J. E. & MENLOVE, F. L. (1967) Vicarious extinction of avoidance behaviour, *Journal of Personality and Social Psychology*, **5**, 16–23.

BANDURA, A. & ROSENTHAL, T. L. (1966) Vicarious classical conditioning as a function of arousal level, *Journal of Personality and Social Psychology*, **3**, 54–62.

BARCIK, J. D. & COLLINS, D. E. (1972) Shock-elicited defensive behavior and passive avoidance performance, *Psychonomic Science*, **28**, 37–40.

BARD, P. (1928) A diencephalic mechanism for the expression of rage with special reference to the sympathetic nervous system, *American Journal of Physiology*, **84**, 490–515.

BARD, P. & MOUNTCASTLE, V. B. (1948) Some forebrain mechanisms involved in expression of rage with special reference to suppression of angry behavior, *Research Publications of the Association for Research in Nervous and Mental Disease*, **27**, 362–404.

BARFIELD, R. J. & SACHS, B. D. (1968) Sexual Behavior: stimulation by painful electric shock to skin in male rats, *Science*, **161**, 392–395.

BARKER, J. C. (1968) *Scared to Death*. London: Frederick Muller.

BARKOW, J. (1978) Culture and sociobiology, *American Anthropologist*, **80**, 5–20.

BARNETT, S. A. (1956) Behaviour components in the feeding of wild and laboratory rats, *Behaviour*, **9**, 24–43.

BARNETT, S. A. (1958) Experiments in 'neophobia' in wild and laboratory rats, *British Journal of Psychology*, **49**, 195–201.

BARNETT, S. A. (1975) *The Rat: A Study in Behavior*. Chicago: University of Chicago Press.

BARNETT, S. A. & COWAN, P. E. (1976) Activity, exploration, curiosity and fear: an ethological study, *Interdisciplinary Science Reviews*, **1**, 43–62.

BARNETT, S. A. & SPENCER, M. M. (1951) Feeding, social behaviour and interspecific competition in wild rats, *Behaviour*, **3**, 229–242.

BARON, A. (1963) Differential effects of fear on activity in novel and familiar environments, *Psychological Reports*, **13**, 251–257.

BARON, A. (1964) Suppression of exploratory behaviour by aversive stimulation, *Journal of Comparative and Physiological Psychology*, **57**, 299–301.

BARRAUD, E. M. (1961) The development of behaviour in some young passerines, *Bird Study*, **8**, 111–118.

BARRON, D. H. (1941) The functional development of some mammalian neuromuscular mechanisms, *Biological Reviews*, **16**, 1–33.

BATESON, P. P. G. (1964a) Changes in chicks' responses to novel moving objects over the sensitive period for imprinting, *Animal Behaviour*, **12**, 479–489.

246

BATESON, P. P. G. (1964b) Changes in the activity of isolated chicks over the first week after hatching, *Animal Behaviour*, **12**, 490–492.

BATESON, P. P. G. (1964c) Effect of similarity between rearing and testing conditions on chicks' following and avoidance responses, *Journal of Comparative and Physiological Psychology*, **57**, 100–103.

BAUER, D. H. (1976) An exploratory study of developmental changes in children's fears, *Journal of Child Psychology and Psychiatry*, **17**, 69–74.

BAUM, M. (1970) Extinction of avoidance responding through response prevention (flooding), *Psychological Bulletin*, **74**, 276–284.

BEACH, F. A., CONOVITZ, M. W., STEINBERG, F. & GOLDSTEIN, A. C. (1956) Experimental inhibition and restoration of mating behavior in male rats, *Journal of Genetic Psychology*, **89**, 165–181.

BEATTY, W. W. & BEATTY, P. A. (1970) Effects of neonatal testosterone on the acquisition of an active avoidance response in genotypically female rats, *Psychonomic Science*, **19**, 315–316.

BECK, A. T., LANDE, R. & BONHERT, M. (1974) Ideational components of anxiety nurosis, *Archives of General Psychiarty*, **31**, 319–325.

BECK, A. T. & RUSH, A. J. (1975) A cognitive model of anxiety formation and anxiety resolution. In: *Stress and Anxiety* (Ed.: I. G. Sarason & C. D. Spielberger). Washington DC: Hemisphere.

BEECH, H. R. & PERIGAULT, J. (1974) Toward a theory of obsessional disorder. In: *Obsessional States* (Ed.: H. R. Beech). London: Methuen.

BELL, R. W. (1974) Ultrasounds in small rodents: arousal-produced and arousal-producing, *Developmental Psychobiology*, **7**, 39–42.

BELL, S. M. (1970) The development of the concept of object as related to infant-mother attachment, *Child Development*, **41**, 291–311.

BEN ARI, Y, & LE GAL LA SALLE, G. (1972) Plasticity at unitary level: II, Modifications during sensory-sensory association procedures. *Electroencephalography and Clinical Neurophysiology*, **32**, 667–679.

BENJAMIN, J. D. (1961) Some developmental observations relating to the theory of anxiety, *Journal of the American Psychoanalytical Association*, **9**, 652–668.

BERECZ, J. M. (1968) Phobias of childhood: etiology and treatment, *Psychological Bulletin*, **70**, 694–720.

BERLYNE, D. E. (1960) *Conflict, Arousal and Curiosity*. New York: McGraw-Hill.

BERMAN, L. (1942) Obsessive-compulsive neurosis in children, *Journal of Nervous and Mental Disease*, **95**, 26–39.

BERMANT, G. (1963) Intensity and rate of distress calling in chicks as a function of social contact, *Animal Behaviour*, **11**, 514–517.

BERNARD, J. A. & RAMEY, C. T. (1977) Visual regard of familiar and unfamiliar persons in the first six months of infancy, *Merrill-Palmer Quarterly*, **23**, 121–127.

BERNSTEIN, I. S. (1964) The integration of rhesus monkeys introduced into a group, *Folia Primatologica*, **2**, 50–63.

BERNSTEIN, S. & MASON, W. A. (1962) The effects of age and stimulus conditions on the emotional responses of rhesus monkeys: responses to complex stimuli, *Journal of Genetic Psychology*, **101**, 279–298.

BERTRAND, M. (1976) The reactions of stumptail monkeys to animals and novel objects. In: *Play: Its Role in Development and Evolution* (Ed.: J. S. Bruner, A. Jolly & K. Sylva). Harmondsworth: Penguin.

BIRKE, L. I. A. & ARCHER, J. (1975) Open field behaviour of oestrous and dioestrous rats: evidence against an 'emotionality' interpretation, *Animal Behaviour*, **23**, 509–512.

BISCHOF, N. (1975) A systems approach toward the functional connections of fear and attachment, *Child Development*, **46**, 801–817.

BITTERMAN, M. E. (1975) Issues in the comparative psychology of learning. In: *The Evolution of Brain and Behaviour in Vertebrates* (Ed.: R. B. Masterton, M. E. Bitterman, C. B. Campbell & N. Hotten). Hillsdale, N. J.: Erlbaum. New York & London: Wiley.

BJERKE, T. & BJERKE, L. G. (1970) Note: Imprintability of Goldeneyes (*Bucephala clangula*), *Psychological Reports*, **27**, 981–982.

BLACK, A. (1974) The natural history of obsessional neurosis. In: *Obsessional States* (Ed.: H. R. Beech). London: Methuen.

BLANCHARD, D. C., BLANCHARD, R. J., LEE, E. M. C. & FUKUNAGA, K. K. (1977) Movement arrest and the hippocampus, *Physiological Psychology*, **5**, 331–335.

BLANCHARD, R. J. & BLANCHARD, D. C. (1968) Escape and avoidance responses to a fear eliciting situation, *Psychonomic Science*, **13**, 19–20.

BLANCHARD, R. J. & BLANCHARD, D. C. (1969a) Crouching as an index of fear, *Journal of Comparative and Physiological Psychology*, **67**, 370–375.

BLANCHARD, R. J. & BLANCHARD, D. C. (1969b) Passive and active reactions to fear-eliciting stimuli, *Journal of Comparative and Physiological Psychology*, **68**, 129–135.

BLANCHARD, R. J. & BLANCHARD, D. C. (1970) Dual mechanisms in passive avoidance I & II, *Psychonomic Science*, **19**, 1–4.

BLANCHARD, R. J. & BLANCHARD D. C. (1971) Defensive reactions in the albino rat, *Learning and Motivation*, **2**, 351–362.

BLANCHARD, R. J., DIELMAN, T. E. & BLANCHARD, D. C. (1968a) Prolonged after-effects of a single foot shock, *Psychonomic Science*, **10**, 327–328.

BLANCHARD, R. J., DIELMAN, T. E. & BLANCHARD, D. C. (1968b) Postshock crouching: familiarity with the shock situation, *Psychonomic Science*, **10**, 371–372.

BLANCHARD, R. J., FUKUNAGA, K. K. & BLANCHARD, D. C. (1976)

Environmental control of defensive reactions to a cat, *Bulletin of the Psychonomic Society*, **8**, 179–181.

BLANCHARD, R. J., FUKUNAGA, K. K., BLANCHARD, D. C. & KELLEY, M. J. (1975) Conspecific aggression in the laboratory rat, *Journal of Comparative and Physiological Psychology*, **89**, 1204–1209.

BLANCHARD, R. J., KELLEY, M. J. & BLANCHARD, D. C. (1974) Defensive reactions and exploratory behavior in rats, *Journal of Comparative and Physiological Psychology*, **87**, 1129–1133.

BLANCHARD, R. J., MAST, M. & BLANCHARD, D. C. (1975) Stimulus control of defensive reactions in the albino rat, *Journal of Comparative and Physiological Psychology*, **88**, 81–88.

BLANCK, A., HÅRD, E. & LARSSON, K. (1967) Ontogenetic development of orienting behavior in the rat, *Journal of Comparative and Physiological Psychology*, **63**, 327–328.

BLEST, A. D. (1957) The function of eyespot patterns in the *Lepidoptera*, *Behaviour*, **11**, 209–256.

BLEST, A. D. (1961) The concept of ritualisation. In: *Current Problems in Animal Behaviour* (Ed.: W. H. Thorpe & O. L. Zangwill). London: Cambridge University Press.

BLIZARD, D. A. (1968) *Autonomic and Behavioural Correlates of Emotionality*, unpublished Ph.D. dissertation, University of Wales (Cardiff).

BLIZARD, D. A. (1971) Situational determinants of open-field behaviour in *Mus musculus*, *British Journal of Psychology*, **62**, 245–252.

BLURTON-JONES, N. G. (1968) Observations and experiments on causation of threat displays of the great tit (*Parus major*), *Animal Behaviour Monographs*, **1**, 75–158.

BOLLES, R. C. (1970) Species-specific defense reactions and avoidance learning, *Psychological Review*, **77**, 32–48.

BOLLES, R. C. (1975) *Learning Theory*. New York: Holt, Rinehart & Winston.

BOLLES, R. C. & COLLIER, A. C. (1976) The effect of predictive cues on freezing in rats, *Animal Learning and Behavior*, **1**, 6–8.

BOLLES, R. C. & WOODS, P. J. (1964) The ontogeny of behaviour in the albino rat, *Animal Behaviour*, **12**, 427–441.

BORCHELT, P. L. & RATNER, S. C. (1973) Development of freezing and immobility, predator defenses, in the bobwhite quail (*Colinus virginianus*), *Behavioral Biology*, **8**, 83–92.

BOURNE, P. G. (1970) *Men, Stress and Vietnam*. Boston: Little, Brown.

BOURNE, P. G. (1971) Altered adrenal function in two combat situations in Vietnam. In: *The Physiology of Aggression and Defeat* (Ed.: B. E. Eleftheriou & J. P. Scott). London: Plenum Press.

BOUSFIELD, W. A. & ORBISON, W. D. (1952) Ontogenesis of emotional behavior, *Psychological Review*, **59**, 1–7.

BOWER, T. G. R. (1974) *Development in Infancy*. San Francisco: Freeman.

BOWER, T. G. R. (1977) *A Primer of Infant Development*. San Francisco: Freeman

BOWER, T. G. R., BROUGHTON, J. M. & MOORE, M. K. (1970) Infant responses to approaching objects: an indicator of response to distal cues, *Perception and Psychophysics*, **9**, 193–196.

BOWLBY, J. (1958) The nature of the child's tie to his mother, *International Journal of Psycho-Analysis*, **39**, 350–373.

BOWLBY, J. (1969) *Attachment and Loss, Vol. 1, Attachment*. London: Hogarth Press.

BOWLBY, J. (1973) *Attachment and Loss, Vol. 2, Separation, Anxiety and Anger*. London: Hogarth Press.

BOYD, H. & FABRICIUS, E. (1965) Observations on the incidence of following of visual and auditory stimuli in naive mallard ducklings (*Anas platyrhynchos*), *Behaviour*, **25**, 1–15.

BRANDT, E. M., BAYSINGER, C. & MITCHELL, G. (1972) Separation from rearing environment in mother-reared and isolation-reared rhesus monkeys (*Macaca mulatta*), *International Journal of Psychobiology*, **2**, 193–204.

BRANNIGAN, C. R. (1972) *Exploratory behaviour in the laboratory rat*, unpublished M.Sc. dissertation, University of Birmingham, England.

BRAUD, W. G. & GINSBURG, H. J. (1973) Immobility reactions in domestic fowl (*Gallus gallus*) less than 7 days old: resolution of a paradox, *Animal Behaviour*, **21**, 104–108.

BREGMAN, E. O. (1934) An attempt to modify the emotional attitudes of infants by the conditioned response technique, *Journal of Genetic Psychology*, **45**, 169–198.

BREMOND, J. C., GRAMET, P., BROUGH, T. & WRIGHT, E. N. (1968) A comparison of some broadcasting equipments and recorded distress calls for scaring birds, *Journal of Applied Ecology*, **5**, 521–529.

BRETHERTON, I. (1978) Making friends with one-year-olds: an experimental study of infant-stranger interaction, *Merrill-Palmer Quarterly*, **24**, 29–51.

BRETHERTON, I. & AINSWORTH, M. D. S. (1974) Responses of one-year-olds to a stranger in a strange situation. In: *The Origins of Fear, Vol. 2* (Ed.: M. Lewis & L. A. Rosenblum). New York & London: Wiley.

BRETT, J. R. & MACKINNON, D. (1954) Some aspects of olfactory perception in migrating adult Coho and Spring Salmon, *Journal of the Fishery Research Board of Canada*, **11**, 310–318.

BRIDGER, W. H. & MANDEL, I. J. (1964) A comparison of GSR fear responses produced by threat and electric shock, *Journal of Psychiatric Research*, **2**, 31–40.

BRIDGER, W. H. & MANDEL, I. J. (1965) Abolition of the PRE by instruction in GSR conditioning, *Journal of Experimental Psychology*, **69**, 476–482.

BRIDGES, K. M. B. (1932) Emotional development in early infancy, *Child Development*, **3**, 324–341.

BROADHURST, P. L. (1957) Determinants of emotionality in the rat: 1, Situational factors, *British Journal of Psychology*, **48**, 1–12.

BROADHURST, P. L. (1960) Experiments in psychogenetics: applications of biometrical genetics to the inheritance of behaviour. In: *Experiments in Personality, Vol. 1, Psychogenetics and Psychopharmacology* (Ed.: H. J. Eysenck). London: Routledge & Kegan Paul.

BROADHURST, P. L. (1972) Abnormal animal behaviour. In: *Handbook of Abnormal Psychology* (Ed.: H. J. Eysenck). London: Pitman.

BRONSON, G. W. (1968a) The fear of novelty, *Psychological Bulletin*, **69**, 350–358.

BRONSON, G. W. (1968b) The development of fear in man and other animals, *Child Development*, **39**, 409–431.

BRONSON, G. W. (1969a) Fear of visual novelty: developmental patterns in males and females, *Developmental Psychology*, **2**, 33–40.

BRONSON, G. W. (1969b) Sex differences in the development of fearfulness: a replication, *Psychonomic Science*, **17**, 367–368.

BRONSON, G. W. (1971) Levels of emotional responsiveness: General discussion. In: *The Origin of Human Social Relations* (Ed.: H. R. Schaffer). London & New York: Academic Press.

BRONSON, G. W. (1972) Infants' reactions to unfamiliar persons and novel objects, *Monographs of the Society for Research in Child Development*, **37**, No. 3.

BRONSON, W. C. (1974) General issues in the study of fear. In: *The Origins of Fear* (Ed.: M. Lewis & L. A. Rosenblum). New York & London: Wiley.

BRONSON, G. W. (1978) Aversive reactions to strangers: a dual-process interpretation, *Child Development*, **49**, 495–499.

BRONSON, G. W. & PANKEY, W. B. (1977) On the distinction between fear and wariness, *Child Development*, **48**, 1167–1183.

BRONSON, W. C. (1975) Developments in behaviour with age-mates during the second year of life. In: *Friendship and Peer Relations* (Ed.: M. Lewis & L. A. Rosenblum). New York & London: Wiley.

BRONSTEIN, P. M. & HIRSCH, S. M. (1976) Ontogeny of defensive reactions in Norway rats, *Journal of Comparative and Physiological Psychology*, **90**, 620–629.

BROOKS, J. & LEWIS, M. (1976) Infants' responses to strangers: midget, adult and child, *Child Development*, **47**, 323–332.

BROOM,, D. M. (1968) Behavior of undisturbed 1- to 10-day-old chicks in different rearing conditions, *Developmental Psychobiology*, **1**, 287–295.

BROOM, D. M. (1969a) Reactions of chicks to visual changes during the first ten days after hatching, *Animal Behaviour*, **17**, 307–315.

BROOM, D. M. (1969b) Effects of visual complexity during rearing on chicks' reactions to environmental change, *Animal Behaviour*, **17**, 773–780.

BROSGOLE, L. (1976) Heat training in the box turtle (*Terrapene carolina*), *Bulletin of the Psychonomic Society*, **8**, 339–340.

BROSGOLE, L. & ULATOWSKI, P. (1973) Heat training in the Mongolian gerbil, *Psychological Reports*, **33**, 275–280.

BROSSARD, M. (1974) The infant's conception of object permanence and his reaction to strangers. In: *The Infant's Reaction to Strangers* (Ed.: T. G. DeCarie). New York: International Universities press.

BROUGH, T. (1969) The dispersal of starlings from woodland roosts and the use of bio-acoustics, *Journal of Applied Ecology*, **6**, 403–410.

BROVERMAN, D. M., KLAIBER, E. L., KOBAYASHI, Y. & VOGEL, W. (1968) Roles of inactivation and inhibition in sex differences in cognitive abilities, *Psychological Review*, **75**, 23–50.

BROVERMAN, D. M., KLAIBER, E. L., VOGEL, W. & KOBAYASHI, Y. (1974) Short-term versus long-term effects of adrenal hormones on behaviors, *Psychological Review*, **81**, 672–694.

BROWN, C. P. (1977) General behavioral inhibition in passive avoidance by chicks, *Behavioral Biology*, **20**, 512–518.

BROWN, J. L & HUNSPERGER, R. W. (1963) Neuroethology and the motivation of agonistic behaviour, *Animal Behaviour*, **11**, 439–448.

BROWN, R. T. (1975) Following and visual imprinting in ducklings across a wide age range, *Developmental Psychobiology*, **8**, 27–33.

BROWN, R. T. & HAMILTON, A. S. (1977) Imprinting: effects of discrepancy from rearing conditions on approach to a familiar imprinting object in a novel situation, *Journal of Comparative and Physiological Psychology*, **91**, 784–793.

BRUSH, F. R. (1957) The effects of shock intensity on the acquisition and extinction of an avoidance response in dogs, *Journal of Comparative and Physiological Psychology*, **50**, 547–552.

BÜHLER, C. (1930) *The First Year of Life*. New York: John Day.

BUTLER, R. A. (1964) The reactions of rhesus monkeys to fear-provoking stimuli, *Journal of Genetic Psychology*, **104**, 321–330.

CALLAWAY, E., III & THOMPSON, S. V. (1953) Sympathetic activity and perception: An approach to the relationship between autonomic activity and personality, *Psychosomatic Medicine*, **15**, 443–445.

CAMPBELL, B. A. & MABRY, P. D. (1972) Ontogeny of behavioral arousal: a comparative study, *Journal of Comparative and Physiological Psychology*, **81**, 371–379.

CAMPBELL, D., SANDERSON, R. E. & LAVERTY, S. A. (1964) Characteristics of a conditioned response in human subjects during extinction trials following a simple traumatic conditioning trial, *Journal of Abnormal and Social Psychology*, **68**, 627–693.

CAMPOS, J., EMDE, R., GAENSBAUER, T. & HENDERSON, C. (1975) Cardiac and behavioural interrelationships in the reactions of infants to strangers, *Developmental Psychology*, **11**, 589–601.

CANDLAND, D. K. (1971) The ontogeny of emotional behavior. In: *The Ontogeny of Vertebrate Behavior* (Ed.: H. Moltz). New York: Academic Press.

CANDLAND, D. K. & CAMPBELL, B. A. (1962) Development of fear in the rat as measured by behavior in the open field, *Journal of Comparative and Physiological Psychology*, **55**, 593–596.

CANDLAND, D. K. & NAGY, Z. M. (1969) The open field: some comparative data, *Annals of the New York Academy of Science*, **159**, 831–851.

CANDLAND, D. K., NAGY, Z. M. & CONKLYN, D. H. (1963) Emotional behavior in the domestic chicken (White leghorn) as a function of age and developmental environment, *Journal of Comparative and Physiological Psychology*, **56**, 1069–1073.

CANNON, W. B. (1915) *Bodily Changes in Pain, Hunger, Fear and Rage*. New York: Appleton.

CANNON, W. B. (1927) The James–Lange theory of emotions: a critical examination and alternation, *American Journal of Psychology*, **39**, 106–124.

CANNON, W. B. (1939) *The Wisdom of the Body, 2nd edition*. New York: Norton.

CARMICHAEL, L. (1970) The onset and early development of behavior. In: *Carmichael's Manual of Child Psychology, 3rd edition* (Ed.: P. H. Mussen). New York: Wiley.

CARMICHAEL, L. & SMITH, M. F. (1939) Quantified pressure stimulation and the specificity and generality of response in fetal life, *Journal of Genetic Psychology*, **54**, 425–434.

CARPENTER, G. (1975) Mother's face and the newborn. In: *Child Alive* (Ed.: R. Lewin). London: Temple Smith.

CARR, A. T. (1970) A psychophysiological study of ritual behaviours and decision processes in compulsive neurosis, unpublished doctoral dissertation, University of Birmingham, England.

CARR, A. T. (1974) Compulsive neurosis: a review of the literature, *Psychological Bulletin*, **81**, 5, 311–318.

CARR, W. J., MARTORANO, R. D. & KRAMES, L. (1970) Responses of mice odours associated with stress, *Journal of Comparative and Physiological Psychology*, **71**, 223–228.

CARROLL, M. E., DINE, H. I., LEVY, C. J. & SMITH, J. C. (1975) Demonstrations of neophobia and enhanced neophobia in the albino rat, *Journal of Comparative and Physiological Psychology*, **89**, 457–467.

CHANCE, M. R. A. & RUSSELL, W. M. S. (1959) Protean displays: a form of allaesthetic behaviour, *Proceedings of the Zoological Society London*, **132**, 65–70.

CHAPMAN, C. & COX, G. (1977) Determinants of anxiety in elective surgery patients. In: *Stress and Anxiety* (Ed.: I. G. Sarason & C. D. Spielberger). Washington, DC: Hemisphere.

CHAZAN, M. (1962) School phobia, *British Journal of Educational Psychology*, **32**, 209–217.

CHEVALIER-SKOLNIKOFF, S. (1974) The ontogeny of communication in the stumptail macaque (*Macaca arctoides*), *Contributions to Primatology*, *Vol. 2*. Basel: Karger.

CHIVERS, D. J. (1969) On the daily behaviour and spacing of howling monkey groups, *Folia Primatologica*, **10**, 48–102.

CHURCH, R. M. (1972) Aversive behavior. In: *Woodworth & Schlosberg's Experimental Psychology* (Ed.: J. W. Kling & L. A. Riggs).

CHURCH, R. M. & BLACK, A. H. (1958) Latency of the conditioned heart rate as a function of the CS–US interval, *Journal of Comparative and Physiological Psychology*, **51**, 478–482.

CICCHETTI, D. & STROUFE, L. A. (1976) The relationship between affective and cognitive development in Down's Syndrome infants, *Child Development*, **47**, 920–929.

CLARK, M. M. & GALEF, B. G. (1977) The role of the physical rearing environment in the domestication of the Mongolian gerbil (*Meriones unguiculatus*), *Animal Behaviour*, **25**, 298–316.

CLOAK, F. T. (1975) Is a cultural ethology possible?, *Human Ecology*, **3**, 161–182.

COGHILL, G. E. (1929) *Anatomy and the Problem of Behaviour*. London: Cambridge University Press.

COGHILL, G. E. & LEGNER, W. K. (1937) Embryonic motility and sensitivity, *Monographs of the Society for Research in Child Development*, **2**, 1–115. (Translation of W. Preyer, Specielle Physiologie des Embryo.)

COHEN, S. E. (1974) Developmental differences in infants' attentional responses to face-voice incongruity of mother and stranger, *Child Development*, **45**, 1155–1158.

COLLARD, R. R. (1968) Social and play responses of first born and later born infants in an unfamiliar situation, *Child Development*, **39**, 324–334.

COLLIAS, N. E. (1952) The development of social behavior in birds, *The Auk*, **69**, 127–159.

COLLIAS, N. E. (1960) An ecological and functional classification of animal sounds. In: *Animal sounds and communication* (Ed.: W. E. Lanyon & W. N. Tavolga). Washington DC: American Institute for Biological Science, Publication No. 7.

COLLIAS, N. E. & JOOS, M. (1952) The spectrographic analysis of sound signals of the domestic fowl, *Behaviour*, **5**, 175–187.

CONNER, R. L. & LEVINE, S. (1969) The effects of adrenal hormones on the acquisition of signalled avoidance behaviour, *Hormones and Behaviour*, **1**, 73–83.

CONNOLLY, K. & SMITH, P. K. (1972) Reactions of pre-school children to a strange observer. In: *Ethological Studies of Child Behaviour* (Ed.: N. Blurton-Jones). Cambridge: Cambridge University Press.

COOK, N. L. (1972) Attachment and object permanence in infancy: a short-term longitudinal study, *Dissertation Abstracts*, **33**, 3280B.

COOVER, G. D., SUTTON, B. R. & HEYBACH, J. P. (1977) Conditioning decreases in plasma corticosterone level in rats by pairing stimuli with daily feedings, *Journal of Comparative and Physiological Psychology*, **91**, 716–726.

COPPINGER, R. P. (1969) The effect of experience and novelty on avian feeding behaviour with reference to the evolution of warning coloration in butterflies: Part I, Reactions of wild-caught adult Blue Jays to novel insects, *Behaviour*, **35**, 45–60.

COPPINGER, P. R. (1970) The effect of experience and novelty on avian feeding behaviour with reference to the evolution of warning coloration in butterflies: II, Reaction of naive birds to novel insects, *American Naturalist*, **104**, 323–335.

CORLEY, K. C., SHIEL, F. O'M., MAUCK, H. P., CLARK, L. S. & BARBER, J. H. (1977) Myocardial degeneration and cardiac arrest in squirrel monkey: physiological and psychological correlates, *Psychophysiology*, **14**, 322–328.

CORNWELL, C. A. (1975) Golden hamster pups adapt to complex rearing odors, *Behavioral Biology*, **14**, 175–188.

CORNWELL, D. & HOBBS, S. (1976) The strange saga of little Albert, *New Society*, 18 March.

CORTER, C. (1976) The nature of the mother's absence and the infant's response to brief separation, *Developmental Psychology*, **12**, 428–434.

CORTER, C., RHEINGOLD, H. R. & ECKERMAN, C. O. (1972) Toys delay the infant's following of his mother, *Developmental Psychology*, **6**, 138–145.

COSTELLO, C. G. (1970) Dissimilarities between conditioned avoidance responses and phobias, *Psychological Review*, **7**, 250–254.

COWAN, P. E. (1976) The new object reaction of *Rattus rattus* L.: The relative importance of various cues, *Behavioral Biology*, **16**, 31–44.

COWAN, P. E. (1977) Neophobia and neophilia: new-object and new-place reactions of three *Rattus* species, *Journal of Comparative and Physiological Psychology*, **91**, 63–71.

COX, F. N. & CAMPBELL, D. (1968) Young children in a new situation with and without their mothers, *Child Development*, **39**, 123–132.

CRAWFORD, F. T. (1977) Induction and duration of tonic immobility, *Psychological Record*, **27**, 89–107.

CROAKE, J. W. (1969) Fears of children, *Human Development*, **12**, 239–247.

CROW, T. J., LONGDEN, A., SMITH, R. & WENDLANDT, S. (1977) Effects of post-training epinephrine injections on retention of avoidance training in mice, *Behavioral Biology*, **20**, 184–196.

CULLEN, J. M. (1972) Some principles of animal communication. In: *Nonverbal Communication* (Ed.: R. A. Hinde). London: Cambridge University Press.

CURIO, E. (1975) The functional organization of anti-predator behaviour in the pied flycatcher: a study of avian visual perception, *Animal Behaviour*, **23**, 1–115.

CURIO, E. (1976) *The Ethology of Predation*. New York: Springer Verlag.

DANA, C. L. (1921) The Anatomic seat of the emotions: a discussion of the James–Lange theory, *Archives of Neurology and Psychiatry (Chicago)*, **6**, 634–639.

DARWIN, C. (1872) *The Expression of Emotions in Man and Animals*. London: Murray. (1904 edited edition).

DAVIDSON, R. J. & SCHWARTZ, G. E. (1976) Patterns of cerebral lateralisation during cardiac biofeedback vs. the self-regulation of emotion: interactions with cognition, *Science*, **190**, 286–288.

DAVIS, K. L. GURSKI, J. C. & SCOTT, J. P. (1977) Interaction of separation distress with fear in infant dogs, *Developmental Psychobiology*, **10**, 203–212.

DAWKINS, R. (1976) *The Selfish Gene*. Oxford: Oxford University Press.

DAWSON, M. E. & FUREDY, J. J. (1973) Cited in : EVANS, I. (1976) Classical conditioning. In: *Theoretical and Experimental Bases of Behaviour Therapies* (Ed.: M. P. Feldman & A. Broadhurst). London: Wiley.

DeCARIE, T. G. (Ed.) (1974) *The Infant's Reaction to Strangers*. New York: International Universities Press.

DENENBERG, V. H. (1964) Critical periods, stimulus input, and emotional activity: a theory of infantile stimulation, *Psychological Review*, **71**, 335–351.

DENENBERG, V. H. & ZARROW, M. X. (1971) Effects of handling in infancy upon adult behavior and adrenocortical activity: suggestions for a neuroendocrine mechanism. In. *Early Childhood: The Development of Self-Regulating Mechanisms* (Ed.: D. N. Walcher & D. L. Peters). New York: Academic Press.

DENNIS, W. (1940) Does culture appreciably affect patterns of infant behaviour?, *Journal of Social Psychology*, **12**, 305–317.

DE TOLEDO, L. & BLACK, A. H. (1968) Heart rate: changes during conditioned suppression in rats, *Science*, **152**, 1404–1406.

DE WEID, D. (1967) Opposite effects of ACTH and glucocorticosteroids on extinction of conditioned avoidance behaviour, *Proceedings of the Internation Congress on Hormonal Steroids, Milan, 1966* (Ed.: L. Martini *et al.*) International Congress Series, No 32. Amsterdam, New York: Excerpta Medica Foundation.

DE WEID, D. (1969) Effects of peptide hormones on behaviour. In: *Frontiers in Neuroendocrinology, 1969* (Ed.: L. Martini & W. F. Ganong). London: Oxford University Press.

DICKINSON, A. (1974) Response suppression and facilitation by aversive stimuli following septal lesions in rats: A review and model, *Physiological Psychology*, **2**, 444–456.

DIETERLEN, F. (1959) Das Verhalten des syrischen Goldhamsters (*Mesocricetus auratus*, Waterhouse), *Zeitschrift für Tierpsychologie*, **16**, 47–103.

DILL, L. M. (1974) The escape response of Zebra Danio (*Brachydanio nerio*), 1: The stimulus for escape, *Animal Behaviour*, **22**, 711–722.

DIMOND, S. J. (1968) Effects of photic stimulation before hatching on the development of fear in chicks, *Journal of Comparative and Physiological Psychology*, **65**, 320–324.

DIMOND, S. J. & FARRINGTON, L. (1977) Emotional responses to films shown to the right or left hemisphere of the brain measured by heart rate *Acta Psychologica*, **41**, 255–261.

DOWNER, J. L. DE C. (1961) Changes in visual gnostic functions and emotional behavior following unilateral temporal pole damage in the 'splitbrain' monkey, *Nature*, **191**, 50–51.

DREWETT, R. F. (1973) Oestrous and dioestrous components of the ovarian inhibition of hunger in the rat, *Animal Behaviour*, **21**, 772–780.

DRIVER, P. M. & HUMPHRIES, D. A. (1970) Protean displays as inducers of conflict, *Nature*, **226**, 968–969.

DUERDEN, J. E. (1906) Death-feigning instinct in the ostrich. *Report of the South African Association for the Advancement of Science*, 1906, 209–212.

DUFFY, E. (1941) An explanation of 'emotional' phenomena without the use of the concept of 'emotion', *Journal of Genetic Psychology*, **25**, 253–293.

DUFFY, E. (1962) *Activation and Behavior*. New York: Wiley.

DUNN, J. (1977) *Distress and Comfort*. London: Fontana/Open Books.

DURHAM, W. H. (1976) The adaptive significance of cultural behaviour, *Human Ecology*, **4**, 89–121.

ECKERMAN, C. O. & RHEINGOLD, H. L. (1974) Infants' exploratory responses to toys and people, *Developmental Psychology*, **10**, 255–259.

ECKERMAN, C. O. & WHATLEY, J. L. (1975) Infants' reactions to unfamiliar adults varying in novelty, *Developmental Psychology*, **11**, 562–566.

EDMUNDS, M. (1974) *Defence in Animals*. Harlow: Longman.

257

EIBL-EIBESFELDT, I. (1965) *Land of a Thousand Atolls: a Study of Marine Life in the Maldive and Nicobar Islands*. London: MacGibbon & Kee.

EIBL-EIBESFELDT, I. (1975) *Ethology: the Biology of Behavior*, 2nd edition. New York: Holt, Rinehart & Winston.

ELLIOT, O. & SCOTT, J. P. (1961) The development of emotional distress reactions to separation in puppies, *Journal of Genetic Psychology*, **69**, 3–22.

ELMADJIAN, F. J., HOPE, J. & LAMSON, E. T. (1957) Excretion of epinephrine and norepinephrine in various emotional states, *Journal of Clinical Endocrinology*, **7**, 608–620.

EMDE, R. N., GAENSBAUER, T. J. & HARMON, R. J. (1976) Emotional expression in infancy: a biobehavioural study, *Psychological Issues*, **10**, Monograph **37**.

ENGLISH, H. B. (1929) Three cases of the 'conditioned fear response', *Journal of Abnormal and Social Psychology*, **34**, 221–225.

EPSTEIN, S. (1971) Heart rate, skin conductance, and intensity ratings during experimentally induced anxiety: habituation within and among days, *Psychophysiology*, **8**, 319–331.

EPSTEIN, S. (1972) The nature of anxiety with emphasis upon its relationship to expectancy. In: *Anxiety: Current Trends in Theory and Research* (Ed.: C. D. Spielberger). New York: Academic Press.

EPSTEIN, S. (1973) Expectancy and magnitude of reaction to a noxious UCS, *Psychophysiology*, **10**, 100–107.

EPSTEIN, S. & CLARKE, S. (1970) Heart rate and skin conductance during experimentally induced anxiety: the effects of anticipated intensity of noxious stimulation and experience, *Journal of Experimental Psychology*, **84**, 105–112.

EPSTEIN, S. & ROUPENIAN, A. (1970) Heart rate and skin conductance during experimentally induced anxiety: the effect of uncertainty about receiving a noxious stimulus, *Journal of Personality and Social Psychology*, **16**, 20–28.

ESSER, A. H. (1971) *Behavior and Environment: The Use of Space by Animals and Men*. New York: Plenum Press.

EVANS, I. (1972) A conditioning model of a common neurotic pattern – fear of fear, *Psychotherapy: Theory, Research and Practice*, **9**, 238–241.

EVANS, I. (1976) Classical conditioning. In: *Theoretical and Experimental Bases of the Behaviour Therapies* (Ed.: M. P. Feldman & A. Broadhurst). London: Wiley.

EVANS, I. & BUSCH, C. J. (1974) The effectiveness of visual and gustatory cues in classical aversive conditioning with electric shock, *Behaviour Research and Therapy*, **12**, 129–140.

EVANS, R. M. (1970) Early aggressive responses in domestic chicks, *Animal Behaviour*, **16**, 24–28.

EVANS, R. M. (1975) Stimulus intensity and acoustical communication in young domestic chicks, *Behaviour*, **55**, 73–80.

EWERT, J.-P. (1970) Neural mechanisms of prey-catching and avoidance behavior in the toad (*Bufo bufo L.*), *Brain, Behavior and Evolution*. **3**, 36–56.

EWERT, J. -P. (1974) The neural basis of visually guided behavior, *Scientific American*, **230**, 34–42.

EYSENCK, H. J. (1968) A theory of the incubation of anxiety/fear responses, *Behaviour Research and Therapy*, **6**, 319–321.

EYSENCK, H. J. (1975) A genetic model of anxiety. In: *Stress and Anxiety* (Ed.: I. Sarason & C. Spielberger). Washington, DC: Hemisphere.

EYSENCK, H. J. (1976) The learning theory model of neurosis – a new approach, *Behaviour Research and Therapy*, **14**, 251–267.

EYSENCK, H. J. & RACHMAN, S. (1965) *The Causes and Cures of Neurosis*. London: Routledge & Kegan Paul.

FABRICIUS, E. (1951) Zur Ethologie junger Anatiden, *Acta Zoologica Fennica*, **68**, 1–175.

FABRICIUS, E. (1962) Some aspects of imprinting in birds, *Symposia of the Zoological Society of London*, **8**, 139–148.

FEHR, F. S. & STERN, J. A. (1970) Peripheral physiological variables and emotion: The James–Lange theory revisited, *Psychological Bulletin*, **74**, 411–424.

FENTRESS, J. C. (1967) Observations on the behavioral development of a hand-reared male timber wolf, *American Zoologist*, **7**, 339–351.

FENTRESS, J. C. (1968) Interrupted ongoing behaviour in two species of vole (*Microtus agrestis* and *Clethrionomys britannicus*), **1**: Response as a function of preceding activity and the context of an apparently irrelevant motor pattern, *Animal Behaviour*, **16**, 135–153.

FENTRESS, J. C. (1973) Specific and nonspecific factors in the causation of behavior. In: *Perspectives in Ethology* (Ed.: P. P. G. Bateson & P. Klopfer). New York: Plenum Press.

FENTRESS, J. C. (1976) Dynamic boundaries of patterned behaviour: interaction and self-organization. In: *Growing Points in Ethology* (Ed. P. P. G. Bateson & R. A. Hinde). Cambridge: Cambridge University Press.

FENZ, W. D. & EPSTEIN, S. (1967) Gradients of physiological arousal in parachutists, *Psychosomatic Medicine*, **29**, 33–51.

FERNANDEZ DE MOLINA, A. & HUNSPERGER, R. W. (1959) Central representation of affective reactions in forebrain and brain stem: electrical stimulation of amygdala, stria terminalis, and adjacent structures, *Journal of Physiology*, **145**, 251–265.

FERNANDEZ DE MOLINA, A. & HUNSPERGER, R. W. (1962) Organization of the subcortical system governing defence and flight reactions in the cat, *Journal of Physiology*, **160**, 200–213.

FINK, M. (1975) Effects of ACTH peptides on memory and brain function, *Psychopharmacological Bulletin*, **11**, 8–11.

FISCHER, G. J. (1970) Arousal and impairment: temperature effects on following during imprinting, *Journal of Comparative and Physiological Psychology*, **73**, 412–420.

FISCHER, G. J. (1972) Sound stimuli and following in a domestic fowl: frequency, rate and duration, *Journal of Comparative and Physiological Psychology*, **81**, 183–190.

FISCHER, G. J. & GILMAN, S. C. (1969) Following during imprinting as a function of auditory stimulus intensity, *Developmental Psychology*, **1**, 216–218.

FISHMAN, R. & TALLARICO, R. B. (1961a) Studies of visual depth perception: 1, Blinking as an indicator response in prematurely hatched chicks, *Perceptual and Motor Skills*, **12**, 247–250.

FISHMAN, R. & TALLARICO, R. B. (1961b) Studies of visual depth perception: 2, Avoidance reaction as an indicator response in chicks, *Perceptual and Motor Skills*, **12**, 251–257.

FLAVELL, J. H. (1977) *Cognitive Development*. New Jersey: Prentice-Hall.

FLESHLER, M. (1965) Adequate acoustic stimulus for startle reaction in the rat, *Journal of Comparative and Physiological Psychology*, **60**, 200–207.

FLOOD, J. F., JARVIK, M. E., BENNETT, E. L., ORME, A. E. & ROSENZWEIG, M. R. (1977) The effects of stimulants, depressants, and protein synthesis inhibition of retention, *Behavioral Biology*, **20**, 168–183.

FOLEY, J. P. (1934) First year development of a rhesus monkey (*Macaca mulatta*) reared in isolation, *Journal of Genetic Psychology*, **45**, 39–105.

FONBERG, E. (1965) Effect of partial destruction of the amygdaloid complex on the emotional-defensive behaviour of dogs, *Bulletin of the Polish Academy of Science (Biology)*, **14**, 719–722.

FONBERG, E. (1968) The role of the amygdaloid nucleus in animal behaviour, *Progress in Brain Research*, **22**, 273–281.

FOWLER, S. J. & KELLOGG, C. (1975) Ontogeny of thermoregulatory mechanisms in the rat, *Journal of Comparative and Physiological Psychology*, **89**, 738–746.

FOX, M. W. (1964) The ontogeny of behaviour and neurologic responses in the dog, *Animal Behaviour*, **12**, 301–310.

FOX, M. W. (1965) Reflex-ontogeny and behavioural development of the mouse, *Animal Behaviour*, **13**, 234–241.

FOX, M. W. (1970) Reflex development and behavioral organization. In: *Developmental Neurobiology* (Ed.: W. A. Himwich). Springfield, Ill.: Thomas.

FRAIBERG, S. (1975) The development of human attachments in infants blind from birth, *Merrill-Palmer Quarterly*, **21**, 315–334.

FRANKENHAEUSER, M. (1975) Experimental approaches to the study of catecholamines and emotion. In: *Emotions — Their Parameters and Measurement* (Ed.: L. Levi). New York: Raven Press.

FREDERICSON, E., GURNEY, N. & DUBOIS, E. (1956) The relationship between environmental temperature and behavior in neonatal puppies, *Journal of Comparative and Physiological Psychology*, **49**, 278–280.

FREEDMAN, D. G. (1967) A biological view of man's social behavior. In: *Social Behavior From Man to Fish*. (Ed.: W. Etkin). Chicago: University of Chicago Press.

FREEDMAN, D. G., KING, J. A. & ELLIOT, O. (1961) Critical period in the social development of dogs, *Science*, **133**, 1016–1017.

FREUD, A. & DANN, S. (1951) An experiment in group upbringing, *Psychoanalytic Study of the Child*, **6**, 127–163.

FRIEDRICH, I., PICKENHAIN, L. & KLINGBERG, F. (1967) Die Entwicklung des Startle-Reflexes in der postnatalen Ontogenese der Ratte, *Acta Biologica et Medica Germanica*, **19**, 605–607.

FRINGS, H., FRINGS, M., COX, B. & PEISSNER, L. (1955) Recorded calls of herring gulls (*Larus argentatus*) as repellants and attractants, *Science*, **121**, 340–341.

FUENZALIDA, C. E. & ULRICH, G. (1975) Escape learning in the plains garter snake *Thamnophis radix*, *Bulletin of the Psychonomic Society*, **6**, 134–136.

FUJITA, O. & HARA, M. (1971) Effects of early rearing conditions and age upon open-field behavior in chicks, *Annual of Animal Psychology*, **21**, 31–42.

FULLER, J. L. (1967a) Effects of the albino gene upon behaviour of mice, *Animal Behaviour*, **15**, 467–470.

FULLER, J. L. (1967b) Experiential deprivation and later behavior, *Science*, **158**, 1645–1652.

FULLER, J. L. & CLARK, L. D. (1966) Effects of rearing with specific stimuli upon postisolation behavior in dogs, *Journal of Comparative and Physiological Psychology*, **61**, 258–263.

FULLERTON, C., BERRYMAN, J. C. & SLUCKIN, W. (1970) Peeping in chicks as function of environmental change, *Psychonomic Science*, **21**, 39–40.

FUNKENSTEIN, D. H. (1956) Nor-epinephrine-like and epinephrine-like substances in relation to human behaviour, *Journal of Mental Disease*, **124**, 58–68.

FUSTER, J. M. & UYEDA, A. A. (1971) Reactivity of limbic neurons of the monkey to appetitive and aversive signals, *Electroencephalography and Clinical Neurophysiology*, **30**, 281–293.

GAENSBAUER, T. J., EMDE, R. N. & CAMPOS, J. J. (1976) 'Stranger' distress: confirmation of a developmental shift in a longitudinal sample, *Perceptual and Motor Skills*, **43**, 99–106.

GAGLIARDI, G. J., GALLUP, G. G. & BOREN, J. L. (1976) Effect of different pupil to eye size ratios on tonic immobility in chickens, *Bulletin of the Psychonomic Society*, **8**, 58–60.

GAINOTTI, G. (1972) Emotional behaviour and hemispheric side of the lesion, *Cortex*, **8**, 41–55.

GAIONI, S. J., HOFFMAN, H. S., KLEIN, S. H. & DePAULO, P. (1977) Distress calling as a function of group size in newly hatched ducklings, *Journal of Experimental Psychology*, **3**, 335–342.

GALEF, B. G. (1970) Target novelty elicits and directs shock-associated aggression in wild rats, *Journal of Comparative and Physiological Psychology*, **71**, 87–91.

GALLUP, G. G. (1974) Animal hypnosis: factual status of a fictional concept, *Psychological Bulletin*, **81**, 836–853.

GALLUP, G. G. (1977) Tonic immobility: the role of fear and predation, *Psychological Record*, **1**, 41–61.

GALLUP, G. G., CUMMINGS, W. H. & NASH, R. F. (1972) The experimenter as in independent variable in studies of animal hypnosis in chickens (*Gallus gallus*), *Animal Behaviour*, **20**, 166–169.

GALLUP, G. G., NASH, R. F. & ELLISON, A. L. (1971) Tonic immobility as a reaction to predation: artificial eyes as a fear stimulus for chickens, *Psychonomic Science*, **23**, 79–80.

GALLUP, G. G., NASH, R. F. POTTER, R. J. & DONEGAN, N. H. (1970) Effect of varying conditions of fear on immobility reactions in domestic chickens (*Gallus gallus*), *Journal of Comparative and Physiological Psychology*, **73**, 442–445.

GANTT, W. H. (1950) Disturbances in sexual functions during periods of stress, *Research Publications of the Association for Research in Nervous and Mental Disease*, **29**, 1030–1050.

GARCIA, J. & KOELLING, R. A. (1966) Relation of cue to consequence in avoidance learning, *Psychonomic Science*, **4**, 123–124.

GARCIA, J., McGOWAN, B. K. & GREEN, K. F. (1971). Sensory quality and integration: constraints on conditioning? In: *Classical Conditioning* (Ed.: A. H. Black & W. F. Prokasy). New York: Appleton-Century-Crofts.

GARCIA, J., McGOWAN, B. K. & GREEN, K. F. (1972) Biological constraints on conditioning. In: *Classical Conditioning II: Current Research and Theory* (Ed.: A. H. Black & W. F. Prokasy). New York: Appleton-Century-Crofts.

GARD, C., HÅRD, E., LARSSON, K. & PETERSSON, V.-A. (1967) The relationship between sensory stimulation and gross motor behaviour during the postnatal development in the rat *Animal Behaviour*, **15**, 563–567.

GAWIENOWSKI, A. M., DENICOLA, D. B. & STACEWICZ-SAPUNTZAKIS, M. (1976) Androgen dependence of a marking pheromone in rat urine, *Hormones and Behaviour*, **7**, 401–405.

262

GELLHORN, E. (1970) The emotions and the ergotropic and trophotropic systems. *Psychologische Forschung*, **34**, 48–94.

GELLHORN, E., CORTELL, R. & FELDMAN, J. (1941) The effect of emotion, sham rage and hypothalmic stimulation on the vago-insulin system, *American Journal of Physiology*, **133**, 532–541.

GESELL, A. L. (1929) The individual in infancy. In: *The Foundations of Experimental Psychology* (Ed.: C. Murchison). Worcester, Mass.: Clark University Press.

GIBSON, E. J. (1969) *Principles of Perceptual Learning and Development*. New York: Appleton-Century-Crofts.

GIBSON, E. J. & WALK, R. D. (1960) The visual cliff, *Scientific American*, **202**, 64–71.

GILLEN, B. (1973) The effect of electric shock upon nonlocomotor measure of exploration, *Bulletin of the Psychonomic Society*, **1**, 121–122.

GILMAN, T. T. & MARCUSE, F. L. (1949) Animal hypnosis, *Psychological Bulletin*, **46**, 151–165.

GINSBURG, H. J., BRAUD, W. G. & TAYLOR, R. D. (1974) Inhibition of distress vocalizations in the open field as a function of heightened fear or arousal in domestic fowl (*Gallus gallus*), *Animal Behaviour*, **22**, 745–749.

GLICKMAN, S. E. & HARTZ, K. (1964) Exploratory behavior of seven species of rodents, *Journal of Comparative and Physiological Psychology*, **58**, 101–104.

GLICKMAN, S. E. & SROGES, R. W. (1966) Curiosity in zoo animals, *Behaviour*, **26**, 151–188.

GLOOR, P. (1972) Temporal lobe epilepsy: Its possible contribution to the understanding of the functional significance of the amygdala and of its interaction with neocortical-temporal mechanisms. In: *The Neurobiology of the Amygdala* (Ed.: E. B. Eleftheriou). New York: Plenum Press.

GOLDBERG, S. (1972) Infant care and growth in urban Zambia, *Human Development*, **15**, 77–89.

GOLDSTEIN, K., LANDIS, C., HUNT, W. A. & CLARKE, F. M. (1938) Moro reflex and startle pattern, *Archives of Neurology and Psychiatry, Chicago*, **40**, 322–327.

GOODALL, McC. (1951) Studies of adrenaline and noradrenaline in mammalian heart and suprarenals, *Acta Physiologica Scandinavica*, **24**, Suppl. 85.

GOODFRIEND, M. & WOLPERT, E. A. (1976) Clinical case report: Death from fright: Report of a case and literature review, *Psychosomatic Medicine*, **38**, 348–356.

GOORNEY, A. B. & O'CONNER, P. J. (1971) Anxiety associated with flying, *British Journal of Psychiatry*, **119**, 159–166.

GOTTLIEB, G. (1968) Prenatal behavior in birds, *Quarterly Review of Biology*, **43**, 148–174.

GOTTLIEB, G. (1971a) Ontogenesis of sensory function in birds and mammals, In: *The Biopsychology of Development* (Ed.: E. Tobach, L. R. Aronson & E. Shaw). New York: Academic Press.

GOTTLIEB, G. (1971b) *Development of species identification in birds: an inquiry into the prenatal determinants of perception.* Chicago: University of Chicago Press.

GOTTLIEB, G. (1973) Neglected developmental variables in the study of species identification in birds, *Psychological Bulletin*, **79**, 362–372.

GOTTLIEB, G. & KUO, Z.-Y. (1965) Development of behavior in the duck embryo, *Journal of Comparative and Physiological Psychology*, **59**, 183–188.

GOULET, J. (1974) The infant's conception of causality and his reactions to strangers. In: *The Infant's Reaction to Strangers* (Ed.: T. G. DeCarie). New York: International Universities Press.

GÖZ, H. (1941) Über den Art und Individualgeruch bei Fischen, *Zeitschrift für Vergelichende Physiologie*, **29**, 1–45.

GRAHAM, D. T. (1972) Psychosomatic medicine, In: *Handbook of Psychophysiology* (Ed.: N. S. Greenfield & R. A. Sternbach). New York: Holt, Rinehart and Winston.

GRAY, J. A. (1970) Sodium amobarbital, the hippocampal theta rhythm and the partial reinforcement extinction effect, *Psychological Review*, **77**, 465–480.

GRAY, J. A. (1971a) Sex differences in emotional behaviour in mammals including Man: endocrine bases, *Acta Physiologica*, **35**, 29–46.

GRAY, J. A. (1971b) *The Psychology of Fear and Stress.* London: Weidenfeld & Nicolson.

GRAY, J. A. (1976) The behavioural inhibition system: a possible substrate for anxiety. In: *Theoretical and Experimental Bases of the Behaviour Therapies* (Ed.: M. P. Feldman & A. Broadhurst). London: Wiley.

GRAY, J. A. & LEVINE, S. (1964) The effect of induced oestrus on emotional behaviour in selected strains of rats, *Nature*, **201**, 1198–1200.

GRAY, P. H. (1962) Verification of Spalding's method for controlling visual experience by hooding chicks in the shell, *Proceedings of the Montana Academy of Science*, **21**, 120–123.

GRAY, P. H. & HOWARD, K. I. (1957) Specific recognition of humans in imprinted chicks, *Perceptual and Motor Skills*, **7**, 301–304.

GRAY, S. J., RAMSEY, C. S. VILLAREAL, R. & KRAKAUER, L. J. (1956) Adrenal influences upon the stomach and the gastric response to stress. In: *Fifth Annual Report on Stress, 1955—1956* (Ed.: H. Selye & G. Hensen). New York: M. D. Publications.

GREEN, J. D., CLEMENTE, C. D. & DEGROOT, J. (1957) Rhinencephalic lesions and behaviour in cats, *Journal of Comparative Neurology*, **108**, 505–546.

GREEN, M., GREEN, R. & CARR, W. J. (1966) The hawk-goose

phenomenon: a replication and an extension, *Psychonomic Science*, **4**, 185–186.

GREEN, P. C. (1965) Influence of early experience and age on expression of affect in monkeys, *Journal of Genetic Psychology*, **106**, 157–171.

GREEN, R., CARR, W. J. & GREEN, M. (1968) The hawk-goose phenomenon: further confirmation and a search for the releaser, *Journal of Psychology*, **69**, 271–276.

GREENBERG, D. J., HILLMAN, D. & GRICE, D. (1973) Infant and stranger variables related to stranger anxiety in the first year of life, *Development Psychology*, **9**, 207–212.

GREENBERG, D. J., HILLMAN, D. & GRICE, D. (1975) Perceptual incongruity and social interaction as determinants of infants' reaction to novel persons, *Journal of Genetic Psychology*, **127**, 215–222.

GRINGS, W. W. & SUKONECK, H. I. (1971) Prediction probability as a determiner of anticipatory and preparation electrodermal behavior, *Journal of Experimental Psychology*, **91**, 310–314.

GRINKER, R. & SPIEGEL, J. (1945) *Men Under Stress*. London: Churchill.

GROSSEN, N. & KELLEY, M. J. (1972) Species-specific behavior and acquisition of avoidance behavior in rats, *Journal of Comparative and Physiological Psychology*, **81**, 307–310.

GROSSMAN, S. P. (1967) *A Textbook of Physiological Psychology*, New York: Wiley.

GRUBB, T. C. (1977) Discrimination of aerial predators by American coots in nature, *Animal Behaviour*, **25**, 1065–1066.

GUHL, A. M. (1958) The development of social organisation in the domestic chick, *Animal Behaviour*, **6**, 92–111.

GUITON, P. (1958) The effect of isolation on the following response of brown leghorn chicks, *Proceedings of the Royal Physical society of Edinburgh*, **27**, 9–14.

GUITON, P. & SLUCKIN, W. (1969) The effects of visual experience on behavioural development in neonatal domestic chicks, *British Journal of Psychology*, **60**, 495–507.

GUTH, S., SEWARD, J. P. & LEVINE, S. (1971) Differential manipulation of passive avoidance by exogenous ACTH. *Hormones and Behavior*, **2**, 127–138.

GUYOMARCH, J. C. (1974) *Les vocalisations des Gallinaces structure des sons et des repertoires ontogenese motrice et acquisition de leur semantique*, doctoral thesis: University of Rennes, France.

HAGMAN, E. (1932) A study of fears of children of pre-school age, *Journal of Experimental Education*, **1**, 110–130.

HALE, E. B. & SCHEIN, M. W. (1962) The behaviour of turkeys. In: *The Behaviour of Domestic Animals* (Ed.: E. S. E. Hafez). London: Balliere, Tindall, Cox.

HALL, C. S. (1934a) Drive and emotionality: factors associated with adjustment in the rat, *Journal of Comparative Psychology*, **17**, 89–108.

HALL, C. S. (1934b) Emotional behavior in the rat: I, defecation and urination as measures of individual differences in emotionality, *Journal of Comparative Psychology*, **18**, 385–403.

HALL, C. S. (1938) The inheritance of emotionality, *Sigma Xi Quarterly*, **26**, 17–27, 37.

HALLAM, R. S. & RACHMAN, S. (1976) Current status of aversion therapy. In: *Progress in Behavior Modification* (Ed.: M. Hersen, R. Eisler & P. Miller). New York: Academic Press.

HALLAM, R. S., RACHMAN, S. & FALKOWSKI, W. (1972) Subjective, attitudinal and physiological effects of electrical aversion therapy, *Behaviour Research and Therapy*, **10**, 1–14.

HALLIDAY, M. S. (1967) Exploratory behaviour in elevated and enclosed mazes, *Quarterly Journal of Experimental Psychology*, **19**, 254–263.

HALLIDAY, M. S. (1968) Exploratory behaviour. In: *Analysis of Behavioural Change* (Ed.: L. Weiskrantz). New York: Harper & Row.

HAMILTON, W. (1964) The genetical evolution of social behaviour, I and II, *Journal of Theoretical Biology*, **7**, 1–52.

HARE, R. D. (1972) Cardiovascular components of orienting and defensive responses, *Psychophysiology*, **9**, 606–614.

HARLOW, H. F. (1960) Affectional behavior in the infant monkey. In: *The Central Nervous System and Behavior* (Ed.: M. A. B. Brazier, Transactions 3rd Conference). New York: J. Macy Jr. Foundation.

HARLOW, H. F. & HARLOW, M. K. (1965) The affectional systems. In: *Behavior of Non-human Primates, Vol. 2* (Ed.: A. M. Schrier, H. F. Harlow & F. Stollnitz). New York: Academic Press.

HARLOW, H. F. & ZIMMERMANN, R. R. (1959) Affectional responses in the infant monkey, *Science*, **103**, 421–432.

HARPER, L. V. (1970) Role of contact and sound in eliciting filial responses and development of social attachments in domestic guinea pigs, *Journal of Comparative and Physiological Psychology*, **73**, 427–435.

HARPER, L. V. (1976) Behavior. In: *The Biology of the Guinea Pig* (Ed.: J. E. Wagner & P. J. Manning). New York: Academic Press.

HARRÉ, R. (1974) The conditions for a social psychology of childhood. In: *The Integration of a Child into a Social World* (Ed.: M. P. M. Richards). Cambridge: Cambridge University Press.

HART, F. M. & KING, J. A. (1966) Distress vocalizations of young in two subspecies of *Peromyscus maniculatus*, *Journal of Mammalogy*, **47**, 287–293.

HARTLEY, P. H. T. (1950) An experimental analysis of interspecific recognition, *Symposium of the Society for Experimental Biology*, **4**, 313–336.

HASKETT, G. J. (1977) The exploratory nature of children's social relations, *Merrill-Palmer Quarterly*, **23**, 101–113.

HASLAM, M. T. (1965) Treatment of an obsessional patient by reciprocal inhibition, *Behaviour Research and Therapy*, **2**, 213–216.

HASLERUD, G. M. (1938) The effect of movement of stimulus objects upon avoidance reactions in chimpanzees, *Journal of Comparative Psychology*, **25**, 507–528.

HAYES, W. N. & SAIFF, E. I. (1967) Visual alarm reactions in turtles, *Animal Behaviour*, **15**, 102–106.

HAYWOOD, H. C. & WACHS, T. D. (1967) Effects of arousing stimulation upon novelty preference in rats, *British Journal of Psychology*, **58**, 77–84.

HEBB, D. O. (1946) On the nature of fear, *Psychological Review*, **53**, 250–275.

HEBB, D. O. (1949) *The Organisation of Behaviour*. New York: Wiley.

HEDIGER, H. (1950) *Wild Animals in Captivity*. London: Butterworth.

HEIMER, L. (1972) The olfactory connections of the diencephalon in the rat, *Brain, Behavior and Evolution*, **6**, 484–523.

HEINZ, G. (1973) Responses of ring-necked pheasant chicks (*Phasianus colchicus*) to conspecific calls, *Animal Behaviour*, **21**, 1–9.

HELLMAN, L. (1971) Introduction. In: *A Month of Saturdays* (By D. Parker). London: Macmillan.

HENKIN, R. I. (1970) The neuroendocrine control of perception. In: *Perception and its Disorders: Proceedings of the Association for Research in Nervous Mental Disease, 32nd edition*. Hamburg: Williams & Wilkins.

HERBERT, M. (1978) *Conduct Disorders of Childhood and Adolescence*. Chichester: Wiley.

HERBERT, M. & SLUCKIN, W. (1969) Acquisition of colour preferences by chicks at different temperatures, *Animal Behaviour*, **17**, 213–216.

HERRNSTEIN, R. J. (1969) Method and theory in the study of avoidance, *Psychological Review*, **76**, 49–69.

HERSOV, L. A. (1960) Persistent non-attendance at school, *Journal of Child Psychology and Psychiatry*, **1**, 130–136.

HESS, E. H. (1959a) The relationship between imprinting and motivation. In: *Nebraska Symposium on Motivation* (Ed.: M. B. Jones). Lincoln, Neb.: University of Nebraska Press.

HESS, E. H. (1959b) Two conditions limiting critical age for imprinting, *Journal of Comparative and Physiological Psychology*, **52**, 515–518.

HESS, E. H. (1973) *Imprinting: Early Experience and the Developmental Psychobiology of Attachment*. New York: Van Nostrand Reinhold.

HESS, E. H. & SCHAEFER, H. H. (1959) Innate behavior patterns as indicators of the 'critical period', *Zeitschrift für Tierpsychologie*, **16**, 155–160.

HESS, W. R. (1957) *The Functional Organization of the Diencephalon*. New York: Grune & Stratton.

267

HILTON, S. M. & ZBROZYNA, A. W. (1963) Amygdaloid region for defense reactions and its afferent path in the brain stem, *Journal of Physiology*, **165**, 160–173.

HINDE, R. A. (1954) Factors governing the changes in strength of a partially inborn response, as shown by the mobbing behaviour of the chaffinch (*Fringilla coelebs*): 1, The nature of the response, and an examination of its course; 2, The waning of the response, *Proceeding of the Royal Society of London, B*, **142**, 306–331, 331–358.

HINDE, R. A. (1959) Unitary drives, *Animal Behaviour*, **7**, 130–141.

HINDE, R. A. (1970) *Animal Behaviour: a Synthesis of Ethology and Comparative Psychology, 2nd edition*. New York: McGraw-Hill.

HINDE, R. A. (1971) Development of social behaviour. In: *Behavior of Non-human Primates, Vol. 3* (Ed.: A. M. Schrier & F. Stollnitz). New York: Academic Press.

HINDE, R. A. (1974) *Biological Bases of Humal Social Behaviour*. New York: McGraw Hill.

HINDE, R. A. (1977) Dominance and role – two concepts with dual meanings, *Journal of Social and Biological Structures*, **1**, 27–38.

HINDE, R. A. & SPENCER-BOOTH, Y. (1971) Effects of brief separation from mother on rhesus monkeys, *Science*, **173**, 111–118.

HINDE, R. A. & STEVENSON-HINDE, J. G. (Ed.) (1973) *Constraints on Learning*. London: Academic Press.

HINDE, R. A., ROWELL, T. E. & SPENCER-BOOTH, Y. (1964) Behaviour of socially living rhesus monkeys in their first sixth months, *Proceedings of the Zoological Society of London*, **143**, 609–649.

HINTZMAN, D. L. (1978) *The Psychology of Learning and Memory*. San Francisco: Freeman.

HIRSCH, J., LINDLEY, R. H. & TOLMAN, E. C. (1955) An experimental test of an alleged innate sign stimulus, *Journal of Comparative and Physiological Psychology*, **48**, 278–280.

HOFFMAN, H. S. & BOSKOFF, K. J. (1972) Control of aggressive behavior by an imprinted stimulus, *Psychonomic Science*, **29**, 305–306.

HOFFMAN, H. S. & RATNER, A. M. (1973) Effects of stimulus and environmental familiarity on visual imprinting in newly hatched ducklings, *Journal of Comparative and Physiological Psychology*, **85**, 11–19.

HOFFMAN, H. S., EISERER, L. A., RATNER, A. M. & PICKERING, V. L. (1974) Development of distress vocalization during withdrawal of an imprinting stimulus, *Journal of Comparative and Physiological Psychology*, **86**, 563–568.

HOFFMAN, H. S., RATNER, A. M., EISERER, L. A. & GROSSMAN, D. J. (1974) Aggressive behavior in immature ducklings, *Journal of Comparative and Physiological Psychology*, **86**, 569–580.

HOFFMAN, H. S., SEARLE, J. L., TOFFEY, S. & KOZMA, F. (1966) Behavioral control by an imprinted stimulus, *Journal of the Experimental Analysis Behavior*, **9**, 177–189.

HOGAN, J. A. (1965) An experimental study of conflict and fear: an analysis of behavior of young chicks toward a mealworm, Part 1, The behavior of chicks which do not eat the mealworm, *Behaviour*, **25**, 45–97.

HOGAN, J. A. (1966) An experimental study of conflict and fear: an analysis of behavior of young chicks toward a mealworm, Part 2, The behavior of chicks which eat the mealworm, *Behaviour*, **27**, 273–289.

HOHMANN, G. W. (1962) The effect of dysfunctions of the autonomic nervous system on experienced feelings and emotions. Paper presented at the Conference on Emotions and Feelings at the New School for Social Research, New York, October.

HOHMANN, G. W. (1966) Some effects of spinal cord lesions on experienced emotional feelings, *Psychophysiology*, **3**, 143–156.

HOOFF, J. A. R. A. M. VAN, (1962) Facial expressions in higher primates, *Symposium of the Zoological Society of London*, **8**, 97–125.

HUGDAHL, K. & OHMAN, A. (1977) Effects of instruction on acquisition and extinction of electrodermal responses to fear relevant stimuli, *Journal of Experimental Psychology*, **3**, 608–618.

HUGDAHL, K., FREDRIKSON, M. & OHMAN, A. (1977) 'Preparedness' and arousability as determinants of electrodermal conditioning, *Behaviour Research and Therapy*, **15**, 345–353.

HUGHES, G. H. & MENZEL, E. W. (1973) Use of space and reactions to novel objects in gelada baboons (*Thercopithecus gelada*), *Journal of Comparative and Physiological Psychology*, **83**, 1–6.

HUGHES, R. N. (1969) Social facilitation of locomotion and exploration in rats, *British Journal of Psychology*, **60**, 385–388.

HUNSPERGER, R. W. & BUCHER, V. M. (1967) Affective behaviour produced by electrical stimulation in the forebrain and brain stem of the cat, *Progress in Brain Research*, **27**, 103–127.

HUNT, H. E. (1897) Observations on newly hatched chicks, *American Journal of Psychology*, **9**, 125–127.

HUNT, J. McV. (1965) Intrinsic motivation and its role in psychological development. In: *Nebraska Symposium on Motivation, Vol. 13* (Ed.: D. Levine). Lincoln, Neb.: University of Nebraska Press.

HURLEY, A. C. & HARTLINE, P. H. (1974) Escape responses in the damselfish *Chromis cyanea (Pisces: Pomacentridae)*: a quantitative study, *Animal Behaviour*, **22**, 430–437.

HUTT, C. (1966) Exploration and play in children, *Symposium of the Zoological Society of London*, **18**, 61–81.

269

HUTT, C. (1967) Effects of stimulus novelty on manipulatory exploration in an infant, *Journal of Child Psychology and Psychiatry*, **8**, 241–247.

HUTT, C. (1970) Specific and diversive exploration, *Advances in Child Development and Behaviour*, **5**, 119–180.

IERSEL, J. J. A. VAN & BOL, A. C. A. (1958) Preening in two tern species, A study on displacement activities, *Behaviour*, **13**, 1–88.

IMPEKOVEN, M. (1976a) Prenatal parent-young interactions in birds and their long-term effects. In: *Advances in the Study of Behavior, Vol. 7* (Ed.: J. S. Rosenblatt, R. A. Hinde, E. Shaw & C. Beer). New York: Academic Press.

IMPEKOVEN, M. (1976b) Responses of laughing gull chicks (*Larus atricilla*) to parental attraction- and alarm-calls, and effects of prenatal auditory experience on the responsiveness to such calls, *Behaviour*, **56**, 250–278.

IMPEKOVEN, M. & GOLD, P. S. (1973) Prenatal origins of parent-young interactions in birds: a naturalistic approach. In: *Behavioral Embryology. Studies on the Development of Behavior and the Nervous System, Vol. 1* (Ed.: G. Gottlieb). New York: Academic Press.

INGLE, D. (1976) Behavioral correlates of central visual function in Anurans. In: *Frog Neurobiology* (Ed.: R. Llinás & W. Precht).

INGRAM, I. M. (1961) The obsessional patient and obsessional illness, *American Journal of Psychiatry*, **117**, 1016–1019.

ISAACSON, R. L. (1974) *The Limbic System*. New York: Plenum Press.

ISAACSON, R. L. & PRIBRAM, K. H. (Ed.) (1975) The *Hippocampus, Vol. 2: Neurophysiology and Behavior*. New York: Plenum Press.

IUVONE, P. M. & VAN, HARTESVELDT, C. (1976) Locomotor activity and plasma corticosterone in rats with hippocampal lesions, *Behavioral Biology*, **16**, 515–520.

IZARD, C. E. (1972) *Patterns of Emotions: A New Analysis of Anxiety and Depression*. New York: Academic Press.

JACKSON, E., CAMPOS, J. J. & FISCHER, K. W. (1978) The question of decolage between object permanence and person permanence, *Developmental Psychology*, **14**, 1–11.

JAMES, W. (1884) What is emotion? *Mind*, **9**, 188–205.

JAMES, W. T. (1952) Observations on the behavior of new-born puppies: 2, Summary of movements involved in group orientation, *Journal of Comparative and Physiological Psychology*, **45**, 329–335.

JANIS, I. L. (1951) *Air War and Emotional Stress*. New York: McGraw-Hill.

JAYNES, J. (1957) Imprinting: the interaction of learned and innate behavior: 2, The critical period, *Journal of Comparative and Physiological Psychology*, **50**, 6–10.

JENNINGS, H. S. (1906) *Behavior of the Lower Organisms*. New York: Columbia University Press.

JEROME, E. A., MOODY, J. A., CONNOR, T. J. & RYAN, J. (1958) Intensity of illumination and the rate of responding in a multiple door situation, *Journal of Comparative and Physiological Psychology*, **51**, 47–49.

JERSILD, A. T. (1933) *Child Psychology*. New York: Prentice-Hall.

JERSILD, A. T. (1943) Studies of children's fears. In: *Child Behavior and Development* (Ed.: R. G. Barker, J. S. Kounin & H. F. Wright). New York: McGraw-Hill.

JERSILD, A. T. (1946) Emotional development. In: *Manual of Child Psychology* (Ed.: L. Carmichael). New York: Wiley.

JERSILD, A. T. & HOLMES, F. B. (1935) Children's fears, *Child Development Monographs No. 20*. New York: Teachers College, Columbia University.

JERSILD, A. T., MARKEY, F. V. & JERSILD, C. L. (1933) Children's fears, dreams, wishes, daydreams, likes, dislikes, pleasant and unpleasant memories. *Child Development Monograph No. 12*. New York: Teachers College, Columbia University. Cited in: JERSILD, A. T. (Ed.) *Child Psychology*. Prentice-Hall, 1960.

JEWELL, P. A. (1966) The concept of home-range in mammals, *Symposium of the Zoological Society of London*, **18**, 85–109.

JOHNSON, A. (1957) School phobia: discussion, *American Journal of Orthopsychiatry*, **27**, 307–309.

JOHNSON, T. N. ROSVOLD, H. E. & MISHKIN, M. (1968) Projections from behaviorally-defined sectors of the prefrontal cortex to the basal ganglia, septum, and diencephalon of the monkey, *Experimental Neurology*, **21**, 20–34.

JOLLY, A. (1966) *Lemur Behavior*. Chicago: Chicago University Press.

JOLLY, A. (1972) *The Evolution of Primate Behaviour*. New York: Macmillan.

JONES, E. G. & POWELL, T. P. S. (1970) An anatomical study of converging sensory pathways within the cerebral cortex of the monkey, *Brain*, **93**, 793–820.

JONES, H. E. & JONES, M. C. (1928) Fear, *Childhood Education*, **5**, 136–143.

JONES, M. C. (1924) The elimination of children's fears, *Journal of Experimental Psychology*, **7**, 383–390.

JONES, R. B. & POWELL, N. W. (1973a) Aversive effects of the urine of a male mouse upon the investigatory behaviour of its defeated opponent, *Animal Behaviour*, **21**, 707–710.

JONES, R. B. & POWELL, N. W. (1973b) The coagulating glands as a source of aversive and aggression inhibiting pheromone(s) in the male albino mouse, *Physiology and Behavior*, **11**, 455–462.

JORMAKKA, L. (1976) The behaviour of children during a first encounter, *Scandinavian Journal of Psychology*, **17**, 15–22.

JOSLIN, J., FLETCHER, H. & EMLEN, J. (1964) A comparison of the responses to snakes of lab- and wild-reared rhesus macaques, *Animal Behaviour*, **12**, 348–352.

271

KAADA, B. R. (1972) Stimulation and regional ablation of the amygdaloid complex with reference to functional representations. In: *The Neurobiology of the Amygdala* (Ed.: B. E. Eleftheriou). New York: Plenum Press.

KAGAN, J. (1970) Attention and psychological change in the young child, *Science*, **170**, 826–832.

KAGAN, J. (1971) *Change and Continuity in Infancy*. New York: Wiley.

KAGAN, J. (1974) Discrepancy, temperament, and infant distress. In: *The Origins of Behavior, Vol. 2: The Origins of Fear* (Ed.: M. Lewis & L. A. Rosenblum). New York & London: Wiley.

KAGAN, J., KEARSLEY, R. B. & ZELAZO, P. R. (1975) The emergence of initial apprehension to unfamiliar peers. In: *Friendship and Peer Relations* (Ed.: M. Lewis & L. A. Rosenblum). New York & London: Wiley.

KARKI, N. T. (1956) The urinary excretion of noradrenaline and adrenaline in different age groups, its diurnal variation and the effect of muscular work on it, *Acta Physiologica Scandinavica*, **39**, Supplement 132.

KAUFMAN, I. C. & HINDE, R. A. (1961) Factors influencing distress calling in chicks, with special reference to temperature changes and social isolation, *Animal Behaviour*, **9**, 197–204.

KAUFMAN, I. C. & ROSENBLUM, L. A. (1969) Effects of separation from mother on the emotional behavior of infant monkeys, *Annals of the New York Academy of Science*, **159**, 681–695.

KEELER, C. E. (1947) Coat colour, physique and temperament, *Journal of Heredity*, **38**, 271–277.

KENNY, A. (1963) *Action, Emotion and Will*. London: Routledge & Kegan Paul.

KIMMEL, C. B., PATTERSON, J. & KIMMEL, R. O. (1974) The development and behavioral characteristics of the startle response in the zebra fish, *Developmental Psychobiology*, **7**, 47–60.

KIMMEL, H. D. (1965) Instrumental factors in classical conditioning. In: *Classical Conditioning* (Ed.: W. Prokasy). New York: Appleton-Century-Crofts.

KING, J. A. (1958) Maternal behavior and behavioral development in two subspecies of *Peromyscus maniculatus*, *Journal of Mammalogy*, **39**, 177–190.

KING, J. A. (1963) Maternal behavior in *Peromyscus*. In: *Maternal Behavior in Mammals* (Ed.: H. L. Rheingold). New York: Wiley.

KIRKMAN, F. B. (1937) *Bird Behaviour*. London: Nelson.

KLARE, W. F. (1974) Conditioned fear and postshock emotionality in vicious circle behaviour of rats, *Journal of Comparative and Physiological Psychology*, **87**, 364–372.

KLECK, R. (1966) Emotional arousal in interactions with stigmatised persons, *Psychological Reports*, **19**, 1226.

KLEIN, R. P. & DURFEE, J. T. (1976) Infants' reactions to unfamiliar adults versus mother, *Child Development*, **47**, 1194–1196.

KLEMM, W. R. (1971) Neurophysiologic studies of the immobility reflex ('animal hypnosis'). In: *Neurosciences Research, Vol. 4* (Ed.: S. Ehrenpreis & O. C. Solnitzky). New York: Academic Press.

KLORMAN, R., WIESENFELD, A. R. & AUSTIN, M. L. (1975) Autonomic responses to affective visual stimuli, *Psychophysiology,* **12**, 553–560.

KLUVER, H. & BUCY, P. C. (1937) 'Psychic blindness' and other symptoms following bilateral temporal lobectomy in rhesus monkeys, *American Journal of Physiology*, **119**, 352–353.

KLUVER, H. & BUCY, P. C. (1938) An analysis of certain effects of bilateral temporal lobectomy in the rhesus monkey, with special reference to 'psychic blindness', *Journal of Psychology*, **5**, 33–54.

KLUVER, H. & BUCY, P. C. (1939) Preliminary analysis of the temporal lobes in monkeys, *Archives of Neurology and Psychiatry*, **42**, 979–1000.

KOLB, B. & NONNEMAN, A. J. (1975) The development of social responsiveness in kittens, *Animal Behaviour*, **23**, 368–374.

KONNOR, M. (1972) Aspects of the developmental ethology of a foraging people. In: *Ethological Studies of Child Behaviour* (Ed.: N. Blurton-Jones). Cambridge: Cambridge University Press.

KONRAD, K. & MELZACK, R. (1975) Novelty-enhancement effects associated with early sensory-social isolation. In: *The Developmental Neuropsychology of Sensory Deprivation* (Ed.: A. H. Riesen). New York: Academic Press.

KONRAD, K. W. & BAGSHAW, M. (1970) Effect of novel stimuli on cats reared in a restricted environment, *Journal of Comparative and Physiological Psychology*, **70**, 157–164.

KOVACH, J. K. & HESS, E. H. (1963) Imprinting: effects of painful stimulation upon the following response, *Journal of Comparative and Physiological Psychology*, **56**, 461–464.

KRAFFT EBBING, R. VON (1897) *Traite Clinique de Psychiatrie*. Paris: Laurent.

KRAMER, G. & ST. PAUL, U. VON (1951) Über Angeborenes and Erworbenes feinderkennen beim Gimpel (*Pyrrhula pyrrhula*), *Behaviour*, **3**, 243–255.

KRUIJT, J. P. (1964) Ontogeny of social behaviour in Burmese red junglefowl (*Gallus gallus spadiceus*) Bonnaterre, *Behaviour*, Supplement **12**.

KRUUK, H. (1972) *The Spotted Hyena: a Study of Predation and Social Behaviour*. Chicago: University of Chicago Press.

KRUUK, H. (1975) Functional aspects of social hunting by carnivores. In: *Function and Evolution in Behaviour* (Ed.: G. Baerends, C. Beer & A. Manning). Oxford: Oxford University Press.

KRUUK, H. (1976) The biological function of gulls' attraction towards predators, *Animal Behaviour*, **24**, 146–153.

KRUUK, H. & TURNER, M. (1963) Comparative notes on predation by lion,

273

leopard, cheetah and wild dog in the Serengeti area, East Africa, *Mammalia*, **31**, 1–27.

KUHLMANN, F. (1909) Some preliminary observations on the development of instincts and habits in young birds, *Psychological Review, Monograph Supplement*, **11**, 49–84.

LACEY, J. I. (1950) Individual differences in somatic response patterns, *Journal of Comparative and Physiological Psychology*, **43**, 338–350.

LACEY, J. I. (1959) Psychophysiological approaches to the psychotherapeutic process and outcome. In: *Research in Psychotherapy* (Ed.: E. Rubinstein & M. B. Parloff). Washington, DC: American Psychological Association.

LACEY, J. I. (1967) Somatic response patterning and stress: Some revisions of activation theory. In: *Psychological Stress* (Ed.: M. H. Appley & R. Trumbull). New York: Appleton-Century-Crofts.

LACEY, J. I. & LACEY, B. S. (1970) Some autonomic-central nervous system interrelationships. In: *Physiological Correlates of Emotion* (Ed.: P. Black). New York: Academic Press.

LADER, M. & TYRER, P. (1975) Vegetative system and emotion. In: *Emotions: Their Parameters and Measurement* (Ed.: L. Levi). New York: Raven Press.

LADER, M. H. & MATHEWS, A. M. (1968) A physiological model of phobic anxiety and desensitization, *Behaviour Research and Therapy*, **6**, 411–421.

LAMB, M. E. (1977) The development of mother-infant and father-infant attachments in the second year of life, *Developmental Psychology*, **13**, 637–648.

LANDIS, C. & HUNT, W. A. (1939) *The Startle Pattern*. New York: Farrar & Rinehart.

LANDSBERG, J.-W. & WEISS, J. (1976) Stress and increase of the corticosterone level prevent imprinting in ducklings, *Behaviour*, **57**, 173–189.

LANG, P. J. (1970) Stimulus control, response control and desensitization of fear. In: *Learning Approaches to Therapeutic Behaviour Change* (Ed.: D. Levis). Chicago: Aldine.

LANG, P. & LAZOVIK, A. D. (1963) Experimental desensitization of a phobia. *Journal of Abnormal and Social Psychology*, **66**, 519–525.

LANGE, C. G. (1885) *Om Sindsbevaegelser, et psykofysiologisk studie*. Copenhagen: Kronar.

LANGER, E. J., FISKE, S., TAYLOR, S. E. & CHANOWITZ, B. (1976) Stigma, staring, and discomfort: a novel stimulus hypothesis, *Journal of Experimental Social Psychology*, **12**, 451–463.

LAPOUSE, R. & MONK, M. A. (1959) Fears and worries in a representative sample of children, *American Journal of Orthopsychiatry*, **29**, 803–818.

LARSEN, S. R. (1965) Strategies for reducing phobic behaviour. Cited in *Psychopathology: Experimental Models* (Ed.: M. Seligman & J. Maser). San Francisco: Freeman. 1977.

LATANE, B. (1969) Gregariousness and fear in laboratory rats, *Journal of Experimental Social Psychology*, **5**, 61–69.

LATANE, B. & GLASS, D. C. (1968) Social and nonsocial attraction in rats, *Journal of Personality and Social Psychology*, **9**, 142–146.

LATANE, B. & SCHACHTER, S. (1962) Adrenalin and avoidance learning, *Journal of Comparative and Physiological Psychology*, **55**, 369–372.

LATANE, B. & WERNER, C. (1971) Social and nonsocial sources of attraction in rats, *Psychonomic Science*, **24**, 147–148.

LATANE, B., POOR, D. & SLOAN, L. (1972) Familiarity and attraction to social and nonsocial objects by rats, *Psychonomic Science*, **26**, 171–172.

LATANE, B., MELTZER, J., JOY, V. & LUBELL, B. (1972) Stimulus determinants of social attraction in rats, *Journal of Comparative and Physiological Psychology*, **79**, 13–21.

LAUTCH, H. (1971) Dental phobia, *British Journal of Psychiatry*, **119**, 151–158.

LAWICK-GOODALL, J. VAN (1968) The behaviour of free-living chimpanzees in the Gombe Stream Reserve, *Animal Behaviour Monographs*, **1**, 165–311.

LAWICK-GOODALL, J. VAN (1974) *In the Shadow of Man*. London: Fontana.

LAZARUS, R. S. (1966) *Psychological Stress and the Coping Process*. New York: McGraw-Hill.

LAZARUS, R. S. (1975a) A cognitively oriented psychologist looks at biofeedback, *American Psychologist*, **30**, 553–561.

LAZARUS, R. S. (1975b) The self-regulation of emotion. In: *Emotions: Their Parameters and Measurement* (Ed.: L. Levi). New York: Raven Press.

LEFEBVRE, L. & SABOURIN, M. (1977) Response differences in animal hypnosis: a hypothesis, *Psychological Record*, **27**, 77–87.

LEHRMAN, D. S. (1953) A critique of Konrad Lorenz's theory of instinctive behavior, *Quarterly Review of Biology*, **28**, 337–363.

LEHRMAN, D. S. (1970) Semantic and conceptual issues in the nature-nature problem. In: *Development and Evolution of Behavior* (Ed.: L. R. Aronson, E. Tobach, D. S. Lehrman & J. S. Rosenblatt). San Francisco: Freeman.

LESTER, B. M., KOTELCHUCK, M., SPELKE, E., SELLERS, M. J. & KLEIN, R. E. (1974) Separation protest in Guatemalan infants: Cross-cultural and cognitive findings, *Developmental Psychology*, **10**, 79–85.

LESTER, D. (1967) Effects of fear upon exploratory behaviour, *Psychonomic Science*, **9**, 117–118.

LESTER, D. (1968) Two tests of a fear-motivated theory of exploration, *Psychonomic Science*, **10**, 385–386.

LEVENTHAL, G. S. & KILLACKEY, H. (1968) Adrenalin, stimulation, and preference for familiar stimuli, *Journal of Comparative and Physiological Psychology*, **65**, 152–155.

LEVI, L. (1965) The urinary output of adrenaline and noradrenaline during pleasant and unpleasant emotional states, *Psychosomatic Medicine*, **27**, 80–85.

LEVI, L. (1972) Stress and distress in response to psychosocial stimuli: Laboratory and real life studies in sympathoadrenomedullary and related reactions, *Acta Medica Scandinavica Supplement* 528.

LEVINE, S. (1970) An endocrine theory of infantile stimulation. In: *Stimulation in Early Infancy* (Ed.: A. Ambrose). New York: Academic Press.

LEVITT, E. E. (1971) *The Psychology of Anxiety*. London: Paladin.

LEVY, D. (1951) Observations of attitudes and behavior in the child health center, *American Journal of Public Health*, **41**, 182–190.

LEWIS, A. (1942) Incidence of neurosis in England under war conditions, *Lancet*, **2**, 175–183.

LEWIS, M. & BROOKS, J. (1974) Self, other, and fear: infants reactions to people. In: *The Origins of Behavior, Vol. 2: The Origins of Fear* (Ed.: M. Lewis & L. A. Rosenblum). New York: Wiley.

LEWIS, M. & ROSENBLUM, L. A. (1974) *The Origins of Behavior, Vol. 2: The Origins of Fear*. New York: Wiley.

LEWIS, M., YOUNG, G., BROOKS, J. & MICHALSON, L. (1975) The beginning of friendship. In: *Friendship and Peer Relations* (Ed.: M. Lewis & L. A. Rosenblum). New York & London: Wiley.

LEWIS, N. & ENGLE, B. (1954) *Wartime Psychiatry*. New York: Oxford University Press.

LEYHAUSEN, P. (1967a) The biology of expression and impression. In: *Motivation of Human and Animal Behavior* (Ed.: K. Lorenz & P. Layhausen). New York: Van Nostrand Reinhold.

LEYHAUSEN, P. (1967b) On the natural history of fear. In: *Motivation of Human and Animal Behavior* (Ed.: K. Lorenz & P. Leyhausen). New York: Van Nostrand Reinhold.

LIBERSON, C. W. & LIBERSON, W. T. (1975) Sex differences in autonomic responses to electric shock, *Psychophysiology*, **12**, 182–186.

LIEBERMAN, M. W. (1963) Early developmental stress and later behavior. *Science*, **141**, 824–825.

LINDSLEY, D. B. (1951) Emotion. In: *Handbook of Experimental Psychology* (Ed.: S. S. Stevens). New York: Wiley.

LITTENBERG, R., TULKIN, S. & KAGAN, J. (1971) Cognitive components of separation anxiety, *Developmental Psychology*, **4**, 387–388.

LIVESEY, P. J. & EGGER, G. J. (1970) Age as a factor in open-field responsiveness in the white rat, *Journal of Comparative and Physiological Psychology*, **73**, 93–99.

LO, W. H. (1967) A follow-up study of obsessional neurotics in Hong Kong Chinese, *British Journal of Psychiatry*, **113**, 823–832.

LOCKARD, R. B. (1963) Some effects of light upon the behavior of rodents, *Psychological Bulletin*, **60**, 509–529.

LORENZ, K. (1937) Uber die Bildung des Instinktbegriffes, *Die Naturwissenschaften*, **25**, 289–331.

LORENZ, K. (1939) Vergleichende Verhaltensforschung, *Zoologischer Anzeiger Supplement*, **12**, 69–102.

LORENZ, K. (1965) *Evolution and Modification of Behavior*. Chicago: University of Chicago Press.

LOUCH, A. R. (1966) *The Explanation of Human Action*. Oxford: Blackwell.

LYNN, R. (1966) *Attention, Arousal and the Orientation Reaction*. Oxford: Pergamon.

MAATSCH, J. L. (1959) Learning and fixation after a single shock trial, *Journal of Comparative and Physiological Psychology*, **52**, 408–410.

MCALLISTER, W. R. & MCALLISTER, D. E. (1971) Behavioral measurement of conditioned fear. In: *Aversive Conditioning and Learning* (Ed.: F. R. Brush). New York: Academic Press.

MCBRIDE, G. (1971) Theories of animal spacing: the role of flight, fight and social distance. In: *Behavior and Environment: The Use of Space by Animals and Men* (Ed.: H. Esser). New York: Plenum Press.

MCCALL, R. B., KENNEDY, C. B. & APPLEBAUM, M. I. (1977) Magnitude of discrepancy and the distribution of attention in infants, *Child Development*, **48**, 772–785.

MACCOBY, E. E. & FELDMAN, S. (1972) Mother-attachment and stranger-reactions in the third year of life, *Monographs of the Society for Research in Child Development*, **37**, No. 1.

MACCOBY, E. E. & JACKLIN, C. N. (1974) *The Psychology of Sex Differences*. Stanford: Stanford University Press.

MCCULLOCH, T. L. & HASLERUD, G. M. (1939) Affective responses of an infant chimpanzee reared in isolation from its kind, *Journal of Comparative and Physiological Psychology*, **28**, 437–445.

MCFARLAND, D. J. (1966) On the causal and functional significance of displacement activities, *Zeitschrift für Tierpsychologie*, **23**, 217–235.

MCFARLAND, D. J. & SIBLEY, R. (1972) 'Unitary drives' revisited, *Animal Behaviour*, **20**, 548–563.

MCFARLANE, J. W., ALLEN, L. & HONZIK, M. (1954) *A Developmental Study of the Behavior Problems of Normal Children*. Berkeley: University of California Press.

MCGREW, W. C. (1972) *An Ethological Study of Children's Behaviour*. New York & London: Academic Press.

MACKINTOSH, N. J. (1974) *The Psychology of Animal Learning*. London: Academic Press.

MACLEAN, P. D. (1949) Psychosomatic disease and the 'visceral brain': Recent developments bearing on the Papez theory of emotion, *Psychosomatic Medicine*, **11**, 338–353.

MACLEAN, P. D. (1972) Cerebral evolution and emotional processes: New findings on the striatal complex, *Annals of the New York Academy of Science*, **193**, 137–149.

MACLEAN, P. D. (1973) Effects of pallidal lesions on species-typical display behaviour of squirrel monkey, *Federal Proceedings*, **32**, 384.

MACLEAN, P. D. (1975) Sensory and perceptive factors in emotional functions of the triune brain. In: *Emotions; Their Parameters and Measurement* (Ed.: L. Levi.) New York: Raven Press.

McNIVEN, M. A. (1960) 'Social-releaser mechanisms' in birds – a controlled replication of Tinbergen's study, *Psychological Record*, **10**, 259–265.

MAIER, S. F., SELIGMAN, M. & SOLOMON, R. L. (1969) Pavlovian fear conditioning and learned helplessness effects on escape and avoidance behaviour of (a) the CS–US contingency and (b) the independence of the US and voluntary responding. In: *Punishment and Aversive Behavior* (Ed.: B. A. Campbell & R. M. Church). New York: Appleton-Century-Crofts.

MALCUIT, G. (1973) Cardiac responses in aversive situation with and without avoidance possibility, *Psychophysiology*, **10**, 295–306.

MALCUIT, G., DUCHARME, R & BELANGER, D. (1968) Cardiac activity in rats during bar-press avoidance and 'freezing' responses, *Psychology Reports*, **23**, 11–18.

MALMO, R. B. (1975) *On Emotions, Needs and Our Archaic Brain*. New York: Holt, Rinehart & Winston.

MARANON, G. (1924) Contribution a l'etude de l'action emotive de l'adrenaline, *Revue Francaise d'Endocrinologie*, **2**, 301–325.

MARGOLIN, S. G., KUBIE, L. S., KANZER, M. & STONE, L. (1943) Acute emotional disturbances in torpedoed seamen of the merchant marine who are continuing at sea, *War Medicine*, **3**, 393–408.

MARK, V. H. & ERVIN, R. R. (1970) *Violence and the Brain*. New York: Harper & Row.

MARKGREN, M. (1960) Fugitive reactions in avian behaviour, *Acta Vertebratica*, **2**, 1–110.

MARKS, I. M. (1969) *Fears and Phobias*. London: Heinemann.

MARKS, I. M. (1977) Phobias and obsessions: Clinical phenomena in search of a laboratory model. In: *Psychopathology: Experimental Models* (Ed.: M. Seligman & D. Maser). San Francisco: Freeman.

MARKS, I. M. & GELDER, M. (1967) Transvestism and fetishism: clinical and psychological changes during faradic aversion, *British Journal of Psychiatry*, **117**, 173–185.

MARLER, P. (1956) Behaviour of the chaffinch *Fringilla coelebs*, *Behaviour*, Supplement No. **5**, 1–184.

MARLER, P. (1959) Developments in the study of animal communication. In: *Darwin's Biological Work* (Ed.: P. R. Bell). London: Cambridge University Press.

MARLER, P. (1965) Communication in monkeys and apes. In: *Primate Behavior: Field Studies of Monkeys and Apes* (Ed.: I. DeVore). New York: Holt, Rinehart & Winston.

MARLER, P. (1968) Visual systems. In: *Animal Communication* (Ed.: T. A. Sebeok). Bloomington: Indiana University Press.

MARLER, P. & HAMILTON, W. J. (1966) *Mechanisms of Animal Behavior*. New York: Wiley.

MARLOWE, W. B., MANCALL, E. L. & THOMAS, J. J. (1975) Complete Kluver–Bucy syndrome in man, *Cortex*, **11**, 53–59.

MARSHALL, G. (1976) *The Affective Consequences of 'Inadequately Explained' Physiological Arousal*, unpublished doctoral dissertation, Stanford University.

MARTIN, R. C. & MELVIN, K. B. (1964) Fear responses of bobwhite quail (*Colinus virginianus*) to a model and a live red-tailed hawk (*Buteo jamaicensis*), *Psychologische Forschung*, **27**, 323–336.

MARUKHANYAN, E. V. (1961) The resistance of motor defensive conditioned reflexes to extinction in dogs, *Pavlov Journal of Higher Nervous Activity*, **11**, 492–500.

MARVIN, R. S. (1977) An ethological-cognitive model for the attenuation of mother-child attachment behaviour. In: *Attachment Behaviour* (Ed.: P. Pliner & L. Kramer). New York: Plenum Press.

MARVIN, R. S. & MOSSLER, D. G. (1976) A methodological paradigm for describing and analysing complex non-verbal expressions: coy expressions in pre-school children, *Representative Research in Psychology*, **7**, 133–139.

MASLACH, C. (1977) Negative emotional biasing of explained arousal. In: *Emotions and Emotion-Cognition Interactions in Psychopathology* (Ed.: C. E. Izard). New York: Plenum Press.

MASLOW, A. (1973) *The Farther Reaches of Human Nature*, Harmondsworth: Penguin.

MASON, J. W. (1975) Emotion as reflected in patterns of endocrine integration. In: *Emotions: Their Parameters and Measurement* (Ed.: L. Levi). New York: Raven Press.

MASON, J. W., MANGAN, G. F. Jr., BRADY, J. V., CONRAD, D. & RIOCH, D. M. (1961) Concurrent plasma epinephrine norepinephrine and 17-hydroxycorticosteroid levels during conditioned emotional disturbances in monkeys, *Psychosomatic Medicine*, **23**, 344–353.

MASON, W. A. (1960) Socially mediated reduction in emotional responses of young rhesus monkeys, *Journal of Abnormal and Social Psychology*, **60**, 100–104.

MATHEWS, A. & SHAW, P. (1977) Cognitions related to anxiety: a pilot study of treatment, *Behaviour Research and Therapy*, **15**, 503–505.

MATUSSEK, P. (1975) *Internment in Concentration Camps and its Consequences*. New York: Springer-Verlag.

MAY, J. (1977) A psychophysiological study of self and externally regulated phobic thoughts, *Behavior Therapy*, **8**, 849–861.

MEIER, G. W. & STUART, J. L. (1959) Effects of handling on the physical and behavioral development of Siamese kittens, *Psychological Reports*, **5**, 497–501.

MEILI, R. (1959) A longitudinal study of personality development. In: *Dynamic Psychopathology in Childhood* (Ed.: L. Jessner & E. Pavenstedt). London: Heinemann.

MELLSTROM, M., CICALA, G. A. & ZUCKERMAN, M. (1976) General versus specific trait anxiety measures in the prediction of fear of snakes, heights and darkness, *Journal of Consulting and Clinical Psychology*, **44**, 83–91.

MELZACK, R. (1961) On the survival of mallard ducks after 'habituation' to the hawk-shaped figure, *Behaviour*, **17**, 9–16.

MELZACK, R., PENICK, E. & BECKETT, A. (1959) The problem of 'innate fear' of the hawk shape: an experimental study with mallard ducks, *Journal of Comparative and Physiological Psychology*, **52**, 694–698.

MENZEL, E. W. (1964a) Patterns of responsiveness in chimpanzees reared through infancy under conditions of environmental restriction, *Psychologische Forschung*, **27**, 337–365.

MENZEL, E. W. (1964b) Responsiveness to object movement in young chimpanzees, *Behaviour*, **24**, 147–160.

MENZEL, E. W. (1965) Responsiveness to objects in free-ranging Japanese monkeys, *Behaviour*, **26**, 130–150.

MENZEL, E. W., DAVENPORT, R. K. & ROGERS, C. M. (1961) Some aspects of behaviour towards novelty in young chimpanzees, *Journal of Comparative and Physiological Psychology*, **54**, 16–19.

MENZEL, E. W., DAVENPORT, R. K. & ROGERS, C. M. (1963a) The effects of environmental restriction upon the chimpanzee's responsiveness to objects, *Journal of Comparative and Physiological Psychology*, **56**, 78–85.

MENZEL, E. W., DAVENPORT, R. K. & ROGERS, C. M. (1963b) Effects of environmental restrictions upon the chimpanzee's responsiveness in novel situations, *Journal of Comparative and Physiological Psychology*, **56**, 329–334.

MEYER, V. (1966) Modification of expectancies in cases with obsessional rituals, *Behaviour Research and Therapy*, **4**, 273–280.

MILLER, B. V. & LEVIS, D. J. (1971) The effects of varying short visual exposure times to a phobic stimulus on subsequent avoidance behaviour, *Behaviour Research and Therapy*, **9**, 17–21.

MILLER, D. E. (1966) *Ontogeny of Approach and Escape Responses and Circadian Activity Rhythms in Domestic Chicks*. Ph.D. Thesis, University of Wisconsin.

MILLER, L. (1952) Auditory recognition of predators, *Condor*, **54**, 89–92.

MILLER, L. C., BARRETT, C. L., HAMPE, E. & NOBLE, H. (1973) Factor structure of childhood fears, *Journal of Consulting and Clinical Psychology*, **39**, 264–268.

MILLER, N. E. (1948) Studies of fear as an acquirable drive: 1, Fear as motivation and fear-reduction as reinforcement in the learning of new responses, *Journal of Experimental Psychology*, **38**, 89–101.

MILLS, M. & MELHUISH, E. (1974) Recognition of mother's voice in early infancy, *Nature*, **252**, 123–124.

MITCHELL, D. (1976) Experiments on neophobia in wild and laboratory rats: a re-evaluation, *Journal of Comparative and Physiological Psychology*, **90**, 190–197.

MITCHELL, D., WILLIAMS, K. D. & SUTTER, J. (1974) Container neophobia as a predictor of preference for earned food by rats, *Bulletin of the Psychonomic Society*, **4**, 182–184.

MITCHELL, G., (1970) Abnormal behavior in primates. In: *Primate Behavior: Developments in Field and Laboratory Research, Vol. 1* (Ed.: L. A. Rosenblum). New York: Academic Press.

MOLTZ, H. & STETTNER, L. J. (1961) The influence of patterned-light deprivation on the critical period for imprinting, *Journal of Comparative and Physiological Psychology*, **54**, 279–283.

MOLTZ, H. ROSENBLUM, L. & HALIKAS, N. (1959) Imprinting and the level of anxiety, *Journal of Comparative and Physiological Psychology*, **52**, 240–244.

MONAHAN, L. C. (1975) *Mother-Infant and Stranger-Infant Interaction: an Ethological Analysis*, unpublished Ph.D. Thesis, Indiana University.

MONTEVECCHI, W. A., GALLUP, G. G. & DUNLAP, W. P. (1973) The peep vocalization in group reared chicks (*Gallus domesticus*); its relation to fear, *Animal Behaviour*, **21**, 116–123.

MONTGOMERY, K. C. (1955) The relation between fear induced by novel stimulation and exploratory behavior, *Journal of Comparative and Physiological Psychology*, **48**, 254–260.

MONTGOMERY, K. C. & MONKMAN, J. A. (1955) The relationship between fear and exploratory behavior, *Journal of Comparative and Physiological Psychology*, **48**, 132–136.

MOOG, F. (1959) The development of function in the adrenal cortex. In: *Comparative Endocrinology* (Ed.: A. Gorbman). New York: Wiley.

281

Moos, R. H. & Engel, B. T. (1962) Psychophysiological reactions in hypersensitive and arthritic patients, *Journal of Psychosomatic Research*, **6**, 227–241.

Morgan, G. A. (1959) Children who refuse to go to school, *Medical Officer*, **103**, 221–224.

Morgan, G. A. & Ricciutti, H. N. (1969) Infants' responses to strangers during the first year. In: *Determinants of Infant Behaviour, Vol. 4* (Ed.: B. M. Foss). London: Methuen.

Morgan, P. A. & Howse, P. E. (1973) Avoidance conditioning of jackdaws (*Corvus monedula*), *Animal Behaviour*, **21**, 481–491.

Morgensen, D. F. & Martin, I. (1969) Personality, awareness and autonomic conditioning, *Psychophysiology*, **5**, 536–549.

Morris, D. (1956) The feather postures of birds and the problem of the origin of social signals, *Behaviour*, **9**, 75–113.

Morris, R. & Morris, D. (1965) *Men and Snakes*. London: Hutchinson.

Morrison, B. J. & Hill, W. F. (1967) Socially facilitated reduction of the fear response in rats raised in groups or in isolation, *Journal of Comparative and Physiological Psychology*, **63**, 71–76.

Morrow, G. R. & Labrum, A. H. (1978) Psychological and physiological measures of anxiety, *Psychological Medicine*, **8**, 95–101.

Mottin, J. L. & Gatehouse, R. W. (1975) Attenuation of novelty preference: Homeostatic arousal or retrograde amnesia?, *Bulletin of the Psychonomic Society*, **5**, 172–174.

Mowbray, J. B. & Cadell, T. E. (1962) Early behavior patterns in rhesus monkeys, *Journal of Comparative and Physiological Psychology*, **55**, 350–357.

Mowrer, O. H. (1939) A stimulus-response analysis of anxiety and its role as a reinforcing agent, *Psychological Review*, **46**, 553–564.

Mowrer, O. H. (1947) On the dual nature of learning and re-interpretation of 'conditioning' and 'problem-solving', *Harvard Educational Review*, **17**, 102–148.

Mowrer, O. H. (1951) Learnable drives and rewards. In: *Handbook of Experimental Psychology* (Ed.: S. Stevens). New York: Wiley.

Mowrer, O. H. (1960a) *Learning Theory and Behavior*. New York: Wiley.

Mowrer, O. H. (1960b) *Learning Theory and the Symbolic Processes*. New York: Wiley.

Moyer, K. E. (1966) Effect of ACTH on open-field behaviour, avoidance, startle and food and water consumption, *Journal of Genetic Psychology*, **108**, 297–302.

Mueller, E. & Lucas, T. (1975) A developmental analysis of peer interaction among toddlers. In: *Friendship and Peer Relations* (Ed.: M. Lewis and L. A. Rosenblum). New York & London: Wiley.

MÜLLER, D. (1961) Quantitative Luftfeind-Attrapenversuche bei Auer- und Birkhühern, *Naturforschung*, **16**, 551–553.

MÜLLER-VELTEN, H. (1966) Uber den Angst-geruch bei der Hausmaus (*Mus musculus* L.), *Zeitschrift für Vergleichende Physiologie*, **52**, 401–429.

MYKTOWYCZ, R. (1974) Odor in the spacing behaviour of mammals. In: *Pheromones* (Ed.: M. C. Birch). Amsterdam & London: North-Holland

MYRBERG, A. A. (1965) A descriptive analysis of the behavior of the African cichlid fish *Pelmatochromis Guentheri (Sauvage)*, *Animal Behaviour*, **13**, 312–329.

NARAYANAN, C. H., FOX, M. W. & HAMBURGER, V. (1971) Prenatal development of spontaneous and evoked activity in the rat (*Rattus norvegicus albinus*), *Behavior*, **40**, 100–134.

NASH, R. F. & GALLUP, G. G. Jr. (1976) Habituation and tonic immobility in domestic chickens, *Journal of Comparative and Physiological Psychology*, **90**, 870–876.

NASH, R. F., GALLUP, G. G. Jr. & CZECH, D. A. (1976) Psychophysiological correlates of tonic immobility in the domestic chicken (*Gallus gallus*), *Physiology and Behavior*, **17**, 413–418.

NASH, R. F., GALLUP, G. G. & McCLURE, M. K. (1970) The immobility reaction in leopard frogs (*Rana pipiens*) as a function of noise induced fear, *Psychonomic Science*, **21**, 155–156.

NATELSON, B. H., SMITH, G. P., STOKES, P. E. & ROOT, A. W. (1973) Changes of plasma glucose and insulin during defense reactions in monkeys, *American Journal of Physiology*, **224**, 1454–1462.

NATHAN, M. A. & SMITH, O. A. (1971) Conditional cardiac and suppression responses after lesions in the dorsomedial thalamus of monkeys, *Journal of Comparative and Physiological Psychology*, **76**, 66–73.

NELSON, M. N. & ROSS, L. E. (1974) Effects of masking tasks on differential eyelid conditioning: a distinction between knowledge of stimulus contingencies and attentional or cognitive activities involving them, *Journal of Experimental Psychology*, **102**, 1–7.

NEWSON, J. & NEWSON, E. (1968) *Four Years Old in an Urban Community*. London: Allen & Unwin.

NICE, M. M. (1943) Studies on the life history of the song sparrow: 2, The behavior of the song sparrow and other passerines, *Transactions of the Linnaean Society of New York*, **6**, 1–328.

NICE, M. M. & TER PELKWYK, J. (1941) Enemy recognition by the song sparrow, *Auk*, **58**, 195–214.

NITSCHKE, W., BELL, R. W. & ZACHMAN, T. (1972) Distress vocalizations of young in three inbred strains of mice, *Developmental Psychobiology*, **5**, 363–370.

NITSCHKE, W., BELL, R. W., BELL, N. J. & ZACHMAN, T. (1975) The ontogeny of ultrasounds in two strains of *Rattus norvegicus, Experimental Aging Research*, **1**, 229–242.

NOIROT, E. (1968) Ultrasounds in young rodents: 2, Changes with age in albino rats, *Animal Behaviour*, **16**, 129–134.

NOIROT, E. (1972) Ultrasounds and maternal behavior in small rodents, *Developmental Psychobiology*, **5**, 371–387.

NOVAK, P. W. & LERNER, M. J. (1968) Rejection as a consequence of perceived similarity, *Journal of Personality and Social Psychology*, **9**, 147–152.

O'BRIEN, T. J. & DUNLAP, W. P. (1975) Tonic Immobility in the blue crab (*Callinectes sapidus*): its relation to threat of predation, *Journal of Comparative and Physiological Psychology*, **89**, 86–94.

OHMAN, A. & BOHLIN, G. (1973) The relationship between spontaneous and stimulus-correlated electrodermal responses in simple and discriminative conditioning paradigms, *Psychophysiology*, **10**, 589–600.

OHMAN, A., BJÖRKSTRAND, P.-A. & ELLSTRÖM, P.-E. (1973) Effect of explicit trial by trial information about shock probability in long interstimulus interval GSR conditioning, *Journal of Experimental Psychology*, **98**, 145–151.

OHMAN, A., ERIKSSON, A. & OLOFSSON, C. (1975b) One trial learning and superior resistance to extinction of autonomic responses conditioned to potentially phobic stimuli, *Journal of Comparative and Physiological Psychology*, **88**, 619–627.

OHMAN, A., ERIXON, G. & LOFBERG, I. (1975a) Phobias and preparedness: phobic versus neutral pictures as conditioned stimuli for human autonomic responses, *Journal of Abnormal Psychology*, **84**, 41–45.

OHMAN, A., FREDRIKSON, M., HUGDAHL, K. & RIMMO, P.-A. (1976) The premise of equipotentiality in human classical conditioning: conditioned electrodermal responses to potentially phobic stimuli, *Journal of Experimental Psychology*, **105**, 313–317.

OKON, E. E. (1970a) The effects of environmental temperature on the production of ultrasounds in unhandled albino mouse pups, *Journal of Zoology, London*, **162**, 71–83.

OKON, E. E. (1970b) The ultrasonic responses of albino mouse pups to tactile stimuli, *Journal of Zoology, London*, **162**, 485–492.

OKON, E. E. (1971) The ·temperature relations of vocalizations in infant golden hamsters and Wistar rats, *Journal of Zoology, London*, **164**, 227–237.

OLIVERIO, A., CASTELLANO, C. & ALLEGRA, S. P. (1975) Effects of genetic and nutritional factors on postnatal reflex and behavioral development in the mouse, *Experimental Aging Research*, **1**, 41–56.

OORTMERSSEN, G. A. VAN (1971) Biological significance, genetics and evolutionary origin of variability in behavior within and between inbred strains of mice, *Behaviour*, **38**, 1–92.

ORCHINIK, C. W., KOCH, R., WYCIS, H. T., FREED, H. & SPIEGEL, E. A. (1950) The effect of thalamic lesions upon the emotional reactivity (Rorschach and behavior studies). In: *Life Stresses and Bodily Disease*, Research Publications of the Association for Research in Nervous and Mental Disease, Vol. 29. Baltimore: Williams & Wilkins.

ORR, D. W. & WINDLE, W. F. (1934) The development of behavior in chick embryos: the appearance of somatic movements, *Journal of Comparative Neurology*, **60**, 271–285.

OSWALT, G. L. & MEIER, G. W. (1975) Olfactory, thermal and tactual influences on infantile ultrasonic vocalization in rats, *Developmental Psychobiology*, **8**, 129–135.

OWINGS, D. H., BORCHERT, M. & VIRGINIA, R. (1977) The behaviour of California ground squirrels, *Animal Behaviour*, **25**, 221–230.

PANTIN, C. F. A. (1935) Facilitation in nerve nets, *Journal of Experimental Biology*, **12**, 119–138.

PAPEZ, J. W. (1937) A proposed mechanism of emotion, *Archives of Neurology and Psychiatry*, **38**, 725–743.

PARADISE, E. & CURCIO, F. (1974) Relationship of cognitive and affective behaviours to fear of strangers in male infants, *Developmental Psychology*, **10**, 476–483.

PARE, W. P. (1969) The effect of adrenalectomy, adrenal demedullation and adrenaline on the aversive threshold in the rat, *Annals of the New York Academy of Science*, **159**, 869–879.

PARKER, G. (1977) Cyclone Tracy and Darwin evacuees: on the restoration of the species, *British Journal of Psychiatry*, **130**, 548–555.

PEARSON, M. (1970) *Causation and Development of Behaviour in the Guinea Pig*, D. Phil. dissertation, University of Sussex.

PFEIFFER, J. E. (1969) *The Emergence of Man*. London: Nelson.

PFEIFFER, W. (1962) The fright reaction of fish, *Biological Reviews*, **37**, 495–511.

PFEIFFER, W. (1963) Alarm substances, *Experientia*, **19**, 113–123.

PFEIFFER, W. (1974) Pheromones in fish and amphibia. In: *Pheromones* (Ed.: M. C. Birch) Amsterdam & London: North-Holland.

PHILLIPS, R. E. & SIEGEL, P. B. (1966) Development of fear in chicks of two closely related genetic lines, *Animal Behaviour*, **14**, 84–88.

PITCAIRN, T. K. (1974) Aggression in natural groups of Pongids. In: *Primate Aggression, Territoriality and Xenophobia: A Comparative Perspective* (Ed.: R. L. Holloway). London: Academic Press.

PITCHER, G. (1965) Emotion, *Mind*, **74**, 326–346.

POLLITT, J. D. (1957) Natural history of obsessional states: a study of 150 cases, *British Medical Journal*, **1**, 194–198.

285

PRATT, K. C. (1945) A study of the 'fears' of rural children, *Journal of Genetic Psychology*, **67**, 179–194.

PRESTRUDE, A. M. (1977) Some phylogenetic comparisons of tonic immobility with special reference to habituation and fear, *Psychological Record*, **1**, 21–39.

PRUITT, W. O. (1965) A flight releaser in wolf-caribou relations, *Journal of Mammalogy*, **46**, 350–351.

RABINOWITZ, F. M., MOELY, B. E. & FINKEL, N. (1975) The effects of toy novelty and social interaction on the exploratory behaviour of preschool children, *Child Development*, **46**, 286–289.

RACHMAN, S. (1968) *Phobias: Their Nature and Control*. Springfield, Ill.: Thomas.

RACHMAN, S. (1974) *The Meanings of Fear*. Harmondsworth: Penguin.

RACHMAN, S. (1976) The passing of the two-stage theory of fear and avoidance: fresh possibilities, *Behaviour Research and Therapy*, **14**, 125–131.

RACHMAN, S. (1977) The conditioning theory of fear-acquisition: a critical examination, *Behaviour Research and Therapy*, **15**, 375–387.

RACHMAN, S. & HODGSON, R. (1974) Synchrony and desynchrony in fear and avoidance, *Behaviour Research and Therapy*, **12**, 311–318.

RADIN, S. S. (1967) psychodynamic aspects of school phobia, *Comprehensive Psychiatry*, **8**, 119–128.

RAFMAN, S. (1974) The infant's reaction to imitation of the mother's behavior by the stranger. In: *The Infant's Reaction to Strangers* (Ed.: T. G. DeCarie). New York: International Universities Press.

RAJECKI, D. W. (1974) Effects of prenatal exposure to auditory or visual stimulation on postnatal distress vocalizations in chicks, *Behavioral Biology*, **11**, 525–536.

RAJECKI, D. W. & EICHENBAUM, H. (1973) Distress and contentment calls of the Peking duckling *(Anas platyrynchos):* duration and intensity, *Perceptual and Motor Skills*, **37**, 547–551.

RAJECKI, D. W., EICHENBAUM, H. & HEILWEIL, M. (1973) Rates of distress vocalizations in naive domestic chicks as an index of approach tendency to an imprinting stimulus, *Behavioral Biology*, **9**, 595–603.

RAJECKI, D. W., IVINS, B. & REIN, B. (1976) Social discrimination and aggressive pecking in domestic chicks, *Journal of Comparative and Physiological Psychology*, **90**, 442–542.

RAKOVER, S. S. (1975) Tolerance of pain as a measure of fear, *Learning and Motivation*, **6**, 43–61.

RAND, A.L. (1941) Development and enemy recognition of curve-billed thrasher, *Bulletin of the American Museum of Natural History*, **78**, 213–242.

RANDALL, P. K. & CAMPBELL, B. A. (1976) Ontogeny of behavioral arousal in rats: effect of maternal and sibling presence, *Journal of Comparative and Physiological Psychology*, **90**, 453–459.

RATNER, S. C. (1967) Comparative aspects of hypnosis. In: *Handbook of Clinical and Experimental Hypnosis* (Ed.: J. E. Gordon). New York: Macmillan.

RATNER, S. C. (1975) Animal's defenses: fighting in predator-prey relations. In: *Advances in the Study of Communication and Affect, Vol. 2; Nonverbal Communication of Aggression* (Ed.: P. Pliner, L. Krames & T. Alloway). New York: Plenum Press.

RATNER, S. C. (1977) Immobility in invertebrates: what can we learn?, *Psychological Record*, **27**, 1–13.

RATNER, S. C. & THOMPSON, R. W. (1960) Immobility reactions (fear) of domestic fowl as a function of age and prior experience, *Animal Behaviour*, **8**, 186–191.

RAUSCH, L. J. & LONG, C. J. (1974) Habenular lesions and avoidance learning deficits in albino rats, *Physiological Psychology*, **2**, 352–356.

RAZRAN, G. (1956) Extinction re-examined and re-analysed: a new theory, *Psychological Review*, **63**, 39–52.

REDICAN, W. K. (1975) Facial expressions in nonhuman primates. In: *Primate Behavior: Developments in Field and Laboratory Research, Vol.4* (Ed.: L. A. Rosenblum). New York: Academic Press.

REICHSMAN, F., ENGLE, G. L. & SEGAL, H. L. (1955) Behaviour and gastric secretion: the study of an infant with a gastric fistula, *Psychosomatic Medicine*, **17** (Abstr.), 481.

RESCORLA, R. A. (1969) Conditioned inhabition of fear. In: *Fundamental Issues in Associative Learning* (Ed.: N. J. Mackintosh & W. K. Honig). Halifax, N.S.: Dalhousie University Press.

RESCORLA, R. A. & SOLOMON, R. L. (1967) Two-process learning theory: relationships between Pavlovian conditioning and instrumental learning, *Psychological Review*, **74**, 151–182.

REVUSKY, S. (1977) Learning as a general process with an emphasis on data from feeding experiments. In: *Food Aversion Learning* (Ed.: N.W. Milgram, L. Krames & T. M. Alloway). New York: Plenum Press.

REVUSKY, S. H. & BEDARF, E. W. (1967) Association of illness with prior ingestion of novel foods, *Science*, **155**, 219–220.

REYNIERSE, J. H. (1960) Effects of CS-only trials on resistance to extinction of an avoidance response, *Journal of Comparative and Physiological Psychology*, **61**, 156–158.

RHEINGOLD H. L. (1969) The effect of a strange environment on the behaviour of infants. In: *Determinants of Infant Behaviour, Vol. 4* (Ed.: B. Foss) London: Methuen.

RHEINGOLD, H. L. & ECKERMAN, C. O. (1969) The infant's free entry into a new environment, *Journal of Experimental Child Psychology*, **8**, 271–283.

RHEINGOLD, H. L. & ECKERMAN, C. O. (1973) Fear of the stranger: a critical examination, *Advances in Child Development and Behavior*, **8**, 185–222.

RICCIUTI, H. N. (1974) Fear and the development of social attachments in the first year of life. In: *The Origins of Behavior, Vol. 2: The Origins of Fear.* (Ed.: M. Lewis & L. A. Rosenblum). New York & London: Wiley.

RICHARDSON, W. B. (1942) Reaction toward snakes as shown by the wood rat *Neotoma albigula*, *Journal of Comparative Psychology*, **34**, 1–10.

RICHTER, C. P. (1953) Experimentally produced behavior reactions to food poisoning in wild and domesticated rats, *Annals of the New York Academy of Science*, **56**, 225–239.

RIGTER, H. & RIEZEN, H. V. (1975) Anti-amnesic effect of $ACTH_{4-10}$; its independence of the nature of the amnesic agents and the behavioral test. *Physiology and Behavior*, **14**, 563–566.

RITCHIE, B. F. (1951) Can reinforcement theory account for avoidance?, *Psychological Review*, **58**, 382–386.

ROBERTS, W. W. (1962) Fear-like behavior elicited from dorsomedial thalamus of cat, *Journal of Comparative and Physiological Psychology*, **55**, 191–197.

ROBIN, A. & MacDONALD, D. (1975) *Lessons of Leucotomy*. London: Kimpton.

ROBSON, K. S., PEDERSEN, F. A. & MOSS, H. A. (1969) Developmental observations of diadic gazing in relation to the fear of strangers and social approach behavior, *Child Development*, **40**, 619–627.

ROCKETT, F. C. (1955) A note on 'an experimental test of an alleged innate sign stimulus' by Hirsch, Lindley and Tolman, *Perceptual and Motor Skills*, **5**, 155–156.

ROGERS, L. J. (1974) Persistence and search influenced by natural levels of androgens in young and adult chickens, *Physiology and Behavior*, **12**, 197–204.

ROHRBAUGH, M. & RICCIO, C. V. (1970) Paradoxical enhancement of learned fear, *Journal of Abnormal Psychology*, **75**, 210–216.

ROHRBAUCH, M., RICCIO, D. V. & ARTHUR, S. (1972) Paradoxical enhancement of conditioned suppression, *Behaviour Research and Therapy*, **10**, 125–130.

ROLLS, E. T. (1975) *The Brain and Reward*. Oxford: Pergamon.

ROLLS, E. T. & ROLLS, B. J. (1973) Altered food preferences after lesions in the basolateral region of the amygdala in the rat, *Journal of Comparative Physiology*, **83**, 248–259.

ROMER, A. S. (1962) *The vertebrate body*. London: Saunders.

ROOD, J. P. (1972) Ecological and behavioural comparisons of three genera of Argentine cavies, *Animal Behaviour Monographs*, **5**, 1–83.

ROSENBLATT, J. S. & SCHNEIRLA, T. C. (1962) The behaviour of cats. In:

288

The Behaviour of Domestic Animals (Ed.: E. S. E. Hafez). London: Baillière Tindall & Cox.

ROSENBLUM, L. A. & ALPERT, S. (1974) Fear of strangers and specificity of attachment in monkeys. In: *The Origins of Behavior, Vol. 2: The Origins of Fear.* (Ed.: M. Lewis & L. A. Rosenblum). New York: Wiley.

ROSENBLUM, L. A. & CROSS, H. A. (1963) Performance of neonatal monkeys on the visual cliff situation, *American Journal of Psychology*, **76**, 318–320.

ROSS, H. S. (1974a) Forms of exploratory behaviour in young children. In: *New Perspectives in Child Development* (Ed.: B. Foss). Harmondsworth: Penguin.

ROSS, H. S. (1974b) The influence of novelty and complexity on exploratory behavior in 12-month-old infants, *Journal of Experimental Child Psychology*, **17**, 436–451.

ROSS, H. S. (1975) The effects of increasing familiarity on infants' reactions to adult strangers, *Journal of Experimental Child Psychology*, **20**, 226–239.

ROSS, H. S. & GOLDMAN, B. D. (1977) Infants' sociability toward strangers, *Child Development*, **48**, 638–642.

ROSS, J. F. & GROSSMAN, S. P. (1977) Transections of stria medullaris or stria terminalis in the rat: Effects on aversity controlled behavior, *Journal of Comparative and Physiological Psychology*, **91**, 907–917.

ROTHBALLER, A. B. (1959) The effects of catecholamines on the central nervous system, *Pharmacology Review*, **11**, 494–547.

ROTTMAN, S. J. & SNOWDON, C. T. (1972) Demonstration and analysis of an alarm pheromone in mice, *Journal of Comparative and Physiological Psychology*, **81**, 483–490.

ROUTTENBERG, G. A. & GLICKMAN, S. E. (1964) Visual cliff behavior in undomesticated rodents, land and aquatic turtles, and cats (*Panthera*), *Journal of Comparative and Physiological Psychology*, **58**, 143–146.

ROVEE, C. K. & KLEINMAN, J. M. (1974) Developmental changes in tonic immobility in young chicks (*Gallus gallus*), *Developmental Psychobiology*, **7**, 71–77.

ROVEE, C. K. & LUCIANO, D. P. (1973) Rearing influences on tonic immobility in three-day-old chicks (*Gallus gallus*), *Journal of Comparative and Physiological Psychology*, **83**, 351–354.

ROVEE, C. K., AGNELLO, A.-M. & SMITH, B. (1973) Environmental influences on tonic immobility in three- and seven-day-old chicks (*Gallus gallus*), *Psychological Record*, **23**, 539–546.

ROWELL, C. H. F. (1961) Displacement grooming in the chaffinch, *Animal Behaviour*, **9**, 38–63.

ROWELL, T. E. (1962) Agonistic noises of the rhesus monkey, *Symposium of the Zoological Society of London*, **8**, 91–96.

ROWELL, T. E. (1972) *Social behaviour of Monkeys*. Harmondsworth: Penguin.

ROWELL, T. E. & HINDE, R. A. (1963) Responses of rhesus monkeys to mildly stressful situations, *Animal Behaviour*, **11**, 235–243.

RUBEL, E. W. (1970) Effects of early experience on fear behaviour of *Coturnix coturnix*, *Animal Behaviour*, **18**, 427–433.

RUSSELL, P. A. (1973a) Open-field defecation in rats: relationships with body weight and basal defecation level, *British Journal of Psychology*, **64**, 109–114.

RUSSELL, P. A. (1973b) Relationships between exploratory behaviour and fear: a review, *British Journal of Psychology*, **64**, 417–433.

RUSSELL, P. A. (1973c) Sex differences in rats' stationary-cage activity measured by observation and automatic recording, *Animal Learning and Behavior*, **1**, 278–282.

RUSSELL, P. A. & WILLIAMS, D. I. (1973) Effects of repeated testing on rats' locomotor activity in the open-field, *Animal Behaviour*, **21**, 109–112.

RUTTER, M. (1972) *Maternal Deprivation Reassessed*. Harmondsworth: Penguin.

RYDÉN, O. (1972) Habituation of the cease-begging response of great tit nestlings (*Parus major*) to different acoustic stimuli, *Psychological Research Bulletin, Lund University*, **12**.

RYDÉN, O. (1973) Conditioning and extinction of begging to auditory stimuli of differing significance, *Psychological Research Bulletin, Lund University*, **13**.

RYDÉN, O. (1974a) Reaction to natural auditory stimuli by wild captured and partly laboratory-reared great tit nestlings (*Parus major*), *Psychological Research Bulletin, Lund University*, **14**.

RYDÉN, O. (1974b) Responses to an alarming auditory stimulus as affected by massive earlier exposure: a combined field and laboratory experiment with great tit nestlings (*Parus major*), *Psychological Research Bulletin, Lund University*, **14**.

RYLE, G. (1949) *The Concept of Mind*. London: Hutchinson.

RZOSKA, J. (1953) Bait shyness: a study in rat behaviour, *British Journal of Animal Behaviour*, **1**, 128–135.

RZOSKA, J. (1954) The behaviour of white rats towards poison baits. In: *The Control of Rats and Mice, Vol. 2* (Ed.: D. Chitty). Oxford: Clarendon Press.

SACKETT, G. P. (1966) Monkeys reared in isolation with pictures as visual input: evidence for an innate releasing mechanism, *Science*, **154**, 1470–1473.

SACKETT, G. P. (1973) Innate mechanisms in primate social behavior. In: *Behavioral Regulators of Behavior in Primates* (Ed.: C. R. Carpenter). Lewisburg: Bucknell University Press).

SACKETT, G. P. & RUPPENTHAL, G. C. (1973) Development of monkeys after varied experiences during infancy. In: *Ethology and Development* (Ed.: S. A. Barnett). London: Heinemann.

SALZEN, E. A. (1962) Imprinting and fear, *Symposium of the Zoological Society of London*, **8**, 199–217.

SALZEN, E. A. (1963) Imprinting and the immobility reactions of domestic fowl, *Animal Behaviour*, **11**, 66–71.

SALZEN, E. A. (1967) Imprinting in birds and primates, *Behaviour*, **28**, 232–254.

SALZEN, E. A. (1969) Contact and social attachment in domestic chicks, *Behaviour*, **33**, 38–51.

SALZEN, E. A. (1970) Imprinting and environmental learning. In: *Development and Evolution of Behavior, Vol. 1* (Ed.: L. R. Aronson, E. Tobach, D. S. Lehrman & J. S. Rosenblatt). San Francisco: Freeman.

SALZEN, E. A. (1978) Social attachment and a sense of security – a review, *Social Science Information*, **17**, 555–627.

SANDERSON, R., LAVERTY, S. & CAMPBELL, D. (1962) Traumatically conditioned responses acquired during respiratory paralysis, *Nature*, **196**, 1235–1236.

SARTORY, G. & EYSENCK, H. J. (1976) Strain differences in the acquisition and extinction of fear responses in rats, *Psychological Reports*, **38**, 163–187.

SATINDER, K. P. (1976) Reactions of selectively bred strains of rats to a cat, *Animal Learning and Behavior*, **4**, 172–176.

SAVAGE, R. D. (1960) *Constitutional Determinants Emotionality in the Rat: An Experimental Investigation of Fear, Frustration and Conflict*, Ph.D. dissertation, University of London.

SCAIFE, M. (1976a) The response to eye-like shapes by birds, II: the effect of context: a predator and a strange bird, *Animal Behaviour*, **24**, 195–199.

SCAIFE, M. (1976b) The response to eye-like shapes by birds, II: The importance of starting, pairedness and shape, *Animal Behaviour*, **24**, 200–206.

SCARR, S. & SALAPATEK, P. (1970) Patterns of fear development during infancy, *Merrill Palmer Quarterly*, **16**, 53–90.

SCHACHTER, S. (1957) Pain, fear and anger in hypertensives and a psychophysiological study, *Psychosomatic Medicine*, **19**, 17–29.

SCHACHTER, S. (1975) Cognition and peripheralist-centralist controversies in motivation and emotion. In: *Handbook of Psychobiology* (Ed.: M. S. Gazzaniga & C. Blakemore). New York: Academic Press.

SCHACHTER, S. & SINGER, J. C. (1962) Cognitive, social and physiological determinants of emotional state, *Psychological Review*, **69**, 379–399.

SCHAFFER, H. R. (1966) The onset of the fear of strangers and the incongruity hypothesis, *Journal of Child Psychology and Psychiatry*, **7**, 95–106.

SCHAFFER, H. R. (1971) Cognitive structure and early social behaviour. In:

The Origins of Human Social Relations (Ed.: H. R. Schaffer). London & New York: Academic Press.

SCHAFFER, H. R. (1974) Cognitive components of the infant's response to strangers. In: *The Origins of Behaviour, Vol. 2: The Origins of Fear*. (Ed.: M. Lewis and L. A. Rosenblum). New York & London: Wiley.

SCHAFFER, H. R. (1977) *Mothering.*London: Fontana/Open Books.

SCHAFFER, H. R. & EMERSON, P. E. (1964) The development of social attachments in infancy, *Monographs of the Society for Research in Child Development*, **29**, No. 3.

SCHAFFER, H. R. & PARRY, M. H. (1969) Perceptual-motor behaviour in infancy as a function of age and stimulus similarity, *British Journal of Psychology*, **60**, 1–10.

SCHAFFER, H. R., GREENWOOD, A. & PARRY, M. H. (1972) The onset of wariness, *Child Development*, **43**, 165–175.

SCHALLER, G. B. (1972) *The Serengeti Lion: A Study of Predator:Prey Relations.* Chicago: University of Chicago Press.

SCHALLER, G. B. & EMLEN, J. T. (1961) The development of visual discrimination patterns in the crouching reactions of nestling grackles, *Auk*, **78**, 125–137.

SCHALLER, G. B. & EMLEN, J. T. (1962) The ontogeny of avoidance behaviour in some precocial birds, *Animal Behaviour*, **10**, 370–381.

SCHIFF, W. (1965) Perception of impending collision: a study of visually directed avoidant behavior, *Psychological Monographs*, **79**, Whole No. 604.

SCHIFF, W., CAVINESS, J. A. & GIBSON, J. J. (1962) Persistent fear responses in rhesus monkeys to the optical stimulus of 'looming', *Science*, **136**, 982–983.

SCHILDKRAUT, J. J. & KETY, S. S. (1967) Biogenic amines and emotion, *Science*, **156**, 21–30.

SCHLEIDT, W. M. (1961a) Über die Auslösung der Flucht vor Raubvögeln bei Truthühnern, *Naturwissenschaften*, **48**, 141–142.

SCHLEIDT, W. M. (1961b) Reaktionen von Truthühnern auf fliegende Raubvögel und Versuche zur Analyse ihrer AAMs, *Zeitschrift für Tierpsychologie*, **18**, 534–560.

SCHNEIRLA, T. C. (1959) An evolutionary and developmental theory of biphasic processes underlying approach and withdrawal. In: *Nebraska Symposium On Motivation* (Ed.: M. R. Jones). Lincoln, Neb.: University of Nebraska Press.

SCHNEIRLA, T. C. (1965) Aspects of stimulation and organisation in approach/withdrawal processes underlying vertebrate behavioral development. In.: *Advances in the Study of Behavior, Vol. 1* (Ed.: D. S. Lehrman, R. A. Hinde & E. Shaw). New York: Academic Press.

292

SCHULMAN, A. H., HALE, E. B. & GRAVES, H. B. (1970) Visual stimulus characteristics for initial approach response in chicks (*Gallus domesticus*), *Animal Behaviour*, **18**, 461–466.

SCHWARTZ, A. N., CAMPOS, J. J. & BAISEL, E. J. (1975) The visual cliff: cardiac and behavioral responses on the deep and shallow sides at five and nine months of age, *Journal of Experimental Child Psychology*, **15**, 85–99.

SCHWARTZ, J. C. (1972) Effects of peer familiarity on the behavior of pre-schoolers in a novel situation, *Journal of Personality and Social Psychology*, **24**, 276–284.

SCHWARTZBAUM, J. S. & GAY, P. E. (1966) Interacting effects of septal and amygdaloid lesions in the rat, *Journal of Comparative and Physiological Psychology*, **61**, 59–65.

SCOTT, J. P. (1958) *Animal Behavior*. Chicago: University of Chicago Press.

SCOTT, J. P. (1962) Critical periods in behavioral development, *Science*, **138**, 949–958.

SCOTT, J. P. (1967) The development of social motivation. In.: *Nebraska Symposium on Motivation* (Ed.: D. Levine). Lincoln, Neb.: University of Nebraska Press.

SCOTT, J. P. (1969) The emotional basis of social behavior, *Annals of the New York Academy of Science*, **159**, 777–790.

SCOTT, J. P. & FULLER, J. L. (1965) *Genetics and the Social Behavior of the Dog*. Chicago: University of Chicago Press.

SCOTT, J. P. & SENAY, E. (1973) *Separation and Depression*. Washington, DC: American Association for the Advancement of Science.

SELIGMAN, M. E. P. (1975) *Helplessness: On Depression, Development and Death*. San Francisco: Freeman.

SELIGMAN, M. E. P. (1970) On the generality of the laws of learning, *Psychological Review*, **77**, 406–418.

SELIGMAN, M. E. P. (1971) Phobias and preparedness, *Behaviour Therapy*, **2**, 307–320.

SELIGMAN, M. E. P. & HAGER, J. L. (Ed.) (1972) *Biological Boundaries of Learning*. New York: Appleton-Century-Crofts.

SELIGMAN, M. E. P. & JOHNSTON, J. C. (1973) A cognitive theory of avoidance learning. In.: *Contemporary Approaches to Conditioning and Learning* (Ed.: F. J. McGuigan & D. B. Lumsden). Washington, DC: Winston.

SELYE, H. (1952) *The Story of the Adaptation Syndrome*. Montreal: Acta.

SERAFICA, A. & CICCHETTI, D. (1976) Down's syndrome children in a strange situation: attachment and exploration behaviors, *Merrill-Palmer Quarterly*, **22**, 137–150.

SHAFFRAN, R. (1974) Modes of approach and the infant's reaction to the

293

stranger. In.: *The Infant's Reaction to Strangers* (Ed.: T. G. DeCarie). New York: International Universities Press.

SHAMD, A. F. (1914) *The Foundation of Character*. London: Macmillan.

SHELDON, M. H. (1968a) Exploratory behavior: the inadequacy of activity measures, *Psychonomic Science*, **11**, 38.

SHELDON, M. H. (1968b) The effect of electric shock on rats' choice between familiar and unfamiliar maze arms: a replication, *Quarterly Journal of Experimental Psychology*, **20**, 400–404.

SHELDON, M. H. (1970) Effect of electric shock on rats' activity in familiar and unfamiliar environments, *Quarterly Journal of Experimental Psychology*, **22**, 374–377.

SHERRINGTON, C. S. (1900) Experiments on the value of vascular and visceral factors for the genesis of emotions, *Proceedings of the Royal Society (London)*. B,**66**, 390–403.

SHERRINGTON, C. S. (1947) *The Integrative Action of the Nervous System*, 2nd edition. New Haven: Yale University Press.

SHIRLEY, M. M. (1933) *The First Two Years: A Study of Twenty-Five Babies, Vol. 3: Personality Manifestations*. Institute of Child Welfare Monograph Series No. 8. Minneapolis: Minneapolis University Press.

SIECK, M. H., BAUMBACH, H. D., GORDON, B. L. & TURNER, J. F. (1974) Changes in spontaneous, odor modulated and shock induced behaviour patterns following discrete olfactory system lesions, *Physiology and Behaviour*, **13**, 427–439.

SILVER, S. I. & KIMMEL, H. D. (1969) Resistance to extinction in classical GSR conditioning as a function of acquisition trials beyond peak CR size, *Psychonomic Science*, **14**, 53–55.

SILVERMAN, A. J. & COHEN, S. I. (1960) Affect and vascular correlates to catecholamines, *Psychiatric Research Reports*, **12**, 16–30.

SIMNER, M. L. (1976) Interflash interval and the chicks' differential attraction toward intermittent light, *Behavioral Biology*, **17**, 355–365.

SIMON, M. E. (1954) Der optomotorische Nystagmus während der Entwicklung normaler und optisch isoliert aufgewachsener Küken, *Zeitschrift für vergleichende Physiologie*, **37**, 82–105.

SKARIN, K. (1977) Cognitive and contextural determinants of stranger fear in six- and eleven-month old infants, *Child Development*, **48**, 537–544.

SLATER, E. P. (1972) *Some Aspects of Exploration and Learning in Three Strains of Mice*, M. Phil. dissertation, University of Sussex.

SLUCKIN, A. M. & SMITH, P. K. (1977) Two approaches to the concept of dominance in preschool children, *Child Development*, **48**, 917–923.

SLUCKIN, W. (1972) *Imprinting and Early Learning*, 2nd edition. London: Methuen.

SMITH, F. V. (1962) Perceptual aspects of imprinting, *Symposium of the Zoological Society London*, **8**, 171–192. .

SMITH, F. V. (1969) *Attachment of the Young: Imprinting and Other Developments*. Edinburgh: Oliver & Boyd.

SMITH, H. M. (1960) *Evolution of Chordate Structure*. New York: Holt, Rinehart & Winston.

SMITH, K. U. & DANIEL, R. S. (1946) Observations of behavioral development in the loggerhead turtle (*Caretta caretta*), *Science*, **104**, 154–156.

SMITH, P. K. (1974) Social and situational determinants of fear in the playgroup. In.: *The Origins of Behavior, Vol. 2: The Origins of Fear* (Ed.: M. Lewis & L. A. Rosenblum). New York & London: Wiley.

SOKOLOV, E. N. (1963) *Perception and the Conditioned Reflex*. Transl. S. W. Waydenfeld. Oxford: Pergamon.

SOLOMON, R. L. & DeCARIE, T. G. (1976) Fear of strangers: a developmental milestone or an overstudied phenomenon?, *Canadian Journal of Behavioural Science*, **8**, 351–362.

SOLOMON, R. L. & BRUSH, E. S. (1954) Experimentally derived conceptions of anxiety and aversion. In.: *Nebraska Symposium on Motivation* (Ed.: M. R. Jones). Lincoln, Neb.: University of Nebraska Press.

SOLOMON, R. L. & WYNNE, L. C. (1954) Traumatic avoidance learning: the principles of anxiety conservation and partial irreversibility, *Psychological Review*, **61**, 353–385.

SOLOMON, R. L., KAMIN, L. J. & WYNNE, L. C. (1953) Traumatic avoidance learning: the outcomes of several extinction procedures with dogs, *Journal of Abnormal and Social Psychology*, **48**, 291–302.

SOLOMON-SHAFFRAN, R. & DeCARIE, T. G. (1976) A more natural approach for use in the evaluation of infants' stranger reactions, *Canadian Journal of Behavioural Science*, **8**, 98–101.

SOLYOM, L., BECK, P., SOLYOM, C. & HUGEL, R. (1974) Some etiological factors in phobic neuroses, *Canadian Psychiatric Association Journal*, **19**, 69–78.

SOUTHWICK, C. H., SIDDIQI, M. F., FAROOQUI, M. Y. & PAL, B. C. (1974) Xenophobia among free-ranging rhesus groups in India. In: *Primate Aggression, Territoriality, and Xenophobia: a Comparative Perspective* (Ed.: R. L. Holloway). London: Academic Press.

SPALDING, D. A. (1873) Instinct: with original observations on young animals. Reprinted (1954) in *British Journal of Animal Behaviour*, **2**, 2–11.

SPELKE, E., ZELAZO, P. R., KAGAN, J. & KOTELCHUCK, M. (1973) Father interaction and separation protest, *Developmental Psychology*, **9**, 83–90.

SPENCE, K. W. (1966) Cognitive and drive factors in the extinction of the conditioned eyeblink in human subjects, *Psychological Review*, **73**, 445–458.

SPITZ, R. A. (1950) Anxiety in infancy: a study of its manifestations in the first year of life, *International Journal of Psycho-Analysis*, **31**, 138–143.

SROUFE, L. A. (1977) Wariness of strangers and the study of infant development, *Child Development*, **48**, 731–746.

SROUFE, L. A., WATERS, E. & MATAS, L. (1974) Contextual determinants of infant affective response. In: *The Origins of Fear* (Ed.: M. Lewis & L. A. Rosenblum). New York & London: Wiley.

STERN, D. N. & BENDER, E. P. (1974) The behavior of preschool children approaching a strange adult: Sex differences. In: *Sex Differences in Behavior* (Ed.: R. Friedman). New York: Wiley.

STERN, W. (1924) *Psychology of Early Childhood*. London: Allen & Unwin.

STETTNER, L. J. & TILDS, B. N. (1966) Effect of presence of an imprinted object on responses of ducklings in an open field and when exposed to a fear stimulus, *Psychonomic Science*, **4**, 107–108.

STODDART, D. M. (1976) *Mammalian Odours and Pheromones*. London: Edward Arnold.

STOTLAND, E. (1969) Exploratory investigations of empathy. In: *Advances in Experimental Social Psychology* (Ed.: L. Berkowitz). New York: Academic Press.

STRAUS, W. L. & WEDDELL, G. (1940) Nature of the first visible contractions of the forelimb musculature in rat foetuses, *Journal of Neurophysiology*, **3**, 358–369.

STRAUSS, H. (1969) Das Zusammenschrecken, *Journal für Psychologie und Neurologie, Leipzig*, **39**, 111–231.

STRAYER, F. F. & STRAYER, J. (1976) An ethological analysis of social agonism and dominance reactions among preschool children, *Child Development*, **47**, 980–989.

STROEBEL, C. F. (1967) Behavioral aspects of circadian rhythms. In: *Comparative Psychopathology* (Ed.: J. Zubin & H. F. Hunt). New York: Grune & Stratton.

STRONGMAN, K. T. (1973) *The Psychology of Emotion*. Chichester: Wiley.

STRUHSAKER, T. T. (1967) Auditory communication among vervet monkeys (*Cercopithecus aethiops*). In: *Social Communication Among Primates* (Ed.: S. A. Altman). Chicago: University of Chicago Press.

SUBERI, M. & MCKEEVER, W. F. (1977) Differential right hemisphere memory storage of emotional and non-emotional faces, *Neuropsychology*, **15**, 757–768.

SUOMI, S. J. & HARLOW, H. F. (1976) The facts and functions of fear. In: *Emotions and Anxiety* (Ed.: M. Zuckerman & C. D. Spielberger). Hillsdale, N. J.: Lawrence Erlbaum.

SVORAD, D. (1957) 'Animal hypnosis' (Totstellreflex) as experimental model for psychiatry, *Archives of Neurology and Psychiatry, Chicago*, **77**, 533–539.

SYMINGTON, T., CURRIE, A. R., CURRAN, R. S. & DAVIDSON, J. N. (1955) The reaction of the adrenal cortex in conditions of stress. In: *Ciba Foundations Colloquia on Endocrinology, Vol. 8, The Human Adrenal Cortex.* Boston: Little, Brown.

SYMMES, D. (1959) Anxiety reduction and novelty as goals of visual exploration by monkeys, *Journal of Genetic Psychology*, **94**, 181–198.

TANAKA, D. (1973) Effects of selective prefrontal decortication on escape behavior in the monkey, *Brain Research*, **53**, 161–173.

TEASDALE, J. D. (1974) Learning models of obsessional-compulsive disorder. In: *Obsessional States* (Ed.: H. R. Beech). London: Methuen.

TEITELBAUM, P. & DERKS, P. (1958) The effects of amphetamine on forced drinking in the rat, *Journal of Comparative and Physiological Psychology*, **51**, 801–810.

TENNES, K. H. & LAMPL, E. E. (1964) Stranger and separation anxiety in infancy, *Journal of Nervous and Mental Disease*, **139**, 247–254.

THOMAS, A., CHESS, S., BIRCH, H. G., HERTZIG, M. E. & KORN, S. (1964) *Behavioral Individuality in Early Childhood.* New York: New York University Press.

THOMPSON, R. W. & GALOSY, R. A. (1969) A one-trial non-shock passive avoidance task for rats, *Behavior Research Methods and Instrumentation*, **1**, 227–228.

THOMPSON, S. K. (1975) Gender labels and early sex role development, *Child Development*, **46**, 339–347.

THOMPSON, W. R. & MCELROY, L. R. (1962) The effect of maternal presence on open-field behavior in young rats, *Journal of Comparative and Physiological Psychology*, **55**, 827–830.

THORNDIKE, E. (1899) The instinctive reaction of young chicks, *Psychological Review*, **6**, 282–291.

TILNEY, F. & CASAMAJOR, L. (1924) Myelinogeny as applied to the study of behavior, *Archives of Neurology and Psychiatry, Chicago*, **12**, 1–66.

TINBERGEN, N. (1951) *The Study of Instinct.* Oxford: Clarendon Press.

TINBERGEN, N. (1952) Derived activities: Their causation, biological significance, origin and emancipation during evolution, *Quarterly Review of Biology*, **27**, 1–32.

TINBERGEN, N. (1953) *Social Behaviour in Animals, with Special Reference to Vertebrates.* London: Methuen.

TINBERGEN, N. (1957) On antipredator responses in certain birds – a reply, *Journal of Comparative and Physiological Psychology*, **50**, 412–414.

TINKELPAUGH, O. L. & HARTMAN, C. G. (1932) Behavior and maternal care of the newborn monkey (*Macaca mulatta* – 'M. rhesus'), *Journal of Genetic Psychology*, **40**, 257–286.

TOLHURST, D. J. (1973) Separate channels for the analysis of the shape and the movement of a moving visual stimulus, *Journal of Physiology, London*, **231**, 385–402.

TORTORA, D. F. & BORCHELT, P. L. (1972) The effect of escape responses on immobility in the bobwhite quail (*Colinus virginianus*), *Psychonomic Science*, **27**, 129–130.

TRACY, H. C. (1926) The development of motility and behavior reactions in the toadfish (*Opsanus tau*), *Journal of Comparative Neurology*, **40**, 253–369.

TRAUSE, M. A. (1977) Stranger responses: Effects of familiarity, stranger's approach and sex of infant, *Child Development*, **48**, 1657–1661.

TREISMAN, M. (1975a) Predation and the evolution of gregariousness, I: Models for concealment and evasion, *Animal Behaviour*, **23**, 779–800.

TREISMAN, M. (1975b) Predation and the evolution of gregariousness, II: An economic model for predator-prey interaction, *Animal Behaviour*, **23**, 801–825.

TRIVERS, R. L. (1974) Parent-offspring conflict, *American Zoologist*, **14**, 249–264.

TUGE, H. (1934) Early behavior of the embryos of carrier-pigeons, *Proceedings of the Society for Experimental Biology and Medicine*, **31**, 462–463.

TUGENDHAT, B. (1960a) The normal feeding behaviour of the three-spined stickleback (*Gasterosteus aculeatus*), *Behaviour*, **15**, 284–318.

TUGENDHAT, B. (1960b) The disturbed feeding behaviour of the three-spined stickleback: Electric shock is administered in the food area, *Behaviour*, **16**, 159–187.

TWIGG, G. (1975) *The Brown Rat*. Newton Abbott: David & Charles.

UDIN, H., OLSWANGER, G. & VOGLER, R. E. (1974) Evidence for a spatial gradient of avoidance behaviour in humans, *Perceptual and Motor Skills*, **39**, 275–278.

UEXKULL, J. VON, (1934) A stroll through the world of animals and man. Reprinted (1957) in: *Instinctive Behaviour: the Development of a Modern Concept* (Ed.: C. H. Schiller). London: Methuen.

UKA, N. (1966) *A Pioneer Study of Physical and Behavioural Growth and Development of Nigerian Children*. Ibadan: University Institute of Education.

URSIN, H., COOVER, G. D., KOHLER, C., DERYCK, M., SAGVOLDEN, T. & LEVINE, S. (1975) Limbic structures and behaviour: Endocrine correlates. In: *Progress in Brain Research, Vol. 42: Hormones, Homeostasis and the Brain* (Ed.: W. H. Gispen, F. B. Van Wimersma Greidanus, B. Bohus & D, de Wied). Amsterdam: Elsevier.

VALENTA, J. E. & RIGBY, M. K. (1968) Discrimination of the odor of stressed rats, *Science*, **161**, 599–601.

VALENTINE, C. W. (1930) The innate bases of fear, *Journal of Genetic Psychology*, **37**, 394–420.

VALENTINE, C. W. (1942) *The Normal Child and Some of His Abnormalities: A General Introduction to Psychology of Childhood*. Harmondsworth: Penguin.

VALENTINE, C. W. (1946) *The Psychology of Early Childhood*. London: Methuen.

VALINS, S. (1970) The perception and labeling of bodily changes as determinants of emotional behaviour. In: *Physiological Correlates of Emotion* (Ed.: P. Black). New York: Academic Press.

VALLE, F. P. (1970) Effects of strain, sex, and illumination on open-field behavior of rats, *American Journal of Psychology*, **83**, 103–111.

VALLE, F. P. (1971) Rats' performance on repeated tests in the open field as a function of age, *Psychonomic Science*, **23**, 333–335.

VALLE, F. P. (1972) Free and forced exploration in rats as a function of between – vs. within – Ss design, *Psychonomic Science*, **29**, 11–13.

VAUGHAN, F. (1968) School phobias. Cited in: BERECZ, J. M., Phobias of childhood: Etiology and treatment, *Psychological Bulletin*, **70**, 694–720.

VESTAL, B. M. (1975) Development of the immobility response (animal hypnosis) in two species of deermice (*Peromyscus*), *Animal Learning and Behaviour*, **3**, 11–15.

VINCE, M. A. & CHINN, S. (1972) Effects of external stimulation on the domestic chick's capacity to stand and walk, *British Journal of Psychology*, **63**, 89–99.

VOLOKHOV, A. A. (1970) The ontogenetic development of higher nervous activity in animals. In: *Developmental Neurobiology* (Ed.: W. A. Himwich). Springfield, Ill.: Thomas.

WADDINGTON, C. H. (1977) *Tools for Thought*. London: Jonathan Cape.

WAGNER, A. R. (1969) Frustrative non-reward: a variety of punishment. In: *Punishment and Aversive Behavior* (Ed.: B. A. Campbell & R. M. Church). New York: Appleton-Century-Crofts.

WALK, R. D. & GIBSON, E. J. (1961) A comparative and analytical study of visual depth perception, *Psychological Monographs*, **75**, Whole No. 519.

WALK, R. D. & WALTERS, C. P. (1974) Importance of texture-density preferences and motion parallax for visual depth discrimination by rats and chicks, *Journal of Comparative and Physiological Psychology*, **86**, 309–315.

WALKER, V. J. & BEECH, H. R. (1969) Mood states and the ritualistic behaviour of obsessional patients, *British Journal of Psychiatry*, **115**, 1261–1268.

WALLEN, R. (1945) Food aversions of normal and neurotic males, *Journal of Abnormal and Social Psychology*, **40**, 77–81.

WALSH, R. N. & CUMMINS, R. A. (1976) The open-field test: a critical review, *Psychological Bulletin*, **83**, 482–504.

WALTHER, F. R. (1964) Einige Verhaltensbeobachtungen an

Thomsongazellen (*Gazella thomsoni*, Gunther, 1884) in Ngorongoro-Krater, *Zeitschrift für Tierpsychologie*, **21**, 871–890.

WALTHER, F. R. (1969) Flight behaviour and avoidance of predators in Thomson's Gazelle (*Gazella thomsoni*, Gunther, 1884), *Behaviour*, **34**, 184–221.

WALTON, D. & MATHER, M. D. (1964) The application of learning principles to the treatment of obsessive compulsive states in the acute and chronic phases of illness. In: *Experiments in Behaviour Therapy* (Ed.: H. J. Eysenck). Oxford: Pergamon.

WANG, G. & LU, T. (1943) The hind brain and the early development of behavior in frogs, *Journal of Neurophysiology*, **7**, 149–162.

WARING, A. E. & MEANS, L. W. (1976) The effect of medial thalamic lesions on emmotionality, activity, and discrimination learning in the rat, *Physiology and Behaviour*, **17**, 181–186.

WASHBURN, S. L. & DEVORE, I. (1961) The social life of baboons, *Scientific American*, **204**, 62–71.

WATERS, E., MATAS, L. & SROUFE, L. A. (1975) Infants' reactions to an approaching stranger: Description, validation and functional significance of wariness, *Child Development*, **46**, 348–356.

WATSON, J. B. (1924) *Psychology from the Standpoint of a Behaviourist, 2nd edition.* Philadelphia: Lippincott.

WATSON, J. B. & MORGAN, J. J. B. (1917) Emotional reactions and psychological experimentation, *American Journal of Psychology*, **28**, 161–174.

WATSON, J. B. & RAYNER, R. (1920) Conditioned emotional reactions, *Journal of Experimental Psychology*, **3**, 1–14.

WEINER, S., DORMAN, D., PERSKY, H., STACH, T. W., NORTON, J. & LEVITT, E. E. (1963) Effect on anxiety of increasing the plasma hydrocortisone level, *Psychosomatic Medicine*, **25**, 158.

WEINRAUB, M., BROOKS, J. & LEWIS, M. (1977) The social network: a reconsideration of the concept of attachment, *Human Development*, **20**, 31–47.

WEISS, B. & LATIES, V. G. (1961) Behavioral thermoregulation, *Science*, **133**, 1338–1344.

WEISS, J., KOHLER, W. & LANDSBERG, J.-W. (1977) Increase of the corticosterone level in ducklings during the sensitive period of the following response, *Developmental Psychobiology*, **10**, 59–64.

WEISS, J. M. (1968) Effects of coping responses on stress, *Journal of Comparative and Physiological Psychology*, **65**, 251–260.

WEISS, J. M. (1970) Somatic effects of predictable and unpredictable shock, *Psychosomatic Medicine*, **32**, 397–409.

WEISS, J. M., MCEWEN, B. S., SILVA, M. T. A. & KALKUT, M. F. (1969) Pituitary-adrenal influences on fear responding, *Science*, **163**, 197–199.

WELKER, W. I. (1956a) Some determinants of play and exploration in chimpanzees, *Journal of Comparative and Physiological Psychology*, **49**, 84–89.

WELKER, W. I. (1956b) Effects of age and experience on play and exploration of young chimpanzees, *Journal of Comparative and Physiological Psychology*, **49**, 223–226.

WELKER, W. I. (1957) 'Free' versus 'forced' exploration of a novel situation by rats, *Psychological Reports*, **3**, 95–108.

WELKER, W. I. (1959a) Escape, exploratory and food-seeking responses of rats in a novel situation, *Journal of Comparative and Physiological Psychology*, **52**, 106–111.

WELKER, W. I. (1959b) Factors influencing aggregation of neonatal puppies, *Journal of Comparative and Physiological Psychology*, **52**, 376–380.

WELLS, M. J. (1968) *Lower Animals*. London: Weidenfeld & Nicholson.

WESTPHAL, R. (1877) Fear of open spaces, *Achiv fur Psychiatrie und Nervenkrankheiten*, **7**, 377–382.

WHITE, A. R. (1967) *The Philosophy of Mind*. New York: Random House.

WILCOCK, J. (1968) Strain differences in response to shock in rats selectively bred for emotional elimination, *Animal Behaviour*, **16**, 294–297.

WILCOCK, J. (1972) Water-escape in weanling rats: a link between behaviour and biological fitness, *Animal Behaviour*, **20**, 543–547.

WILLIAMS, C. D. & KUCHTA, J. C. (1957) Exploratory behavior in two mazes with dissimilar alternatives, *Journal of Comparative and Physiological Psychology*, **50**, 509–513.

WILLIAMS, D. I. & RUSSELL, P. A. (1972) Open-field behaviour in rats: effects of handling, sex and repeated testing, *British Journal of Psychology*, **63**, 593–596.

WILLIAMS, E. & SCOTT, J. P. (1953) The development of social behavior patterns in the mouse, in relation to natural periods, *Behaviour*, **6**, 35–64.

WILSON, G. & NIAS, D. (1976) *Love's Mysteries*. London: Open Books.

WIMERSMA GREIDANUS, T. B. VAN & DE WEID, D. (1969) Effects of intracerebral implantation of corticosteroids on extinction of an avoidance response in rats, *Physiology and Behaviour*, **4**, 365–370.

WIMERSMA GREIDANUS, T. B. VAN & DE WIED, D. (1971) Effects of systemic and intracerebral administration of two opposite acting ACTH-related peptides on extinction of conditioned avoidance behaviour, *neuroendocrinology*, **7**, 291–301.

WOLE, J. & RACHMAN, S. (1960) Psychoanalytic evidence: the case of Little Hans, *Journal of Nervous and Mental Disorders*, **131**, 135–145.

WOLF, S. & WOLFF, H. G. (1943) *Human Gastric Functions: An Experimental Study of a Man and His Stomach*. Oxford: Medical Publications.

WOLFF, P. H. (1969) Crying and vocalisation in early infancy. In: *Determinants of Infant Behaviour, Vol. 4* (Ed.: B. M. Foss). London: Methuen.

WOLIN, L. R., ORDY, J. M. & DILLMAN, A. (1963) Monkeys' fear of snakes:

301

a study of its basis and generality, *Journal of Genetic Psychology*, **103**, 207–226.

WOLPE, J. (1958) *Psychotherapy by Reciprocal Inhibition*. Standford: Standford University Press.

WOLPE, J. & RACHMAN, S. (1960) Psychoanalytic evidence: a critique based on Freud's case of Little Hans, *Journal of Nervous and Mental Disease*, **131**, 135–145.

WOOD, C. D. (1958) Behavioural changes following discrete lesions of temporal lobe structures, *Neurology*, **8**, 215–220.

WOODWORTH, R. S. & SHERRINGTON, C. S. (1904) A pseudoaffective reflex and its spinal path, *Journal of Physiology*, **31**, 234–243.

WYNNE, L. C. & SOLOMON, R. L. (1955) Traumatic avoidance learning: Acquisition and extinction in dogs deprived of normal peripheral autonomic feedback, *Genetic Psychology Monographs*, **52**, 241–284.

WYNNE-EDWARDS, V. C. (1962) *Animal Dispersion in Relation to Social Behaviour*. Edinburgh: Oliver & Boyd.

YARROW, L. J. (1967) The development of focused relationships during infancy. In: *Exceptional Infant, Vol. 1* (Ed.: H. J. Hellmuth). New York: Brunner/Mazel.

YERKES, R. M. & YERKES, A. W. (1936) Nature and conditions of avoidance (fear) responses in chimpanzees, *Journal of Comparative Psychology*, **21**, 53–66.

YOUNG, J. Z. (1971) *An Introduction to the Study of Man*. London: Oxford University Press.

YOUNGSTROM, K. A. (1938) Studies on the developing behavior of Anura, *Journal of Comparative Neurology*, **68**, 351–379.

ZAJONC, R. B., MARKUS, H. & WILSON, W. R. (1974) Exposure, object preference, and distress in the domestic chick, *Journal of Comparative and Physiological Psychology*, **86**, 581–585.

ZARROW, M. X., PHILPOTT, J. E., DENENBERG, V. H. & O'CONNOR, W. B. (1968) Localization of ^{14}C-4-corticosterone in the 2-day old rat and a consideration of the mechanism involved in early handling, *Nature*, **218**, 1264–1265.

ZBROZYNA, A. W. (1960) Defense reactions from the amygdala and the stria terminalis, *Journal of Physiology*, **153**, 27P–28P.

ZEIGLER, H. P. (1964) Displacement activity and motivational theory: a case study in the history of ethology, *Psychological Bulletin*, **61**, 362–376.

ZELAZO, P. R. & KOMER, M. J. (1971) Infant smiling to non-social stimuli and the recognition hypothesis, *Child Development*, **42**, 1327–1339.

ZENER, K. (1937) The significance of behavior accompanying conditioned salivary secretion for theories of the conditioned response, *American Journal of Psychology*, **50**, 384–403.

ZIMBARDO, P. G., EBBESON, E. D. & MASLACH, C. (1977) *Influencing Attitudes and Changing Behaviour*. London: Addison-Wesley.

ZUCKER, I. (1965) Effect of lesions of the septo-limbic area on behaviour of cats, *Journal of Comparative and Physiological Psychology*, **60**, 344–352.

Author Index

304

306

307

308

Jersild, A. T., 112, 128, 167, 188, 189, 222
Jersild, C. L., 189
Jewell, P. A., 105
Johnson, A., 204
Johnson, T. N., 52
Johnston, J. C., 234
Johnston, R. E., 120, 209, 210, 211
Jolly, A., 101, 105
Jones, H. E., 92, 167
Jones, M. C., 92, 166, 167
Jones, R. B., 49, 120
Joos, M., 146, 147
Jormakka, L., 188
Joslin, J., 93, 121
Joy, V., 115

Kaada, B. R., 48, 49, 53
Kagan, J., 167, 169. 170, 171, 172, 177, 178,
    182, 183, 187, 191, 195, 198
Kalkut, M. F., 158
Kamin, L. J., 211, 231
Karki, N. T., 38
Kaufman, I. C., 103, 113, 114, 146
Kearsley, R. B., 182, 187
Keeler, C. E., 158
Kelley, M. J., 52, 64, 104, 106, 110, 119
Kellogg, C., 133
Kennedy, C. B., 171
Kenny, A., 3, 8, 9, 23
Kety, S. S., 42
Killackey, H., 158
Kimmel, C. B., 129, 131, 135
Kimmel, H. D., 211
Kimmel, R. O., 129, 131, 135
King, J. A., 143, 149, 157
Kirkman, F. B., 138, 142
Klare, W. F., 103
Kleck, R., 102
Kleiber, E. L., 41
Klein, R. E., 176, 193
Klein, R. P., 177
Klein, S. H., 147
Kleinman, J. M., 145
Klemm, W. R., 145, 146
Klingberg, F., 135
Klorman, R., 102
Kluver, H., 45, 47, 49
Kobayashi, Y., 41
Koch, R., 54
Koelling, R., A., 123, 212
Köhler, C., 50, 53, 154
Kolb, B., 154

Komer, M. J., 171
Konnor, M., 193
Konrad, K., 162
Korn, S., 171
Kotelchuck, M., 183, 193
Kovach, J. K., 131
Kozma, F., 147
Krafft-Ebbing, R. Von, 205
Krakauer, L. J., 29
Kramer, G., 97
Krames, L., 102
Kruijt, J. P., 131, 137, 141, 150, 152, 153, 159,
    162
Kruuk, H., 88, 95, 100
Kuchta, J. C., 112
Kuhlmann, F., 132, 138, 142, 157
Kuo, Z.-Y., 130

Labrum, A. H., 232
Lacey, J. I., 37, 42, 58, 60, 70
Lader, M., 26, 224
Lamb, M. E., 176
Lampl, E. E., 183, 190
Lamson, E. T., 37
Landis, C., 91, 135
Landsberg, J. W., 154
Lang, P. J., 32, 58, 213
Lange, C. G., 25, 26, 28, 36
Langer, E. J., 102
Lapouse, R., 190
Larsen, S. R., 218
Larsson, K., 133, 134
Latane, B., 114, 115, 158
Laties, V. G., 103
Lautch, H., 123, 214, 220
Lawick-Goodall, J. Van, 102, 120
Lazarus, R. S., 13, 19, 29, 30, 31, 33
Lee, E. M. C., 51
Leeper, R., 13
Lefebvre, L., 68
Le Gal La Salle, G., 49
Legner, W. K., 129
Lehrman, D. S., 121
Lerner, M. J., 102
Lester, D., 58, 111, 193
Leventhal, G. S., 158
Levi, L., 33, 37
Levine, S., 42, 43, 50, 53, 61, 158
Levis, P. J., 225
Levitt, E. E., 25, 27
Levy, C. J., 109
Levy, D., 179

309

310

311

313

314

Subject Index